More praise for
INSIDE THE VC AND THE NVA

"A pair of American veterans, one an infantryman, the other a military historian, have teamed up to produce a singular book on the Vietnam War. This is a front-slope view of the war as seen by the grunts on the other side. As Pogo was wont to say: we have seen the enemy and he is us."

—PROFESSOR DOUGLAS PIKE
Author of *Viet Cong*

"Lanning and Cragg's excellent study provides a detailed portrait of the VC and NVA soldiers and why they fought the way they did; this effort has removed much of the mystery surrounding the foe that our nation fought for over twenty years."

—*Military Review*

"Impeccably researched, unbiased, and revealing. This fills a gap."

—*Kirkus Reviews*

"Accessible to the general reader but usable by the serious scholar, this is the year's first Vietnam book that belongs in virtually any collection on the war."

—*Booklist*

Also by Michael Lee Lanning:
Published by Ivy Books:

THE ONLY WAR WE HAD: A PLATOON LEADER'S
  JOURNAL OF VIETNAM
VIETNAM 1969–1970: A COMPANY COMMANDER'S
  JOURNAL
INSIDE THE LRRPS: RANGERS IN VIETNAM
INSIDE FORCE RECON: RECON MARINES IN
  VIETNAM
THE BATTLES OF PEACE

Also by Dan Cragg
Published by Ivy Books:

THE SOLDIER'S PRIZE

INSIDE THE VC AND THE NVA

THE REAL STORY OF NORTH VIETNAM'S ARMED FORCES

Michael Lee Lanning and Dan Cragg

IVY BOOKS • NEW YORK

Ivy Books
Published by Ballantine Books
Copyright © 1992 by Michael Lee Lanning and Dan Cragg
Map copyright © 1992 by Random House, Inc.

Library of Congress Catalog Card Number: 91-58640

ISBN 0-8041-0500-6

Manufactured in the United States of America

First Hardcover Edition: August 1992
First Mass Market Edition: January 1994

For Leslie and Mucho,
Faithful Companions on
Our Ten-Thousand-Mile Route

CONTENTS

FOREWORD

The partnership between Lee Lanning and Dan Cragg that produced this book was established with a handshake during a visit to a hillside Civil War campsite in Alexandria, Virginia, in the spring of 1988—but the paths that led there and to this book actually began long ago and half a world away.

For Lee Lanning, although he certainly was not aware of it at the time, the initial concept of this study was forcefully delivered on a bullet-swept, artillery- and bomb-pocked piece of jungle southeast of Xuan Loc, South Vietnam, in August 1969. His platoon, part of Charlie Company, 2nd Battalion, 3rd Infantry, 199th Light Infantry Brigade, had overrun a bunker complex of the 33rd NVA Regiment after a bitter fight. While searching the body of one of the NVA casualties, Lanning discovered a thin, cardboard-covered journal illustrated ornately with drawings of flowers and jungle wildlife. Despite his initial urge to keep the diary as a souvenir, he complied with his unit's standard operating procedures and turned it over to intelligence channels for analysis.

Experience had taught Lanning that this was the last he would ever see of the journal. Although intelligence officers were always crying for information from the field, especially for items such as this diary, they seldom shared their analyses with the men who risked their lives to get the material for them. Much to his surprise, however, a translated copy of the captured journal was forwarded to Lanning several months and many firefights later. Reading the daily entries about long marches, illness, danger, fear and homesickness did more to humanize the enemy for Lanning than any other event of the war because the brief journal writings portrayed a young soldier not unlike himself.

When Lanning returned home, he stored away the translated diary along with his own journals, other scraps of paper, and pieces of gear that represented his time in combat—the age-old ritual of forgetting and moving on with life performed by every soldier home from the wars. There the items stayed neglected for more than fifteen years, until 1984, when he rewrote his combat journals into what was published as *The Only War We Had: A Platoon Leader's Journal of Vietnam* and *Vietnam 1969– 1970: A Company Commander's Journal.* In digging through that memorabilia, Lanning was once again amazed by the similarities between his own journals and that of the dead North Vietnamese soldier.

Dan Cragg's experience of Vietnam was much different from Lanning's. He first went there in 1962 to serve with the American advisory detachment to the 5th Infantry Division, Army of the Republic of Vietnam, U.S. Military Assistance Advisory Group. The war in those days was just dangerous enough to be exciting.

Cragg returned to Vietnam in 1965 and for a time worked for General William C. Westmoreland's command historian at Military Assistance Command, Vietnam, headquarters in Saigon. Part of his job there was to screen documents for use in the annual command histories. The most fascinating of all the papers to cross Cragg's desk in those days were translated copies of the personal diaries of VC/NVA soldiers. Slowly, a picture of the enemy's face began to take shape in his mind—not unlike the picture Lanning was forming. Wouldn't it be interesting, he remembers thinking, to put together a collection of these diaries? However, almost all the translations were classified at the time and Cragg was not to pursue his idea.

Two decades later both of us were living in the Washington, D.C., area and were between writing projects when we were introduced to each other by Owen Lock, then senior editor of Del Rey Books. It did not take long for us to discover our shared interest in the soldiers of the VC/NVA and we quickly agreed to collaborate. It also did not take long to conclude that our former enemies deserved a much more detailed study than one told through an anthology of captured journals alone. The more we investigated the subject, the more we realized that virtually everything thus far written about the VC/NVA had been done by "academics," "graybeards," and "think tankers" who, despite good intentions, had never smelled gunpowder, seen the enemy in the peep sight of an M-16 rifle, or suffered the hardships, frustrations, and sacrifices of the soldier's life in wartime.

We believe this book to be an important contribution to the historiography of the Vietnam War. Historians of the war have divided themselves into two major camps—those who believe the key to victory was in counterinsurgency or counterguerrilla warfare, and those who maintain that the war could have been won through conventional means if they had been applied with more determination and rigor. The former school emphasizes psychological warfare, land reform, nation building, and other social programs as essential adjuncts to victory—"winning the hearts and minds" of the population by getting the support of the people *first*, and then handling the guerrillas with a combination of police and military operations.

The advocates of the big battalions, on the other hand, argue that the loyalty of the population in South Vietnam was never seriously in question and that probably from 1965, but certainly from 1968, onward, the military conduct of the war was totally in the hands of the North Vietnamese high command, who sent conventional, not guerrilla, forces to fight in South Vietnam. These analysts maintain that if we had succeeded in completely stopping the flow of men and supplies coming into South Vietnam from Cambodia and from North Vietnam via the Ho Chi Minh Trail, the Communist forces in the South could have been utterly destroyed. Allied firepower would have won the war because the Communist political infrastructure could never have survived without its military arm to protect it.

We believe both arguments have merit although personally we've pitched our tents closer to the camp of the big battalion people than to that of the "hearts and minds" advocates. But both systems of thought have built into them one glaring error— they maintain that if *we* had done this or *we* had done that then *we* could have won the war. Neither gives much consideration to the enemy's intentions and what *he* did to thwart our military and political initiatives. We believe that the North Vietnamese politburo controlled the events in South Vietnam to a surprising and hitherto unexpected extent. No analysis of the war can be complete without considering that dimension. We believe our book is unique because it considers not how we Americans lost that war but how the Communists won it.

During the war, the RAND Corporation recorded more than 2,600 interviews with VC/NVA POWs and defectors. We drew heavily upon these interviews because, despite the growing accessibility today of Vietnam to Westerners, we felt that those wartime observations, perceptions, and feelings represent more realistically what really happened to the participants than what may have evolved in their memories after the passage of twenty years. It is our personal observation that the accuracy and honesty of war stories tend to decline in inverse proportion to the amount of time that separates the teller from his tale.

The RAND material, while it represents a valuable archive of largely unexploited raw information on life in the VC/NVA, must be used with extreme caution. The RAND interviewers were looking for certain things, we for others, and although the people who did the interviewing were native Vietnamese linguists, they were neither trained interrogators nor military intelligence analysts—they were relatively sophisticated city people who in the main were less familiar with the countryside of their own land than the average American infantryman who had to live in it. Most of them were not even familiar with the nuances of the special vocabulary the Communist soldier used, and this is glaringly evident in the ambiguities and mistakes in the English transcriptions of some of the interviews.

We made every effort to compare the RAND data—and the analyses based upon it—against other sources and the reader will find these listed in the Source Notes and Bibliography that follow the text.

With our six and one-half years' combined experience on the ground in Vietnam, more than forty-two years' service in the United States Army, and eight previously published books on the military, we knew almost from the time of our first meeting that we had to write this book. In retrospect, we realized that our editor, Owen Lock, knew it, too, and had brought us together for this purpose.

More than twenty years have passed since our part in the Vietnam War. Even today, it is hard for us to look at pictures taken of our erstwhile foes, snug and seemingly unconcerned in their jungle hideouts, and not want to call in napalm and artillery. But we have mellowed over the years and researching this book has done much to dispel our prejudice and ignorance about our former enemies, to the point where we are confident that we can present an honest, accurate picture of what it was like to be a grunt on the other side. If some readers find hints of lingering resentments, we offer no apologies or explanations—it was simply not that kind of war. Likewise, nothing in this book should be construed as deprecating in any way the valor or dedication of the free world forces, particularly the armed forces of the Republic of South Vietnam, who fought beside us in that war. This is, after all, a book about our Communist enemies, not our allies. Where we feel our enemy deserves praise, we have given it; where not, we have said so.

Finally, if that battle in August 1969 had gone differently and a member of the 33rd NVA Regiment had found Lanning's diary, we hope it would have humanized him to the enemy as much as theirs have for us and, hopefully, for you who read this book. We think that it will for, in the final analysis, no one really understands soldiers, be they friend or foe, as well as other soldiers.

M.L.L., Tempe, Arizona
D.C., Springfield, Virginia
March 1992

AUTHORS' NOTE

The terms Viet Cong (VC) and North Vietnamese Army (NVA) are used throughout this text rather than the more proper National Liberation Front (NLF) and People's Army of Vietnam (PAVN). This choice was made because of the general readership's greater familiarity with the former terms than the latter ones.

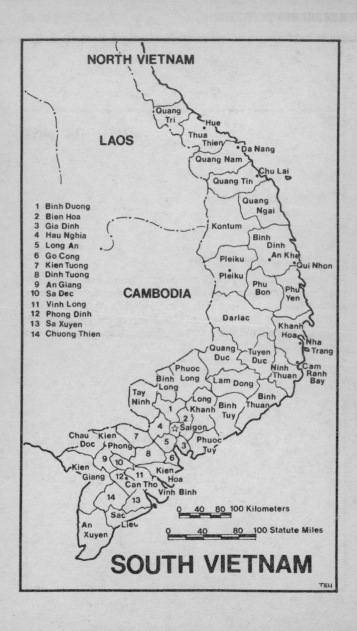

NORTH VIETNAM

LAOS

Quang
Tri
Hue
Thua
Thien
Da Nang
Quang Nam
Chu Lai
Quang Tin
Quang
Ngai
Kontum
Binh
Dinh
An Khe
Pleiku
Qui Nhon
Pleiku
Phu
Bon
Phu
Yen

CAMBODIA

Darlac
Khanh
Hoa
Nha
Trang
Quang
Duc
Tuyen
Duc
Ninh
Thuan
Cam
Ranh
Bay
Phuoc
Long
Lam Dong
Binh
Long
Tay
Ninh
Long
Khanh
Binh
Tuy
Binh
Thuan
1
2
Saigon
4
Phuoc
Tuy
Chau
Doc
Kien
Phong
7
5
3
9
8
6
10
Kien
Hoa
Kien
Giang
12
11
Can Tho
Vinh Binh
14
13
Sac
Lieu
An
Xuyen

1 Binh Duong
2 Bien Hoa
3 Gia Dinh
4 Hau Nghia
5 Long An
6 Go Cong
7 Kien Tuong
8 Dinh Tuong
9 An Giang
10 Sa Dec
11 Vinh Long
12 Phong Dinh
13 Sa Xuyen
14 Chuong Thien

0 40 80 100 Kilometers

0 40 80 100 Statute Miles

SOUTH VIETNAM

TEH

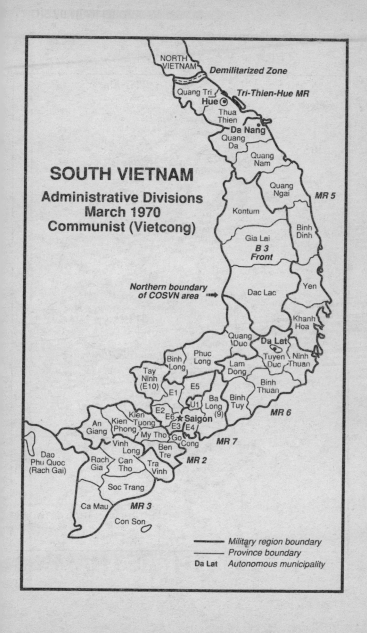

SOUTH VIETNAM

**Administrative Divisions
March 1970
Communist (Vietcong)**

NORTH
VIETNAM

Demilitarized Zone

Quang Tri

Tri-Thien-Hue MR

Hue ◉

Thua
Thien

Da Nang

Quang
Da

Quang
Nam

Quang
Ngai

MR 5

Kontum

Gia Lai

*B 3
Front*

Binh
Dinh

← *Northern boundary
of COSVN area* ⇒

Dac Lac

Yen

Khanh
Hoa

Quang
Duc

Da Lat

Binh
Long

Phuc
Long

Tuyen
Duc

Ninh
Thuan

Tay
Ninh
(E10)

E5

Lam
Dong

E1

Binh
Thuan

E2

U1

Ba
Long
(9)

Binh
Tuy

Kien
Tuong

E6

★ Saigon

An
Giang

Kien
Phong

E3

E4

MR 6

My Tho

Go
Cong

MR 7

Vinh
Long

Ben
Tre

Dao
Phu Quoc
(Rach Gai)

Rach
Gia

Can
Tho

Tra
Vinh

MR 2

Soc Trang

Ca Mau

MR 3

Con Son

―――― *Military region boundary*

―――― *Province boundary*

Da Lat *Autonomous municipality*

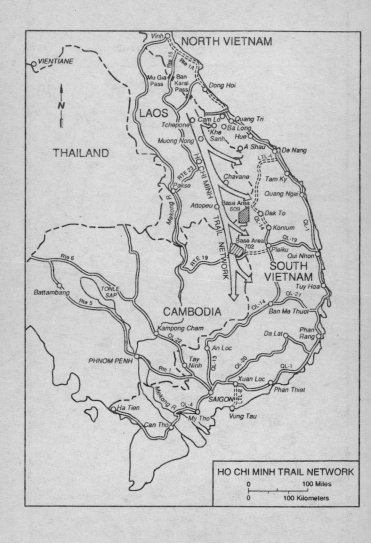

HO CHI MINH TRAIL NETWORK

0   100 Miles

0   100 Kilometers

1

IN THEIR OWN WORDS

In the minds of many Americans who fought in the Vietnam War, the soldiers of the Viet Cong and the North Vietnamese Army were supermen who could see in the dark, move silently and invisibly in all types of terrain, survive a week on a handful of rice, and willingly sacrifice their own lives if they could take a capitalist with them. Other Americans scoff at this description, viewing the VC/NVA as ignorant, emaciated, subhuman peasants who used terror as a weapon and who rarely had the will or courage to stand and fight.

Somewhere between these two descriptions lies the truth. Unfortunately, while focusing on national objectives, international alliances, decisive battles, and senior leaders, most studies of the Vietnam War leave soldiers of the VC/NVA as faceless and impersonal as the body-count reports used by the Americans to judge the war's progress.

In reality, the men and women of the VC/NVA were neither super- nor subhuman. In many ways they shared feelings and reactions similar to soldiers of other times and wars—fear, hardship, boredom, and homesickness know no ethnic or geographic boundaries.

Access to captured records and archives, as well as availability of defeated leaders who formulated policy, have assisted historians in re-creating and recording the events and personalities involved in other American-fought wars. In Vietnam, where victory was not attained, these sources are not available. However, a wealth of documents was captured on the battlefield during the conflict. Along with extensive interviews with prisoners recorded at the time, these documents provide insight into the VC/NVA tactics, planning, and day-to-day life-style.

In addition to various military documents, many personal diaries and letters of the VC and NVA were captured or found during the war. Despite being against the "Disciplinary Rules for Military Security" to keep journals, many—if not most—of the VC/NVA recorded their thoughts and innermost feelings at one time or another during the war. Generally, the Communist soldiers explained that they kept diaries because they realized the importance of their cause and wanted to record their experiences for their families and friends. Other reasons, not easily expressed or acknowledged but familiar to all soldiers, are that writing in a journal was frequently a way of combatting boredom, calming fears, and expressing emotion.

The following excerpts from VC/NVA diaries, letters and reports are but a few examples of the thoughts and feelings of the soldiers of the VC/NVA. They are the writings of ordinary men and women caught up in an extraordinary event who are otherwise little different from the common people that have always made up armies since the beginning of armed conflict.

Mai Van Hung was an NVA draftee who began his journey down the Ho Chi Minh Trail in the summer of 1965. His thoughts about food shortages, disease, homesickness, and the fear of death were recorded in his diary[1] over the next eighteen months. Fighting in the Central Highlands, Hung and his unit encountered elements of the U.S. 25th Infantry Division on March 14, 1967. The Americans found the journal on the battlefield following the fight. Whether Hung survived the action is not known.

August 24, 1965
Nghe An

I am leaving the camp tonight. My heart is filled with love for my homeland. I pledge to achieve victory before returning to my hometown.

The holiday [North Vietnam's national day] was not celebrated as it had been in the past. We did not have the day off. Instead, we kept negotiating the ten-thousand-mile route. We will keep going until we achieve reunification. Then we will be entitled to days of happiness. . . .

> October 12, 1965
> *Quang Binh*

How happy I was to meet a comrade from my place of birth while on the way to combat duty. We were moved beyond words because we had not heard from each other for 180 days. We exchanged small gifts and confided in each other. But the sacred moments we spent together went by quickly. Again we set off on our way to duty. How sad we were then to be separated from each other! The last wishes and the last looks back, then we melted away into the jungle.

I wonder when we will be able to see each other again! Not until the country's reunification! That day is too long in coming. We do not know whether we will still be alive to see it. We hold no hope of life. No words can express the hardships of our lives. I feel pessimistic and downhearted! Can anyone understand my inner feelings?

> November 16, 1965
> *Rear Base*

We had hoped for a few days' leave when we reached this place, but it did not materialize. The imperialists have robbed us of everything. Our hard lives are deprived of happiness. Everything is despair. What will our lives be like tomorrow? It will be very hard and unfair if our lives tomorrow are the same as they are today!

How frustrating life is! To whom should I unburden myself? In whom should I confide? Who can understand my pent-up feelings? No one could possibly, except us, the soldiers!

> November 24–25, 1965

Upon reaching the territory of Military Region V, we thought we would be granted one or two days of rest and recuperation, but we were not. For two days and nights the war raged fiercely close to us. Bombs and bullets rained on the jungles and mountains of this heroic land. . . .

The war has taken the lives of so many North Vietnamese youths. The Party and the country have lost so many beloved sons who sacrificed their lives for the cause of the Party. This great loss, suffered by the Party and the country, is also a great loss for the families of the dead.

Their families have still not been informed. But some day they will receive the sad news, and their suffering will be immense.

This is only the initial phase. Yet many men are demoralized. More than 50 percent have been sick. How dark life is! When can we return to the North!

Dear Mom:

I miss so much being away from you. I also miss my brothers, sisters, uncles, and aunts. But I have to make the sacrifice of my life for the [country's] future.

Please understand me. Away from home, I wish that I could write you in order to ease your anxiety. But I cannot. So please wait patiently until the day of reunification. Please take care of yourself and do not be sad anymore.

Dear Mom! My life is plagued with hardships and bereft of happiness. How I long for the day of reunification when I will return to live a happy life. I have no other wish.

Dear Mom! How wretched and hopeless my life is! I do not want to live any longer. But when I think of our family and my brothers and sisters, I know I must make the effort.

I feel a lump in my throat, unable to convey my thoughts to you. I can ask no one to send my words to you. How bitter my feelings are! Good-bye, Mom!

Dear Brother Minh:

Only four months have elapsed; yet it seems to me that we have been separated for years. . . . I cannot say how much I miss you. I reminisce with sadness about the good old days in the North. Please, forgive me for the wrongs I have done.

January 1, 1966
Gia Lai [NVA name for Pleiku Province]

The days and the months are passing helplessly. I am pining away in eternal grief and sorrow. Homesickness comes over me when I imagine that my loved ones are impatiently looking forward to hearing from me and to seeing me back home. I imagine that my younger brothers and sisters often talk about me, and that they go out to greet me as I come home in the evening. But all of this is illusion. The day of return is too far away, if, indeed, such a day still exists! By then my younger brothers and sisters will have grown up. My mother will be very old because she worried about me so often.

For my part, since the day I left home, there has not been a single moment that I have not thought of my family. How I miss the days I spent at home with my brothers and sisters! I wish I could go home. How I hate this war.

The barren land of Gia Lai Province does not appeal to me. There is nothing that endears me to this place, which they dub the second Homeland!

No vegetables or meat can be found here. We have nothing for food except salt, salted shrimp paste, and dried fish. How unbearable life is! Worse still there exists no stream in which to bathe except a mudhole large enough for a water buffalo to wallow in. How dreary is the life of a member of the Liberation Army! There is nothing for the Lunar New Year Celebration! I feel sad beyond words. If I only had some friends in whom to confide my homesickness and to unburden my hopes for a better tomorrow.

January 24, 1966

For the past five months I have not heard from my family nor have I been able to write home. How is everyone in my family? So many questions I would like to ask keep piling up in my mind. No words are enough to say how much I miss my mother, brothers, and sisters. I wish the day of reunification would draw near so that I could have a chance to see them again.

In February 1966, an American unit overran a base camp of the 7th Battalion of the Quyet Tam Regiment. Among the captured materials was the eighteen-page booklet[2] of Ha Xuan Dai, an NVA medic assigned as a filler to the VC unit. Dai, whose fate is unknown, wrote of his medical training and his first combat.

November 11, 1965

Last night, I was weary when I went to get rice. I had to carry a heavy burden for a great distance in one hour.

It was cold, then I went to Regiment to get rice, bandages, and cotton to prepare for the forthcoming battles.

November 15, 1965

A meeting was held in order to disseminate combat resolutions. Tonight, there was a medical meeting of the battalion to work out command orders.

November 16, 1965

There was a meeting of Group Chapter to pledge our determination to win. At 1300 hours we gathered the whole unit to study the battlefield on a sand table, assign missions, establish a signal organization and a military hospital.

November 17, 1965

Early in the morning, observation planes and helicopters were roaring in the sky. F-102 and F-105 fighters bombed the Mo Duc and Duc Pho districts in Quang Ngai Province. Then the RVN [South Vietnamese] troops landed by helicopters.

November 18, 1965

This morning, I sterilized medical instruments, syringes, and needles. By 2300 hours tonight, we will attack the post of A.54. It will be my first battle to exterminate the enemy. It is a long wait until the firing time.

November 19, 1965

Last night, we would have attacked Post 7 of A.54, had the enemy not withdrawn from it at 1500 hours on 18 November.

November 20, 1965

Our unit prepared to attack A.48 and two enemy strongpoints at Mo Duc district, Quang Ngai Province.

November 21, 1965

We started early in the morning. The whole Quyet Tam Regiment attacked a post located at the crossroads of Route 5 and National Route 1, near the railroad.

Group 7 attacked Thu mountain and the Nam-Bac hamlet. We were marching the whole day. It rained and was very cold. Everything was wet, including medicine. We moved to the staging area at 0200 hours on 22 November, and opened fire at 0345 hours. The 72nd unit attacked Thu mountain, the 73rd, 71st, 74th, and 75th attacked the hamlet. At last, the enemy left the hamlet but massed his forces at Thu mountain. The 72nd could not win the battle. We continued to fight until early in the morning on the 22. Then we retreated at 0400 hours.

November 22, 1965

It was almost dawn but we had not yet won the battle. We had to retreat toward Bac Son. Enemy aircraft bombed us. There were many wounded. Company comrades Thanh of Company 2 and Anh of Company 4 were killed. Tonight, we moved into the jungle.

November 23, 1965

I stayed at the foot of the mountain, about two kilometers from an enemy post, to take care of our wounded. M-113 APCs [armored personnel carriers] began to sweep near the foot of the mountain. Only one hundred meters separated them from our shelter; it seemed as if we would be captured.

Helicopters, observation planes, and F-105s bombed near us throughout the day. We could not eat or drink.

November 26, 27, and 28, 1965

I spent three days in the Nui Lon forest. I had two attacks of fever. I was very tired and could taste nothing. It rained and rained for three days. I thought of everything. I missed my mother, my grandmother, and the family and was home-sick. I felt like crying. I was miserable beyond expectation.

December 3, 1965

The fever has gone. On December 2, I marched moving from the old position to the new one. I felt tired after the long trip on foot. It rained torrentially.

December 9, 1965

We received the order to lay an ambush on Route 5.

December 13, 1965

We spent the last four days recuperating and preparing for combat.

December 27, 1965

The whole group liberated the Minh Long district from enemy control. We collected large amounts of medicines and booty. I was very happy. This was my second battle.

January 30, 1966

I engaged in a counterassault battle with M-113s. It was a most fierce battle. We retreated to Duc Pho, Quang Ngai province. Two comrades, Nho and Dao, were missing. Bao was wounded. Khanh was left on the battlefield to take care of wounded. I was in charge of the mission to look after the whole battalion. It was very hard. We were out of rice, ammunition, bandages, and cotton. How long would it take us to break up the 8,000-man sweep operation of the enemy. I don't know. The Party will provide leadership.

In May 1967, units of the U.S. 9th Infantry Division captured the official records and personal files of the 514th VC Regiment in the Mekong Delta.[3] With the documents were letters received as well as correspondence prepared for mailing. Many of these were the property of a young man by the name of Be Danh who corresponded regularly with members of a support group known as the Mothers of the National Liberation Front Fighters. Other letters were to female acquaintances whom Danh greeted as "sister," the common term of friendship. It is worth noting that despite his words of affection and dedication, Danh may not have been entirely honest. In his papers were the names and addresses of a total of thirty-four young women with whom he apparently corresponded on a regular basis.

December 1965
Dear Mothers:

Tonight I can't go to sleep. I keep thinking of one thing and another. I'm lost in thought under the moonlit sky of the twelfth lunar month. While all the other young men are sleeping peacefully, your son is clutching a carbine in his hands, and is looking toward the enemy post. Once in a while, a strong gust of wind chills me to the marrow. I think of the waning winter and the coming spring. Nothing has been changed, and we are indifferent to the spring that is approaching.

I recall that before, each time flowers bloomed indicating that spring was coming, everyone was excited and thrilled to welcome a beautiful spring.

This spring, how can we be happy when the Americans are still sowing so many sorrows and miseries, and when thousands of tons of bombs are falling on our Fatherland, destroying and setting houses on fire, stripping the trees bare of leaves, forcing the people to flee and wander from place to place, and reducing them to a life of privation and hardship? How can I be happy when I think of all this? Wherever we go, we see only destruction—heaps of ashes and debris where warm and happy homes used to be. What are we going to do? When the country is plunged into a sea of fire, the only thing we can do is to transform our hatred into action and make use of all our strength to bring a spring of victory to the people. When victory is achieved, we will rebuild the bridge that links North and South, no matter what, so that North and South will be united again, and so that the loved ones who are now separated will be united again—they are all anxiously looking forward to that.

This spring your children on the front line have only this letter, sent over the long distances to the rear area, to inquire about our mothers and to wish them good health and strong energy to live forever and to enjoy a spring of victory and glory in 1966.

Your son,
Be Danh

My dear Sister:

Tonight, July 13, 1966, I went on operation, marching over a 10,000-mile route. It was raining and the path was very slippery. I had to carry a heavy load, and so had to proceed very slowly and carefully on the muddy path in the middle of an isolated and deserted forest. Our column of troops, back from a victorious battle, were the only people moving in the forest. The sky was without stars and hung like a black blanket overhead. The night was pitch black and quiet. I heard the chirping of crickets and insects, a sad song echoing in the quiet night.

At that moment I thought of you in the rear area, and wondered if you and all the other older and younger sisters knew the hardships that your brother had to go through. I wondered whether you were sleeping peacefully or sitting at the openings of shelters, ready to take cover if you were bombed? I thought that the latter was the more likely. I wondered whether you talked about your brothers on the front line, or whether you had forgotten completely about them. I thought that the latter was also more likely, because just a few days ago, when I met you, my oldest sister, you didn't recognize me. You had forgotten me completely. You had to look at me for a long time before you could recognize me, your younger brother. This, of course, hurt the love and friendship between you, my visiting sister, and me, Be Danh. But I wasn't mad at you, my dear sister. I thought that our feelings toward each other were sacred, and I considered your visit as a delicious spiritual food for me, your brother, on the front line. We are separated by 10,000 miles, and when we meet it is only for a few short seconds. Our emotional needs therefore cannot be fulfilled; is this not true, my dear sister? I think that you understand this better than I.

Good-bye to my very dear sister. Loving you forever.

Your brother, Be Danh

Another letter[4] in the documents captured from the 514th VC Battalion demonstrates the importance of the Revolution over mere personal concerns. The letter from Phuong Trinh to Sau Kim, dated March 25, 1967, also relates how the women of the Viet Cong were as dedicated to victory as the men.

March 25, 1967
My dearest:

I have received your letter. My commander has also received your letter asking for permission to marry me. Please forgive me for not having replied to you sooner. You must have been waiting anxiously for my reply.

My love, I accept your marriage proposal, but let me tell you something. Both of us understand very well the importance of marriage. Marriage will make one happy or unhappy for one's entire life. Loving you means that I have thought things out and that I have reflected on this matter very seriously. My acceptance of your marriage proposal is therefore certain. Your letter proposing to me shows that you are sincere and that you really want to marry me. I thank you for this. But, my dearest, our situation does not allow us to get married soon!!! Please understand me. To put on a dress, one has to pull it over the head first. I don't want to make my parents sad, and I don't dare to make them sad because of me. Besides, I think that—it will be incorrect to say that we're still too young—we are in the prime of our lives, a time that should be devoted to serving society, contributing all our strength to the *Party and to the Fatherland*. We belong to the generation that is advancing speedily forward and that is scoring many achievements on the battlefield. I am determined to sacrifice my personal life and emotions to make my parents happy, and also to be able to continue marching on the Revolutionary path that I'm following.

If we wait longer, this will enable us to gauge the faithfulness of us both, to see which of us is really sincere and faithful. Do you see any difficulties for yourself if we do this? Are you mad at me? As for me, I have definitely made up my mind. I've given all my love to you. As long as I continue fighting under the Party flag, I'll remain your own. Self-respecting and loving people will remain faithful to the ones they love; this is a proof of their dignity. I'll wait for you and remember you forever. . . . Sometime in the future, or when the country is reunified, you and I will be reunited. How precious will our love be then! Do you agree, my love?

I'm going to stop here. I send you my unspoken, but profound and faithful love. I wish you good health, happiness, and steady progress. Missing you and sending you thousands of kisses.

Yours,
Trinh

Nguyen Van Nhung was a private in the 33rd NVA Regiment. He was killed by elements of the U.S. 199th Light Infantry Brigade southwest of Xuan Loc in August 1969. Among Nhung's personal effects was a thin cardboard-covered diary[5] containing brief daily entries dating back to his days as a trainee in the North during January of the same year. Most of the soldier's writings merely recorded the length of time of each day's march, mountain ridges scaled, poor food, and air attacks. Others, listed here, are a bit more meaningful.

January 1969
> 5th—Started combat tactical training, prepare to go to South Vietnam to liberate my country.
> 29th, 30th—Received my equipment in preparation to go liberate my country. Spent a three-day pass at home with my family.

February 1969
> 9th—Begin to move South by rail.

20th—Go to Cu Nam Bo Thanh (V) by boat.

26th—March from 0700 hours until 1200 hours, arrive at #27 station, take a bath in a stream.

March 1969

1st—Walking very toilsome, crossed two slopes.

6th—Arrived at station at 1100 hours, this station had been attacked by Special Forces and bombing had destroyed it.

7th—Today crossed entry and exit point into South Vietnam, carry ten days' [worth] of dry food.

8th—We got up very early and moved out. We were cooking rice when the jet fighters came in and dropped a lot of bombs, but we withdrew safely.

9th—We got up at 0600 hours and left from here. We felt pretty good today because no air strikes came our way.

11th—On the way to the station we saw many jet fighters. We arrived at 1200 hours [near Khe Sanh area]. It is very hot at night.

16th—We stayed at this station for rest. We saw a movie at this station.

20th—It is very hot today. I felt pain in my legs. We didn't stop for any rest. Sorry about that.

April 1969

5th—It took me six hours to get to station 73. My friends Van and Nen are sick and must stay here.

7th—It took me five hours to go to station 74. We have to carry rice for twenty days. Very tired.

May 1969

24th—We are waiting here. I don't have anything to do. It is making me homesick.

28th—B-52 air strike nearby.

June 1969

25th—Good-bye to everybody. I and another comrade have to go to G-7 Military Region. There were difficulties and sadness when we left our group.

26th—We walked all day long from K-7 to K-6. We try to keep going.

30th—I'm going to K-1. It is becoming difficult for me.

July 1969

2nd—We had a day of rest. We did not get any rice today.
Maybe tomorrow.

3rd—I almost died by B-52.

4th—After B-52 air strike we moved to V-10. We moved
very fast and forgot to eat. It's sad today.

19th—I must run away. I almost died again by B-52.

24th—I feel very tired. I have a back pain and feel very
sick.

25th—I am worried about my health. I don't want to miss
my next move.

26th—Crossing operation at Dong Nai River. It rained and
the way very muddy. I am suffering very much.

August 1969

2nd—I get malaria. I can't eat anything, only drink water.

10th—B-52 strike is very close to our position.

11th—I sat all day in my bunker.

12th—Movement operation was often attacked and had to
come back.

13th—Everything is ready for running away when we see
enemy coming.

Fears, hardship, pride, and belief in a cause were not limited
only to the VC and NVA who faced the Americans. South Vietnamese troops were opposed by equally dedicated enemies—
from the very beginning of the war. After a fight at Daktrum on
September 3, 1961, ARVN forces found a diary[6] in the uniform
of a North Vietnamese who was accompanying a Viet Cong
unit.

May 4, 1961

Leaving temporarily the beloved North to return to my native South to liberate my compatriots from the yoke of misery
imposed by US–Diem. This has been my ideal for a long time.

August 6, 1961

A few lines to remind me of this remote place! Not enough
rice; meals tasteless because there is not enough salt; clothing
is not warm enough for this very high peak.

Nevertheless, in his determined heart, the fighter for liberation of the South remains faithful to the Party, to the people
of the South, and he remains faithful to his only love.

August 14, 1961

Memory!

One afternoon which is turning into evening. I am sitting on the peak of a high mountain. This is a famous scenic place. This is the highest peak of the whole chain of mountains, and it is all covered with mist. All this scenery arouses nostalgia in my heart! I try to recall my life since I was a young boy.

I answered the call of the Party when I was very young, and what did I do for the people of my village? I devoted myself to the people. I took part in propaganda and aroused the people to carry out the policy of the Party and the Government and helped organize village defense and fighting forces. On March 25, 1954, I began my fighting career and I contributed my part in fighting the French Expeditionary Force. With the army of Interzone 5, I saw the end of the war on July 20, 1954, and then on April 26, 1955, I left my native place and all the ties with my family and friends to go North as a victorious fighter.

Since that day, my spirit has matured together with that of the regular army. We have built up a beautiful and prosperous and strong North; the construction sites and factories spring up quickly everywhere under a bright sky and under the superior socialist regime. Close to me there was a unique source of consolation in my life. My life was beautiful, my happiness immeasurable. Enough to eat; warm clothing in my daily life; earning a living was fairly easy; often I enjoyed songs and dances which deal with the healthy life of all the people in the North and with the maturity of the army.

December 15, 1961

On the call of the Party, I returned to my beloved Fatherland! My life returned to normal. I enjoyed again the peaceful atmosphere and my happiness. I continued training daily for the defense of the territory of the North and for the continuation of the liberation of the South. But I was back with my only love. Hurrah! How happy and how sweet. But my life could not continue that way!

For the third time my life turned to war again. For the liberation of our compatriots in the South, a situation of boiling oil and burning fire is necessary! A situation in which husband is separated from wife, father from son, brother from brother is necessary. I joined the ranks of the liberation army in answer to the call of the Front for Liberation of the South.

Now my life is full of hardship—not enough rice to eat nor enough salt to give a taste to my tongue, not enough clothing to keep myself warm! But in my heart I keep loyal to the Party and to the people. I am proud and happy.

I am writing down this story for my sons and my grandsons of the future to know of my life and activities during the Revolution when the best medicine available was the root of the wild banana tree and the best bandage was the leaf of rau lui, when there was no salt to give taste to our meals, when there was no such food as meat or fish as we enjoy in a time of peace and happiness such as I have known and left behind.

2

THE VIETNAM ENIGMA

For most Westerners, everything about the Communist soldier in Vietnam was an enigma distorted by ignorance and obscured by a fog of misunderstanding. Those who fought him, including the Americans and the French, had little comprehension of the warrior they faced and, unfortunately, frequently had little desire to learn more about him.

Confirming the axiom that those who fail to study history are doomed to repeat it, America and her allies committed the same mistake that led to the defeat of so many other foreigners in Indochina over the centuries by underrating the enemy. All too often, those who did make some effort to gain an understanding of the VC/NVA studied them only in the context of the "now" instead of investigating the cultural, sociological, and military heritage that over the millennia have molded the Vietnamese people.

In fact, there is no great mystery. The tenacity, courage and patience of the VC/NVA are no puzzle to those who know the history of their country. The first Americans did *not* arrive in Vietnam in 1960; Westerners had been visiting there for nearly two centuries before U.S. combat forces arrived in great numbers.

The first recorded European to visit what is now Vietnam was an envoy from the Roman emperor Marcus Aurelius Antoninus,

who visited the Red River Delta in A.D. 166. Other evidence
that Western culture reached Vietnam in the second century A.D.
is provided by a Roman medal with the likeness of the Emperor
Antonius Pius (Marcus Aurelius's immediate predecessor), dated
A.D. 152, unearthed at Oc Eo, in southernmost South Vietnam.
The visit of Marcus Aurelius's envoy was noted in the annals of
the Giao-chi, as that region was known to the Chinese. It is
believed that later Europeans, mispronouncing "Giao-chi,"
created the word "Cochin," to which "China" was annexed,
providing the name, Cochinchina, by which Vietnam was known
in the West for many centuries. It should be noted that the term
"Giao-chi" was used by the Chinese in a derogatory sense,
meaning "the people whose toes point outward."[1]

The first American diplomatic mission to Vietnam arrived off
the coast of Phu Yen Province, not far from Cam Ranh Bay, on
the warship U.S.S. *Peacock* in January 1833. Aboard was Ed-
mund Roberts, President Andrew Jackson's envoy to "the courts
of Cochinchina." Roberts experienced much difficulty present-
ing his credentials to Emperor Minh Mang and the imperial
court in Hue.* This was due in part to the fact that his papers
had to be carried overland to the court, and the mandarins who
acted as intermediaries insisted on arguing endlessly over the
ceremonial forms of the translations, which were in Chinese,
the official court language. These difficulties were compounded
by the multilayered and slow-moving Vietnamese bureaucracy.
Another factor, one that no doubt influenced these proceedings
(and one that certainly influenced subsequent Vietnamese-
American relations), was the fear Vietnamese have of failure:
the Vietnamese never make any important decision without
careful, lengthy study and consideration. By the time word was
finally sent that the emperor would receive Roberts and his mission, the Americans had already sailed away in disgust.[2]

Roberts again attempted to present his mission to the imperial
court on his homeward voyage three years later. After the *Peacock* landed at Danang, Minh Mang sent an official delegation
to greet the Americans; however, Roberts was too ill to receive
them. Roberts died shortly afterward, apparently unaware of the
offer to meet with his delegation. The Vietnamese did not be-

*Hue, formerly Phu Xuan, only became home to the imperial court in 1802, when
moved there by the Emperor Gia Long. Thus, American journalists who anguished
over the destruction of the "ancient imperial city of Hue" during the fighting there
in 1968, failed to realize that as a capital, Hue was younger than Washington, DC.

lieve the envoy was really sick but thought he had deliberately snubbed them. Relations between the Americans and the Vietnamese were off to a bad start.

Communications between the two countries would improve little over the following years. The United States would continue to send officials to Vietnam up to the bitter end in 1975. They would, in the words of the historian Ellen Hammer, "like Roberts . . . not only fail to bridge the gap in communication between the two cultures; they would not even realize that such a gap existed."[3]

Closer contact between Americans and Vietnamese during the fifteen years of the Vietnam War did little to improve understanding. Some U.S. officials and military leaders were able to develop an empathy for, and an understanding of, the Vietnamese, but unfortunately they were in the minority. Even those enlightened few were much more likely to become knowledgeable only about the methods and intentions of their South Vietnamese allies while remaining ignorant of the Viet Cong and North Vietnamese.

While the ordinary American foot soldier had little opportunity to develop personal relationships with the Vietnamese or learn about their culture—he had a war to fight and was right in the middle of it for most of his Vietnam tour—the same is not true of those who occupied the highest positions in the U.S. government. A pervasive ignorance of Vietnamese culture was bad enough, but much more critical and damaging was the total lack of comprehension by the senior elected and appointed officials of how determined the enemy was to win the war.

Even the most cursory study of Vietnamese military history reveals their willingness to suffer whatever casualties over whatever period of time necessary in order to win. The Communists in Vietnam outlasted their enemies because in terms of the Vietnam conflict the Americans were just not prepared to think of victory in terms of total war. Quite simply, the Communists were prepared to lose for a longer period of time than the Americans were prepared to win.

THE VIETNAMESE AS WARRIORS

Throughout their history, the Vietnamese have been quick to pick up the sword to defend or extend their borders. According to Vietnamese lore, the first Vietnamese dynasty, that of the Hong Bang, was established in North Vietnam in the year 2879

B.C. under a king known as Kinh Duong Vuong. He was succeeded by his son, Lac Long Quan, who in turn married an immortal, Au Co. From these two sprang the one hundred Hung Vuong kings of the Hong Bang dynasty who ruled for 2,622 years.[4]

Vietnamese independence first came to an end in 111 B.C. when the armies of the Chinese Western Han dynasty conquered the Kingdom of Nam Viet. In A.D. 39 the Chinese yoke was briefly thrown off after a rebellion led by two sisters, Trung Trac and Trung Nhi, who ruled until defeated by a Chinese army in A.D. 43. Rather than suffer the humiliation of capture, the sisters committed suicide. Subsequently the Trung sisters became powerful symbols of resistance to foreign domination. In fact, the story of the Trung sisters' sacrifice is so inspirational to the Vietnamese that even the Communists have held it up as worthy of emulation in the modern revolutionary struggle.[5]

Vietnam remained under Chinese control for the next nine hundred years. This was a period marked by numerous unsuccessful revolts—in A.D. 220, 248, 542, 589, and 602. It was also a time during which the Chinese culture became more and more integrated into that of the conquered people of Vietnam.

Finally, in 938, taking advantage of the power vacuum created by the fall of the T'ang dynasty, the Vietnamese successfully defeated their Chinese overlords at the Battle of Bach Dang. With the exception of an interlude of Chinese domination from 1406–1428, the Vietnamese retained their independence until their submission to the French in 1883.

This period of nine hundred years of independence was not peaceful, but rather, in typical Vietnamese fashion, marked by a succession of coups and usurpations, civil war, and expansionism. Under the Ly emperors (1009–1225) the Vietnamese seized territory from the Kingdom of Champa (Central South Vietnam) and repulsed invasions from both China and Cambodia. The most significant acquisition occurred in 1069 when Emperor Thanh Tong seized from Champa the present central region of southern Vietnam and renamed it Dai Viet (Greater Viet). This same area was renamed Viet Nam in 1802 by Emperor Gia Long.[6]

The wars between the Kingdom of Champa and Annam (from An-Nam, or "Pacified South," as Vietnam was known to the Chinese) were prosecuted with great intensity and bitterness by both sides. The only peace between the two occurred during the Mongol invasions of 1257–1287, when the two kingdoms coop-

erated for their mutual defense. The truce ended in 1287 with
the Second Battle of Bach Dang, in which one of the greatest
heroes of Vietnamese military history, Tran Hung Dao, deci-
sively defeated the invaders.[7]

Peace, as usual in Vietnam, was not lasting. Reconquered by
the Chinese in 1406, the Vietnamese chafed under their rule
until led in revolt by Le Loi, a man much noted at the time for
his honesty, courage, and charity. He also proved to be a superb
military strategist. Le Loi conducted a ten-year guerrilla war
against the Chinese that ended in the reassertion of Vietnam's
independence in 1428. The Le dynasty lasted for 360 years.[8]

The Vietnamese inexorably continued extending their empire
southward under the Le emperors (1428–1788). Qui Nhon came
under their control in 1602, Phan Rang in 1653, Saigon in 1696,
Phan Thiet in 1697, Ha Tien in 1714, and the Khmers finally
ceded the fertile Mekong Delta region in 1757.[9]

The nineteenth century brought Western enemies to Indochina. In 1858, France, acting in accordance with the dictates
of her own expansionist and colonial aims, seized Danang from
the Nguyen emperors (1802–1945). The French took Saigon in
July 1861; the Delta region was annexed in 1867. With occasional assistance from their former Chinese enemies, the Vietnamese resisted the imposition of French rule valiantly, but to
no avail. In 1883 an expeditionary force brought northern Vietnam under French control. Vietnamese independence officially
came to an end under the Treaty of Qui Mui on August 25, 1883.

In time the French takeover was nearly total. By 1938 virtually all foreign investments in Vietnam were in French hands.
French economic policy throughout Indochina was geared to
the benefit of metropolitan France. Her colonies in Southeast
Asia became not only a source of raw materials for her domestic
industries but also a protected market for the goods those industries produced.[10]

In terms of its impact on Vietnamese culture, the French
conquest had even more far-reaching effects. The mandarinate—
the governing bureaucracy modeled on the Chinese system—
suffered a decline in prestige and influence as it was supplanted
by French colonial managers and administrators. The introduction of Western technology also brought Western ideas of self-
determination that impelled educated Vietnamese to question
their own traditional social values. French schools gradually
replaced those based on Chinese models so that Western values

and outlooks were placed in direct confrontation with the traditional ones.

The result of these developments was the creation of a society divided into three classes. At the top were a small number of Vietnamese—intellectuals, professionals, and landowners—who found themselves totally immersed in French culture and dependent upon French patronage. The vast majority of the population, which merely submitted itself to colonial rule, formed the second class. An underclass, derived from the first two groups and influenced by Western ideas of political radicalism, formed the third class. Regardless of class and acceptance of the new culture, it is interesting to note that during World War I France was so much in control of the lives of the Vietnamese people that 100,000 of them were sent to the Western Front to fight under the tricolor.[11]

As French hegemony continued to solidify, the colonial government did not try to reform Vietnamese institutions as much as replace them. Nguyen emperors, descendants of the magnificent Gia Long, were allowed to stay on their throne but as figureheads only. Soon, the Imperial Court degenerated into a social gathering around a puppet ruler, and servile and corrupted mandarins.[12] Despite the family's impotence, the last Nguyen, Bao Dai, served as emperor until being forced to abdicate under pressure by the Viet Minh in 1945.

The half century following the consolidation of French power in the 1880s was a time of revolts, rebellions, and resistance. While causes and objectives differed from incident to incident, each was characterized by the rising tide of Vietnamese nationalism. Ironically, while the French were attempting to impart their values and benefits to the Vietnamese, they were also sowing the seeds of their eventual defeat—and that of America as well. Combining the political radicalism of the French Revolution and the dogma of Karl Marx and Friedrich Engels with their ancient tradition of resistance to foreign domination, the Vietnamese once again prepared to expel the invaders.

In the immediate aftermath of World War II, with the fall of Vichy France, the Vietnamese again seemed in control of their own country. The Viet Minh seized control in Hanoi, Hue, and Saigon. One observer even claims to have seen evidence that the Viet Minh actually changed the name of Saigon to Ho Chi Minh City at that time. It was not until December 1946 that the French were able to reassert their power in Vietnam. Now fighting under the Viet Minh, the Vietnamese nationalists prepared to expel the French.[13] Time was once again a factor the Viet Minh were willing to exploit. It would take eight years for the First Indochina War to culminate with the surrender of the French forces at Dien Bien Phu. Here, near the village of Muong Thanh, in a remote valley in northwestern North Vietnam, a Vietnamese Communist siege force—estimated at 49,500 combatants and 55,000 support troops—battled a fortified French airhead with a garrison of barely 13,000 for fifty-six days in 1954.[14] When the French forces finally surrendered at 1740 hours local time, May 7, 1954, 10,000 prisoners were taken. The victory had not come cheaply, costing the Viet Minh nearly 23,000 casualties.[15]

For the next two decades the Communist triumph at Dien Bien Phu haunted America and her South Vietnamese allies. It was a rallying cry and an inspiration for the North Vietnamese and their Viet Cong cousins. If they had beaten the West once, they could do it again. As the historian and long-time Vietnam observer Bernard Fall wrote in a slightly different but still very appropriate context, "It is hard to argue with Dien Bien Phu."

Yet the Americans learned little from the tenacity, patience, and sacrifice of the Viet Minh against the French. In 1968, General Vo Nguyen Giap, North Vietnam's top military officer and former commander-in-chief of the army that overwhelmed Dien Bien Phu, stated that 500,000 of his men* had died to date in the struggle to conquer South Vietnam.[16] An American analyst estimated in 1975 that between 1965 and 1972 possibly as many as 851,000 VC/NVA died in South Vietnam.[17] Even the lower estimate—500,000 Communist soldiers killed—is approximately ten times the total deaths (battle and nonbattle) U.S. forces suffered in Vietnam from 1959 to 1975.

For the body-counting Americans, victory certainly seemed at hand in 1968. However, few Westerners seemed to understand that to their enemy, dying in defense of the Vietnamese homeland was an honored death.[18] The following example of the fighting spirit and sacrifice of the Viet Minh in the First Indochina War would have served the Americans well as an object lesson.

On March 15, 1954, a sergeant in the 7th Algerian Rifles

---

*This figure may have been a correct estimate or Giap may have thought it was, but the distinct possibility remains that he merely pulled it out of the air, to impress the West with North Vietnam's determination to win the war. When Stanley Karnow asked him the same question in Hanoi in 1990, he refused even to hazard a guess. "We still don't know," is all he would say. An aide later confided to Karnow that "at least a million of their troops perished, the majority of them in the American war."

surrendered his men on top of Strongpoint Gabrielle, overlooking Dien Bien Phu. In good French, a Communist officer ordered him and his men to the rear. The sergeant asked how they were to get across the barbed wire and minefields. "Just walk across the bodies of our men," the officer told him. About eight hundred dead and dying Viet Minh, cut down in the final assaults on Gabrielle, lay in front of the sergeant's trench. One of them looked up at the prisoners; they saw his lips moving and they hesitated to use him as a stepping stone. "Get going," the Viet Minh officer said. "You can step on him. He has done his duty for the Democratic Republic of Vietnam."[19]

What enabled the Communists to endure such punishment? There are many answers, but the ultimate explanation lies in Vietnam's long tradition of commitment, sacrifice, and endurance in war. This martial spirit was encapsulated by Nguyen Du in his epic poem, *The Tale of Kieu*: "Tu fought his one last fight on earth/to show them all a soldier's dauntless heart . . . then dropped his body on the field like trash."[20]

THE LAND

Unlike many other parts of the world, Vietnam has little direct strategic importance to the West. At the time of the war it seemed to many Americans that all the resources and bloodshed invested to keep the South free were hardly worth it.

Vietnam stretches like a long figure S down the eastern coast of the Indochinese peninsula, from China (8° 30′ north latitude) to the Gulf of Siam (23° 24′ north latitude). The country's coastline is approximately 1,400 miles long. Vietnam lies entirely within the tropical zone, its northern border being on the same latitude as Havana, Cuba. To the east are the Gulf of Tonkin and the South China Sea; to the west Laos and Cambodia. The southernmost tip of Vietnam, the Ca Mau (Mui Bai Bung) Peninsula, juts into the Gulf of Siam.

The combined population of Vietnam in 1973 was estimated at 42,435,000 (19,954,000 in the South and 22,481,000 in the North). Hanoi's population in 1974 was estimated at 600,000; Saigon's in 1973 was 1,825,297. The years since the end of the Second Indochina War have been quite "fertile." In 1987 the population of the Socialist Republic of Vietnam (SRV) was estimated at 63,585,121.

In 1954 the two Vietnams were partitioned at the 17th Parallel, along the Ben Hai River (Song Ben Hai). Until April 30,

1975, this area was known as the Demilitarized Zone, or the DMZ.

Of Vietnam's 127,000 square miles of land area (approximately the size of New Mexico), only about 25 percent is actually under cultivation. More than 30 percent of the country is covered by forests and jungles.

In the north the most heavily populated and cultivated region is in the Red River Delta area. The central part of the country consists mainly of highlands formed by the Chaine Annamitique, where peaks rise from 3,000 to 10,000 feet. These mountains stretch from about 50 miles north of Ho Chi Minh City (formerly Saigon) for 750 miles north into China. The bulk of the population in this central area of the country resides in a narrow strip between the mountains to the west and the South China Sea in the east.

The southern part of Vietnam is characterized by the Mekong Delta, a 26,000-square-mile alluvial plain formed by the five branches of the Mekong River. This region is under intense cultivation and is known as the "rice bowl of Southeast Asia."

The climate in Vietnam is hot and humid the year round, although the humidity and temperature are somewhat lower in the Hanoi area than in the southern parts of the country. Average rainfall in Hanoi is 72 inches per year; 128 inches fall at Hue on the average; and Ho Chi Minh City averages 80 inches per year. The southern part of the country is hot all year round. While there is some industry in Vietnam, especially in the north, its people are primarily dependent on agriculture, principally rice cultivation. About 85 percent of the Vietnamese people earn their living from farming.

While the seasonal monsoons sometimes bring serious flooding and destruction of property—often accompanied by heavy loss of life—nature has provided the Vietnamese people a lush and generally tranquil land. The climate permits year-round agricultural activities that, if managed properly, are capable of producing rich food surpluses. Add to this the bounty of the sea that forms Vietnam's eastern limits and the result is a land of plenty, not poverty and hardship.[21]

THE PEOPLE

Neither the geography nor the climate of Vietnam is so extreme or harsh as to make survival there an uncompromising struggle with the forces of nature. It is not an environment that one expects to produce a hardy, military people capable of total commitment to warfare. The key to understanding these warlike traits lies not in geography but in the history of the Vietnamese people, the dynamics of their society, and their political education—particularly that of the men and women who led the Communist movement.

Under the entry entitled "Annam," an anonymous contributor to the Thirteenth Edition (1926) of the *Encyclopaedia Britannica* had this to say about the Vietnamese people:

> The Annamese is the worst-built and ugliest of all the Indo-Chinese who belong to the Mongolian race . . . his skin is thick; his forehead low; his skull slightly depressed at the top . . . his nose is not only the flattest, but also the smallest among the Indo-Chinese; his teeth are blackened and his gums destroyed by the constant use of betel-nut. They cherish great love of their native village and cannot remain long from home. A proneness to gambling and opium-smoking, and a tinge of vanity and deceitfulness, are their less estimable traits. On the whole they are mild and easy-going and even apathetic, but the facility with which they learn is remarkable.

Alan Brodrick, an Englishman who traveled widely in Vietnam before World War II, quotes an early French settler describing the Vietnamese as cowards who displayed no military prowess, who were "a dirty, cruel, obsequious, thievish, quarrelsome people" and the women "especially bad-tempered."[22]

Brodrick, however, was a keen observer in his own right* and he admitted a prejudice in favor of the Vietnamese, attributing their bad reputation in great measure to the political subjugation under which the French colonial administration forced them to live. Many American GIs would agree with Brodrick in his assessment that the Vietnamese are "incredibly deft and unclumsy, they are noiseless in their movements and so quick to comprehend that the slightest gesture or hint is understood."[23]

The educated Vietnamese understood how foreigners, especially the French, viewed them—Brodrick's sympathy notwith-

---

*Brodrick also took the trouble to learn something about the Vietnamese language. He was amused to discover that the Vietnamese pronunciation of his name, "Bu-Dit," sounds just like a frequently used obscenity in their language that translates closely to "kiss my ass" in English. "Annamese are delighted to find that I have so friendly and home-like a patronymic," he wrote.

standing. A Vietnamese patriot, in a letter to the French governor-general of Indochina dated August 15, 1906, was unrestrained in his bitterness:

> Whether in newspapers, or in letters, or in conversations, the French always hold us in hatred and contempt. They consider us not merely as savages, but as dogs and swine. Not only do they not treat us as equals, but to them we are something dirty and stinking to be avoided. During these years any mandarin who dares to object to a French administrator, no matter how right his objection may be, is insulted scornfully. More than a few poor people in the countryside have been beaten to death by Frenchmen. Everyone realizes that the French consider us as animals and brutes; everyone is angry, but who dares to voice his anger?[24]

Sixty years later, many Americans would come to share the low opinion of the Vietnamese held by the French before them. During the war American soldiers invented or borrowed a host of derogatory terms they applied to the Vietnamese people: Dink, dip (short for dipshit), gook, gooker, gooner, little men, Luke the Gook, ricebelly, riceburner, slant, slanteye, slope, slopehead, zip, and zipperhead.

Americans were also guilty of thinking that "all Vietnamese look alike." To the soldier from a melting-pot nation like the United States, where multiracial and varied ethnic backgrounds were represented, it was not unusual for the "sameness" of the Vietnamese to be noted. Typically, the average Vietnamese male is 61 or 62 inches in height and weighs around 120 lbs. He has straight black hair, high cheekbones, a broad face and round head with dark eyes characterized by the Mongolian single eyelid fold. The Vietnamese people have brown skin that varies from a light to medium hue.

The ethnic Vietnamese are a homogeneous people whose historic origins go back beyond 300 B.C. One theory of their origin is that they are descended from a prehistoric mixture of peoples native to the Indochinese peninsula and Mongolian immigrants from South China. Another holds they come from a mixture of Indo-Malayan and Chinese peoples. Whichever theory is correct, the influence of China upon the Vietnamese, ethnically and culturally, has been paramount.

About 15 percent of the people of Vietnam belong to ethnic minorities, the largest of these being the Chinese. In the South there is also a large Cambodian minority. In addition to these groups, an estimated 800,000 Montagnards, or primitive hill people, lived throughout the Chaine Annamitique during the war.

The Vietnamese language, which has been spoken in that region for more than two thousand years, consists of three major dialects: northern, central, and southern. These dialects differ in vocabulary, pronunciation, and tonal pattern, with great divergence occurring even between adjacent villages. While a person native to Saigon can understand a native of Hanoi with little difficulty, the different way each pronounces the same words is distinctive and quite recognizable.

The spoken language uses tones in which the distinction between words is made according to the use of different levels of pitch. Thus, *nha tho*, depending upon how it is pronounced, can mean either a church or a whorehouse. These variations were an endless source of amusement to Americans just learning the language, but to the Western ear unfamiliar with spoken Vietnamese, it always sounds at first like twittering gobbledegook. American GIs often referred to it as "gookamese."

In the written language, these tones are indicated by a series of diacritical marks placed over or under vowels. The Vietnamese first learned writing from the Chinese about two thousand years ago. While Chinese writing was used in official state affairs until the early years of this century, over the years the Vietnamese applied their own meaning and pronunciation to the ideograms. This form of writing is known as *chu nom*. During the sixteenth century, the French missionary Alexandre de Rhodes devised a system of writing Vietnamese using Roman letters—known as *quoc ngu*—which became in time the system that has now entirely replaced *chu nom* in everyday life.

NORTHERNERS VERSUS SOUTHERNERS

Vietnamese people often think of themselves as divided into three distinct regional groupings: Northerners, from the Red River Valley of what was formerly North Vietnam; Centralists, from the southern part of North Vietnam and the northern region of South Vietnam; and Southerners, from the Saigon and Mekong Delta areas of South Vietnam.[25] This deeply rooted regionalism often gave rise to stereotypes and resultant conflicts. Sometimes these differences resulted in harmless banter, much like a New Yorker kidding a Texan. But in the pressure-cooker environment of small combat units where soldiers were forced into close contact with one another, the good-natured teasing sometimes turned nasty: the Northerners saw their Southern compatriots as indolent bumpkins, wastrels, spendthrifts, and at worst, cowards; the view from the South was that the Northerners were overbearing snobs, puritans, misers, and at worst, cowards.

Complicating this situation was the presence of the "regroupees," or ethnic South Vietnamese who went north for training and indoctrination, often for periods of many years. When they finally infiltrated back south, these men sometimes found themselves having difficulty being identified with or understood by natives of either north or south. The regroupees were known as "autumn" people. As a VC assistant platoon leader, himself a regroupee, explained: "They were Southerners who left for North Vietnam in the autumn of 1954, after the Geneva Agreement was signed."[26]

The Viet Cong cadres recruited in South Vietnam after 1958 seemed particularly resentful of the regroupees, often complaining about their arrogance and perceived rapid promotions. The ex–Viet Minh who stayed behind in the South believed the regroupees had lived comfortably in North Vietnam while they were enduring persecution under Ngo Dinh Diem's government. According to a Viet Cong cadre, "The returnees from North Vietnam consider the South Vietnam cadres their lackeys. They are very arrogant, and I myself have been ordered by them to do this or that."

A district-level official added, "The Southern cadres and fighters endured hardships for years while [the regroupees] were enjoying themselves in the North where peace prevailed. And now, when the struggle has already been started in the South, they come to command and show themselves to be overbearing, etc."[27]

The regroupees were in a particularly difficult position. Not only did they have to endure resentment from their fellow Southerners but also from the Northerners as well. A senior-lieutenant regroupee stated that the Northerners often spoke disparagingly of men like himself:

The North Vietnamese cadres blame the South Vietnamese, "The Southern guys only know how to have fun." Sometimes they used local terminology to insult one another, "The regroupees stink like shrimp sauce." The Southerners were quick to reply, ''Those Northern stinkers are miserly. They consider money [everything]. They are cowards like land crabs.''

The senior-lieutenant, an intelligent and perceptive individual, further explained his perspective on the North-South conflict:

The South Vietnamese consider the North Vietnamese flatterers, servile flatterers, always nodding to show their submission and never conceiving any idea of fighting for their rights. The North Vietnamese consider the South Vietnamese as lacking Revolutionary ethics, never being satisfied with anything, having a weak standpoint, always fighting.*

These disagreements were ''a lot more pronounced'' in the Party Chapter meetings:

In the units from the company echelon up, if there is no South Vietnamese in the echelon committee or in the Party committee, the South Vietnamese will consider their prestige reduced. They see themselves as having been overpowered and having no one who understands their feelings and fights for them. . . . [A]t every election for a new term for the Party committee echelon, the South Vietnamese always voted for the South Vietnamese Party members. Those arguments and fights, even though not openly known, are secret and very drastic.[28]

Because both regroupees and Northern cadres were assigned throughout the National Liberation Front (NLF), these disagreements and resentments were fairly widespread. A medical aid man in a VC local-force battalion reported that his battalion chief of staff, a Northerner, was openly snubbed by the men when he criticized them.

They retaliated by ignoring him socially. For example, if the men were drinking tea, they would invite the Southern cadres if these people happened to be around, but they would ignore the Northerner and the regroupee. The men usually displayed

*This informant was true to the stereotype in at least one respect: He beat up his North Vietnamese battalion political officer (see Chapter 8).

their fondness for the Southern cadres noisily in front of the "infiltrators" just to make the latter feel miserable and out of place.[29]

A VC main-force platoon leader expressed more resentment for his Northern counterparts, stating:

Most of our fellow fighters in South Vietnam were dissatisfied and always parried and thrust with those cadres who came from North Vietnam and who often underestimated them. They [the fighters in South Vietnam] used to say: "Don't think that because you came from the North you may behave toward us as our fathers do."[30]

"Sometimes I had a few of them as friends," another Southerner said of the Northern cadres, "and sometimes they were good men. But usually, they talked too much. They thought of themselves as VIPs. They felt superior; we had to do what they told us."

Still another soldier noted one more contrast by saying that although he found Radio Hanoi broadcasts easy to understand and interesting, they were spoiled for him because he didn't like the North Vietnamese accent used by the broadcasters. "The accent is too hard," he said, "so when I heard it, I didn't like it. It didn't sound good to me. Often when we would listen to the broadcasts, and would hear the Northern accent, we would turn the radio off."[31]

On at least one occasion this animosity boiled over into open defiance of military discipline and actual rioting. The incident involved about three hundred regroupees who had been evacuated to North Vietnam for treatment of war wounds. In mid-March 1959 these men became highly dissatisfied with the treatment accorded them by the government of North Vietnam, especially the reduction of subsidies and their reclassification as ordinary workers to be paid according to their assignments and actual work performed. Previously the regroupees had enjoyed a special classification when integrated into the civilian work force, one which entitled them to higher wages—which they considered fair compensation for their sacrifices.

Known as Recuperation Group 78, the Southern dissidents nominated a committee of twenty men to go to Hanoi and represent their case before the military high command and Prime Minister Pham Van Dong. Refused permission to enter the prime minister's office, the delegation demonstrated before the ministerial palace until an aide agreed to see three of them. Despite their efforts, evidently nothing came of the meeting.

Meanwhile, their comrades back in Thanh Hoa ran amok, rioting and destroying private property, robbing the local villagers, and reportedly even raping some of the local women. The insurrection had to be put down by three companies of armed troops. A senior lieutenant, also a regroupee, who participated in quelling this disorder, tried to reason with some of the rioters he found lounging in a coffee house near the Tranh Hoa railway station. He recalled:

> We hadn't finished talking when they pushed the chairs away and threw the glasses at us. Then some grabbed chairs and others sticks to beat us. We tied all six of them up and carried them in hammocks back to the Tranh Hoa elementary school. After that, they were sent to the Secret Service. Such fighting happened everywhere. The disorder caused a lot of conflict between the Northern and Southern people. There could not be any possible union even though some of the invalids who were leaders were shot. Their bodies were thrown into the Ma River.[32]

No doubt this particularly ugly incident was remembered by all sides and reinforced the negative stereotypes, but there is no evidence that these regional animosities, real as they were and nasty as they could sometimes become, ever really harmed the ability of the VC/NVA to cooperate successfully in joint military operations. As an NVA captain put it, "These conflicts happened between individuals and didn't affect the government's policies or their missions."

THE VIETNAMESE VILLAGER

The majority of the Vietnamese people both north and south—85 percent—live in countryside villages. A natural result of this demography was that the vast majority of the soldiers of the VC and the NVA were "country people."[33] This provided but one more contrast between Americans, who were much more likely to be from an urban environment, and their Vietnamese enemies. One commentator has observed of the West that "the tough countryman . . . for whom the rigors of campaigning differed little from the grinding hardship of everyday life, is a disappearing commodity in the northern hemisphere."[34]

Village life is important both culturally and politically. An old Vietnamese adage states that "the authority of the emperor stops at the village gates." Prior to the French conquest, the village operated as a unit of local government, "an informal association of families," traditionally independent, that became largely autonomous in the fifteenth century, when the imperial court withdrew its officials from the villages.[35]

The socioeconomic composition of the Vietnamese village during the war years consisted of tenant farmers and small proprietors with a small middle class and a still smaller number of wealthy landowners who derived their income from leasing and subleasing the land under their control. It has always been the members of this last group who have exercised leadership in the village society and they are the ones who act as the guardians of the village traditions.[36] These traditions are maintained through the village council (in South Vietnam, prior to 1956, the village chiefs) and include not only making decisions concerning village society, but also certain sacred functions and rituals associated with the village Cult of the Guardian Spirit and the annual observation of celebrations and festivals marking the end of the harvest.[37]

A characteristic of village life is that it fosters group solidarity where the life patterns of each individual are tied to those of the other members of the community. The concept of "face" among the Vietnamese is based on one's acceptance by the group/village. Loss of face means rejection by the community—a loss of confidence by society. This is not a peculiar aspect, as one might think, of the "mysterious" East. Most Americans and other Westerners avoid public rejection as assiduously as any Vietnamese villager; likewise, most consider public recognition a good thing. On the other hand, in the West, with its tradition of individualism, going against public opinion is often fully acceptable conduct. However, in Vietnam the threat of rejection, and/or being cut off from the family, is a common method of instilling obedience in Vietnamese children. This threat is so powerful that it is seldom necessary to subject Vietnamese children to corporal punishment.

To the villager, any outside authority who oppressed the people or allowed them to be oppressed lacked any form of legitimacy. This is in keeping with the basic principles of Confucianism, which frame morality in terms of man's duty and obligation—to the state, the family, his fellows. To the Vietnamese, the authority who conducts himself with arrogance, cruelty, and injustice is obeyed only to the extent that obedience can be enforced. The Confucian concept of civic responsibility is expressed succinctly in the collected sayings of Confucius published in the West as the *Analects*.

> Tzu-lu asked about government. The Master said, Lead them; encourage them! Tzu-lu asked for a further maxim. The Master said, Untiringly.[38]

Throughout the years of French domination, these cultural patterns persisted in the villages despite important economic and social changes.[39] Gerald C. Hickey observed of Khanh Hau village in South Vietnam's Mekong Delta in 1964 that:

> The traditional values, practices, and rituals continue to be honored and observed, and they are being transmitted to the younger generation as they were in the past. The ordinary villager clings to the familiar. His primary concerns are his family and perhaps his farm, and in his war-weary world, his will is the will to survive.[40]

In the minds of some Western observers, the Vietnamese villager's attachment to his land took on almost mythical proportions. Frances FitzGerald relates the story of an old farmer who refused to be evacuated from his ancestral lands because "for him to leave the land would be to acknowledge the final death of the family—a death without immortality."[41] Although this story is likely true, Hickey notes that the people living in the village of Khanh Hau in 1964 were immigrants whose ancestors had settled in the area scarcely a century before. As a succession of Vietnamese emperors extended their rule over new lands, their people settled in the conquered territories, forming new villages.

The image of Vietnamese families, happily toiling over the same ricefields for a thousand years of history and suffering terrible culture shock if separated from those ancestral lands is highly exaggerated. In 1954, an estimated one million Vietnamese fled the North to seek freedom in the fledgling Republic of South Vietnam. The North Vietnamese soldiers who came down the Ho Chi Minh Trail to fight their Southern brothers and the Americans, knew they were probably giving up family associations and village life forever—sacrificing everything for the Revolution. "Go South and die," they whispered among themselves, with no mention of village and tradition.*

Many Americans saw the villager and the Vietnamese people in general as passive, fatalistic, unresponsive to change, and even lazy. A joke popular among Americans in Vietnam in the '60s satirized this in light of a U.S. government effort to introduce into the countryside a breed of chicken that would lay bigger eggs. The American birds upbraided their Vietnamese "counterparts" in the henhouse, pointing out that their eggs, larger and better in every way than those laid by the Vietnamese hens, earned two piasters (2P) more in the marketplace. The Vietnamese chickens only shrugged and replied, "Why break your ass for only two P?"

This view of the Vietnamese was also reflected in the many quotations from Rudyard Kipling's *The Ballad of East and West*—prominently displayed in American military clubs and bars during the war throughout South Vietnam—warning: "Oh, East is East, and West is West, and never the twain shall meet" and

> *Now it is not good for the Christian's health*
> *to hustle the Aryan† brown,*
> *For the Christian riles, and the Aryan smiles*
> *and weareth the Christian down;*
> *And the end of the fight is a tombstone white*
> *with the name of the late deceased*
> *And the epitaph drear: "A fool lies here*
> *who tried to hustle the East."*

That the Vietnamese often displayed stoicism in the face of personal tragedy and disappointment, and a fatalistic attitude toward life in general, was a common perception by the American community in Vietnam. But few understood these traits in context. The bamboo plant, a national symbol of the Government of South Vietnam, was frequently adduced as proof of Vietnamese indifference to political fortune. To the Vietnamese, the bamboo is a symbol of the common man's (and the Southerners hoped the nation's) survivability: he "bends with the

---

*Interestingly, since the fall of Saigon on April 30, 1975, another estimated one million Vietnamese from all walks of life have fled a reunified Vietnam to escape the tyranny engendered by that costly victory.
†"Asian" in the Vietnam War versions.

wind.'' This willingness to accommodate external pressures (defecting from one side to the other, for example) was seen by many Americans as gross opportunism, whereas it actually reflected the belief that since man is forced to react to circumstances beyond his control, then the individual must do everything he can to take advantage of them: ''Heaven gives weal or woe/yet from the human heart it also springs/As Heaven shapes our fate we lend a hand.''[42]

Paul Berman noted that while ''belief in the efficacy of individual action, on the one hand, and resignation to destiny, on the other,'' seem contradictory to the Western mind, it is not so for the Vietnamese. He coined the phrase ''pragmatic fatalism'' to describe this trait.[43] Thus, the Vietnamese city dweller who asked an American friend to buy him a watch in the PX so he could sell it on the black market for a profit saw this not as an act of disloyalty or duplicity, but as merely taking advantage of circumstances. Similarly, the villager who woke up with a gun sticking in his face generally did what was ordered, regardless of his private political convictions or who was holding the weapon.

Religion and superstition also played important roles in forming the attitudes of the Vietnamese villager. While Buddhism is the predominant religion in village life as well as throughout Vietnam in general, it coexists peacefully with other religions, sects, and cults such as Christianity, Hinduism, Islam, Chinese ancestor worship, and animism. Animism is the belief in the ubiquity of good and evil spirits that must be constantly propitiated, which has pervaded Vietnamese village life since prehistoric times.

Along with this widespread belief in the existence of spirits, the Vietnamese also place much stock in astrology. Many Vietnamese from all walks of life never make any important decisions without first consulting an astrologer. Americans who are tempted to laugh at this should reflect that horoscopes are a permanent feature in just about every newspaper published in the United States. The impact of astrology on the decision-making process in the Reagan administration is still being debated.

While Confucianism is the predominant ethical philosophy of Vietnamese life, Buddhism is the society's major organized religious force. The two systems complement each other nicely.

In Buddhism, suffering in life is necessary to attain, through a series of incarnations in successive lives, the degree of virtue needed to achieve Nirvana—a state of endless serenity when birth, death, and rebirth no longer occur. Suffering occurs due to desire, which is always frustrating because it can never be totally fulfilled. But desire can be suppressed by leading a virtuous life. Virtue is accumulated by leading a strictly moral, mentally disciplined life oriented toward obtaining wisdom and insight.

This outline of Buddhist doctrines and principles is necessarily broad. One should remember that Buddhism is based on a system of highly developed cosmological principles. It is doubtful, however, to what degree the average Vietnamese villager understands these principles or even cares about them. His chief contact with Buddhism is at the local temple where time-honored rites and ceremonies are conducted. Lest this statement be misconstrued as a slight against the Vietnamese villager, we hasten to add that most Americans find it easier to remember the names of the Seven Dwarves than the Ten Commandments.

However, Buddhism does not teach "fatalism" in the sense that it preaches resignation to an inexorable fate or predetermined destiny. It teaches that the endless cycle of birth, death, and rebirth can be broken; it teaches that hard work and virtue have their rewards. In this sense, Buddhism is no more "fatalistic" than Christianity, which also stresses the corruption of worldly desire.

Thus the Vietnamese villager lives in a world where the dead occupy a prominent place in the affairs of the living. Anyone who has witnessed Vietnamese mourning a departed loved one knows they welcome death no more than any Westerner, but they live with it more comfortably than most Americans. The Vietnamese lives in a world where he knows he must bow to forces—family and government authority, society, the actions of warring armies and of nature—stronger than himself, but he is quick, when circumstances permit, to exercise individual initiative. He lives in a world where acceptance of authority is taught from birth but also where the proper exercise of that authority is by a strict code that carries a distinct set of obligations.

In short, the Vietnamese villager's world is one where his ability to act as an individual, if circumscribed, is far from being denied to him totally. While his outlook, opinions, and conduct have been shaped by ancient tradition and practice, he is no automaton without a mind of his own. During the Vietnam War, the side that understood these circumstances and was able to exploit them had a distinct edge on motivating its forces.

VIETNAMESE LEADERSHIP

An old joke couched in the terms of a riddle asks for the difference between the Boy Scouts and the U.S. Army. The answer is that the Boy Scouts have adult leadership. No similar jokes were told about the VC/NVA side because the Vietnamese Communists had good leaders who knew their people and how to motivate them.

The difference between the leadership of the two Vietnams can be summed up in one simple word: Effectiveness. The Republic of South Vietnam was poor while the Communist leadership was excellent. This is not to say that the men who led the Republic of South Vietnam were all evil, corrupt, and incompetent, although some were; neither is it to say that the men who led the Democratic Republic of Vietnam and the National Liberation Front had the love of their people, lived monastic lives of self-sacrifice and self-denial, and operated according to a brilliant strategy devised by politico-military geniuses, although that was true of Ho Chi Minh.

The fact is that the post-1954 government of the Republic of South Vietnam was never as successful as the Communists in asserting the control over the population required to sustain itself. Weakened and wearied by twenty years of continuous war and the stress of external pressures, the moral fiber of society in non-Communist Vietnam simply broke down. In the final years this poor stepchild of the West became totally dependent on the United States, attempting half-hearted and ineffective reforms while trying to fight a war against a determined and resourceful enemy. With American political moralists constantly looking over their shoulders, the South Vietnamese leaders in the end were reduced to giving lip service to any idea they thought would pacify their American benefactors.

From 1967 to the final battles, Nguyen Van Thieu was president of the Republic of South Vietnam. When Thieu was a colonel in the Army of the Republic of Vietnam, he commanded the 5th Vietnamese Infantry Division in 1962–1963 and was an innovative and dynamic military commander.[44] But a man who knew him as president wrote, "He could not . . . grasp what had happened in the United States . . . as he failed to grasp what was happening to him in his own country. . . . Thieu could not summon the stature to look beyond himself. . . ."[45]

Not so Ho Chi Minh. Even his enemies praised him fulsomely.

In addition to his remarkable intelligence, Ho is endowed with an outstanding personality. He has in fact all the qualities necessary in a leader, and his austerity, perseverance, iron determination and whole-hearted devotion to the cause of the Revolution are an inspiration to all who serve under him and to the nation as a whole.[46]

When Truong Nhu Tang first met Ho Chi Minh in Paris as a young man, he was captivated:[47]

I had never thought of myself as a person especially sensitive to physical appearances, but Ho exuded a combination of inner strength and personal generosity that struck me with something like a physical blow. He looked directly at me, and at the others, with a magnetic expression of intensity and warmth. Almost reflexively I found myself thinking of my grandfather. There was that same effortless communication of wisdom and caring with which my grandfather had personified for us the values of Confucian life.

To the masses he was *Bac Ho*—"Uncle Ho"—but he was also utterly ruthless and implacably cruel when he had to be. In June 1925, for a reward of 100,000 piasters, he betrayed the Vietnamese nationalist Pham Boi Chau to the French, thereby collecting some badly needed revenue for his political activities and at the same time eliminating a potentially dangerous rival.[48] Under his leadership, the Vietnamese Communist Party routinely engaged in extortion, torture, and murder. Many of the Vietnamese who saw this side of Uncle Ho did not like him at all. Years after his death a North Vietnamese dissident commemorated Ho's birthday, May 19, with these verses:[49]

> *Today, the nineteenth of May*
> *I thought o' writing about Him!*
> *Things started to smell like Him*
> *When I stopped—*
> *Better things to do!*
> *Up his ass!*

Nonbelievers aside, Ho's captivating charm and iron will, combined with his political and organizational genius, made him one of the most formidable national leaders of modern times. With his leadership of the Vietnamese Communist Party for over twenty years, it is small wonder that even the lowest-ranking cadres became imbued with such single-minded determination and devotion.

"The Viet Communists established a leadership system that largely overcame the Vietnamese trait of internecine conflict," one U.S. analyst has written.[50] They did this, under Ho Chi Minh's leadership, by restructuring Vietnamese society to refocus the loyalty of the people. Where that loyalty had traditionally belonged to the family and the village, the Vietnamese Communists succeeded in diverting it largely to the Communist Party. Ho Chi Minh wrote in 1960:[51]

> In the beginning it was patriotism and not communism which induced me to believe in Lenin and the Third International. But . . . I came to realize that socialism and communism alone are capable of emancipating the workers and downtrodden people all over the world. For the Vietnamese Revolution and people, Marxism-Leninism is . . . a real sun which lights the road to final victory, to socialism and communism.

Another analyst has written that the Workers Party of Vietnam[52]

> is led not by men and women who came from the workers' class, but rather by the descendants of Confucian scholars, many of whom participated in the traditionalist and promonarchist resistance movements against the French in the late nineteenth century.

Ho Chi Minh, Vo Nguyen Giap, Pham Van Dong, all were the sons of Vietnamese Confucian scholars, men imbued with the mandarin view of public service, "exemplary scholarship, personal integrity, and faithfulness toward what [they] deemed the obligations of public office."[53]

Another important difference between the leadership of the two Vietnams is that the Communist leaders, while they accepted large amounts of military aid and even manpower from their Communist-bloc allies, were never beholden to those benefactors to justify how they used it.

Not so the Republic of South Vietnam, whose government was constantly under pressure to clean up corruption and distribute American aid more equitably among its people, not to mention prosecuting the war successfully. On August 5, 1974, the U.S. Congress placed a $1 billion ceiling on military aid to South Vietnam and six days later pared that to $700 million. In 1973 military aid to South Vietnam had been $2.8 billion; two years later it was down to only $300 million.[54] After January 1975, just when North Vietnam was building up its forces in the South for the final campaign, the U.S. Congress denied President Ford's supplemental budget request of $522 million in military aid to South Vietnam, forcing such an ammunition shortage upon the ARVN that eventually some units were reduced to firing only three artillery rounds per gun per day. With friends like that, the South Vietnamese did not need enemies, but unfortunately, they had them and they were tenacious and dedicated.

*There is no profound difference between the farmer and the
soldier.*

—MAO TSE-TUNG

*To lead into battle a people that has not first been instructed
is to betray them.*

—CONFUCIUS, *ANALECTS*, XIII, 29

3

THE BAMBOO SOLDIERS:
RECRUITING AND TRAINING

In late 1962, an American adviser to a South Vietnamese infantry division operating in the III Corps Tactical Zone remarked
that the enemy was "being hunted like rats. They can't get away
from our firepower. I almost feel sorry for them. This is the
beginning of the end for the VC."[1] Thirteen years later, after a
forty-five-day blitzkrieg that destroyed the ARVN as a fighting
force, Viet Cong and NVA forces marched triumphantly into
Saigon. Behind them lay a bloody trail strewn with the bodies
of hundreds of thousands of their comrades. How could the
Communists tolerate such losses and still emerge the victor? The
answer to that question goes a long way toward explaining how
the Vietnamese Communists progressed from being "hunted
like rats" to becoming the only army the United States of America could not defeat.

So long as an army can be maintained in the field, defeat is
never inevitable. A classic example of this principle, one well
known to all Americans but somehow forgotten in the complex-
ities of Vietnam, is that of the Continental Army of the American Revolution. General Washington was constantly plagued
with manpower shortages—especially in the desperate campaigns of 1776 and 1777—when he literally watched his army
disintegrate around him. On the eve of the Battle of Trenton on
December 26, 1776, he faced Cornwallis's 8,000 British regulars with only 3,000 Continentals. Five years later, Lord Cornwallis surrendered to Washington's Franco-American army at

Yorktown. As long as Washington could keep a force under arms, the British could never win.

Comparisons between the American Revolution and the Vietnamese Communists' "revolution" are tenuous, and to carry them too far would be irresponsible. There is no similarity, for instance, between the way Americans recruited for their army during the Revolutionary War and the way the Vietnamese Communists recruited for theirs in the Vietnam War. Moreover, Ho Chi Minh was no George Washington, despite the claims made by his apologists in the West. Differences aside, the primary similarity is that to win a war one must defeat the enemy's army.

Another way to describe America's predicament in Vietnam is to compare the Americans to the champion boxer who goes into the ring as the odds-on favorite to win, only to lose after fourteen grueling rounds of pounding his adversary because he was too exhausted to answer the final bell, his opponent meanwhile battered and bloody but still on his feet.

It is estimated that during the period 1965–1972 the VC/NVA cumulative personnel losses from all causes (combat deaths, deaths from wounds, desertions, and prisoners) amounted to 1.298 million men. Based on the best estimates available, the VC/NVA combat death toll averaged 100,000 men per year, 1965–1972, ranging from a low of 35,000 men killed in 1965 to a high of 157,000 in 1969.[2]

Despite heavy combat casualties and attrition from disease, defection, and capture, the VC/NVA were always able to deploy an effective fighting force in the South. While the intensity of the fighting fluctuated throughout the course of the war, according to the season and the combat effectiveness of individual units in local areas, so long as the Communists maintained an army in the field they could never be defeated. This was accomplished in part by controlling the frequency of combat contacts*

---

*Between early 1966 and August 1967, RAND Corporation interrogators, interviewing over three hundred POWs and defectors, discovered that these soldiers had experienced an average of only 2.6 combat engagements during the preceding twenty-six months. In contrast, during the period of January 1966 through August 1967, the U.S. Army's 1st Cavalry Division (Airmobile) alone participated in six major combat operations—MASHER/WHITE WING, PAUL REVERE II, BYRD, IRVING, THAYER II, and PERSHING—totaling more than 560 days of combat operations for the division's units. During the period of August 18, 1965, through August 31, 1967, U.S. ground forces in Vietnam spent a total of approximately 2,900 days engaged in *major* combat operations. (See Konrad Kellen, *A View of the VC: Elements of Cohesion in the Enemy Camp in 1966–1967* [RM-5462-1-ISA/ARPA], Santa Monica,

but also by drafting recruits from among the eligible manpower pool of the North Vietnamese population and through vigorous recruiting and coercion in the South.

The Vietnamese Communist Party in both the North and the South was totally committed to its goals. One analyst has noted:

> The organization of life in North Viet Nam has much in common with organization in the Viet Cong "liberated zones" of the South. The Party's general approach in both North and South Viet Nam appears to be total mobilization of the population in the service of its objectives.[3]

THE NORTH VIETNAMESE SOLDIER

In 1966, four million of North Vietnam's eighteen million people were men between the ages of fifteen and forty-nine, one half of whom were classified as fit for military service. At that time the draft age in North Vietnam was eighteen years of age. Approximately 175,000 males turned eighteen each year during the war, and of those, 100,000 were considered fit for military service.[4]

The total strength of North Vietnam's military forces in mid-1966 was estimated at 475,000 personnel—250,000 in the regular army supplemented by paramilitary organizations consisting of another 225,000. In 1966, the Military Assistance Command, Vietnam (MACV), estimated that North Vietnam had 58,000 men in the South, about 10 percent of whom were used as fillers for VC units. Two years later MACV estimated 200,000 North Vietnamese troops were in South Vietnam of whom approximately 66,000 were fillers for Viet Cong units.[5] One reason North Vietnam could spare so much manpower was that it had a lot of help in the form of reinforcement from China.[*6]

The military manpower needs of the NVA were met principally through conscription. During wartime all able-bodied males in North Vietnam between the ages of sixteen and forty-five were eligible for the draft. Registration took place during

CA: The RAND Corporation, November 1969, p. 76; and Shelby L. Stanton, *Vietnam Order of Battle*, New York: Exeter Books, 1981, pp. 9–10).

*In May 1989, the China News Service reported that during the 1960s the People's Republic of China had sent 320,000 troops to North Vietnam. Regardless of how these troops might have been integrated into the North Vietnamese Army's order of battle, they were a significant reinforcement of Hanoi's troop strength during the war.

the first five days in January of the year each draftee became eligible. This was followed by a medical examination after which those men found physically fit for military service returned home to await induction—which normally took place the following December.

Men also volunteered for military service. There is some evidence that volunteers as young as fifteen were accepted into the North Vietnamese Army.[7] An NVA sergeant who rallied to the Government of Vietnam in March 1967 reported that some young men who lied about their age did not fool all the recruiters:

> Nowadays, many young men lie about their age, making themselves older, so that they can be accepted into the army. The morale of the young men in the North is very high. Many seventeen-year-olds volunteered and, when refused, came home crying.[8]

Draft deferments were granted for the physically disabled, sole remaining sons, and individuals who could prove they were the principal support of a family. Party officials, students, and technicians with special skills could also be deferred. Men granted medical deferments were usually reexamined after a year and then inducted or further excused.[9]

Another class of exemption was based on membership in the Vanguard Youth, a quasi-military volunteer labor organization for males between the ages of sixteen and thirty. Also exempted from the draft were ethnic Chinese, although they were permitted to volunteer for military service.

However, during the course of a long and costly war, some exceptions were recognized. One ex-NVA soldier recalls that although supposedly excused from military service because he was a sole-surviving son, he was still drafted—at age twenty-eight.[10] Another sole son, captured in the South in August 1967, claimed his status did not defer him either. "You could say I was forced to join the army," he told his interviewers.[11] First called up in 1957, at age nineteen, another NVA private, later captured in the South, recalled that he had failed to pass the induction physical, "so I stayed home until I was twenty-eight years of age," when he was finally pronounced fit for military service and drafted.[12] Still another soldier adds, evidently without rancor, that young men with political connections were able to get student deferments by being sent overseas to study. "The chairmen of every one of Hanoi's precincts . . . got their sons out of the country to study."[13] But an NVA squad leader who rallied in July 1967 stated that at his school over a hundred men entered the army before he did. Of the three hundred remaining, he said, "They were ready to enter the army whenever the order was received."[14]

Volunteering for the Vanguard Youth did not always mean avoiding the regular army. An ex-NVA sergeant who volunteered for the group to avoid conscription was drafted anyway, after two years of what he considered "wasted" service in a Hanoi-based labor battalion.[15]

Induction into the regular military included a commitment for the duration of the conflict. Early in the war the service obligation for men drafted into the North Vietnamese military forces was set at two years for the army, three for the air force and four for the navy. However, by mid-1965, because of the commitment of troops to fight in South Vietnam, active service obligations were extended indefinitely.[16]

PAY AND ALLOWANCES

Pay and rations for the Communist soldiers and allowances for their families were generally meager but adequate. The North Vietnamese government provided some assistance to the dependents of married men who were serving in the army. Members of farming families, including elderly parents, received NVN$12* a month; families living in small towns NVN$15; and city dwellers NVN$18.[17] It cost the North Vietnamese government NVN$1.20 per day to feed a soldier while he was in the North.[18] In addition, a private in basic training earned NVN$6 a month, a sergeant NVN$12.[19] "There was more than enough rice for us. We had a good diet," an NVA private stated.[20] Another soldier noted the difference between army and civilian rice rations:

> For example, when I went to visit my uncle in Hanoi, I learned their family only got seven kilos of rice a month. I learned

---

*It is very difficult to estimate how much the North Vietnamese dong was worth in U.S. currency. At the time these figures were given, the official exchange rate for the South Vietnamese piaster was seventy-three to one U.S. dollar. Because the South Vietnamese economy was much stronger than that of North Vietnam at the time, the sums mentioned here can only have amounted to pennies or mere fractions of U.S. cents in the international market.

that the teachers in the high schools . . . might get fourteen
kilos a month, whereas I got twenty-one kilos.[21]

TRAINING

Upon induction, the initial period of training for most recruits
lasted an average of three months and consisted of the basic
"school of the soldier" and infantry tactics. "I was taught to
behave as a soldier," an NVA squad leader recalled.[22] An NVA
PFC who rallied in South Vietnam in May 1967 stated that during his two months of basic training in the North, he learned
about infantry combat tactics, "that is to say, squad assault,
platoon air-defense activities; we also learned how to roll, to
creep, to crawl, to shoot, to use the bayonet, to throw grenades."[23] A corporal squad leader captured in June 1967 described his training in terms familiar to all soldiers, "walking
in step with others, saluting, shooting at targets, crawling, rolling, attacking, defending, digging foxholes, shooting with heavy
machine guns."[24]

Political indoctrination courses were an integral part of basic
training and lasted an average of two weeks.[25] A PFC captured
in August 1967 stated that during his political indoctrination he
attended lectures and viewed films—among them two entitled
The People's War and *The Party's War Policy.*[26]

Despite its relatively short duration, this political training was
intense and straightforward. One POW explained what he
learned:

> The long and short of it is this: The soldier's supreme duty is
> to fight on the side of the Revolution. The Revolution has
> given independence to one half of the country, but there still
> remains the other half. We can't live in the North in indepen-
> dence and let our fellow countrymen in the South live in
> slavery.[27]

But this political indoctrination did not turn the NVA soldier
into a doctrinaire automaton, spouting Marxist theories. Rather,
it was designed to tell him why he was fighting. One analyst
deduced:

> Though he holds and expresses a wide range of views on
> domestic and foreign affairs, often in harmony with prevail-

ing Communist tenets, he is no hard-core, across-the-board Communist. But he has learned to live with the Communist system prevailing in his native land, and conveys the impression that his parents and neighbors are not unhappy with it either.[28]

Some newly inducted soldiers trained at special recruit depots while others were sent directly to active units where they were trained by their unit cadre. All organizations of the North Vietnamese Army followed rigorous training programs and some, such as engineer and air defense units, actually got to practice their skills in combat without going South. One NVA PFC, whose air defense unit was assigned to guard two bridges in North Vietnam's Ha Trung District, Thanh Hoa Province, recalled that his position was attacked by U.S. aircraft "more than ten times" before the unit withdrew to receive three months' training on the 12.7mm anti-aircraft machine gun prior to infiltrating South.[29]

Specialized training was also given to selected individuals. An NVA PFC who rallied to the GVN in May 1967 stated that after two months of infantry combat training he was sent to a radio communications course where he was taught to operate different kinds of radio equipment (the 71-, 702-, and K63-type radios) and learned Morse code.[30] One captured lieutenant, an assistant company commander, attended a communications course for officers that lasted nine months.[31] A corporal who rallied in July 1967 stated that he was trained for "rear base-service" duties in 1965. This sophisticated course in army administration and government organization lasted nine months and taught him "how to keep records, how the government's budget is allotted to different agencies and to the Army, how to train rear-base cadres, and how much a fighter earned per month and so forth."[32]

A lieutenant in the rear services who was captured in March 1967 was trained as a logistician in a school near Hanoi where he studied specialized subjects "such as medical administration, food supply, financial affairs, dietetics, military procurement, and bookkeeping." The officer, who had first joined the army in 1953, and was discharged after being seriously wounded fighting against the French in Laos, was recalled to active duty in 1963. He infiltrated into South Vietnam in 1966, only to find himself ill-prepared for his duties:

I didn't receive any training before being sent to the South.
Only infantry and regular units received special training . . .
being in a specialized section, I wasn't given any training
before going South. In actual fact, what we had learned [at
the logistics school in Hanoi] we were not able to apply when
we were in the South, the fact being that, in the South, we
operated in the mountains and jungles. Indeed, in the South
the transportation and supply of matériel had to be made by
men rather than by cars and trucks, as we had learned in the
North.[33]

Perhaps the grossest example of how the exigencies of wartime forced the North Vietnamese to misuse highly trained military personnel is that of a squad leader in a signal unit who
joined the NVA in June 1959. Following three months of infantry training, he was sent to the naval training center in Hai Ninh
Province. There he received seven months' naval training and,
in May 1960, attended the Intermediate Navigation School of
the Sea Communications Service in Haiphong. This training
lasted twenty months and taught him about electric engines and
marine motors. Wounded during an American air strike in April
1965, he convalesced until December, when he was assigned to
a naval repair shop, where he was placed in charge of repairing
boats and ships. But his wounds did not permit him to cope with
this kind of labor-intensive work, so he was transferred to a shop
specializing in making "rank insignia, shoulder boards, army
hat insignia, insignia for collars, medals, and military uniforms" until December 1966, when he was assigned to an NVA
signal battalion.* He left for the South with his unit in January
1967. In April they arrived at their destination in Quang Ngai
Province, South Vietnam. The long-suffering sailor deserted a
month later.[34]

Another soldier, drafted in February 1962 and also a veteran
of fighting in Laos, was assigned to a rear-services unit when
selected to attend a seven-month course for security officers. "I
learned how to carry out an investigation, how to spot enemy
Rangers and frogmen, to guard the coast, and to keep security
in the rural areas. We were supposed to watch the people for
possible traitors among them." This soldier rose to the rank of

*This man may have been telling the truth but old soldiers will recognize here a
pattern common to all armies: A soldier is often sent to "the front" because he
managed to displease some powerful military superior in the rear.

sergeant before he defected in July 1967 simply by walking across the Ben Hai River and turning himself in at the first checkpoint on the other side of the Demilitarized Zone.[35]

After selection for infiltration South, training intensified for most units. This included political indoctrination, physical conditioning, some instruction in enemy weapons and mines, and additional proficiency training with their own weapons. "Shooting at moving targets was part of the training. . . . I learned how to shoot in the dark," a senior sergeant and assistant platoon leader stated.[36] A corporal who had been a carpenter in civilian life remembers that "everyone tried to attain marksmanship" in his infantry unit.[37]

A corporal medical aidman who infiltrated with an infantry sniper unit stated that they trained for eleven months before coming South, two months of basic military training and nine months special weapons training:

> Most of the men in my unit had K-45 rifles equipped with telescopic sights, and they used them in the training. Those weapons were said to come from Hungary. Being a medic, I had a special duty in my company. I had no rifle, so didn't have to practice shooting. But when I had spare time, I used to watch friends in their target practice and, from time to time, was allowed to do some shooting.[38]

A corporal in an NVA engineer unit was given extensive training in disarming enemy mines:

> There are many ways to remove a mine. But in all these methods we use a "thuon" to detect a mine trap first, and then we remove the mine step by step. A "thuon" is a long and pointed iron rod with which one can poke at the ground to see whether there is a mine trap underneath the mine itself. For, according to your usual mine-laying methods, underneath a mine you often lay another mine as a trap which endangers those removing the mine. The basic method to remove all kinds of mines consists of three steps: (1) to detect the mine trap, (2) to cut the ignition cords if the mine is equipped with them, and (3) to take out the fuse, and then get the mine.[39]

Even those units that did not receive much specialized military training before infiltration underwent intensive physical conditioning, "strengthening our legs for the long march South," as an NVA officer candidate put it.[40]

"We also practiced walking long distances while carrying heavy loads. Each evening we walked for one or two hours carrying heavy loads," said one NVA private.[41] These loads averaged from forty-five to sixty pounds, or the approximate weight of the equipment, weapons, and ammunition each soldier was required to carry with him while infiltrating. In some cases the loads used in training weighed up to seventy pounds.[42]

Being selected for infiltration South also meant extra food and pay during the preparation phase. Soldiers were paid NVN$60 per month during this time (approximately five times the pay of a sergeant in a unit not selected for infiltration). A sergeant captured in May 1965 stated that while training for infiltration his food ration was NVN$1.80 per day (0.70 from his monthly pay with the remaining 1.10 paid by the government). He spent a total of NVN$21 on food each month and was free to spend the rest as he pleased. The North Vietnamese government used the remainder of the ration supplement to buy meat and fish, beer, cigarettes, and candy for the troops. The soldiers were also assured that the government would "pay for all expenses incurred by our families when they got sick (expenses for food and medicine). The soldiers' parents who were too old to work would be granted a monthly allowance."[43]

An important aspect in understanding the training and motivation of the ordinary NVA soldier is that while he was in most cases from an agrarian background, he was not an illiterate. An analysis of interviews with two hundred POWs and defectors indicates that more than half (115) had some secondary school education while only one was actually illiterate.[44] Only twelve of these men came from an "upper class" of North Vietnamese society (defined as bourgeoisie, landowner, and rich farmer).[45]

The NVA soldier was also highly motivated and willing to follow his leaders. Between 1963 and November 1969, only 1,700 North Vietnamese soldiers (less than one percent) defected to the South Vietnamese side, despite intensive propaganda efforts to get them to do so. During that same period, 150,000 Viet Cong defected. "Everyone who has spoken with the NVA—if only for a few minutes—vouches for the excellence of their morale, which is not accidental," one analyst determined.[46]

From this data there emerges a picture of the North Vietnamese Army soldier as a man trained in conventional-warfare tactics and weapons. Surprisingly, missing from his program is any special emphasis on jungle warfare or survival training. One analyst concluded from this at the time that the NVA therefore had not been adequately prepared for the battles they faced in the South.[47] This criticism crumbles in the face of two facts: Inured as he was to the hard work and deprivation that characterized agrarian and village life in North Vietnam, the NVA soldier was prepared from birth to face the hardships of military operations in South Vietnam's jungles and mountains; and what he had to learn about surviving in the jungles of South Vietnam he learned well enough to win his war, and he learned these skills not in the classroom but in the jungle itself.

THE VIET CONG SOLDIER

Because of the political/military situation in South Vietnam, the National Liberation Front was forced to institute military recruitment and training programs radically different from those that worked so well in the North.

Competition with the Government of South Vietnam for manpower was a reality that affected VC recruitment. In early 1966 the strength of the ARVN was 585,000, or 3.6 percent of South Vietnam's total population. As of January 1, 1965, there were approximately 4.3 million South Vietnamese males between the ages of fifteen and forty-nine, about half of whom were fit for military service. All males in South Vietnam between the ages of eighteen and thirty-seven were subject to conscription. During the war approximately 140,000 males came of draft age each year.[48] While the ARVN's strength remained approximately ten times that of the Viet Cong throughout the war—according to U.S. estimates—it was always able to meet its force-level requirements. This was because the GVN controlled most of the population centers of South Vietnam and was able to replace its losses from a draft-eligible manpower pool.

The Viet Cong were not so fortunate. In June 1966, the Military Assistance Command, Vietnam, estimated total Viet Cong combat strength at 46,000 personnel.*[49]

---

*These figures do not include VC infrastructure or irregular forces. Tachmindji (p. 788) reports total VC combat strength for 1966 as 64,000 personnel. Tachmindji's figures have been "retroactively adjusted," presumably to include some of those forces not in the MACV Order of Battle Summary. This practice—excluding infrastructure and irregular forces from the Enemy Order of Battle summaries—was taken

As noted earlier, MACV also estimated that in 1966 approximately 10 percent of the personnel in Viet Cong units were North Vietnamese "fillers." The practice of using NVA soldiers to reinforce VC combat units continued throughout the war to the point that by mid-1968 one out of every three men in VC battalions was North Vietnamese.[50]

While it is not often possible to separate Viet Cong losses from those of the NVA, total VC combat-strength figures show a gradual decline between 1965 and 1972. From 46,000 combat troops in mid-1966 (MACV Order of Battle Summary), the Viet Cong force in South Vietnam had shrunk to only 25,000 by January 1973.[51] Another source shows a similar decline, from a high of 64,000 men in 1966 to a low of 24,000–35,000 by 1972.[52] These figures are stark evidence why, as the war dragged on, the Viet Cong was forced to change its recruiting policy from one based initially and exclusively on volunteers to one that relied more and more on kidnapping young men in order to fill its ranks.

The methods of the Viet Cong recruiters can be illustrated by examining a composite case represented by young Nguyen, a resident of Ga Chet, a hamlet just outside the village of Suc Lo, Bu Lon Province, southwest of Saigon in the Mekong Delta region.

Young Nguyen has lived all his young life in Ga Chet hamlet. He has been once to the provincial capital, a city of 15,000 inhabitants some twenty kilometers away from Suc Lo Village, but otherwise he has not traveled much. A few families in his hamlet own radios and occasionally he has seen some Saigon newspapers, but he has little interest in the political events taking shape in the nation's capital. He does know that the Saigon government is fighting the Viet Cong in the countryside and while there have been no major military operations as yet in his home district, it lies in a contested area and he understands that someday he will become involved in the war. In short, he is an impressionable young man with no fixed political views.

because it was felt at the time that those forces played little or no role in U.S. combat operations (see Lewy, pp. 74–75). In the opinion of some analysts, however, this was a serious flaw inasmuch as by this accounting method many Americans in combat units were killed by nonexistent forces: During operations CRIMP (January 1966), CEDAR FALLS (January 1967), and JUNCTION CITY (February–March 1967), many of the U.S. casualties were caused by headquarters, headquarters support, and local-force units, not the enemy maneuver battalions (Tourison).

Nguyen has just turned eighteen, so he knows he is a prime candidate for either the Army of Vietnam (ARVN) or the Viet Cong. His is a poor family and he works hard in his father's tiny ricefields. He has attended school in the nearby village for only four years and is literate. He would have liked to have had more schooling, but he is more concerned with wanting to buy a bicycle. An uncle on his mother's side of the family is serving on the village committee in an NLF-controlled village some distance from his own.

Suc Lo Village and its hamlets are nominally under the control of the Government of South Vietnam (GVN), but the VC have had no trouble penetrating Ga Chet at night and conducting propaganda activities among its people. At these sessions the Viet Cong cadres routinely ask for volunteers. "Would you run away and let others fight the enemy for you?" they ask. "We are becoming more and more powerful," they tell the people, "and soon we will drive off the Americans and achieve national reunification of our country." They exhort them: "Do something for the right side, work for your people's happiness and at the same time secure a better future for yourself." Sometimes they are entertained by troupes of singers and dancers, and Nguyen likes these sessions particularly. One or two of his contemporaries have already responded to the call and joined up with the VC.

While Nguyen has never seen an American, his feelings toward the GVN Self Defense Corps (SDC) garrison in the nearby village are ambivalent. These men slouch about the village and pay little attention to him. They seem the perfect picture of mercenaries by which the Viet Cong cadres describe them. Once, some of them beat up a friend of Nguyen's for no reason except that he had been strolling about the village in the evening. It is dangerous at times even to look at an SDC the wrong way in public. "We wouldn't swap one of our fighters for twenty of them," a VC cadre once said. Nguyen can't help but contrast the conduct of the SDC men with that of the NLF cadres, who are always polite and talk sweetly to the people. He knows the NLF men are not with the Front for pay and benefits, and he believes them when they say they are of the people themselves and therefore genuinely love them. Nguyen has no reason to doubt this. The VC cadres he has seen have always been civil and solicitous toward the people. He remembers one occasion when a smiling cadre used his own handkerchief to wipe the nose of a small child.

There is something else about these NLF recruiters that appeals to Nguyen. They are no longer humble farmers but men with a mission, doing important work. They carry weapons and handle them with easy familiarity. They are men with power and respect, and there is no way young Nguyen can imagine *them* kowtowing to fat village elders or SDC hoodlums. And moreover, they are asking Nguyen to join with them!

Nguyen's father has made it clear that he does not particularly like the village chief, whom he considers arrogant. The chief even went so far once as to curse Nguyen's father in public because he had complained about having to work longer hours on some village project than other, more affluent villagers. Also, Nguyen harbors a vague resentment against the members of the village council who are fatter, work less, and have more than his father, who has never known anything in this life but the incessant toil of farming. Certainly, the sons of these men are better off than young Nguyen. Perhaps unknown even to himself, this resentment is being gradually solidified by the VC propaganda lectures Nguyen has attended. But still, he does not want to leave home. His place is with his father.

Then one day Nguyen is visited at home by two NLF cadre, a man and a woman. The man talks nicely at first. "You will soon be drafted by the GVN," he tells Nguyen. "Are you willing to die for the Americans? If you are conscripted, it's the same as a death sentence. The government will send you to the Central Highlands and you will never see your family again. Now, we think you'd make a good fighter for the Front and if you join us, you might well save your life." These people, he is surprised to learn, know Nguyen and his family very well; obviously they took the time to investigate his background. This is both flattering and comforting, and Nguyen feels at ease in their company. But unknown to young Nguyen, the personal approach is merely the first step in any well-planned clandestine operation to recruit new people, whether as spies or soldiers. By noting his likes and dislikes and other personal characteristics, the VC recruiters have successfully made the first big step in gaining his confidence.

"What is 'the Revolution'?" Nguyen asks at one point. "It is to chase out the imperialists," the man replies. "If we are victorious, you will never have to be a slave to anyone and your family will be shown the respect it deserves." Nguyen thinks immediately of the village chief and the SDC men who protect him.

The woman, older than Nguyen but younger than his mother, tells him that she joined the Front to fight against the enemies of the Vietnamese people. "Is it right," she asks, "that young men like you sit at home with your families?" He is very embarrassed by this accusation because how can a man do less than a woman? This plays directly on the traditional male-female role models of Vietnamese society, which have always produced strong (but not publicly aggressive) women. Nguyen would have been impressed by this particular woman because here she is performing tasks not normally associated with females in his experience.*

Nguyen remembers his uncle and his friends who have already joined the NLF. Even some of the girls in the hamlet have asked him when he plans to join the Front!

The pair visits Nguyen's home on several more occasions, each time for a period of several hours, plying him with the same themes. They tell him that in the Front he will receive special education and training and will earn respect. They assure him that if he is faithful and proficient, he will rise in rank and responsibility. Finally the woman says, "You can't sit on the fence forever," and the man, apparently losing his patience, upbraids him, "You are a young man living in a country in danger! You must defend it! I myself have left my own family to serve the Front! But here you are, hiding your face in your mother's skirts! You don't even deserve to live!"

This is too much! Nguyen is only eighteen and he had begun these sessions more than half convinced that the NLF was on his side anyway. Profoundly embarrassed but enthusiastic at the same time, he takes the plunge and joins the Liberation fighters.

The story of young Nguyen is a composite of many of the methods used by VC recruiters to persuade young men to join their cause. These techniques were extremely effective—and when the VC recruiters adopted an individual approach and turned on the charm full force, they often proved irresistible, even in the face of bitter personal resentment. One actual example of joining the Front despite previous negative experience is that of the son of a GVN hamlet chief whose father had been executed by

---

*The Communists in Vietnam recruited women as a wartime necessity. As a result, they may unwittingly have sown the seeds of their own Vietnamese womens' liberation movement (Tourison interviews).

the Viet Cong. The party secretary made a point of personally
visiting the potential recruit to explain the reasons and necessity
for the execution. The young man remembers:

> In the beginning I was very hurt and angry with them for
> killing my father. I quarreled with them. Then they told me
> that because my father had done wrong in serving as hamlet
> chief and thereby "working against his own class interests,
> against the poor classes," he had to be punished. But he also
> said that the faults of the father should not be visited upon
> the son. They talked to me and to people like me whose
> relatives were killed, in order to eradicate all their hatred of
> the VC. They talked to a point where I felt that they were
> right. I no longer felt hurt. . . . I came to hate my father even
> though I didn't know exactly what he had done.[53]

While this example is admittedly extreme, it illustrates how the
Viet Cong used psychology not only to win over a reluctant recruit but also to separate him from his family loyalty. The persuasive Viet Cong agents convinced the young man to transfer
the spirit and scope of his family loyalty to the Party. The transfer
of one's loyalty, as previously noted, is the goal of all clandestine
recruiting programs.* This "disassociation" effect was an integral part of the "bonding" process to which each new recruit
for the Viet Cong was subjected, and it is one of the primary
reasons why many of them stayed in the ranks despite coercion,
deception, harsh treatment, and terrible living conditions.

Many of the men who did ultimately become disillusioned
and deserted the Viet Cong did so to rejoin their families. The
VC leadership quickly realized that thwarting this tendency was
vital to their cause. When disassociation failed to work, the VC
succeeded in substituting camaraderie and the authority of the
Party for that of family. Their highly restrictive leave policy
helped reinforce each man's closeness to the others in his unit.
Because family loyalty is so much a part of every person's being
in Vietnamese society, once the transfer of loyalty to the Front
was complete, men saw most actions of the Party as justified
and good for them, much as children raised in the Confucian

---

*Among Vietnamese Communists today, those who have defected and subsequently
revealed publicly the internal problems and power struggles of the Party are considered particularly reprehensible because they have dared to bare "family" (Party)
business to strangers.

way accept parental punishment and criticism as proper and beneficial.[54]

The story of young Nguyen also illustrates the political ambiguity of the Vietnamese villager. One analyst has noted that:

> In the eyes of the Vietnamese villagers, there is no clear distinction between the legitimacy of the government and . . . the Viet Cong. Because identification is focused on the family and village, the government is not seen, as it is in the Western tradition, as a unique object of loyalty. It is simply one of a number of forces which attempts to assert its rights, coerce the peasants, and exert its will. . . . The idea of two governments is not an odd one to Vietnamese villagers. That is the way they talk about the GVN and the VC. We should not . . . be surprised (that) men who joined the Viet Cong . . . will be effectively loyal to it.[55]

A 1968 survey* of 491 former Viet Cong (POWs and defectors) revealed the following on why they joined the Viet Cong.[56]

REASONS GIVEN†	% OF SURVEY
1. Economic and social frustrations	32
(49% of the men in this group listed promise of advancement in the VC system as their primary motive; 29% were unemployed)	

*It should be noted that inasmuch as these respondents were defectors or prisoners, their responses to the questions might reveal what they thought their interrogators *wanted* to hear. The questions also seem couched in terms more relevant to Westerners than Vietnamese. Note that none said they joined because they hated the Americans.
†It is interesting to contrast (not to draw any parallels) the findings of this survey with those conducted among American youths at about the same time. A 1967 survey of 1,495 American high school seniors conducted for the U.S. Army Recruiting Command revealed that 40 percent of the respondents would enlist for better job opportunities. Nineteen percent thought army service would make them "more mature," while only 5 percent listed "patriotic reasons" for motivation (Ketchum, MacLeon & Grove, Inc., *Youth Attitude Trend Survey*, May 1967, pp. 8, 10). Discounting such factors as government oppression, a yearning for social justice, and the fact that these opinions were given *before* entering the military, these young Americans were drawn to U.S. Army service for similar reasons and in about the same percentages as their Vietnamese counterparts were attracted to the Viet Cong. The Simulmatics Corporation study, *Improving the Effectiveness of the Chieu Hoi Program*, op. cit., likewise noted that "Men who join the VC for purely ideological reasons are exceedingly rare." (p. 107)

2. Personal oppression by the GVN   28
   (This includes acts of oppression against
   family members. One respondent cited
   being slapped in the face in public by an
   ARVN officer)
3. VC recruitment   20
   (These respondents were characterized as
   "young and naïve," looking for
   excitement or adventure)
4. Social justice   11
   (This includes perceptions of inequality of
   wealth and corruption of GVN officials
   and soldiers)
5. Family-peer pressure   6
   (Here themes of economic-social
   frustration reappear)
6. Other   3

Up to 1963, VC recruiting in South Vietnam was almost totally from among eligible volunteers—and standards for acceptance were quite high. The preferred age range was seventeen to thirty. Men may often have been enticed to join by the promise of service close to home.* However, after 1963, recruiters were instructed to lower the required health standards and apply force to draft-age men to enlist in the Viet Cong. The upper age limit for recruits was also raised from thirty to forty.[57]

The decision to rely more heavily on a levy than on volunteers seems to have been made sometime in 1964. At this point, with the continually deteriorating South Vietnamese political situation, the VC were expanding their forces and stepping up their attacks. The VC levy included all otherwise eligible men eighteen to thirty-five years of age for "service for the duration." Even those disqualified for combat service as a result of wounds often found themselves reassigned to rear-echelon units (particularly food production), where they continued to serve. This system was enforced systematically by the Viet Cong, allowing few exemptions (sole surviving sons, for example, but in practice these exemptions were seldom invoked or recognized).[58] The promises of service in the home district were soon dropped because of the exigency of the war. Villagers were instead escorted away to training centers and service with remote units.[59]

---

*However, in the Viet Cong the path to advancement and prestige for ambitious and spirited recruits lay with service in main-force, not local-force or guerrilla units (Tourison).

A survey of ex–Viet Cong in 1967 revealed that 66 percent of them claimed to have been drafted. According to a former platoon leader:

> In Ben Tre province the VC are militarily very strong this year, because everywhere they force the population to yield a proportionate number of men for their troops and they no longer use propaganda to get men to enlist.[60]

One individual, who claimed to have been a member of a platoon that accompanied district cadres around Binh Duong Province on their monthly recruiting missions, stated that the drives brought in from ten to seventy young men a month and "if the person concerned objected stubbornly . . . he would be tied up and taken away anyway."[61]

A company commander and former member of the district military committee in Vinh Binh Province stated in an April 1965 interview that between 1960 and 1963, the provincial Party committee had no trouble meeting its monthly quota of forty to forty-five recruits, but that since 1964 only about 30 percent of the quotas had been met. He reported:

> Formerly, the selection of new recruits or fighters was very careful, based on the social class of each individual. They had to undergo a testing period, and elements with low morale were rejected. The men received military training before being assigned to a combat unit. Now, the screening of new recruits is careless, and their training is given in proportion as they are assigned to combat units as replacements. The new fighters joining my unit in the last six months before my capture had very little combat experience and therefore their fighting was weak.[62]

The morale and quality of new recruits for the VC varied according to time and place. A platoon leader who rallied in March 1967 described the new recruits in his unit as men who were

> quite capable and they had high morale. Thus, the old fighters and the cadres didn't have to spend too much time guiding them in combat and thus decrease their own fighting ability. The old fighters and the cadres said that the new recruits had the ability and the spirit to fight.[63]

TRAINING

The amount of training received by Viet Cong recruits ranged from none to quite sophisticated, depending on the particular type of unit or activity to which they were assigned. It must also be noted that the amount and quality of training varied from area to area based on the availability of training cadre. Shortage of trainers was a continual problem for the VC.[64] The least well-trained were the members of the part-time guerrillas. What training these men received was often "on the job." An eighteen-year-old village guerrilla from Tuy Hoa District, Phu Yen Province, stated in April 1965 that from September to December 1964, he was not even armed.

> During that period, we had the mission to stand guard . . . at the entrance of (our) hamlet. If we saw the ARVN coming we should beat on the gong so that the cadres could hide themselves. We had also to sharpen the spikes and plant them around the mountain.[65]

In January 1965, the Viet Cong cadres finally issued the recruit a firearm, but he never got to use it. During an attack on his village only a month later, he became so frightened he hid under a bed and was captured.

A squad leader in another village in Tuy Hoa District reported that all the men in his unit had been members of the Republican Combat Youth—a paramilitary organization sponsored by the South Vietnamese government—"so all of us knew how to fire a rifle," he said. "Later, we shot one or two bullets just to give warning and not to fight, and after shooting we vanished."[66]

Still another Viet Cong, recruited into a hamlet guerrilla unit in Tuy An District of Phu Yen Province, was assigned guard duties. At night his three-man cell and some militiamen stood guard in the hamlet. At four A.M. they climbed a nearby mountain to watch for approaching ARVN troops. At seven A.M. they would descend the mountain and undertake their daily work routine. If the enemy was sighted, they were "to fire a few shots to warn the villagers and the village cadres." On March 9, 1965, this man took his family, two oxen, some clothes, and forty kilograms of rice and defected.[67]

However, it was not unusual for these paramilitary soldiers to be transferred to local- or main-force units, where their rudimentary military training was supplemented by unit training.

A deputy company commander and acting company political officer captured in July 1967 stated that the training his men had received was not formal

> because we had no permanent place to stay. Our unit moved often. Furthermore most of the members in my unit had been guerrillas before they were transferred . . . and they had some training before.

The unit training these men did receive consisted of basic infantry tactics, "how to walk through a village and through the people's homes, get through a fence, and so on."[68]

Captured documents pertaining to the training program for recruits assigned to the Viet Cong units operating in Dinh Tuong Province, in the Mekong Delta region, reveal a well-organized and ambitious schedule. In early 1966 the provincial military affairs committee directed that recruits were to receive eight days' training before assignment to a battalion. Six days were devoted to military training such as close-order drill, firing positions, bayonet drill, and grenade throwing. The remaining two days were to be devoted to political training. There were three training sites in the province, each operated by a cadre of thirteen men. During 1964–1965 each course trained approximately seventy recruits but later the cycles consisted of between thirty and sixty trainees. Because of ammunition shortages, marksmanship training consisted mostly of dry-fire exercises.

When recruits were assigned directly to a battalion, they were sent to a platoon where they would train in the battalion campsites, under the direction of the battalion command staff. Ideally, these cycles were to last one month, with seven days of political indoctrination and twenty-three days of military training. The political training consisted of teaching the recruits about the mission of their unit; NLF policy, proselytizing, and leadership; and army traditions. Their military training was to include use and maintenance of weapons; grenade throwing; fortifications and camouflage; movement procedures; individual, cell, and squad tactics; sanitation; protective measures against toxic chemicals; military discipline; guard and patrol duty; liaison; reconnaissance; and POW escort.

The assistant chief of staff for operations of the 5th VC Division issued instructions in which he established the following as the minimum training required for a battalion to perform effectively:

—Marksmanship and weapon familiarization.
—Techniques of armored vehicle destruction.
—Ambush tactics.
—Surprise attack.
—Anti-heliborne or paratroop tactics.

The schedule for specialized training programs was ambitious. Squad and platoon leader training were to last three and five months, respectively, and were to consist of 20 percent political training emphasizing the build-up of unit strength and the development of flexibility, vigilance, and determination.

Training operators of crew-served weapons (heavy machine guns, recoilless rifles, mortars) was to last four months with emphasis on proper maintenance and firing of the weapons. The duration of signal training varied by classes: radio-maintenance, fourteen months; signal squad leader's course, six months; Morse code training, six months; radio repair class, twelve months.

Sappers were trained in squad-, platoon-, and company-sized groups for periods varying from three to six months. These courses taught the use and handling of explosives, wiring of mines, methods of hiding batteries, mine repair, evading mine sweepers and detection, and observation and reconnaissance techniques.

Ideally, village guerrillas were to receive twenty to thirty days additional refresher training each year, to be divided equally between political and military subjects. Guerrilla self-defense units were to be trained in sniper fire, trench warfare, use of grenades and mines, tunneling, and construction of homemade weapons; district companies were to be trained to defend against countersweep operations, conducting surprise raids, trench fighting, ambushing, demolition work, and psychological warfare.

The potential training capability for the Viet Cong in Dinh Tuong Province was estimated at 400 per year for the three-month signal courses; 390 per year for the heavy weapons courses; and 200 per year for the advanced squad leader's courses.

In theory, the Viet Cong believed that political and military training should be given equal consideration, but in practice, military training received more emphasis. In the hard reality of war, where VC main-force unit replacement requirements often exceeded the manpower supply available, raw recruits often received their only real training in actual battle.[69]

As noted, the duration and quality of Viet Cong training varied with time and circumstance. A demolition expert assigned to a local-force unit that operated in Sa Dec Province attended a two-month training program with seventy others. During this course the students lived in the villagers' houses and classes "were held in the garden."[70] A squad leader in a main-force battalion who rallied in May 1967 described the training he received in Long An Province in 1962:

> This training center was located in the [Plain of Reeds]. . . .
> It consisted of many wood-framed and thatched-roof barracks
> patterned after the civilian structures and built at an interval
> of thirty to one hundred meters between each other. The cen-
> tral board of administrators and instructors included five men.
> There were about two hundred trainees in this center and they
> were organized into squad-size units for better training and
> operations. Rice and supplies were issued to the squads and
> the squads were responsible for their cooking. At five o'clock
> each day, there was one hour of physical training. After stay-
> ing for fifteen days at this center, I was sent along with ten
> others to the Battalion.

Upon arrival at his unit, this man received company training, when military operations would permit. "In my unit," he stated, "I was employed in combat operations and training off and on, so after about seven months, I felt I was ready and qualified." Contradicting the myth that all Viet Cong were expert jungle fighters, this squad leader stated that he

> was only trained for operations in the lowland area. I was
> trained in how to use a rifle and an automatic rifle, how to
> fight as part of a three-man cell, and as part of a squad.[71]

A main-force acting platoon leader who defected in May 1967 recalled the assistant platoon leader's course he attended in An Xuyen Province in the fall of 1963:

> The . . . course was taught by a Mobile Infantry School . . .
> which included four instructors and thirty students [and] never
> stayed fixed in one area. It often mixed with the civilian com-

munities along the river banks. For food allowances, each student received one liter of rice and NVN$1.50 per day.

His military training included use of rifles, submachine guns, and automatic rifles; crawling techniques; lessons in squad, platoon, and company tactics in combat; lessons on assault operations against both fortified positions and field positions; and staging ambushes. Because the school kept moving, sophisticated training facilities were impossible, but upon graduation this officer-recruit was satisfied that he had received good training.

I felt I had made much progress in the military and political sciences and that I was fully capable of leading a platoon-size unit. My morale was one of ardor and enthusiasm.

At a later period the same soldier added that the men in his unit were given training on the art of living in the jungle and jungle warfare.[72]

A former company commander of a district regional-force unit in the Central Highlands who rallied in May 1967 received his basic training along with 150 other draftees in 1960. The training center was in a forested area with permanent structures where three cadres conducted the training. In March 1963, the officer was sent to a three-month platoon leader's course in a forested area in Pleiku Province, where the men lived in thatched houses. One hundred men attended this course conducted by three instructors. The students trained in shifts, one half going to classes while the other half carried supplies.

In February 1965 he attended a six-month company commander's course at the same training site. This time there were four instructors for 150 trainees, who again trained in shifts, half attending classes while the rest carried supplies. The men were informed that the Front was shifting its tactics from special to conventional warfare by reinforcing regional, main and provincial forces and equipping them with "all types of modern weapons like cannons, mortars, and artillery."* After these courses, the officer felt he had gotten "more experience for

---

*This is consistent with the guerrilla phase of the war being prosecuted by the NLF prior to Washington's decision to commit U.S. combat troops to the war in South Vietnam on the one hand, and Hanoi's decision to commit itself to conventional war on the other.

combat, and in combat, I felt I was well trained enough to be able to control my men."[73]

A physician's assistant* assigned to a main-force unit who defected in February 1967 attended medical training courses for a total of twenty-four months between early 1962 and July 1966—first a six-month nursing school and later an eighteen-month course for physician's assistants. During this latter course of instruction, he studied physiology, internal and external medicine, pharmacology, obstetrics and pediatrics, acupuncture, hygiene, and "professional management." His practical training consisted of performing an operation on a dog. "We cut off some inches of its intestines and then tied the two ends together. About two weeks later, the dog was well again." This man said his instructors told him that "we couldn't hope to know everything in detail, but should learn the main points and after we had returned to our units, we could continue our learning there."[74]

A main-force captain who served four years as a cadreman at a platoon leader's school situated in a locale controlled by the Front noted how often the classes were interrupted by enemy action. He stated that the village where the school operated was bombarded almost every night, in a "free and unrestricted" manner, although damage to the school facilities and personnel was never serious.[75]

This officer also reported a change in the emphasis of training at his school over the years. "In recent years," he told his interrogator, "student candidates for platoon leader positions were often told that they might not lead one platoon, but possibly command an entire company."[76]

Food for the students and cadre at this school was purchased on the local market and while it "was never as good as the food at home," it was acceptable and the sacrifice of quality served "as a reminder of our ultimate mission." Between training cycles some cadre asserted they hired themselves out to the local farmers to make extra money, helping with harvesting and even transporting the crops to market.[77]

The school had its own cooking facilities:

*This term translates *yi si* in Vietnamese, or "medical technician," although in VC units, prior to the availability of certified medical doctors with NVA units coming to the South, the *yi si* were often the most qualified medical personnel in provincial and regimental medical units (Tourison).

normally a small barracks with a slanted roof. We have three
meals a day: breakfast at 0600 hours, lunch at 1200 hours,
and supper at 1800 hours. Students on barracks duty had to
prepare the meals, while other students went to the training
fields.[78]

Another interesting aspect of life at this school—and a surprising exception to the policy that prevailed almost everywhere else
in the system—was that the cadre and students were allowed to
have visits from their families.

There was no rule and no denial of visits. However, to the
poorer students, the school would advise infrequent visits
because they involved large expenditures and ate up the family budget. I would even say the school policy on family visits
was a bit too generous. The school provided food and housing
for visitors and entertained them throughout their stay at the
school.[79]

It is interesting to compare these assessments of Viet Cong advanced and specialized training with the statements of a cadreman who was a member of a three-man basic training team.
This individual, a regroupee from North Vietnam (who because
of his years in the North may have harbored some prejudice
against his fellow Southerners), operated in Binh Dinh Province
before his capture by South Korean forces in October 1966. He
instructed four cycles of basic trainees for the Viet Cong, one
in 1964, two in 1965, and one in February and March 1966.
Because his job was strictly military instruction, he claimed no
knowledge of his charges' political sophistication—but it cannot
have been high, judging from the degree of illiteracy among the
men he trained.

The fighters were between sixteen and twenty-six. The majority of them were single. They were all Southerners. There
were former GVN draftees among them. Their cultural level
was low, the majority were unable to read and write. I knew
that because I didn't see them take notes. They were in good
health, attended the courses regularly but didn't ask questions.* They respected discipline as any other new recruits

* Actually, the taking of notes during training was not encouraged by NLF cadres, nor
were the men expected to ask questions. In the first place, the trainees were expected

would. It's the same on both sides. I trained only new recruits. They were in the provincial forces. Those who were between eighteen and twenty-six were often former guerrillas. There were some who were homesick or afraid of death, but they didn't ask to be discharged and go home. Each training course was attended by forty to seventy trainees.

When asked to compare the recruits of 1966 with those of 1964 and 1965, the cadre said, "There was no difference in their age. The 1966 trainees were more receptive because the majority of them had been guerrillas, but they were still inferior to the people in the North. . . ."[80]

Illiteracy and lack of formal education among Viet Cong recruits was a problem. The median educational level of the VC was less than two and a half years, and illiteracy ran from 5 to 15 percent.[81] The VC leadership realized this shortcoming and its political officers were charged with organizing literacy programs. The political officers were given the task because the Party considered such "cultural instruction" an integral part of political indoctrination. Regular evening classes were held, military situation permitting, and soldiers were obliged to attend, participate in classwork, and do daily homework assignments.[82] The VC referred to these as "cultural classes," and they included more than just instruction in reading. Instruction in arithmetic was also part of the curriculum with problems as complex as:

A rectangle plot of land measures 45m long and 35m wide. Two roads, each 1.50m in width, are built one along the length of the land and the other along the width of the land. What is the remaining surface area of the plot of land?[83]

An assistant platoon leader in a VC main-force unit described these sessions:

These courses, held in every unit, ranged from elementary to primary education. In my unit, they were held three times a week and lasted for about two hours each time, if we were

to memorize their lessons by rote and they were told that if the Party wanted them to know something, they would be informed, so therefore questions were discouraged. Secondly, it was symptomatic of the security paranoia that infected the NLF that men who asked too many questions or took notes could be subjected to embarrassing scrutiny by the cadres.

not tied down by other missions. Illiterates were taught in groups of three. The more literate soldiers were taught in larger groups. There were about ten illiterates in my company.[84]

"It may not provide village schools," one analyst has commented on the NLF's promise of educational programs for the South Vietnamese villagers, "but it still provides extensive and in some ways excellent training to its own members."[85]

As has been shown, the Viet Cong training program ranged from reading classes for illiterates through year-long courses on the repair and maintenance of complicated signal equipment. Most training was fairly routine, but the unusual was also provided. A young soldier interviewed in February 1965 told of a twenty-eight-day sabotage course he attended with a dozen others during the month of October 1964 at a VC safe house somewhere near Cu Chi.[86]

At instruction time, each one of us came and settled in a hammock screened by dark nylon material, thus preventing us from seeing one another. I could only hear my comrades when they put questions to their instructors. That's why I thought there were three or four women and seven or eight men.

The training was divided into two parts, political indoctrination and sabotage techniques. During the latter, the instructors approached each hammock individually and gave the occupants personal guidance:

We learned to handle a pistol—its different parts, aiming, and firing—and a grenade (aiming [sic], throwing). We spent a longer time on explosives: powder and plastic. We learned how to use them and to reckon their destruction force.

The class had only one pistol with which to practice and no marksmanship training was provided. "We took it apart to know its different parts . . . how to cock it, take aim, and fire. The same applies to the grenade." The class never detonated any of the explosives.

The students could not see the instructor who gave them their political lectures because he was always careful to speak to them from behind a partition. On the duties of a saboteur, he told them:

> We must avoid recognizing a comrade in the presence of a third party. If we run into a comrade in the street or in a public place, we must never greet him nor look at him. If unfortunately we are caught by the enemies, we should never furnish them with information on our organization, our work, our comrades.* The less said, the better, for the more we speak, the more torture we'll get. When we are sent to a certain region, we must try to behave as the local people do in eating, drinking, dressing, recreation. If we want to get acquainted with someone, we must first of all conduct a personal investigation as to his habits, likes, and dislikes. For example, if he's fond of "Cai Luong" performances (a form of opera, very popular in Vietnam) we can talk about them; or if he likes horse-racing, we'll humor him on it and so on. But we must strictly keep him in the dark so far as our connection with the Front is concerned.

The budding saboteur's day began at seven A.M. with breakfast followed by instruction from eight to noon and then lunch. Instruction resumed at two P.M. and continued until half-past five. Supper was served at six. From nine P.M. to ten P.M. a self-criticism session was conducted after which everyone retired for the night. Each meal cost the Front two South Vietnamese piasters (at that time the exchange rate was seventy-three piasters to one U.S. dollar) and was prepared by three young men (not students) specially detailed as cooks. The students lived apart, in separate cottages, and the nighttime self-criticism sessions included only the residents of each respective cottage.

This insistence on secrecy was rigidly enforced:

> We couldn't even see one another nor speak to our classmates. I wasn't allowed to go out of the house. During the rest time I could only move about the house or walk up and down the front yard enclosed with a hedge. Whenever I had to go out to the convenience or have a bath at the well not far from the house, I had to cover my head with a towel pretending to keep off the sun but in truth it was to hide my face.

*Fortunately for this account, the soldier did not learn this lesson well.

THE RECRUITMENT OF WOMEN

Male/female roles in the Vietnamese family are well-defined. The father is the household head and leader of the family while the mother is expected to attend to family financial matters, housekeeping, and the raising of children. While the woman's power traditionally has been wielded behind the scenes, in the home or family environment she is often a dominant figure, arguing and disputing with her husband vociferously. But in public, the traditional Vietnamese woman always appears to agree with and follow her husband's judgment. In Vietnamese society, aggressive women are frowned upon.

Vietnamese men are taught to hold women in high respect. One analyst has noted that "the Viet Cong is skillful in exploiting the appeal of girls and the prestige of woman revolutionaries, using them chiefly in recruiting and indoctrination, but also in hamlet and village guerrilla units, and occasionally . . . in combat operations involving local VC forces."[87]

Viet Cong women generally served in support roles, such as administration, nursing, intelligence; others cooked, helped build fortifications and transport supplies. While the Viet Cong adhered to a strict moral code, it has been asserted that "joy girls" devoted to the sexual gratification of the troops were at times allowed into the camps.[88]

A Viet Cong main-force captain who rallied in February 1967 stated that in order for women to be recruited into the NLF they had to be unmarried, "not even engaged, and members of the proletariat." He noted a 60 percent drop in the number of female volunteers between 1962 and 1967. "The fierceness of the war apparently has discouraged the women's willingness to serve," he explained. When asked if VC women did any actual fighting he answered:

Women recruited as fighters fought like their male counterparts. In Ben Tre Province there was a company consisting entirely of women and led by a woman officer, named Thu Ha. Thu Ha was a first lieutenant and was well known for her skill in manipulating automatic rifles. She was credited with having overrun a series of five GVN forts in Ben Tre Province in the early days of the uprising [1962].

The captain told his interrogator that this female unit had been later inactivated because it became understrength due to defections and desertions.[89]

A thirty-one-year-old female assistant company leader of a local-force unit who rallied in June 1967 (six months pregnant at the time) claimed, among many other military distinctions, to be something of a Viet Cong Annie Oakley, "the most accurate shooter of the class" in her platoon leader's course. Informed that for every three "congratulatory certificates" she would earn one medal and that after the Revolution each medal would be worth forty thousand piasters, she "determined to get rich by fighting hard." During her seven years of service in the Viet Cong, this woman claimed to have earned "forty-three congratulatory certificates and eleven medals. Each time I donned my uniform for an operation, my chest was red with medals. You'll probably think that I'm immodest," she stated, "but the truth is that, as far as I know, no company cadre has been more decorated than I."

This woman's valor brought her to the attention of Madame Nguyen Thi Binh or Dinh,* identified as "the military zone's deputy chief of staff," with whom she became good friends. In recognition of her valor Madame Dinh presented this "female Audie Murphy" with her personal sidearm, a Colt revolver, and an engraved gold band. "I had treasured it for a long time," she confessed, "but not long ago, I was forced to sell it for nine hundred piasters because I was broke."

Unlike her male counterparts, this soldier claimed never to have attended any political indoctrination classes.

> I'd be bored to death listening to people talk politics. When the order came to me, stating that I had to come to such and such a place to make propaganda to the people, I'd refuse, saying that I had a headache.[90]

The interrogator of this woman reported that she was a "chatterbox throughout the interview." However, if only half of what she reported is true, then she more than fulfilled the role expected of Viet Cong women—to "inspire a man, to challenge

---

*A Madame Nguyen Thi Dinh is identified by Douglas Pike (*The Viet Cong*), as deputy commander of the NLF army. Actually, this woman was the "fifth deputy commander" of the NLF, somewhat less than second in command (Tourison). In the interview typescript, this woman's name is spelled both ways.

his pride by their own valor and the strength of their revolutionary commitment.''[91]

Another woman, who was the leader of the Duc Hoa District Party Committee, was highly respected by the VC main-force captain quoted earlier in this section:

> Revolutionary-wise, madame had a high sense of duty and devotion. When visiting you and your family, if she saw that you were behind in your work, she would go all out to help you. If your children were dirty, she would bathe them and care for them as if they were her own, giving them sweets and candies and money, etc.

This officer attributed madame's success to her thorough training in "politics," or the art of dealing with people, "as were all the Communist cadres." This extraordinary woman of Duc Hoa later died of tuberculosis.[92]

CONCLUSIONS

The Viet Cong and North Vietnamese soldiers were largely rural men with, by American standards, little formal education. For most, their first experience of life in the jungles and mountains of Vietnam came only after army induction. Their formal military training mostly ignored jungle warfare or survival techniques and what Americans call "unconventional warfare" training. Some Western analysts have postulated that if only the U.S. leaders had emphasized unconventional, counterguerrilla tactics instead of conventional military operations, America could easily have beaten the Vietnamese Communists at their own game. This conclusion ignores the fact that given Hanoi's determination to win the war as well as its Communist-bloc support in that goal, reorientation of U.S. strategy to emphasize "unconventional" warfare would have made absolutely no difference in the war's ultimate outcome.

However, the VC/NVA soldiers were trained in conventional small-unit infantry tactics and weapons, and what they did not learn in formal settings was taught to them by their unit cadres or was picked up during actual combat operations. When they were not fighting (which was most of the time) or digging in or carrying supplies, they trained and practiced for operations and studied. Even with a war going on all around them, the Viet

Cong were still able to detach men from their units and send them to formal training courses.

Most of these men were draftees: The Northerners went because it was expected of them, the Southerners because they often had little choice in the matter. Once in the ranks they were kept there by intensive political indoctrination and the simple fact that few men readily desert the comrades with whom they have shared hardship and danger.

America and her allies believed that manpower, firepower, logistics, and technology in and of themselves were sufficient to guarantee victory in Vietnam. Throughout the war and until this very day, the Vietnamese Communists have maintained that an important factor that guaranteed their victory was the Americans' lack of will to win a protracted conflict. The Communists prevailed because they placed their trust in the most reliable and oldest tool of warfare: the individual soldier. The bamboo plant, which to the Vietnamese people represents endurance and survival in the face of adversity, is a fitting symbol for these hardy soldiers.

> *"Tonight, July, 16, 1966, I went on operation, marching over a 10,000-mile route."*
>
> FROM A VIET CONG SOLDIER'S
> LETTER TO HIS SWEETHEART[1]

4

THE INFILTRATION SOUTH

THE 10,000-MILE ROUTE

A popular "barracks story" among American servicemen in Southeast Asia during the war featured "Nguyen Nguyen" and his transformation from rice-paddy farmer in the Red River Valley of North Vietnam to NVA soldier in the South. According to one version of the story, Nguyen was drafted at age eighteen and spent three months in basic training. Unfortunately, Nguyen had never seen a rifle before, much less fired one, and he had great difficulty learning fundamental soldiering skills. Despite extra training, including hours of orientation on dedication to Uncle Ho and his native land, Nguyen's leaders determined that the best way for the former rice farmer to serve the Fatherland was as an ammo bearer.

After a brief visit home, Nguyen reported to his unit and was issued a backpack with four 82mm mortar rounds. Along with an extra uniform, a bag of rice and a canteen of water, Nguyen's load was now over a hundred pounds. Nguyen, who weighed only a few pounds more than his pack, squared his shoulders, and with country, village, and family in his thoughts, headed south to help liberate his cousins from the coils of capitalism and oppression by the Americans.

The first few days of Nguyen's journey were uneventful except for the raw sores that developed from the rubbing of the pack straps on his shoulders. Along with his unit, Nguyen shuttled between river boats, trucks, and an occasional foot march as he covered the first two hundred miles. Late one evening, as Nguyen's squad was getting off of a Russian-made truck, his sergeant told him that they were nearing the Laotian border just north of the DMZ. From there onward, they would move on foot.

Their timing was not so good. It was the middle of the monsoon season and the daily rains kept Nguyen soaked. As the days passed and the journey progressed, Nguyen began to weaken. Twice he had to stay behind to recover from bouts of malaria before joining new units. Another time Nguyen wandered lost in the jungle for two days after a B-52 strike had killed the rest of his squad and dazed the young private. Bites and stings from mosquitoes, ants, and scorpions became almost as routine as picking fat, blood-sucking leeches off his body.

At a way station in Cambodia, Nguyen learned that his destination was Long An Province near Saigon. Nguyen, who now weighed less than his pack due to short rations, malaria attacks, and the early stages of beri-beri, wondered how he was going to make it on feet that were blistered and becoming infected.

That afternoon things got worse. American jets screamed out of the sky dropping bombs and napalm. Nguyen's best friend, who had been walking with him for the last two weeks, was burnt alive. Nguyen's lungs were seared by the hot-burning napalm, but he was able to crawl to safety in a water-filled bomb crater.

Things did not get any better the next day. Shortly after one of the guides had told Nguyen's group that they had crossed the border into South Vietnam, helicopter gunships spotted the column. Rockets and bullets cut the jungle and another couple of Nguyen's friends to pieces. That night, huge artillery shells exploded around Nguyen's foxhole. It was little comfort when a cadre told him the American gunners did not know that they were there but were merely shooting "Harassing and Interdictory" (H&I) fires.

With a malarial fever of over 103 degrees, little food, two more air attacks, and an artillery barrage to his credit, Nguyen reached his objective one morning exactly four months after his departure from Hanoi. Outside of the hamlet of Cam Ho, Nguyen reported to his new unit, which at the time was attacking a small government outpost. Minutes after arrival, Nguyen unloaded his heavy pack and handed his four mortar rounds to his new squad leader. Much to Nguyen's surprise, the four rounds were fired one after the other in less than a minute. Then the squad leader turned to him, and with a smile said, "Good job, Nguyen. Now go back and get four more."

As with most barracks tales, there are both truth and fantasy in Nguyen's story. Once an NVA soldier arrived in the South he would not be sent back north. He was there for the duration. For many, a trip back north for more ammo might not have seemed as cruel a mission as indicated in the tale of Nguyen.

In the early years of the war, entry into South Vietnam from the North was not too difficult. Establishment in 1964 of the Ho Chi Minh Trail, leading from North Vietnam into Laos and on into Cambodia, made the journey easier yet. Infiltrators could also cross the lightly defended DMZ, or enter the South by means of the virtually unpatrolled coastline.

North Vietnam began to export its Revolution to the South in the late 1950s. Vo Nguyen Giap, defense minister and commander-in-chief of the Vietnamese People's Army, explained in the January 1960 issue of the Lao Dong Party journal, *Hoc Tap*, that "The North has become a large rear echelon of our army. . . . The North is the revolutionary base for the whole country."[2]

Initially, the majority of the infiltrators were regroupees, ethnic South Vietnamese who had gone North after the partition of the country in 1954. These were soon followed by native North Vietnamese officers, political officers, and cadre sent South to organize and train the guerrillas. Access to South Vietnam was so easy during this period that one of the major infiltration routes was directly across the DMZ. This route crossed the Ben Hai River (the natural border between North and South Vietnam) at Bo Ho Su, went southeast to cross Highway 9, and on to a jungle way station known as Number 8, or Calu, in Quang Tri Province. Another day's march south was Ba Ngai Station, Number 25, with more stations stretching all the way to the Mekong Delta region.

On March 29, 1961, ARVN troops raided the Calu station, capturing documents that detailed traffic through the outpost over the previous six months. According to the documents, from October through March, 1,840 infiltrators had crossed the DMZ and then rested at Calu before proceeding south.[3]

Infiltration from the sea during the early days was accomplished with comparative ease, as on June 5, 1961, when five NVA cadre were captured on the beach at An Don in a small fishing vessel that had set sail from Dong Hoi, North Vietnam.

One of the prisoners, a thirty-four-year-old lieutenant, revealed that this was his seventeenth trip to the South, bringing in men and documents and taking messages back north.[4]

By 1965, escalation of U.S. involvement in the war turned the DMZ into an impenetrable barrier and closed the sea lanes by water and air patrols. The only route south became the Ho Chi Minh Trail, but this caused no real hardship as the Trail, which was actually a network of paths, trails, and roads paralleling the borders of Laos, Cambodia, and South Vietnam, was more than adequate to the task.

Actual work to develop the Ho Chi Minh Trail and build way stations along the route was begun in the spring of 1959 by members of the NVA 301st Division. The first infiltrators to enter the South via the trail did so in August of the same year.[5]

The subsequent high rate of traffic on the Ho Chi Minh Trail is reflected by the growing numbers of NVA soldiers in the South. In 1964 the number was only 6,000. By 1967 this number had grown to 69,000 and to over 100,000 by 1969.[6] Considering replacement for casualties, as well as new units committed to the war, at the height of the conflict, the Trail was the route for as many as 60,000 infiltrators per year.

The trip down the Ho Chi Minh Trail did not, of course, begin with a recruit's entry into the army. Weeks of tactical and political training preceded the time when a soldier was selected to journey south. The actual selection process for infiltration is somewhat unclear, although several methods have been identified.

"Everyone who went south was a volunteer," was the claim of many captured officers as well as being the general "party line" in Hanoi. Although some of the NVA who went south certainly were volunteers, their numbers were small. In fact, the trainees seldom were given the opportunity to volunteer at all. When they completed their training, they were simply ordered south. About as close as the NVA got to mass volunteerism was the result of carefully planned rallies which emphasized the wrongs committed by the invading Americans and the suffering of their Vietnamese brothers in the South. A twenty-one-year-old private, captured in November 1964, recalls that at the conclusion of one of these emotionally packed and skillfully conducted meetings, a "whole group of two hundred men volunteered to go south."[7]

Volunteerism in any army is often difficult to define. Soldiers rarely, if ever, have any definite control over their own fate and their responses to questions often reflect that uncertainty. A popular answer North Vietnamese soldiers gave about why they went south was "I was chosen." Depending on the respondent, this answer was related with pride, resignation, or sarcasm.

In the early 1960s, before the huge buildup of northern forces in the South, whether one was "chosen," "volunteered," or "ordered" was often a moot point. A twenty-six-year-old private captured in July 1964 stated, "I was chosen to attend a military training course in Nghe An. The authorities did not inform us that we were going to be sent south. My comrades and I were very happy to attend an officer's training school. Upon completion of the training, however, the director of the training told us we would be going south shortly to help liberate the Southerners. It was only then that we knew we were going south."[8]

Cadres selecting men to go south usually tried to explain to them why they were so chosen. The common explanation was that their brothers and sisters in the South, miserable and unhappy, were anxiously awaiting liberation. Often it was added that by going south a soldier was actually protecting the North* as well as fighting to expel the Americans and to reunify the two Vietnams. Nearly every speech included the theme that they must go south to "liberate" their countrymen from the American "imperialists."

Upon being informed of their selection to go south, the reactions of the NVA recruits differed little from other soldiers sent to the front in previous wars. First was a feeling of sadness because of the impending long separations from home and family mixed with a second reaction, which was fear of never returning. Third, and most important, was the acceptance of what the recruit considered to be an obligation to his country.

Along with danger and obligation, those selected to go south also felt a sense of adventure. One sergeant, who trained recruits and eventually went south himself, stated, "They're all young, and the young love to travel."†

A twenty-three-year-old assistant squad leader, perhaps

---

*Propaganda was not limited to one side during the war. In the United States at the time, both military and civilian supporters of American involvement in Vietnam often gave the explanation that "It is better to fight Communism in Southeast Asia than on the beaches of California, Washington, and Oregon."

†Again, the similarities among all armies are apparent. A common response in the U.S. Army as to why join up or volunteer for duty in Vietnam was "Fun, travel, adventure." "FTA," in its much more popular form, also means "*Fuck the Army*."

showing more naïveté than revolutionary zeal, claimed, "I was curious and wanted to see beautiful South Vietnam."[9]

Despite grand words about patriotism, love of country, and belief in cause, most young men selected for duty in the South had a mixture of emotions. Typical was a twenty-three-year-old private who initially summarized his reaction to his selection by saying, "I felt that it was my duty to go. I had to comply with national policy." However, when asked if he really wanted to go south the private responded, "No. I was leading a peaceful life in the North where there was no war.* Therefore, I did not want to go south where I was likely to get killed."[10]

Along the same lines, a twenty-two-year-old sergeant reports, "To tell the truth, I was very worried about our trip south. But I had no choice since it was my duty to go. I didn't want to go. . . . However, if the other men could go, why couldn't I who was in no way different from them? Besides, I was a youth who had been enjoying ten years of peace, so I could not sit still watching the South Vietnamese people, who had been suffering for ten years, go on enduring their suffering."[11]

Not all selectees were as resigned or stoic in their reaction. According to a nineteen-year-old private, captured in November 1965, "I think that only 20 percent were enthusiastic about going south. The remaining 80 percent did not want to go. About 10 percent of the men boldly returned their personal effects and weapons and asked to go home." Not wanting to go, or refusal to do so, did not, however, prevent the journey south. The private continues: "They were indoctrinated and educated. They were criticized in front of their squads and platoons. After some time they agreed to go south."[12]

Another twenty-six-year-old private, captured in July 1964, tells a similar story. "I was very sad because I did not want to leave my family. But the cadre mobilized my spirit and told me that I could not stay behind because all my comrades were going. He said I was strong and healthy, so I should go south. My comrades were all very sad at first, but the cadres mobilized their spirits and then they began to feel all right about it. They were all enthusiastic, and willing to go south in the end."[13]

Despite this "mobilization of spirits" by the cadres, some of

---

*When the Americans began their bombing of North Vietnam, many soldiers felt that there was reason to stay home to defend the skies against the U.S. aviators. These bombings also inspired the motivation to fight either in the North or South to avenge friends and family who had been killed or maimed.

the recruits still attempted to avoid the journey south to the war. A twenty-one-year-old private recalls, "When we were informed about our trip south, five or six of us deserted. I returned home, but the army sent a truck to my village and took me away forcibly. The women and boys in my village made fun of me and said it was ridiculous for a youth like myself who had the good fortune to be chosen to go south to refuse to leave the North and to escape home. So I had to go."

Although the young private did eventually go south, apparently his training and the comments from his fellow villagers made little long-term impression. After only four months in the South, the private rallied to the government of South Vietnam.[14]

Actual notification of selection to go south varied from training center to training center and unit to unit as well as with the phase of the war. In the early years, regular members of the People's Army of Vietnam were selected, informed, moved to a staging area, and then given additional military and political training. This training usually lasted two to three months for privates and a month longer for noncommissioned officers. Oddly, one of the biggest deficiencies in this training was a lack of jungle or survival instruction.

As the war wore on, and the vast majority of all recruits were sent south (with the exception of those selected for the air force, air defense, and navy units, and for those sent to Laos for service in the 312th and 316th NVA divisions), the selection process occurred during the basic training phase. Upon completion of the training the newly chosen recruit was usually allowed a brief visit home before his departure south. This was not always the case, however. If immediate replacements were needed in the South, no home leave before departure was granted. In fact, many NVA soldiers related that upon the completion of their training, they immediately began the journey south although they did not know their destination until they were well on their way.*

Training in the staging area was intense, with as much emphasis placed on why the soldier was being sent south as on what to do after he arrived there. A nineteen-year-old private,

---

*The NVA were able to maintain a sophisticated personnel replacement system that met the manpower requirements of units in the South throughout the entire war. Neither those intelligence sources at the time nor studies since have adequately revealed how this system apparently was able to anticipate personnel requirements for officers, NCOs, and special skills, or how it was able to train and dispatch these individuals to the South (Tourison).

destined to be captured after only one month in the war zone, reported that in the staging area, "I studied about the situation in the South. I was told that the South Vietnamese were suffering an American invasion, and that they were living in misery."[15]

A twenty-four-year-old private adds, "The 'political training' course is mainly concerned with the soldier's duties. The long and short of it is this: The soldier's supreme duty is to fight on the side of the Revolution. The Revolution has given independence to one half of the country, but there still remains the other half. The Revolution is going on in the South. North Vietnamese fighters must go there to fight on the people's side to free them from the yoke of American imperialism. Vietnam is indivisible. We can't live in the North in independence and let our fellow countrymen in the South live in slavery."[16]

Despite the cadres' tales about American aggression and reports of the poor state of affairs in the South, NVA soldiers were informed that most of the South Vietnamese countryside was already in the hands of the Revolution. According to the training camp cadre, the South Vietnamese would welcome the soldiers from the North with open arms as liberators.

About the fighting abilities of the American and ARVN soldiers, the NVA were told a variety of stories. The ARVNs reportedly had poor morale and would rarely stand and fight. Reports of the ARVNs running in battle and surrendering in company strength were common. According to the cadre, the Saigon "puppet troops" fought primarily for money rather than for a just cause like the Revolution.

The Americans were said to be better fighters and to be armed with weapons superior to those of the French. Even the accounts that criticized the fighting abilities of the Americans acknowledged that the United States had powerful artillery and air power.

Truth was not a necessary ingredient, however. Stories were told about Americans routinely killing and/or torturing prisoners, often dismembering bodies and regularly performing other acts of brutality. The NVA were indoctrinated to believe that "if we were captured by the Americans, we would have our intestines cut out."[17]

Another training camp tale stated that American soldiers were cannibals and ate children. One fourteen-year-old NVA soldier, captured in 1967, told his interrogators that he feared that he would be eaten. The frightened boy added, however, that he thought that because he was so emaciated from months in the jungle that at least he would have to be fattened up before being consumed.[18]

Other stories of American cruelty related that POWs were put in bags and thrown into the sea to drown. One tale, which was a bit more farfetched, stated that prisoners were sent as laborers to Korea to replace the ROK force fighting in Vietnam. Perhaps the most bizarre of the stories was that POWs and ralliers were placed in a mysterious machine that turned them into Negroes.[19] This outlandish story was quite frightening to the North Vietnamese peasant who identified dark skin color with barbarism and racial inferiority.*

Oddly, while the NVA trainee received much information on the barbarism of the American soldier, he was also told that the non-military people of the United States were supportive of the Revolution and that they were opposed to the conflict and wanted U.S. troops withdrawn from the war zone. Cadre and high-ranking officers bragged about "winning the war on the streets of New York and campuses of New England."

The NVA trainee also received news of his allies. Briefings were held detailing the Sino-Soviet split, with the blame usually placed on the part of the Soviet Union. Despite the difficulties between the two Communist giants, the NVA were told that both would continue to support the Revolution. This was always qualified, however, to emphasize that the Soviets and the Chinese would support North Vietnam with supplies, arms and food—not actual combatants. A private, nineteen years old when captured in November 1965, best describes this relationship by saying, "We were told that Russia and Communist China, being in the same camp as the Front, supported the Front . . . but that the Front was heroically fighting the American imperialists on its own. By so doing, the Front was carrying on the heroic tradition of the Vietnamese people, who, in the past, have risen many times to drive out the foreign invader on their own. The cadres said that the Front did not as yet need food, weapons, or ammunition from friendly countries, and that, when the Front needed them and requested them, these countries would give them to the Liberation movement."[20]

Despite the common image of the Communist proletariat as

---

*An example of this bigotry is the superior attitude of all Vietnamese toward the Montagnards and Cambodian and Chinese minorities. Dark skin is also a socioeconomic stigma among the Vietnamese. Laborers and farmers tanned in the sun while the upper classes could afford to remain indoors.

robots believing all their government's propaganda, the typical NVA recruit was often skeptical of what he was told. Soldiers reported accepting some and discounting other information as propaganda. While most of the recruits stated that they at least pretended to believe the lectures by the political cadre, they did not accept all of it as the truth, or even of much interest. The response of a nineteen-year-old private, captured in March 1965, is what might be expected from a trainee of any army. He relates, "When the political cadre gave his lecture, we did not listen to him carefully. He was standing there talking, and we were down here pinching one another, smoking cigarettes, and fooling around."[21]

The principal training center for NVA destined for the South was southwest of Hanoi at Xuan Mai. After 1964, when requirements for troops in the South increased, soldiers were also trained at units spread all across North Vietnam. Although several infiltration routes were used between the training areas and the war zone, one avenue dominated. After training and/or home leave was completed, the soldiers moved by truck, train, or boat to Vinh, a coastal city about halfway between Hanoi and the DMZ. From there they traveled by truck to the next stop, which was the last major city north of the DMZ—Dong Hoi. There, especially during the early years of war, the soldiers often stayed several weeks to undergo additional training. Moving again by truck, the infiltrators then rode west from Dong Hoi to the Laotian border. Until 1964, all personnel were stopped at the border to be re-equipped and issued black civilian pajamas to replace their NVA uniforms. All personal papers, letters, notebooks, and other identifying matter were turned over to North Vietnamese border authorities. This practice ceased when the increasing number of NVA heading down the Ho Chi Minh Trail became general knowledge—despite the fact that it would be years before North Vietnam admitted that their soldiers were in South Vietnam.

Without the stop for uniform exchange, the NVA infiltrators did not necessarily know when they left their home country and entered Laos. Often their first knowledge that they were no longer in North Vietnam was when their units entered the Laotian town of Techepone. Techepone, located near the border of South Vietnam a few miles south of the DMZ, was the northern terminus of the Ho Chi Minh Trail. It was also the last cluster of civilization the NVA infiltrators saw before entering the jungle for the long journey south.[22]

The size of the infiltrating groups ranged from as small as five men to as large as five hundred. More typical were groups of forty to fifty loosely organized into a platoon or small company. Except for the larger battalion-size groups, the organization for the infiltration had little importance. Once the groups arrived in the South, most were generally reassigned to units already established. Beyond attempting to keep the men in the three-man cells basic to all Communist organizations, assignment to the units was rather arbitrary.

Responsibility for the infiltration from North Vietnam and through Laos belonged to the NVA 559th Command Group, named after the date of its formation, May 1959. The 559th was in charge of the infiltrators all along the Ho Chi Minh Trail and did not release this responsibility until turning over the new soldiers to the appropriate military regional headquarters in South Vietnam.

Group 559 operated a series of way stations from deep inside the Panhandle of North Vietnam down the length of the Ho Chi Minh Trail into South Vietnam. These way stations were situated at approximately one-day march intervals—ten to twenty kilometers—depending on the terrain. The 559th provided complete infiltration support, including air defense, road repair and construction, communications, medical support, vehicles, security and guides. At its maximum strength, the 559th was a small army within itself, composed of an estimated 50,000 troops assigned to fifteen units the size of regiments and known as *binh trams*. Each *binh tram* consisted of two air-defense battalions armed with 37mm, 14.5mm, 12.7mm, and 23mm guns, and an SA2 missile battalion in addition to two engineer battalions, two truck transportation battalions, a signal battalion, a communications/liaison battalion, a security battalion, a medical battalion, and a food-production unit.[23]

Guides from the commo/liaison battalions led the infiltrators along the various trails. Prior to 1965, local guides were used. As a security measure, these guides met infiltrating units halfway between way stations, led them to their home station, and after rest and food, led them halfway to the next station. This procedure ensured that the guides had no knowledge of the exact location of any way station except their own. Local guides were often from nearby mountain tribes who had allegiance to neither North nor South Vietnam. Their cooperation was secured either under the threat of death or by bribery with food—or both. After 1965, when the trail became fully operational, local guides were replaced by regular members of the *binh tram*s organic to the 559th.

For security reasons, locations of way stations were identified by a series of letters and numbers without reference to nearby landmarks or villages. Most common of the designations was a number preceded by the letter "T," which stood for *tram*, the Vietnamese word for "station." The number after the "T" usually represented the sequence of the station from the trail's beginning point or crossing into South Vietnam. For example, "T-31" would be the designation for the thirty-first station along a certain trail. Infiltrators were rarely aware of their actual location but the station number was known to them. Typical journal entries include "arrived at Station #25 at 1200 hours," "overnighted at Station #51," and "moving to T-13."[24]

Another numbering system used along the trail was for infiltration passes and for infiltrating unit designations. Each soldier was issued an infiltration pass by the Central Reunification Committee prior to his departure for South Vietnam. This document was 2½ by 4 inches in size, was printed on glazed paper, and included the soldier's name and unit. Each pass was serial-numbered so that the first and third digits always added up to seven. Infiltration units received a special designation for use during the move South. It was preceded by the letter "D," for *doan*, or "group," and followed by numbers such as "D-512."[25]

During the early years of the war, the Ho Chi Minh Trail extended only as far into Laos as required to allow border crossings into the South Vietnamese provinces of Quang Nam, Quang Tri, Tua Thien, and Kontum. This limit of advance into Laos was the result of the Royal Laotian Government's strict neutrality guaranteed by the United States and the Soviet Union. The North Vietnamese had no desire to anger their friends and supporters in Moscow. It was not until unrest in the government of Laos weakened its control over its eastern provinces that the NVA took advantage by further encroaching into Laos and extending the arms of the trail deeper into "neutral" territory.

What had begun as a narrow pathway grew to wide roads improved with gravel, bridges, and pipeline systems for fuel. In places where natural foliage did not provide adequate camouflage, additional trees and bushes were planted or were carefully woven into overhead lattices so that the trail could not be observed from the air.

Despite the story about Nguyen and his mortar rounds, most of the infiltrators did not carry any extras beyond items for their own care and comfort. On their persons or in their rucksacks, the NVA soldiers going south typically each carried two green uniforms, a pair of black pajamas, two pairs of underwear, rubber sandals or canvas boots, a canteen, and a small entrenching tool. For sleeping, each carried a cotton tent coated on one side with tarlike asphalt. With the addition of cotton or nylon cords the tent could also be used as a hammock. A thin nylon or plastic sheet for warmth or further protection from the rain rounded out the personal gear.

When the infiltrators departed North Vietnam, they received five to seven days' rations, a small packet of medicines (mostly antimalaria pills), field dressings, and three to seven magazines of ammunition for their rifles. When food and medicine ran out, more was issued at the way stations. Heavy crew-served weapons were not carried on the journey but rather were issued to the soldier from reserve stocks stored near the border-crossing sites in Laos and Cambodia. An exception to this was infiltration by newly committed battalions and regiments, which did carry their own crew-served weapons.

The dangers encountered along the Ho Chi Minh Trail were many and varied. Contrary to popular American beliefs that the NVA were native jungle fighters, most NVA recruits came from the metropolitan Hanoi area and from the rice farms along the Red River and the South China Sea. Except for small-scale logging operations, the average North Vietnamese had no reason to ever enter the jungle. Therefore, most of the difficulties for the new Liberation fighter revolved around homesickness, illness, disease, and the discomforts of nature itself.

For many of the infiltrators, the Ho Chi Minh Trail was their first experience in the jungle. The dampness, oppressive heat, and rotting vegetation combined with leeches, scorpions, centipedes, ants, and the other seemingly limitless types of biting, stinging, sucking insects made the jungle most inhospitable. In addition, venomous snakes, including cobras and bamboo vipers, waited in tree branches, under logs or in the grass for their next victims.* Within a few days after beginning their journey south, most infiltrators caught cold and with little more than

---

*Of all the dangers in the jungle, snakes perhaps received the most notice for the least cause. Although poisonous snakes were common in the jungles and rice paddies, none was aggressive and practically all species did their best to avoid humans. Accounts of soldiers on either side being bitten by snakes were rare; however, the fear of such attacks was a real danger in itself.

aspirin to treat themselves, many developed pneumonia—especially during monsoon season.

Even more threatening on the trail were the swarms of mosquitoes. While the bites themselves were bad enough, mosquitoes carried one or more of the malaria strains that prevailed in Southeast Asia. The incubation time from exposure to symptoms was a matter of weeks. As a result, many of the infiltrators were weak with chills and fever before they even reached the war zone.

Although the NVA were issued malaria pills containing chloroquine, primaquine, and dapsone—the same ingredients that were in the capsules used by the Americans—they nevertheless frequently contracted the disease. This was due primarily to shortages of the pills, which had to be taken regularly to be effective against certain strains of the disease. Another important reason, just as the Americans learned, was that the pills in many cases merely masked the symptoms of malaria instead of preventing the disease. Against still other strains of malaria there were no known preventive measures.

Along with malaria, the infiltrators could look forward to the possibility of contracting yellow fever, beri-beri, tuberculosis, and other tropical diseases, some unknown even to medical science. Also, poor sanitation led to bouts of dysentery, ring worm, and internal parasites.

The maladies and dangers facing the young NVA infiltrator on the Ho Chi Minh Trail were compounded by acute homesickness. For the teenage soldier whose entire life had revolved around village and family, the psychological impact of journeying to a far-away war—with little hope or promise of returning—was great. Nearly every diary and interview of the infiltrators is filled with references to being lonesome for family members and concern that they would never again return to their homes.

Illness and homesickness caused many of the infiltrators to request of their cadres and/or guides permission to return to the North. Without exception their requests were denied. The new Liberation fighter soon learned that the Ho Chi Minh Trail was a one-way route. There would be no return until victory was achieved and the two Vietnams reunited under the leadership of Hanoi.

The best a sick infiltrator could expect was to remain at a way station until he recovered. This had little appeal because it meant that fellow cell members and friends from training would move on and perhaps never be seen again. Once the sick soldier recovered, he was reassigned to the next unit on its way through.

Although the natural dangers of the Ho Chi Minh Trail that existed in the early years continued, far greater perils surfaced in 1965 when American bombers and fighters began to attack it routinely. Day and night, targets spotted by visual means or by sophisticated ''people sniffers'' responding to body heat and excretions came under constant bombardment and strafing. Fighter jets swooped down to tree-top level while B-52s dropped tons of bombs from altitudes so high that the men on the ground were unaware of the attack until the jungle erupted around them.

Soon the Ho Chi Minh Trail was marked by bomb craters and scorched earth. Destroyed trucks and equipment littered the sides of the trail as did the graves of infiltrators who never lived to see South Vietnam and fight for the liberation of their Southern brothers and sisters.

The bombing, in addition to killing or wounding many of the infiltrators, demoralized the survivors. One infiltrator who came South in 1967 recalls:

We arrived at Thanh Hoa Province [just north of the DMZ], crossed the river with the ferry boat, and were warned that there would be many, many strafing attacks. My battalion was the First Battalion and we were not attacked, but the Third Battalion got hit pretty badly. Many wounded, forty were killed, very tragically killed. We slept in the daytime and we walked at night. Many trucks were moving at night. One time I saw a truck burn after a rocket attack. We had several close calls with bombing but they missed us. But the trip was tragic because as we went further down the road we could see the destruction that had been reaped. There were many buildings and houses, homes in ashes, the road was a mess, the effect on morale was bad. It got more dangerous as we got closer to South Vietnam. Coming to the border, the bombing and strafing got so strong that we had to take to the mountain routes.[26]

Daytime aerial attacks on the trail became so severe that eventually the NVA moved primarily at night. At times they rerouted the trail to better camouflaged areas. Despite the best efforts of American air power, however, Hanoi continued to send its young soldiers to negotiate every painful, dangerous, dirty inch of what seemed to them to be a ten-thousand-mile route.

Time required for an infiltrator to make his way down the Ho Chi Minh Trail from North Vietnam to the war zone depended on the phase of the war, the time of year, the requirement for replacements in the South, and his ultimate destination. One of the first groups to use the trail took fifty-five days to make it from Hanoi to Quang Ngai Province.[27] By the dry season of 1969, with the need for replacements to replenish units devastated by the disastrous Tet Offensive still critical, infiltrators made it from near Hanoi all the way to Xuan Loc, east of Saigon, in only thirty days.[28]

Whatever the infiltrators encountered on their way down the Ho Chi Minh Trail, their troubles did not end when they arrived in South Vietnam. More air strikes, helicopter attacks, and artillery barrages as well as ARVN and U.S. infantry patrols awaited them. Moreover, the NVA did not find South Vietnam to be what they expected.

In the North, the recruits had been told that two thirds to three fourths of South Vietnamese territory was in the hands of the Front and that three fourths to nine tenths of the population supported them. Except for those arriving in the final months of the war, the infiltrators found these claims completely without merit. Villagers did not welcome the newly arriving NVA with open arms, and the new freedom fighters soon discovered that the jungle was the only place of refuge—and they had received little or no training on how to adapt to their new environment. Instead of joining with their South Vietnamese brothers against the imperialist Americans as they had been told to expect, they found themselves more often facing their ARVN brothers on the battlefield. The infiltrator was soon aware that the war was far from being finished and that he faced a large and growing number of ARVN and U.S. forces. Instead of being welcomed as a liberator, he quickly had to adjust to the high possibility of a long war, a great danger of being killed, and the likelihood of an extended absence from his village and family.[29]

Despite these problems and revelations, the NVA had little option but to go on fighting. Although areas of the Ho Chi Minh Trail were reported to be as much as two feet deep in Chieu Hoi (open arms or surrender) leaflets, of those captured less than 20 percent of the infiltrators claimed even to be aware of the program. Their cadres had told them not to look at the leaflets, and like good Revolutionary soldiers, most had complied.[30]

For those NVA who might have been aware of the Chieu Hoi program, the few who were interested feared that their defection would preclude their return North and/or that reprisals would be taken against their families. As for the rest of the infiltrators, while the situation might not have met their expectations, it made little difference. Once in the South, it was time for the infiltrator to fight—and survive.

5

ORGANIZATION

No study of the VC/NVA organization can be complete without an investigation of the political structure of North Vietnam. The Vietnamese Communist leadership distinguished little between their political and military operations, with the exception that the political always took priority. Individuals held positions of leadership both in the government and in the military, and they rarely made a distinction between roles when they made decisions or issued orders.

The integration of the political and military leadership roles by the Vietnamese Communists dates to the beginnings of the Communist movement in Vietnam. Working first as the Indochinese Communist Party (ICP) established in 1930, members planned political strategy and then fought for fifteen years until they could take over the Vietnamese nationalist movement during the turmoil and political vacuum that followed World War II. The Vietnamese Communist movement, under a variety of names but always with the same ultimate goal—unifying Vietnam— battled the French, Americans, South Vietnamese, and other Free World forces for thirty years before accomplishing their objective.[1]

In 1945 the ICP was dissolved and a succession of Communist groups composed the core of the movement until March 3, 1951, when the Dang Lao Dong (Vietnamese Workers Party) officially took over. It was under this banner that Party leaders in Hanoi directed, controlled, and supplied the entire war efforts of both the VC and the NVA.*

All control of the VC and the NVA—political and military— ultimately came from the Central Committee of the Lao Dong Party through subordinate organizations arranged along territorial lines. For example, the Central Committee controlled the NVA High Command, which trained and deployed all regular and reserve troops of the North Vietnamese Army while still in North Vietnam. The Liberation Army was never anything more than an extension of the NVA. Depending on geographical area of assignment in South Vietnam, some NVA units remained under control of North Vietnam after their infiltration into the South while others were resubordinated. For instance, in the summer of 1966, NVA forces came directly across the DMZ. These forces were organic to the NVA High Command but were assigned to the operational control of the B5 Front for that particular operation.[2]

The Central Committee in Hanoi formed and controlled the People's Revolutionary Party (PRP) in South Vietnam. The PRP in turn controlled the National Front for the Liberation of South Vietnam, which was more commonly known as the National Liberation Front (NLF). The NLF "controlled" its VC military forces through the Central Office for South Vietnam (COSVN), which also reported directly to the Central Committee. While some experts dispute the "legitimacy" or even the existence of the NLF and the PRP, the best evidence suggests that they in fact did exist, did exercise authority over the Viet Cong forces, and did lose power and status as the war wore on. The NLF and PRP had virtually no role whatsoever in the final victorious offensive and the reunification of the two Vietnams.

Any look at the NLF and PRP must also be qualified by recognizing that the two organizations were puppets of Hanoi's Lao Dong Party and that the primary purpose of their existence

---

*It is not the intention of this book to conduct an in-depth study of Vietnamese political movements or to study closely the higher echelons of military and government leadership beyond how they directly affected the combat soldiers who actually fought the war. Other books, particularly Michael Conley's *The Communist Insurgent Infrastructure in South Vietnam: A Study of Organization and Strategy* (Washington, D.C.: The American University, 1967), and Douglas Pike's *Viet Cong* (Cambridge, MA: The M.I.T. Press, 1968) and *PAVN: People's Army of Vietnam* (Novato, CA: Presidio Press, 1986) go into great detail on the political/military development and are recommended.

was to give legitimacy to the claim of a people's revolution in the South rather than admit the conflict was led and fought by soldiers from the North.[3]

NVA units, trained and equipped in the North, were conventional military organizations. Infiltrated into South Vietnam, they maintained their same unit organization throughout the war. While unit organization remained the same, the unit designation changed frequently—as often as every six months. This was to hide its identity from enemy intelligence and order-of-battle experts. Although the NVA units occasionally crossed into Cambodia or Laos to rest and refit, they remained in or near the war zone for the duration. Replacements for casualties came to the unit down the Ho Chi Minh Trail.

While NVA units often worked through COSVN or three other similar politico-military-logistic headquarters—formed in the Central Highlands, along the DaNang–Cam Ranh Bay coast line, and the provinces near the DMZ in preparation for Tet of 1968— their chain of command was always direct to Hanoi. Every unit, regardless of size, was directly answerable through its chain of command to the NVA High Command.

Viet Cong forces were organized into full military and paramilitary units modeled after the Chinese Revolutionary Armed Forces. Publicly these units were under the direction of the PRP Central Committee; however, in reality, COSVN, under leadership of the Lao Dong Party, was in command of all VC activities. COSVN controlled the Viet Cong units through three interzone headquarters that were divided into seven subheadquarters zones. Direct control of the Liberation units was further subordinated to thirty provincial committees that were also responsible for spreading propaganda and indoctrinating the civilians in their provinces. The provincial committees controlled district committees that in turn directed village and hamlet cells.[4]

The elite of the Viet Cong were the main-force units, which reported to one of the interzone headquarters or directly to COSVN. Main-force units were composed of full-time soldiers, many of whom had been trained in the North and infiltrated into the South. A majority of the main-force fighters were Party members and most could read and write. Called "hard hats" by the Allies and South Vietnam civilians because many wore the pith helmets common to NVA regulars, main-force units usually operated as battalions that could join to form multibattalion forces for a particular campaign.

Ranking just below the main-force units were the regional or territorial forces. The regional forces were also composed of full-time soldiers but differed from the main forces in that most of their men were indigenous to the area in which they served. They were generally not as well educated as the main-force soldiers and were not as likely to be Party members. The regional forces rarely were larger than company size and operated under the control of the district-level headquarters.

The final category of VC are aptly described as primarily "farmers by day and soldiers by night." These village, hamlet, or local guerrillas, as they were known at different times and in different areas, were composed mostly of those too old or too young to join the regional and main-force units. Organized into militia units under the control of village or hamlet Front leaders, these guerrilla organizations usually operated in groups as small as three-man cells and occasionally as large as platoons. Although the village guerrillas did conduct some military operations, such as sniping and emplacing booby traps, they were engaged more often in supporting the regional- and main-force units and in collecting intelligence and providing an armed presence in the villages to destabilize GVN political control. Wearing the black pajamas typical of farmers all across the country, the guerrillas kept their weapons and equipment hidden in houses, tunnels, or watertight containers submerged in streams or rice paddies.[5]

When compared to the organizations of the armed forces of the United States and other Western nations, the VC and NVA system may at first seem complicated. While this was true, the political and military organization of the Liberation forces conformed to classic Communist patterns: strong central authority at the top, decentralized operations at the lower levels. As in all Communist countries, the Party—in this case the Lao Dong Party—exercised complete control over all levels of the government, political and military.[6]

The VC/NVA force structure was composed of combat units, administrative service forces, irregulars, and politico-military infrastructure. Some of the units were full-time regulars while others were part-time guerrillas, with still others composed of impressed laborers who may or may not have had any loyalty to the Revolution.

Exactly how many VC and NVA participated in the war is impossible to calculate. Numbers of the VC/NVA were much debated at the time and since by order-of-battle experts as well as the news media and other analysts. Difficulties in determining head counts are compounded by the fact that NVA infiltrating in 1964 and 1965 were at times assigned as "fillers" to Viet Cong units while in the later years VC were added to the ranks of regular NVA units. A further impediment to establishing an accurate order of battle is that many VC units were destroyed during Tet of 1968 and their ranks subsequently filled by NVA replacements even though the units continued to carry their VC designations.

Despite these difficulties, U.S. intelligence officers were able to establish fairly accurate estimates of VC/NVA strengths by listing categories of "regular combat forces," "administrative services," and "guerrillas," with subcategories for VC and NVA. In 1964, USMACV estimated the size of Communist forces in South Vietnam at 180,000. This number steadily rose to a high of 290,000 to 340,000 in 1968. During the final years of the war the numbers ranged from 195,000 to 308,000.[7] (For a detailed account of VC/NVA numbers by year and category, see Appendix A.)

The tactic of avoiding offensive combat unless conditions were favorable for victory allowed VC and NVA units to remain dispersed and come together in large units only for major offensives. Guerrilla units rarely operated in organizations larger than a twelve-man squad. A single main-force or NVA battalion might be spread out over twenty to thirty kilometers with platoons and companies occupying separate sectors. Numbers of soldiers assigned to the units varied according to the time of the year, the intensity of combat, and the phase of the war.

Despite these various configurations and manning levels, the principal VC and NVA combat organization was based on a triangular system. Three men made up a cell, three cells a squad, three squads a platoon, three platoons a company, three companies a battalion, and three battalions a regiment. This "system of three" continued through division, corps and army. The triangular system was not totally rigid. It was not unusual for the "system of three" to vary from a "system of two to five."[*]

The typical VC/NVA infantry battalion was composed of a command staff, three infantry companies, one combat support company, and three separate platoons—one each for signal, re-

---

*This triad system with a flexibility of reducing or expanding from two to five subunits was not unique to the VC/NVA. The same technique of organization was used by the U.S. Army, the ARVNs, and the vast majority of the world's other ground military forces.

connaissance, and sapper operations. (In some instances the recon and sapper platoons were combined.) At maximum strength the battalion consisted of 450 to 600 men, but typically it fought understrength. The organization was flexible enough for the battalion to be considered combat ready with as few as 300 soldiers present for duty.

Representing the bulk of the battalion's combat power were the three infantry companies—each composed of 60 to 130 men organized into three platoons and a company headquarters section. Weapons assigned at the company level were dominated by small arms such as the AK-47 and the SKS rifles. The heaviest weapons at the infantry company level were RPD 7.62mm light machine guns and rocket-propelled grenade launchers (RPGs).

Heavy weapons, such as 81- and 82mm mortars, 57- and 75mm recoilless rifles, and 12.7mm machine guns, were found in the battalion's combat support company. These weapons, assigned to sections, squads, and platoons within the combat support company, could be deployed independently but were more typically attached to the infantry companies. Members of the combat support company were also responsible for the emplacement of mines and booby traps.

Overall command, control, and administration of the battalion was conducted by the headquarters staff, which was headed by the battalion commander, assisted by his executive officer, and the everpresent political officer and cadre. The signal, reconnaissance, and sapper platoons, separate from the infantry companies, were directly responsible to a member of the battalion staff—usually the chief of staff.

The mission of the signal element was to provide and maintain communication from the battalion commander to his subordinate units and to his superior regimental headquarters while in camp, on the move, or in battle. When the units were in static situations, signal element members laid telephone wires connecting the battalion to its companies and platoons. Because radios were in short supply and could not be shielded from Allied direction finders, telephones and runners were virtually the exclusive means of communications between battalions and subordinate units. Typically, however, each battalion was issued one radio for voice communications with its regimental headquarters. Even this set was used only when telephone lines were not yet laid or when it was not practical to use couriers.

Reconnaissance platoons assigned to combat battalions were

responsible not only for reconnaissance but also for guiding and covering troops on the march. Because of the danger of their missions, members of the recon units (whose duties included mapping of terrain; locating water sources, campsites, routes of march, and avenues of withdrawal; and surveillance of enemy units) were generally considered elite troops. Also, recon soldiers were more likely to be Party members than others of the battalion. The VC/NVA claimed this was due to the recon men's skills and dedication, but it was actually more a result of their independent missions, which offered greater opportunities for desertion and/or defection; assured party loyalty was an important factor in a man's assignment to a reconnaissance unit.

Sapper platoons originally served with infantry battalions to clear obstacles and lead attacks on built-up positions. In the years after Tet of 1968, except for the 1972 Easter Offensive and prior to the final offensive, the VC/NVA virtually abandoned attempts to overrun U.S. or ARVN positions by frontal attacks. An interim tactic during these rebuilding years was to stage raids by sapper units. To accomplish this, sapper platoons were combined into companies and battalions that operated independently from the infantry battalions. When the infantry units had a need for sappers, a unit of platoon size was attached for the specific mission.

Before formal acceptance into the sapper units, soldiers received as much as three months' additional training at a special base near Son Tay, in North Vietnam, or on the job with their unit in the South. They learned how to move quietly to penetrate bases surrounded by mines, barbed wire, and detection devices, and how to use all types of explosives. Typical of the sappers' skill was their attack on Liberty Bridge, defended by U.S. Marines near the DMZ in March 1969. During the attack, the sappers infiltrated past five manned listening posts and reached the bridge without setting off a single one of the more than three hundred trip flares and anti-intrusion devices surrounding their objective.[8]

Control and discipline of the VC and NVA troops within each unit was based upon careful evaluation of what each individual thought, how he performed, and how he got along with his comrades. This was facilitated by three mechanisms or approaches—close supervision, criticism/self-criticism, and use of three-man cells. Supervision of subordinates, including monitoring morale, willingness to follow orders, and ability to get along with fellow soldiers, was not unique to the VC/NVA.

While the leaders' basic responsibilities of watching over subordinates are typical in all armies, what was unusual about the VC/NVA techniques of supervision was the absoluteness of the cadres' watching every action and monitoring even the thoughts and moods of the Front soldiers. In any army, a soldier gives up a certain amount of privacy. In the Liberation army, the lack of privacy, both in action and in the mind, was total. What could not be directly observed about an individual was investigated by questioning fellow soldiers and the soldier himself.

Surprisingly, the soldiers did not seem to resent the close supervision (or perhaps those who did resent it were quickly "reeducated"). According to a twenty-year-old VC private captured in August 1968, "The cadres did watch over all the troops. They watched over the way of talking, the behavior, and combat spirit of the troops to see if they had good or bad morale. The cadres did it personally. They [the soldiers] all knew they were being watched by the cadres. It did not bother them. They became more friendly with each other because of the knowledge of being watched."

A twenty-nine-year-old VC private, captured a month earlier, adds that they were closely watched because the cadres "were afraid the men would rally or desert home. Everyone knew he was being watched. They had to be cautious in their speech. If anyone had any hidden thoughts, for example, to desert home, he would have to conceal it until he was able to have a good opportunity to escape."

More information about the process of supervision is offered by a twenty-six-year-old cadre member captured in September 1968. When asked about his role in watching over his men, the junior officer and Party member stated, "It is not correct to use the word 'watch.' The cadre only supervised the daily activity of the three-man cell, the troops [themselves] watched over and knew the actions of the others." The officer added that the men knew they were being watched but "their reaction was to work more zealously in order to display their high morale."[9]

An extension of the constant supervision techniques for maintaining discipline was criticism/self-criticism. Front soldiers were constantly being indoctrinated in the importance of the liberation of the South, the need to destroy the Americans and their South Vietnamese "puppets," and in their own role as hero, patriot, friend, and protector of the people. Daily, and with special sessions following every combat action, each soldier listened as his leaders and comrades reviewed his performance, motivation, and morale. First, the leaders critiqued the soldier, detailing his positive and negative actions. This was followed by similar observations from his comrades. The session concluded with the soldier being given the opportunity to explain his actions and to react to the criticism received. The essential, and required, part of the discussion was the soldier's acknowledgment of faults and weaknesses—in both thought and deed—and his promise to work hard at self-improvement.[10]

Typical of military units based on the Maoist Chinese Communist model, self-criticism *("Phe Binh")* was a part of the VC and NVA units from their very beginnings. The VC/NVA conducted these sessions through reviews and discussions of actions at all levels. These sessions, known as *Kiem Thao,* were not only for the private soldier but also for the cadre and unit commanders. While Phe Binh was directed primarily toward the motivational and disciplinary problems of the individual, Kiem Thao* concentrated on resolving organizational problems and leadership difficulties.[11]

Although various ranks might attend the same Kiem Thao session, lower ranks normally did not criticize higher. Non-Party members were not allowed to comment on the actions of Party members of equal or lower rank. Despite this minor bit of "favoritism," the Kiem Thao system, by all accounts, was successful in maintaining cohesion, morale, and fighting ability.

VC and NVA of all ranks accepted Kiem Thao. According to an NVA master sergeant who was a Party member and twenty-eight years old when captured in November 1968, "I was pleased when the company cadres criticized me for my mistakes because, thanks to them, I could make corrections."

As for criticism sessions of his subordinates, the sergeant continued, "I could not see any better method to correct the errors of the troops. At the beginning the person criticized was pretty upset. However, the troops gradually realized that it was a good method. After each criticism session I noticed that the discipline was improved and personal sentiments were better. The sessions were very democratic. They helped the troops to observe discipline strictly, thus correcting their morale and thoughts."

A twenty-six-year-old junior NVA officer adds, "In self-

---

*Many documents outside of Vietnam at the time and since use Phe Binh and Kiem Thao interchangeably to mean any criticism/self-criticism session. To be completely accurate, it is acceptable to use Kiem Thao to mean Phe Binh, but never the converse.

criticism sessions, I promised I would make corrections, and after that I felt relaxed. Criticism is a good method, and it is a token of mutual affection in a unit. If there were any errors we would help each other to correct and avoid them. Criticism is always fair because it is based on the ideas of several people and of the group, not of a single person or a few people. Criticism sessions helped the respective persons make corrections; thus they were not angry or discouraged.''

Serious errors of judgment and of exhibited cowardice were criticized along with seemingly minor faults. A twenty-three-year-old VC company executive officer, captured in September 1968, admits, ''After the Tet Offensive I was criticized after being lightly wounded in Cholon [the Chinese section of Saigon] while trying to withdraw hurriedly from the battlefield. Upon reaching the unit home base, I had no idea of the actual strength of my platoon and I was not able to help any wounded get away. I was criticized for having a passive attitude, being an egoist, fleeing alone, and not helping fellow fighters while I was still able to help them.''

About the criticism itself, the officer recalled, ''I did not feel depressed, nor discouraged, because I admitted I was too scared and ran away although the wound on my hand was not serious. Upon reaching home base, I felt I was guilty because I was an assistant platoon leader, I was only lightly wounded and turned to flee, leaving behind many seriously wounded soldiers who were close to where I was.''

Although it was absolutely necessary for soldiers to admit their faults and promise to improve themselves, the Kiem Thao sessions did allow the person being criticized to offer reasons for his failures or inadequacies. The VC officer who ran with a minor wound at Tet explained, ''Actually I ran out of ammunition. I was afraid that if I moved deeper I would not be able to find a way out, and then I might be killed or captured.''

Even those at the bottom of the rank structure agreed that the Kiem Thao system was good. An eighteen-year-old private stated, ''When a person whose defects were not criticized made a mistake or had a shortcoming, he could never realize his mistake and thus could never correct his defects. So I think the criticism is good. To be criticized means to receive assistance from the men in the squad. Without criticism one might not know one's shortcomings and consequently make even bigger mistakes. So the persons involved in the criticism never got mad. On the contrary, they felt enthusiastic for being helped by their comrades.''

A VC private first class, who was twenty-eight years old when captured in November 1968, added, ''Yes, it has a good effect. I would compare criticism sessions to a mirror with which I could look at my face. If my face had a stain, I could see it through the mirror in order to clean it up.'' The VC soldier concluded that he thought criticism helped to make his unit better, but he explained that benefits were not always immediate, stating, ''Some men were angry at first, especially the ones who had too much self-pride. But after a few days they will have forgotten about it and later on, little by little, they will have realized that the criticism session is necessary.''

Kiem Thao sessions were designed to correct ''incorrect thoughts,'' which was the basis for critiquing poor actions and morale. A twenty-one-year-old VC private, captured in September 1968, explains, ''Let me give you an example. For some reason I do not like you and think you are bad. But I keep this to myself and think that I am right. Now, in this meeting, I criticize you and you defend yourself. Other people will listen to us and join in the discussion. This way will help us know each other better, and thus our friendship will be consolidated.''[12]

Self-criticism, admission of faults, and promises to try to do better were the first steps to please superiors. After the Kiem Thao session, the VC officer who ran from the battle for Cholon was allowed to continue to lead his soldiers. He rose in rank from assistant platoon leader to platoon leader and company executive officer in the six months between the running incident and his later capture.

Although cadre and other leaders certainly made ''on-the-spot corrections,'' and both admonished and praised their soldiers on an individual basis, Kiem Thao was the primary action tool used to handle transgressions—whether minor ones, such as being late for a work detail, or major ones, such as losing a weapon or not performing bravely in combat. Kiem Thao was seen by all ranks as a fair, equitable system that was essential to morale and combat readiness.

While close scrutiny and Kiem Thao were essential elements of supervision, the ultimate means of control of the VC/NVA soldiers was their organization into three-man cells where each member of the cell constantly observed the other two. From induction, each soldier was taught that his three-man collective team was more important than his individual rights or desires. The three members of the cell were expected to share work, recreation, food, and personal thoughts as equals. If one member's morale was low, the others cheered him up. If one became ill, the others tended to him. If wounded or killed in battle, fellow members of the cell were expected to risk their lives to rescue their comrade or to retrieve his body.

In short, the three-man cell enforced a bonding akin to brotherhood, which was essential for coping with fear in battle and boredom in camp. Many cells* formed in the NVA training camps remained unchanged during infiltration and remained together until casualties or disease thinned their ranks.

The use of the cell as the cornerstone for VC/NVA unit organization varied little with the time or phase of the war. Although there is some evidence that the cohesion within the cell was looser in some units than in others while in camp, all organizations heavily relied on the three-man cell to act as a team during combat.[13]

Three-man cells, along with Kiem Thao and the constant supervision by the cadres, removed any possibility of privacy for the VC/NVA private. While Americans may view the deprivation of privacy as a dehumanizing control tactic, the VC/ NVA saw the system as essential. A twenty-one-year-old NVA private first class was a member of a three-man cell for a year before his capture in August 1968. According to the PFC, "The three-man cell was very helpful to me. For example, during the infiltration south, the other men in my cell gave me a lot of assistance such as carrying my gun and ammunition or other items for me when I was tired or sick. The attitude of the other men in the cell was so encouraging that I was even more determined to endure the hardships in order to arrive in the South."

VC and NVA soldiers depended on their fellow cell members in combat as well as in camp. A three-year veteran of the NVA before his capture in September 1968 stated, "The others took

*Although all armies rely on some type of cell or team as their lowest formal organization, only the VC/NVA and the Chinese forces—who developed the system prior to the Korean War—have made the members of the three-man cell so dependent upon each other. The comparable U.S. Army unit in actual organization is the infantry squad fire team composed of four or five soldiers. In actual performance, the only U.S. concept that even closely resembles the three-man cell is the two-man "buddy system" employed by the Army's Infantry School Ranger Department. Ranger students are paired from the beginning of the class and the two soldiers are expected to be together and share everything for the duration of the course.

good care of me. When I was wounded the first time on an operation, the other two men helped me to get out from the battlefield.''

An eighteen-year-old private, captured after a year in the South, added, ''In combat the three men in the cell always kept close to each other. They moved forward together and withdrew together in case they had to. But it also helped the men do their work when not in combat. When I had a problem, the other men in the cell helped me to solve it. When I quarreled with someone, the other two men helped me to calm down and explained to me what the problem was. When I got sick, the other two men called the medic and got medicine for me.''

Another NVA private explained, ''When not in combat, work to be done would be assigned to the cells. I think human beings have a tendency to work with friends rather than working alone. Three heads are better than one, as you know.''

A VC officer, Party member, and veteran of more than two years in the Front before his capture, explained the usefulness of the cell system to unit leaders: ''I was a company executive officer. Though I lived among the men, I did not have the time to talk with every man in my company in order to know what he thought or how he worked. It was the three-man cell system that helped me better understand the men's spirit.''

Another summation of the system was offered by a twenty-two-year-old NVA sergeant with three years of battle experience before his capture in late 1968. According to the sergeant, ''The purpose of the three-man cell was to consolidate the men's morale and fighting spirit. A big unit like a platoon or a company could not hold meetings regularly. Therefore the big unit divided into cells, the cells held meetings every day, regularly, and the men in the unit had better opportunities to consolidate the morale of each other and to motivate their fighting spirit. The three-man cell helped the men to carry out their assignments properly. It helped the men go into combat enthusiastically and helped them to carry out noncombat duties.''

The sergeant concluded by explaining how the cell system also made his job as a leader easier, stating, ''It helped me to fulfill my task. My job with my battalion [the 34th NVA Battalion] was to keep records on the unit's strength. During combat the squads had to keep me informed of the number of men killed or wounded so I could report to my commander. Since the cell had only three men, it was easy for them to know whether anyone among them was killed or wounded.''[14]

Of all the aspects that combined for the eventual victory by the VC/NVA forces, the success of the three-man-cell system stands out as a deciding factor. Its importance is emphasized by the words of the men themselves in interview after interview where they said, in effect, that the cell system made them feel "We are like brothers, even closer than brothers."[15]

Although the cell was the smallest organized unit, it rarely operated by itself. The basic unit for maneuver and operations, and the smallest normally given an independent mission, was the squad. Led by a sergeant, who was assisted by a corporal, a squad was generally composed of three cells but occasionally varied from two to four. While soldiers within a cell were responsible only for the welfare and morale of themselves and their fellow cell members, the duties of the squad leader were much more extensive.

Squad leaders were responsible for the welfare and state of mind of their men as well as the day-to-day tasks of camp life and preparation for battle. Specific jobs included ensuring the squad properly fortified and camouflaged its positions, maintained its weapons and equipment, and practiced good personal hygiene, and observed the "regulations and rules of the Armed Forces." In addition to these requirements, the squad leader also had to oversee the squad's study of military and political subjects, to ensure that good relations were maintained with other squads in the unit, and to make sure criticism/self-criticism sessions were held.[16]

The soldiers within a cell and squad could look forward to a fair promotion system based on achievement and merit. Although there were examples of nepotism based on family or village origins, particularly among the Viet Cong, a Front recruit could usually depend on advancing from private to private second class (or combatant, as it was frequently called) to the grade of private first class. All that was expected for promotion to these ranks was to obey orders, work hard, display the ability to assume additional responsibility and, of course, continue to survive.[17]

Further advancement within the VC/NVA promotion system was not so simple because the Liberation forces were not organized strictly along military lines. Promotions to the rank of assistant squad leader and higher brought political as well as military responsibilities. Although some noncommissioned officers and officers concentrated almost entirely on military or political tasks with little overlap, the vast majority assumed the role of leader and teacher in both. The military chain of command and discipline were critical; however, the ultimate high command and authority was the Party.

Virtually every soldier holding the rank of squad cadre and above belonged to the Youth Group or the Party, and many privates were also members. Generally, any unit—even one as small as a squad—that operated independently was required to have a Party member in charge. In larger units operating together, such as an infantry battalion, Party membership was required at the company officer level and above. It was almost impossible for a soldier to advance above the rank of assistant platoon leader without the benefit of Party membership. In the isolated cases where a non-Party member did advance, it was never in the position of troop leadership.

Soldiers of the North Vietnamese Army belonged to the Lao Dong Party and Viet Cong were members of the People's Revolutionary Party. Although the names of the two parties were different, little else was; the PRP was merely a Southern extension of the Lao Dong Party. The primary purpose of the PRP was to provide the façade of a civil war in the South. In fact, VC and NVA alike referred only to the "Party" with no other formal name. On questioning, they were as likely to refer to the "Communist Party" as to the Lao Dong or PRP.

Full Party membership was not gained easily. Although considered "Party members," youths between the ages of sixteen and twenty-five first joined Labor Youth Groups responsible for their political education and indoctrination.[18] Depending on the time and stage of the war, in a typical NVA combat unit 90 percent of its soldiers were Party members—30 percent "full members," 60 percent Labor Youth Group Members. Party membership in Viet Cong units ranged from 5 to 21 percent full members and 10 to 59 percent Labor Youth Group members. The higher of these numbers were in the main-force units with decreasing membership in local forces and the militia.[19]

THE CADRE SYSTEM

For many, a confusing factor in the study of the VC and NVA rank structure is the use of the word "cadre." In some instances, the term applied to the political teams that recruited for the Viet Cong; in other cases, cadre referred to instructor groups who trained new soldiers. Further complicating the understanding was that normally anyone with the rank of assistant squad leader and above was referred to as cadre. While the use of "cadre" was common for many aspects of the VC/NVA leadership, its most precise definition is in its context of the politico-military nature of all leadership positions. From assistant squad leader to general officer, every VC/NVA leader—or cadre—was responsible for the military proficiency and the political education and motivation of his subordinates. Each leader had two roles so entwined that to those unfamiliar with the VC/NVA they may have seemed indistinguishable from one another.

Requirements for selection as cadre and for promotions within the leadership chain reflect this duality of purpose. "Talent and virtue" were considered essential characteristics for officers. A captured VC platoon leader explained, "A person with talent is a person who fights with enthusiasm, who participates in dangerous and challenging activities, who has initiative in war tactics, who can devise and improvise many schemes and plans to beat the enemy, with the minimum of losses for his own unit. In one word, talent means principally the talent to fight the war. Virtue on the other hand means that a person must show proof of moderation, endurance, etc."

Adding more to the subject was a VC company commander who stated, "In the Revolution if you want to become a cadre, you not only have to be talented, you have to be virtuous as well. Talents alone don't help you to become a cadre, nor do virtues. . . . A good educational background can't guarantee you a cadre position either. The Front's motto is 'You reach maturity in fighting, you reach maturity in smoke and fire.'"

Bravery in combat had its costs, and the attrition of cadre members was the price. The death of leaders meant promotions for those of lesser rank; however, this was not always in the best interest of the unit. Frequent battles and the resultant loss of leaders often meant less qualified individuals had to take command. A VC platoon leader, talking about the large number of casualties in his unit in 1965–1966, stated, "The quality of the cadre in the regiment is not as high as it used to be. A lot of good cadres have died over the years, and they were replaced by cadres from lower levels. For example, if a company cadre was killed in action, a platoon cadre didn't go through a special training course for company cadres [and] he would be less competent than his predecessor."

Although cadres, especially those of senior rank, seldom were demoted for military reasons, they could lose something even more important—their Party membership. Cowardice or failure to display "proper virtue" could lead to a cadre finding himself suddenly a non-Party member. A platoon leader, captured in 1966, recalled that his assistant company commander was expelled from the Party for a second offense of "consorting with women." Although he was allowed to retain his rank, he was forbidden to attend Party meetings and therefore to learn in advance of future operations. The officer eventually felt so ineffectual and ashamed that he requested a transfer to another battalion.[20]

Along with talent and virtue, a VC or NVA soldier desiring to join the Party and ultimately to become a cadre member had to be literate. Education above basic literacy was not, however, considered as important as being able to carry out political directives well. Three to six years of schooling was the average for the Viet Cong, with one or two additional years being typical among the NVA cadre.[21]

Class status and socioeconomic background of a cadre/Party member candidate was important, but their influence was opposite of what might be expected in other armies. In the VC/ NVA, lower-class and poverty origins were looked upon favorably. Inclusion of those from other groups that the Communists viewed as reactionary—landowners, intelligentsia, etc.—was required because the Party wanted all groups represented in its "united front." Although recruits for the Revolution were sought from all classes, it was advantageous for advancement to truly be a representative of the people.

Complaints, especially by the Viet Cong, about slow promotions for men from "high class" backgrounds were numerous. A VC private, captured in late 1966, reported, "My superiors didn't trust me too much because I came from a landlord family, and they treated me not very well. I took part in a battle and we were successful, but they didn't promote me because of my background."

Another VC private, captured during the same time period, added, "I know of one man who joined the Viet Minh in 1945 and has fought for them ever since, but because he comes from a landlord family, he still is an ordinary member. He has never been allowed to join the Party. This man used to cry terribly because he had sacrificed everything, including his parents, for the Party, but he had never been allowed to become a Party member. When there was a meeting of Party members, this man was never allowed to attend, but he could stand nearby and sometimes he could hear what they said. When the Party members attacked and insulted the landlords, he would feel very miserable."[22]

Party membership was fundamental to the position of political officer in the Revolutionary army. In the VC and the NVA, there were parallel structures of command at all echelons down to company level. In each case, the political cadre dominated the military cadre.

The political officer was a hybrid institution of the VC/NVA modeled after that of the Soviets. Political cadre were not directly in the military chain of command but had their own separate rank and command structure. The military chain of command made no decision without consulting the political cadre.

This superiority of political over military cadre was noted by a VC officer in 1967 who stated, "The military were responsible for military operations but ordinarily those operations were carried out in order to satisfy the political cadre. The political cadre always had the last word and always made the final decision."

Another VC cadre said, "The battalion commander was supposed to be in charge of everything, but in reality, it was the political cadre who had more power, because he is really a Party member. The political officer, who was the assistant to the battalion commander, made reports on discipline, morale, and so forth. He also made psychological warfare and military proselytizing, and would send reports to Party headquarters."

More explanation is offered by another VC cadre who stated, "In my experience, despite their exterior appearances, the political cadre have been much nastier in their dealings with the population than the military cadre. It is the political cadre who hold the real power. It is they who make the decisions which are based on political considerations. It is the Party that directs and it is the Party that decides on the activities of all the organizations in the government. This includes the military."[23]

Contrary to American studies of military organizations and the various principles of leadership developed over the years that emphasize unity of command, the dual command system of the VC/NVA did work—up to a point. Although disagreements between political and military cadre certainly occurred, there was never any doubt that the political cadre would have the last word. Another factor that ensured the system's workability was that military cadre were often selected for political positions and, on occasion, a political officer would, usually after a promotion, go on to command a military unit at a higher level.

THE POLITICAL OFFICER

A political officer and an assistant political officer were assigned at every level from the High Command down to each company. Platoons subordinate to a company did not have a political officer, but those platoons that operated independently did have one assigned. Political officers were also found in army headquarters and in all territorial military headquarters. The political officer and his assistant did not operate alone. They were assisted by a staff that was generally equal to that of the parallel military headquarters. For example, the political staff of an infantry regiment was composed of twenty-one men—about the same number as the combat staff.

The political cadre participated in combat and often played a direct role during battle. Their tasks included maintaining the spirit of the fighters and offering leadership by word and example. Political officers, in addition to offering advice and, often, orders to the military cadre leaders, could also serve as counselors/confessors to the soldiers. They listened to troubles, consoled those with personal or family problems, and constantly extolled the virtue of the Party and the Revolution. Political officers also served as the conduit of information from the Party and higher-ranking political staffs.

Selection as a political officer was considered a great honor. Each candidate was carefully screened for dedication to the Party and assessed on his skills as a political leader. Political talent, virtue, and bravery on the battlefield—the same criteria used in promotion to military cadre rank—were the critical characteristics. Political officers were usually selected from the ranks of platoon leaders. The importance and appreciation of the unit's military mission on the part of political cadre were outlined in a memorandum captured early in 1967. According to the document,

> The important condition for successful accomplishment of the political task in the training service requires the political cadre to make efforts in improving his military knowledge. When possessing a firm military knowledge, the cadre will be able to fulfill his political mission. Without military knowledge he misses the power for carrying out his mission. For that reason the military training is a requirement for the Political Officer; moreover, the military science is so com-

plicated that the person in charge must possess a good knowledge to complete his assigned mission.[24]

Training was also important for the political officer following his selection. A former VC political officer recalls:

All the men who were selected to take a training course to become political officers usually were the platoon cadres, platoon leaders, or assistant platoon leaders. Company political officers were usually platoon leaders or assistant platoon leaders, who were sent to take a political training course for about six months or one year at 'R'* to become Battalion political officers. Regiment political officers were also selected from the Battalion political officers to study at 'R' for about one year.[25]

Fighters and military cadre often disagreed on the quality and performance of their political cadre. Some political officers were described as ''gentle, affable, friendly'' and they were universally liked and respected by the men. Others were not considered so kindly. When questioned about the political cadre, a regroupee first lieutenant, captured in September 1968, answered:

In the unit everybody had to keep in mind the proverb which says, 'The political task is the primary task, and the morale motivation is the first mission.' This meant that the political task was more important than any other. The political task was composed of different activities, and the morale motivation was the most important activity in the political task. Morale motivation was always an important mission. If a man carried a rifle but he didn't know why he was fighting and whom he was fighting for, or what purpose he was following, this wouldn't bring to himself or anyone else any good thing, regardless of how modern his weapon was. He would have to know whom he was fighting for and how great his task was. If all the men in the unit fully understand their obligations and the purpose of the fighting, they would fight the war and carry out their other tasks very enthusiastically. And the Revolution, of course, would be served.[26]

*Code name for a regional training center.

When asked if the political officer in his unit had any faults, a thirty-eight-year-old former deputy battalion commander responded:

> As a human being of course he had faults. But the only fault I found in the political officer of my unit was that he sometimes got hot-tempered with his subordinate cadres when the results of their assignments were not satisfactory. Generally, he was a very nice and gentle person, especially when everyone in the unit did his work well. Then the cadre used to talk and joke to the men in the unit very cheerfully.[27]

The respondent, who was a Party member, in answer to whether he thought the political officer was sincere and told the fighters the truth, concluded:

> I believe what the political officer in my unit said but I knew that he was not 100 percent sincere because he had to motivate the men's morale and if he was sincere and told everything, the victory news together with the defeat news, the men's morale might deteriorate. In carrying out this task I realized that he must not be completely sincere. For instance, he told us about the good results of the general offensive [Tet of 1968] which had brought about the Paris talks. I believe this because the radio and the newspapers told us all about it. But he told us that we won, both militarily and politically, during the general offensives, which I did not believe very much. The fact that led me to not believe him was that we were not able to take the big cities as we had planned to, and after Tet we were attacked many times in our areas.[28]

A twenty-one-year-old VC squad leader, after his capture in October 1968, when asked about his political officer, stated:

> The political officer was a native of South Vietnam, a man of very high character . . . he was responsible for the political education and motivation of the men . . . his mission was very important. He was responsible for the good morale of the men without which the men's unit would have broken up. . . . He was a nice person, always used correct language. He was gentle and never harsh to the men . . . he was never rude so everyone liked him . . . he was well qualified . . . he was especially good at political education; that means he

knew how to boost the men's morale. The men did what he told them to do. Thanks to his political education I understand more about the Front policy. That was good for me. The political officer succeeded in boosting the men's morale. Thanks to his education the men's spirits were more stable and they were more determined to fight. The number of deserters dropped. That was good for the unit.[29]

Another supportive of his political officer was a twenty-three-year-old NVA private first class who said, "The political officer was a very gentle and very pleasant person. No one ever complained about him. We all liked him and considered him our eldest brother."[30]

Another NVA private first class, who was eighteen and a Youth Group member when captured in late 1968, was not so positive, stating:

We all obeyed his orders, but I don't think the men liked him very much. He used to talk too much, especially during the night meetings when we were all tired and he kept on talking. He said we would go on trying harder and harder. We should go on trying harder and harder, doing this, avoiding this . . . which we all knew already. Young fighters did not enjoy listening to lengthy speeches.[31]

Another VC private had an even more practical critique of the political officers, saying, "The political cadre was not entirely successful in influencing the spirit and behavior of the men. That was because the war became fierce in my area [late 1968 in the Delta] and many people couldn't refrain from fearing the rigors of war."[32]

Despite a few complaints, many of the VC/NVA had nothing but the highest regard for the political cadres. Perhaps the most extreme praise for the results of the work done by the political cadre was expressed by an assistant squad leader captured in January 1969. According to the twenty-one-year-old VC:

Of the number of men in my company, twelve had been killed in a sweep operation by the ARVN troops in August. Among them were the company commander and the political officer, but the remaining troops still had high morale. None of them seemed discouraged, frightened, or wanted to defect or rally.

I think this was due to the effects of the political indoctrination by the political officer.[33]

Positive feelings were not only felt for the political cadre by the Liberation fighters but also for the military cadres. Typical of these were those expressed by a VC local-force soldier who stated:

As far as I know, the cadres of my company were very nice to the fighters. They treated the fighters in a most friendly manner. I can say that most of the fighters liked their cadres. Of course, a minority disliked the cadres because the latter offended them in some way. When the fighters successfully carried out the orders, they were praised and commended, but there were those who got criticized because they didn't do their work well, and they resented being criticized.[34]

A main-force platoon leader, who worked his way up through the ranks, said of his feelings while a private:

All felt they [the cadres] deserved to be our leaders and we had therefore great confidence and trust in them. They [the fighters] felt that the cadres must have proved themselves worthy before being appointed to the position they were holding.[35]

REGIONAL FRICTIONS*

While relations between political and military cadres and the fighters were generally good, interaction between the VC, the NVA, and the regroupees was not always as positive. A former VC civilian provincial official, speaking of strained relations early in the war, explained, "The Winter [Southern] cadres often despised the Autumn [regroupee] cadres because they [the former] have fought for over ten years in the South in hardship, and now the Autumn cadres who had lived in peace for a long time in the North come to be their leaders. The Autumn cadres [were] confident in the education, training, and knowledge they'd obtained so they encroached upon the Winter cadres."[36]

Basis for friction between Southerner and Northerner was best described in a lengthy account by an NVA cadre who stated,

*For a general discussion of this subject, see Chapter 2, The Vietnam Enigma.

The Southern cadres are resolved to end the war in South Vietnam as quickly as possible in order to return to civilian life and live like the others. According to the Northerners, the Party can only win through a combination of political and military action. They do not pay attention to the problem of time. They work slowly. According to the Northerners, you cannot resolve the war through purely military means. The Northerners consider themselves better trained than the Southerners in politics, military affairs, and experience on the battlefield. There are always arguments between the Northerners and the Southerners.

Additional information, with even more obvious bias, is offered by the same soldier:

The Southern military cadres are fond of employing human-wave tactics. They don't use proper military tactics, which is why there are so many men killed. The Northerner cadres always lead very orderly and strict lives. The Southerners are too free-thinking and they change their minds very frequently. Their morale also fluctuates. They do not have enough discipline and they do pretty much what they want. If they want to eat and drink, they will eat and drink, and they do not follow any orders.[37]

Differences, complaints, and disagreements between the various Revolutionary groups had little negative impact on their overall effectiveness. Problems were solved by good leadership, strong discipline, and the liberal use of the Kiem Thao sessions. The organization and implementation of the VC and NVA military structure within the Party was uniquely suited to the Revolution. Despite extreme hardships, a formidable enemy, and a war that seemed to be without end, this framework was to see the VC/NVA through to victory.

CRITICISM, CELLS, AND THE CONFUCIAN WAY

The Vietnamese, with their tradition of personal loyalty within the hierarchal structure of the family unit, were particularly well suited to the Kiem Thao and three-man-cell concepts. Maintaining good relationships with others, demonstrated through etiquette and ritual, is a basic concept of the Confucian ethical system which holds that in order for a person in a superior role to be treated properly himself, he must first treat his subordinates with propriety. Thus the persuasive, constructive criticisms of the Kiem Thao sessions described above by these VC/NVA soldiers would not have seemed at all improper to most of them.* They were conducted in the same way a father might instruct his wayward sons or an older brother his younger siblings—to correct their behavior in order to bring harmony and honor to the family. Soldiers in the cells gave to one another the same loyalty and support expected of brothers. As the Vietnamese family was to the village, so the cell was to the military unit.

The less-respected political officers "talked too much," or got "hot-tempered" with their subordinate cadres, like officious bureaucrats. But in general, the VC/NVA cadre and political officers were acutely aware of the necessity of proper conduct toward their men. Cadre had to display "proper virtue" and moderation at all times, be brave, be hardy, and be literate. Political officers were "gentle, affable, and friendly" persons of "high character" who always used "correct language" and avoided rudeness when dealing with the men. The best of them became like "eldest brothers" to the men, a very important and revealing description connoting a kind of familial relationship between the men and their political officer and one of deepest respect and affection between Vietnamese males.

This is not to suggest that Vietnamese society was particularly susceptible to the influence of Communist doctrine because of its Confucian foundations—capitalism and democracy were made to work in Vietnam just as effectively as Marxism-Leninism. The thriving market places in the now defunct Republic of South Vietnam and the success of hundreds of thousands of Vietnamese refugees in the West since 1975 are but two examples of the successful implementation of the former. However, the key to understanding how any political system works is in knowing how power and leadership are exercised within that system. The Communists found in Vietnam a fertile ground for their doctrines because that country's social system is based on a system of hierarchies where individual free will is given less importance than decisions made by groups. The

---

*In fact, these sessions seem almost like group therapy, and are also somewhat reminiscent of the "rap" sessions that were the rage in the U.S. Army during the 1970s. But in contrast to the latter, which were meant to "clear the air" and relieve racial tensions, the Kiem Thao sessions were an important technique for attitude reorientation and behavior control.

Communists simply supplanted the Confucian hierarchies with their own.

In short, these men conducted themselves according to many of the ideals of the traditional mandarin scholars who were once the backbone of Vietnam's royal dynasties. The men who composed the top leadership of the Vietnamese Communist Party understood their Confucian heritage well because they were educated in it and were the sons of fathers who actually lived according to its precepts. Understanding their countrymen and their society so well, these leaders were able to adapt these ancient principles of social conduct to their own purposes, one of the major reasons they ultimately achieved victory.

6

EQUIPMENT, ARMS, AND SUPPLIES

As the war progressed, equipment, arms, and supplies of the VC/NVA evolved in a manner similar to that of their logistics system. Beginning in the late 1950s, the VC relied on outdated equipment, primitive weapons, and leftover ammunition from the war against the French. In the early 1960s, the VC supplemented these stocks with supplies captured from the armed forces of South Vietnam and with arms and equipment infiltrated from North Vietnam. By the mid-1960s, when the war escalated upon the commitment of U.S. ground troops, the VC and infiltrating NVA units were equipped and armed with the most modern weapons and supplies Communist nations could provide. A war previously fought by improvising with whatever was available gave way by 1966 to a war fought by supply-line efficiency.

UNIFORMS

The basic combat uniform of the NVA was a simple green shirt and a pair of trousers made of lightweight cotton. Two button-down pockets were on the breast of the shirt while the pants had "hand pockets" from the belt to the thigh. Some uniforms had two button-down pockets on the seat of the trousers while others had none. Buttons were of plain green plastic.

117

Similar uniforms in dark blue and various shades of brown and khaki were also issued. Except for units that had recently infiltrated from the North, soldiers in the same organization frequently wore different colored uniforms or mixtures of the various shades because of nonstandard local procurement. Typically, an NVA soldier had only one spare uniform, which he carried in his pack. He also carried a sweatshirt-type overgarment, particularly in the highlands, for the chilly nights typical of the region. Most of these shirts were dark blue though some were in various shades of green and brown.

Black pajamas, more frequently associated with the VC than the NVA, were also issued to the regulars from the North. The loose-fitting pajamas—made of silk, cotton, synthetics, or blends of these materials—were usually worn in camp, not during field operations.

The Viet Cong main-force units used many of the uniforms of the NVA after 1965—especially those made of khaki-colored material. However, the black pajamas or a mixture of various civilian attire was much more typical. Top priority in uniform selection for the VC was to permit them to blend in with the local population.

Neither the NVA nor the VC maintained clothing depots. Storage and stockpiling of arms and ammunition were much too important to dedicate space and manpower to maintain extra uniforms. Instead, clothing was issued as soon as it was manufactured in the various VC/NVA-controlled villages.

Adornments for the uniforms of both the NVA and VC were almost nonexistent. Badges of rank or branch of service were rarely worn or even carried. (For examples of NVA rank, see Appendix B.) Within the VC, position titles existed, but insignia of these ranks did not. Most of this lack of attention to uniform decorations was simply a matter of convenience—living in the jungle was tough enough without spending valuable time on uniform upkeep. Another reason for not wearing rank was to avoid identifying officers and noncoms to American and ARVN snipers.*

---

*Like their opponents, U.S. infantry soldiers rarely wore the usual garrison patches and sew-ons during field operations.

EQUIPMENT

The belts and belt buckles worn by the NVA/VC displayed both a uniqueness and a fascinating variety.[1] Besides holding up the wearer's trousers, belts were used along with a web harness and straps for carrying ammo pouches, canteens, side arms, and medical packets. Belt materials included webbed cotton, nylon, leather, and soft brown plastic. Early in the war, webbed cotton and leather were prevalent but nylon became much more common in the later years due to its durability in the humid jungles.

Belt buckles—made of nickel, nickel alloy, brass, dull aluminum, or steel with a thin plating of chrome—were usually the two-piece interlocking design and, like the belts, were manufactured in China. The stamped five-pointed star buckle worn by officers and NCOs was the most popular battlefield souvenir for U.S. and Allied troops.

Footgear for the NVA was primarily ankle-high green canvas Chinese Communist boots that resembled high-top tennis shoes. Among the VC, the "Ho Chi Minh sandal,"* with soles made of old tire treads and held to the foot with fabric or rubber cords, was popular. Another common type of footgear for both VC and NVA was rubber or plastic shower shoes or thongs made in Taiwan, Hong Kong, and North or South Korea.

Occasionally the VC and NVA wore no shoes at all. Many recruits in the North and South came straight off the farms, where shoes were not practical in the wet rice paddies and/or not affordable on limited incomes.

The most common headgear of the VC was the conical woven-reed hat typically worn by farmers and peasants. These hats were manufactured throughout Southeast Asia and available in every market; however, if necessary, the VC could weave his own headgear from whatever fibers were available.

For the NVA soldiers, a sun helmet† made of pressed cardboard or cork covered with cloth was the primary hat. The sun helmet had a simple plastic headband for size adjustment and a chin strap made of thin leather with a small adjustable aluminum buckle. Although no protection from flying bullets or shell fragments, the helmet was quite adequate in protecting its wearer from sunlight and rain. Some of the hats sported the circular

*Ho Chi Minh sandal is, of course, the American name for the footwear. To the VC and NVA, they were referred to as *binh tri thien*.
†Most U.S. soldiers erroneously referred to the sun helmet as a "pith helmet" because it resembled the headgear of nineteenth-century British soldiers.

metal or plastic insignia of a five-pointed star on an enameled scarlet background edged with a gold wreath made to look like rice stalks.* This device, worn on the front center of the helmet, was a normal part of the uniform for NVA soldiers in the North. It was unusual, however, for it to be worn at all in the South, and if it was, it violated established policy.

Generally the sun helmet was tan; however, it was also produced in tints of brown or green. Whatever the shade, the hats had the tendency to fade after long exposure to sunlight, resulting in little consistency in color.

One of the most interesting facts about the sun helmet is that it is one, if not the only, piece of the NVA gear that was totally manufactured in North Vietnam.[2] Small factories, primarily in the Hanoi area, produced the unique helmets.

On occasion NVA forces were also issued a variety of soft caps. Many of these, which came in shades of olive drab and tan, were similar to the "Mao cap" worn throughout China and by NVA units posing as Pathet Lao in Laos. The most unusual soft cap was made of green cotton cloth with a sun flap in the back in addition to a bill at the front. The sun flap could be folded into the cap by means of a snap when not in use. Some of these caps also had ear flaps that could be secured on top of the cap or below the chin with a plastic button.

Steel helmets were a rarity among the NVA and almost non-existent for the VC. A few captured French metal helmets were available early in the war, while in the later years some NVA units infiltrating south were issued steel helmets made in the Soviet Union.

Equipment to carry water, food, ammunition, and other supplies varied greatly with the geographical region of the country, the length of time the unit had been organized, and the phase of the war. Since the VC/NVA were constantly on the move, everything had to be portable and lightweight. Few, if any, items not absolutely essential to the survival of the unit were carried.

The typical VC/NVA backpack, made of dark-green cotton or canvas, differed from American rucksacks in that it had heavy straps sewed directly to it rather than it being supported by a metal frame. Manufactured in China, North Korea, or Hong Kong, the pack had a large, primary compartment, surrounded

---

*A similar cap insignia was worn by the North Vietnamese Navy with the addition of an anchor and a star on a purple background. The Air Force sported wings with the star on a sky-blue background.

on the outside by two to five small pouches. Each of the pockets was covered by a flap that could be secured by means of straps and metal buckles. As with most of the VC/NVA equipment, the packs were void of any markings except for an occasional inking of letters and numbers called "factory markings."

Another common carrying device was the Chicom chest pouch or vest that was designed to accompany the AK-47 assault rifle. Made of dark green or tan canvas and leather, the pouch had in its center front three large pockets, each capable of holding one thirty-round banana-type magazine. Two smaller pockets on each side of the magazine pouches held extra loose ammunition and rifle-cleaning equipment. The pockets had flaps that fastened to a cord loop with either wooden or plastic toggle buttons.

Ammunition pouches designed to hold ammo for the Chicom carbine Type 56, or for the SKS, its Soviet equivalent, could be worn either across the chest or attached to the belt. Made in China of green cotton fabric or canvas, these pouches had ten pockets that were each designed for two ten-round clips of 7.62mm ammunition. In reality, some of these pouches were often left empty for comfort and extra ammo carried in the pack.

Various other packs and pouches designed to transport ammo were also used. Many of these were adapted in the field to a particular need or its bearer's desires to carry extra ammo, grenades, and food. Others were homemade or pieced together from odds and ends of equipment captured from or discarded by the Americans. VC and NVA alike were much more interested in the practicality of their equipment than its appearance or uniformity.

One item nearly always found inside or strapped to the pack was an entrenching tool. Because of artillery and air strikes, the NVA and VC had to spend much of their time below ground. The most common shovel was the Chicom-manufactured one, with a blade five or six inches in width on a handle nineteen to twenty inches long.

Canteens issued to the VC/NVA were one-liter pumpkin-shaped aluminum containers painted black or dark green with reddish-brown or black Bakelite-type screw-on caps. Owners often scratched their names, units, or other artwork on the otherwise unadorned metal and used thin cotton straps to secure the canteens to their belts or to suspend them over their shoulders. Other canteens came complete with green cotton cloth covers that provided insulation, muffled noises, and made for easier carrying. Many of the canteens were manufactured in Communist China and were so marked.

In the later years of the war, replacement canteens, also produced in China, were made of molded green plastic complete with a five-point raised star in a circle. Another canteen, rarer than the other two, made of rubber-covered cloth, had the advantage of a built-in carrying handle and was collapsible for easier storage when empty.

WEAPONS

Unlike most of the VC/NVA clothing and individual equipment, which originated in Southeast Asia or China, weapons, although primarily from the Communist-bloc countries after 1967, came from every corner of the globe. During the early years, the VC had to resort to weapons captured from the Japanese and French. As supplies began to arrive from the North, new weapons from the various Communist nations appeared as well as surplus Allied and Axis weapons left over from World War II (with some even dating back to the First World War finding their way to Vietnam). Given a minimum amount of care, weapons have a long life span. Often rifles and pistols manufactured for one war see service in several more before being destroyed or worn out.*

It is likely that by 1965, and certainly by Tet of 1968, every NVA soldier in South Vietnam was armed with the most modern weapons of Soviet design and manufacture, or at least Chicom copies. Although the VC guerrilla still carried a variety of weapons, main-force units after 1965/1966 were armed in the same manner as their NVA counterparts.

The basic weapon of the VC/NVA was the Soviet 7.62mm assault rifle AK-47 (Kalashnikov) or its Chicom copy, the 7.62mm assault rifle Type 56. Although the Chicom Type 56 predominated in many units and areas, Allied forces referred to the assault rifle as the AK-47 regardless of origin. Capable of firing in the semi- or fully automatic mode at the flip of a switch, the AK-47 and Type 56 were issued in several basic configura-

---

*Despite the influx of modern weapons in the later years of the war, quality weapons were still carried regardless of their age and origin. One of the authors (Lanning) captured a German P-38 9mm pistol, each part complete with the eagle and swastika proofmark of the Third Reich, from the deputy commander of the 274th VC Regiment in November 1969. (See *Vietnam, 1969–1970, A Company Commander's Journal*, Ivy Books, 1988, pp. 63–64.)

tions. One model had a conventional wooden buttstock while another had a folding metal stock. Other copies, usually differing only in markings, were made in North Korea, Czechoslovakia, Hungary, Poland, Yugoslavia, Bulgaria, East Germany, and Rumania.[3] (For a complete description and characteristics of weapons, see Appendix C.)

As for semiautomatic rifles, the Soviet 7.62mm carbine model SKS (Simonov) was both common and popular. Fed by a ten-round integral clip, the SKS had an effective range of four hundred meters. The Chicom copy of the SKS, the 7.62mm carbine Type 56, or CKC as it was often called due to the Vietnamese misreading of the cyrillic alphabet (C for S), differed little from the SKS except for manufacturer's markings.[4]

Other assault rifles, submachine guns, and carbines of various calibers and capabilities were also part of the VC/NVA arsenal. Weapons sold, resold, captured, or given away often ended up in the hands of enemies of the original manufacturer. U.S.-made .30 caliber M-1 (semiautomatic) and M-2 (semi- and full automatic) carbines and .45 caliber Thompson M1928A1 submachine guns found their way into the hands of the VC/NVA by way of capture as well as international gun sales. In similar manner, additional weapons from the Soviet Union, East and West Germany, Australia, Denmark, the United Kingdom, France, Belgium, Japan, and China were procured.

Despite this proliferation of weapons, as the years passed, the AK-47 and the SKS or their Sino-Soviet-bloc copies became the dominant individual weapons. Their availability was one important factor for their dominance; however, an even more important factor was that of ammunition resupply. The AK-47 and SKS both used the Soviet 7.62mm M43 or Chicom Type 56 cartridges whereas the other weapons varied from 7.62mm and 9mm to .45 caliber—and often the ammunition was not interchangeable even between similar caliber weapons.

This interchangeability in ammunition influenced the VC/NVA selection of the Soviet 7.62mm light machine gun RPD (Degtyarev) and its Chicom twin, the light machine gun Type 56. The RPD's one hundred–round metallic belt, which fit inside a drum mounted below the gun, used the same ammo as the AK and SKS. These ammo drums could be changed in seconds by an experienced gunner. The rapid reloading capability, combined with the rate of fire of 150 rounds per minute, allowed the RPD to deliver a great amount of firepower delivered by a gunner who usually had an assistant to help in carrying extra ammunition, reloading, and to take over in case the primary gunner became a casualty.

Other machine guns, varying from 7.5mm to 12.7mm and dating back as far as World War I, were employed by the VC/NVA. Some of these weapons were mounted on metal or rubber wheels while others were carried by one man or a team of two or more. The larger-caliber, heavy machine guns were used as antiaircraft weapons in addition to ground support. However, because of their size and weight, these weapons were usually employed at large defensive positions or near the various borders where they could be quickly extracted to safety.

The VC/NVA carried pistols and revolvers, but as on most modern battlefields, they were more useful as a sign of rank than for offensive or defensive purposes. Officers, political staff, and occasionally senior noncommissioned officers carried side arms. The Soviet TT-33 and the Chicom 7.62mm models 51 and 54 pistols were the most common,[5] but again, as with other weapons, virtually every industrialized nation's arms were represented.

While the types of pistols varied, holsters were fairly consistent. The Chicom Model 54 holster was a "universal" carrier for all types of pistols and revolvers. The holster was made of reddish-brown leather or a similarly colored plastic over heavy cloth lined with dark-blue or gray corduroy fabric. It had a large flap over the top that could be secured with an eyelet to a brass or aluminum post. An exterior pocket held an average-size pistol magazine. The magazine pouch cover closed with a brass or aluminum button sometimes embossed with a five-pointed star. Webbed straps sewed to the back of the holster allowed it to be worn on the belt or fixed with leather straps and worn as a shoulder holster.

Regardless of the individual weapon, the VC/NVA always carried cleaning gear for maintenance. Each kit consisted of a three- to four-inch-long cylinder containing a bore brush, a patch ram, patches, and cleaning rod sections of eight to twelve inches that could be screwed together. The cylinder itself doubled as the handle for the cleaning rod. Some of the kits included extra firing pins and/or drift pins. Cleaning kits for the larger machine guns contained basically the same components but were wrapped in dark cloth pouches that had sections for the different parts.

Each cleaning kit included a rifle oil and solvent container referred to as an "oiler." The sheet metal or aluminum circular oiler was about two inches in diameter with a divider inside that separated it into two compartments. Dual metal screw-on caps at the top of the oiler allowed access to each of the sections. These oilers, made in China and the Soviet Union, bore raised letters on the front that translate "Alkaline Solvent/Oil" in either Chinese ideograph or Russian cyrillic characters.

VC/NVA mortars varied from 60mm to 160mm. The most common were the Soviet 82mm mortar M-1937 and its copy, the Chinese Communist 82mm mortar Type 53. Both of these smoothbore, drop-fired weapons had ranges of over three kilometers. Composed of a sight, tube, bipod, and base plate weighing a total 123 pounds, the 82mm mortar required a crew of three and one additional ammunition bearer.

Another of the more popular VC/NVA mortars was the French Stokes-Brandt 60mm M-1935 mortar and its various copies including the U.S. 60mm mortar M-2 and the Chinese Nationalist 60mm mortar Type 31. The three differed little and fired any type of 60mm mortar ammunition. With a weight of about forty pounds, the mortar could be fired by one man; however, a crew of two was the general practice.

Although the VC/NVA rarely stood and fought against Allied armor and mechanized units, they had antitank weapons in their inventory. Used more as antipersonnel weapons than for their intended purpose, the most common were the Soviet antitank grenade launcher RPG-2 and its Chicom copy, the grenade launcher Type 56. A modernized version, the Soviet antitank grenade launcher RPG-7 and its Chicom copy, the grenade launcher Type 69, were also widely used.

All four of these weapons were 40mm with the capability of penetrating more than six inches of armor at a range of a hundred to five hundred meters. The RPG-2 looked like a pipe with a pistol grip and trigger while the RPG-7 appeared the same except for a six-inch-diameter funnel-shaped aperture at the rear of the tube. Ammunition also differed: the RPG-2 round was fin-stabilized while the RPG-7 projectile was finless. Interestingly, both weapons and their Chicom copies could only be fired right-handed. A gas escape hole on the right side of the weapon in the area of the firing mechanism housing released enough blast to be fatal to the left-handed shooter.

A weapon the VC used with great effectiveness against populated areas and large installations such as airfields was the 122mm rocket. Also known as the Soviet DKZ-B antibuilding, antipersonnel free-flight missile, the 122mm rocket consisted of three components: an eight-foot launch tube that weighed about forty pounds; a folding tripod mount; and the rocket itself, which was about six feet in length and carried a one-hundred-pound high-explosive warhead. These were fin-stabilized missiles with a range of approximately 10,000 meters. A panoramic sight and fitted quadrant gave them some degree of accuracy, but when they were used against civilian targets, which they frequently were, aiming was deliberately indiscriminate in order to use them most effectively as weapons of terror.

Similar use was made of Chicom 107mm, H-12 rockets and Soviet 140mm rockets. The 41.75-pound 107mm had a range of 8,300 meters while the 140mm weighed about 65 pounds with a maximum range of 10,000 meters. Both of these rockets were designed to be fired from multiple-tube launchers, but with modifications could be fired individually.

Although the weapons of the VC/NVA were quite diverse, perhaps no greater variety was found than in their selection of hand grenades. Grenades manufactured in the Soviet Union, China, and their satellites were supplied to both VC and NVA units. A small number of grenades was actually manufactured in North Vietnam from components supplied by Communist-bloc nations. Still another source was jungle workshops in South Vietnam, Cambodia, and Laos, where grenades were made of discarded C-ration cans, soft drink and beer containers, and other items picked up from dumps and vacant camps. One popular container was a red six- to eight-ounce tin can that originally held mackerel packed in tomato sauce. Filler consisted of bits of metal, nails, and glass mixed with TNT, potassium nitrate, black powder, and/or picric acid.

Many of these explosives came from dud bombs and artillery shells that the shop workers carefully defused and sawed open. Several workshops in Gia Dinh and Hau Hgia provinces in early 1967 were able to produce more than one thousand grenades each month with only fifteen to twenty-five workers assigned. In addition to grenade manufacture, these same workers were responsible for the reloading of small-arms ammunition, the repairing of weapons, and the making of various mines and booby traps.[6]

Grenades imported from other countries varied in style from the long-handled potato masher and the oblong pineapple to the round baseball. Russian and Chinese grenades were usually painted shades of brown while those from other countries were dark green and black. Homemade as well as imported grenades used two basic types of fuse systems. A striker-release system similar to the one in U.S. grenades was most common while a pull-friction type was also used—particularly in the homemade models. The latter method was employed by pulling a string that caused a friction start, much like striking a match. This method was used, however, only when firing devices for the striker-release system were not available, because the pull-friction method was often unreliable in the damp jungles and wet rice paddies.

While they were seldom or never used in actual combat, knives of various types were carried by both the VC and NVA. The more common types were a cross between a hunting and kitchen or butcher knife. Blade length was commonly four to six inches. Handles of wood, bamboo, or plastic were at times wrapped in hemplike cord, heavy cotton, or nylon string. Nearly all of these extremely poor-quality knives were manufactured in small plants or cottage industries in North Vietnam. Knives made in the field from pieces of downed helicopters or metal from other aircraft were also carried at times.

More common than knives were short machetes with blades of twelve to eighteen inches. These, too, were often homemade but were generally of a little better quality metal. Machetes, like the knives, were little used in combat but rather were employed to clear areas for camps, to chop bamboo for building items, and to hack through thick jungle. One machetelike item often found with the VC and NVA was a thin six- to eight-inch blade fixed to the end of an 18- to 24-inch hardwood stick. This cutting tool was actually made in South Vietnam for use in tapping rubber trees by scoring the trunk as high as the tool would reach. Many of these knives were confiscated by the VC/NVA from the rubber-plantation workers.

Booby traps were a primary weapon of the VC guerrillas but were seldom used by the regular NVA units. Typical VC booby traps were pressure or pressure-release devices added to dud artillery and mortar rounds, or even to unexploded bombs weighing hundreds of pounds. Most common were hand grenades rigged with instant fuses triggered by trip wires. While the punji pit, filled with sharpened bamboo stakes soaked in human waste, received much notice in the press, in reality it and other nonexplosive devices were rare after the North began its concentrated supply efforts to the VC in 1965.

After NVA units began arriving in the South, regular mines, including antipersonnel and antitank, became common. Pressure mines containing shaped explosive charges of C-3, C-4, or TNT were laid on roads and trails frequented by Allied vehicles. Various Soviet and Chicom antipersonnel mines similar to the U.S. Claymore were used to defend base camps or to spring ambushes. The usual internal configuration for the mines was a circular pattern of projectiles, resembling a wasp nest, backed with explosive. These were capable of being rigged like a booby trap and left unattended or they could be "command-detonated" using a wire hooked to a battery. The mines ranged in size from two pounds to more than forty and contained projectiles as small as a BB or as large as a man's thumb. Some of the jungle workshops were capable of making copies of the imported mines.

The nature of warfare employed by the VC/NVA did not lend itself to the use of artillery and/or armor forces for much of the conflict. Except for the siege of Khe Sanh—which could be supported from Laos—the attack on Lang Vei in 1968, and sites opposing U.S. Marine bases across the DMZ, artillery was little used until the Easter Offensive of 1972 and the final push on Saigon in 1975. The same was true for the use of tanks and mechanized vehicles.

When the VC/NVA were finally strong enough to pursue conventional warfare, artillery and tanks were readily available—principally from the Soviet Union. Various howitzers and field guns were used with the 122mm gun being the most common. The most numerous tanks were the Soviet amphibious tank PT-76 with its 76mm main gun, the medium tank T-34/85 with an 85mm gun, and the medium tank T-54 with a 100mm gun.

Whatever the weapon carried and regardless of the source, there is no doubt that NVA units infiltrating into the South by 1965 were more than adequately armed. The weapons of the VC units followed. In a survey conducted of Viet Cong POWs in late 1965, 94 percent of the main-force and 74 percent of the local-force Viet Cong reported that their weapons were adequate to meet their mission requirements.[7] Guerrilla forces, however, reported a weapons-satisfaction rate of only 33 percent at the time because of their antiquated arms. This low ratio, however, improved dramatically over time with virtually all VC forces carrying modern weapons by 1967.

COMMUNICATIONS

Communications of the VC/NVA were extremely austere—especially when compared with the extensive use of AM and FM radios by the Allied forces.* An NVA or main-force VC infantry company had only one radio for maintaining communications with its battalion headquarters. This was supported by a field telephone wire system laid between battalion and each company when the units were stationary for any length of time.[8] If time and assets were available, the telephone wire network was extended to the platoons.

The primary tactical voice communications radio used by the VC/NVA at the battalion-to-regiment level was the Chicom Type 71 B transceiver, which had a range of approximately fifty kilometers. This radio was replaced in the mid-1960s by the improved Chicom Type 63 transceiver. For communications from regiment to higher echelons, the VC/NVA relied on the Chicom radio set, Model 102E, which had an estimated range of 125 kilometers. Soviet equivalents of these radios were also employed. Communications equipment captured or stolen from the Allies, particularly FM PRC 10s, 25s, and 77s, were also used. However, these U.S.-made radios were not frequency-compatible with the Chicom and Soviet models and were therefore limited in their use.[9]

Telephone wire included U.S.-made WD-1, which was frequently left behind when Americans abandoned fixed positions and fire bases. A gray plastic-coated wire made in China was also used. The telephones themselves were U.S.-made TA-312s or similar sets of Soviet design—Suchotsk Model TA 1-43 or Chicom models E0754 and Q-07.1.

The limited number of radios and telephones were backed up by the principal means of communication—couriers. In actual combat, virtually all messages by both main-force VC and the NVA were transmitted by this method. Runners carried verbal and written reports and requests from platoon to company and orders from company to platoon. Company messengers performed similar missions between their unit and battalion.

In the less rigidly organized VC local force and guerrilla units, couriers were used almost exclusively. This commo-liaison system or communications network relied on women, children, and

*An American infantry platoon of thirty or so men typically carried three to six radios. Company commanders were surrounded by a mass of radio antennas with different sets keyed to company, battalion, and fire-support frequencies.

old men carrying messages between specific points. Each courier was familiar with only his portion of the communications route so that if he or she was captured, only a limited part of the total network would be compromised. A VC commo-liaison officer captured in the fall of 1966 explained:

> The VC village secretary received orders from the district VC secretary, who in turn sent messages to the cadres who were staying in the hamlets. In each hamlet there is a fixed place where I would come with my message. At that place there was a man who would know me. He was in touch with the cadres of that hamlet and he would deliver the orders to the cadre. I gave the message to this man, not to the cadre. I knew, therefore, the fixed place and I knew this man, but I did not know the cadres. The cadres in turn, at some other time, went to another place to pick up the messages.[10]

Another method of communication was signal shots fired by small arms. Units in remote jungles, where no Allied forces were present, fired shots to assist link-up operations or as warnings as they approached built-up areas or defensive positions. Rifle shots were also a common means for landing zone and trail watchers to report the presence of Allied patrols.

FOOD

Regardless of the weapon and equipment in hand, the proficiency and life span of the VC/NVA soldier was often more dependent upon what he had in his stomach. Food supply was a constant problem, yet the stereotype of the enemy starving in the jungle, popular among Allied troops, was simply not true. Although there were certainly shortages of rations at times, overall the VC/NVA had adequate, albeit boring, food.

The basic item of consumption by the VC/NVA, like their ARVN enemies and the general population of Southeast Asia, was rice. This was supplemented, particularly in the mountainous regions where little rice was raised, with sweet potatoes, manioc, and corn.[11] Salt and *nuoc mam*, a pungent sauce made from fermented fish, were the primary seasonings. Fresh and dried fish of all types were added to the diet with a small perch-like species known as anabas being the most common. Meat, if from domestic markets, was nearly always pork. Rat, monkey, snake, and anything else that could be caught or snared in the jungle was added to the pot. Vegetables and fruits native to the paddies or jungle were also included in the diet of VC/NVA who were always alert for forage that would add to their meals.

Sources of food were almost exclusively from within South Vietnam. Rice was taken from local farmers as tax payment or was donated by sympathetic or coerced villagers. Food was also purchased from villagers and from markets in the liberated zones. Crops were planted and tended by the VC/NVA in remote areas for their own supply.

Oddly, some of the rations consumed by the VC/NVA were grown, packaged, and shipped by the United States. Large amounts of wheat, flour, rice, cooking oil, and canned meat were given to the South Vietnamese by the Agency for International Development (AID). The food, by gift, sale, or theft, made its way into the hands of the insurgents.*

Food was prepared in the early morning or late evening in an underground cooker called a "guitar" system or Hoang Cam–type stove that prevented aerial detection. The guitar system consisted of a deep, covered hole in the ground with long underground vents made of bamboo to dissipate the smoke. Food preparation was accomplished at the cell or squad level with members alternating as cooks. When units were in bivouac or base camp, cooking was done at the company level.

One of the primary difficulties was not in procurement of the food but in finding time to prepare it properly. Rice preparation is time consuming and under- or overcooking makes it less than palatable. One VC private in 1965 reported, "The rice we cooked was either burnt or uncooked. The rice didn't get cooked because we had to put out our fires when aircraft appeared. By the time we could start a new fire, it was too late and the rice would not get cooked. For me, eating uncooked or burnt rice was the worst hardship."[12]

Rice and other rations were cooked in one- to two-liter aluminum or tin pans that were part of each cell's gear. Food was served in rice bowls made of aluminum or ferrous metal with a porcelain or enamel glaze. Some of the latter had marble green and white designs or other decorations in white or blue. Others had folding wire handles that allowed the bowls to double as

---

*Recapture of the AID goods by Allied troops led to widespread rumors that the agency supplied the VC/NVA directly. Few American soldiers had anything kind to say about AID after continually finding sacks and cans of food marked with its clasped hands logo and "Donated by the People of the United States of America" legend alongside "Agency for International Development."

ladles. The only marking on these bowls was an occasional light-blue bird design on the bottom of the bowl that was likely the mark of its North Vietnamese manufacture.[13] (For more details on food procurement and supply, see Chapter 7, Logistics.)

Water, both for consumption and sanitation, was not generally a problem for the VC/NVA. Rivers, canals, and streams cover South Vietnam and for half of each year, daily monsoon rains add to them. Villages and hamlets had wells and/or large pottery jugs that held twenty-five or more gallons of water collected from roof run-off. During dry periods, in the high mountains, or in the salt water–covered Delta areas, the VC/NVA learned to collect water from bamboo stalks, the trunks of banana trees, and other vegetation.

Water, particularly that from dirty or contaminated sources, had to be boiled before consumption though frequently water was boiled to brew a weak "green" tea as much as for purification. Tea not consumed immediately was placed in a canteen to be drunk cold or reheated later.

The NVA and VC were equally addicted to one native product of America—tobacco. Up to one half of the Liberation soldiers smoked, and that number would have likely been larger if cigarettes had been provided for free, as they were to the American troops. U.S. menthol brands, especially Salems and Kools, were the most desired by the Vietnamese of both sides. Due to the lack of availability of American brands and their cost on the black market, the VC and NVA more commonly smoked Gauloises Caporals. Made in France and introduced during the French colonization of Southeast Asia earlier in the century, the blue-packaged Caporals were plentiful in the local markets—in both the North and South. One distinct advantage of the nonfiltered Caporals was that they were so strong that even the most dedicated smoker was encouraged to cut down.

MEDICAL

Medical supplies were critical for the VC/NVA units, living as they did in the jungle, making frequent exhausting moves, suffering attacks from the air and ground, subsisting on a diet at times deficient in the proper nutrients, and exposed to every tropical disease endemic to Southeast Asia. Although there is no evidence that there was a shortage of medical supplies in North Vietnam, there were times in the South when battle and illness depleted them to the point where the medical staff could not properly perform their duties.

A regroupee medical cadre, who had completed three years of medical school in Hanoi before being sent south and later captured in Quang Tri Province in 1966, reported, "In the hospital, the patients were 80 percent sick and 20 percent wounded. Most of the sick had either malaria or vitamin deficiencies and the third major illness was combat fatigue, which was a malady of the nervous system due to battle, bombardment, noise, and a great deal of pressure. In the unit, as many as 80 percent of the men were sick with malaria, beri-beri, or combat fatigue."[14]

While different percentages were given in different areas and at different times during the war, 25 to 30 percent of the VC/NVA consistently complained of shortages in medical supplies. Medical care itself was not usually the problem, but rather the lack of medicines and bandages. (For a complete description of the VC/NVA medical system, see Chapter 7, Logistics, and also Chapter 8, Life in Camp and Bivouac.) Typical of these complaints was that of a VC private captured in Long An Province in December 1968. According to the soldier, "[the VC] didn't have good medical care because supplies were not adequate."[15]

Interestingly, problems with shortages of medical supplies were compounded by the conflict between traditional Oriental medical practices and Western methods. Some Vietnamese supported traditional medical treatments based on herbs and plants, refusing Western medication. Although there were traditional practitioners of Oriental medicine among the NVA, they too were faced with shortages because they were not familiar with the flora of South Vietnam and could not always find the needed ingredients for their medicines and cures.[16]

Medical supplies were obtained from the same Communist-bloc countries that provided much of the other VC/NVA war-fighting material, as well as from Laos and Cambodia. Additional sources were the various "neutral countries" like the Scandinavian nations, Switzerland, and others that sent "humanitarian aid" in the form of medical supplies to North Vietnam. North Vietnam also manufactured some drugs such as novocaine, atropine, and malaria remedies. These, as well as those of some of the Communist countries, were packaged in glass vials two to three inches long with a half-inch diameter. The ends of the vials were pointed where the glass had been heat-sealed. To open the vial, it had to be broken.

Although this prevented resealing, it did ensure that the contents were not contaminated.[17]

Drugs and medical supplies were also purchased on the South Vietnamese open and black markets. Many of the black-market items came directly from the U.S. transports at the docks of Saigon and Cam Ranh Bay. Another locally procured item that proved useful as field dressings and bandages were sanitary napkins.[18]

Despite the acknowledgment and criticism of medical supply shortages, most VC/NVA defended the adequacy of medical care provided. The key to this appreciation for the medics was based not so much on what was available but rather on how it was presented. VC/NVA medics were quite attentive to their patients. Tender loving care was the watchword and was often substituted for supplies and facilities.[19]

In the final analysis, the only acceptable evaluation of VC/NVA equipment, weapons, and supplies is that they were more than adequate. There is no doubt that at times there were shortages and inadequacies that impacted the day-to-day life of the VC/NVA. However, it must be remembered that most of the time the VC/NVA were not seeking immediate victory but rather were merely trying to survive. Patience and time were the key to victory, not ammunition and aggressiveness.

Interestingly, when the VC/NVA were at their initial peak (from 1967 through Tet of 1968), ammunition, weapons, supplies, and manpower were so much in surplus that the enemy was able to abandon its guerrilla and small-unit tactics and assume conventional large-scale warfare. The result was their death, defeat, and destruction throughout South Vietnam. Although Tet was ultimately a strategic victory—primarily because of its effect on further eroding the support of the war by the U.S. populace—it was a tactical disaster on the battlefield. For the VC/NVA, Tet of 1968 was a reminder that it was better to be occasionally hungry or short of ammunition in a jungle hideaway than to have a full stomach and extra ammo and attempt to slug it out with Allied units toe to toe.

7

LOGISTICS

In addition to positive morale and motivation of its forces, any country must have a sound logistical base if it harbors hopes of victory in war. At first glance, it would seem improbable that the North Vietnamese and Viet Cong could supply, support, and care for a large army pitted against the world's strongest nation. However, logistics of the Vietnam War, like practically every other aspect of the conflict, defied the traditional military axioms and doctrine of belligerents in previous wars.

Though North Vietnam was one of the world's poorest nations in agriculture and industry, it possessed a characteristic even more important than food and material goods—a national will to focus the entire country's assets on the war effort. According to Vo Nguyen Giap, minister of defense and commander-in-chief of the North Vietnamese Army, "The Vietnamese people's war of liberation proved that an inefficiently equipped people's army, but an army fighting for a just cause, can, with appropriate strategy and tactics, combine the conditions needed to conquer a modern army of aggressive imperialism."[1]

Although Giap did not credit the support from other sources that made his army far better than "inefficiently equipped," the total effort of the people of North Vietnam cannot be discounted in any analysis of their victory over the Saigon government. Practically everyone in North Vietnam worked either directly or indirectly to support the war. Sacrifices were expected and revolutionary zeal abounded. Slogans such as "Prepare for the Worst," "There Is No True Peace Without True Independence," and "Defend the North and Liberate the South" were written on walls, printed on leaflets, issued as postage stamps, and painted on banners, as well as inscribed in the hearts of the people.

Students in North Vietnam* took pledges known as the "three readies" by which to measure their dedication. For students the "readies" included (1) ready to fight and fight valiantly, ready to enlist in the armed forces; (2) ready to overcome all difficulties, to stimulate production work and studies, under any circumstances whatsoever; and (3) ready to go anywhere and perform any task required by the Motherland.

Women of all ages took a similar pledge known as the "three responsibilities." They included (1) replace the men, free them for combat duty; (2) take charge of the family, encourage husband and children to leave for the front; (3) serve or take part in combat when necessary.

Eventually the "three responsibilities" were exported to the women of the VC in the South and expanded to the "five pledges." The pledges included (1) to fight well against the Americans and their puppets; (2) to produce well and to exercise strict economy in production; (3) to feed the war wounded and look after them; (4) to carry out family tasks well, to look after and educate the children properly; and (5) to be virtuous and behave properly.[2]

However, despite these lofty pledges, the victory achieved by the NVA and VC was not a case of national will succeeding without a strong logistical base. Although the logistics of the VC/NVA were in many ways as different as other aspects of the war, their system of supply, support, and transportation was key to their ultimate victory.

Austere logistics and extended lines of communications were nothing new to the VC/NVA. In a massive study of strategic

---

*Despite the commitment of its people to the war, North Vietnam, like the United States, had its privileged class. During the war as many as 25,000 young men and women of North Vietnam were sent to study abroad—primarily to the Soviet Union and Communist China, but also to France and other western European countries. Not surprisingly, many of these draft-exempt students were the children of high-ranking government and military officials.

lessons learned in Vietnam conducted by the BDM Corporation in the late 1970s, its authors concluded:

> Inspired by Ho Chi Minh and led by General Vo Nguyen Giap, the Viet Minh survived Japanese occupation in World War II and defeated and evicted the French colonialists. Subsequently, the Communist Vietnamese leadership outlasted America's eight-year combat effort in Southeast Asia, and finally reunited Vietnam by force of arms. A major factor contributing to their success was the remarkable logistical support structure they created in an integrated network of bases, sanctuaries, and lines of communications. Indeed, the sanctuaries gave them the trump card that enabled them to fight a protracted war and outlast the United States' commitment to the Republic of Vietnam. [3]

COMMUNIST-BLOC SUPPORT

Credit for the logistical support does not, however, by any means lie entirely with North Vietnam and their Viet Cong agents in the South. The VC/NVA war efforts, as well as the economy in the North, were supported extensively by the People's Republic of China (PRC), the Soviet Union, and other Communist nations. Support from China to the Viet Minh began in 1950 with the transfer of weapons and equipment captured in Korea. According to the renowned Indochina observer Bernard Fall, enough U.S. weapons to arm several Viet Minh divisions had been captured by the Chinese in Korea by October 1950. [4] This support of arms and supplies continued after the conclusion of the Korean War to aid the Viet Minh against the French in the First Indochina War.

Following the Viet Minh victory, the PRC continued aid to a total of more than $670 million during the decade before 1965. When the war with the United States began to escalate, PRC support increased from $110 million in 1965 to $225 million in 1967. During subsequent years the PRC provided from $150 million to $200 million annually. [5]

Soviet support of the Viet Minh began in the early 1950s with delivery of trucks via China. Based on economic needs and a growing distrust of their closer Chinese neighbors, the North Vietnamese established closer ties with Moscow in 1957. Following a visit to Hanoi by Soviet Marshal Voroshilov in May of that year, support from the USSR increased at a rate so rapid that it outdistanced the PRC in one year. Despite the fact that after the Sino-Chinese split of the 1950s the Soviet Union had to send most of its aid by water rather than by land across China, its support was more than double that of the PRC during the next ten years.[6]

Soviet military and economic aid totaled $365 million from 1954 to 1964 but sharply increased to $295 million in 1965 alone. This number nearly doubled to $510 million in 1966 and rose to a high of $705 million in 1967. During the remaining years of the war, Soviet aid averaged $420 million per year.[7]

LOGISTICAL BASES

While the Viet Minh, followed by the North Vietnamese after the defeat of the French, continued to actively pursue aid from both the Soviets and the Chinese, they made efforts on their own to establish logistical bases for the anticipated liberation of the South. Following the separation of the two Vietnams after the First Indochina War, the Viet Minh in the South buried large quantities of weapons, ammunition, and other equipment in protective containers for future use. Other Viet Minh retreated to jungle hideaways in the South rather than move to North Vietnam in accordance with the peace agreements. These strongholds were located in the Plain of Reeds, Rung Sat, and U Minh Forest in the Delta; War Zones C and D and the Iron Triangle near Saigon; and in the mountains near Na Trang and the jungles of Quang Ngai Province. They would remain the logistical bases for the VC/NVA for the rest of the war.[8]

In addition to their in-country bases, the VC/NVA also established logistic sites as well as command and control bases in Laos and Cambodia during the years between the ouster of the French and the fight against the Americans. These bases were integrated into the Ho Chi Minh Trail and other avenues into South Vietnam. For example, work by the North Vietnamese in Laos commenced in 1959 when the 70th Battalion of the 559th Transportation Group began building troop shelters and supply points along the Ho Chi Minh Trail at approximately one-day-march intervals.[9]

NVA forces began moving into the northern border provinces of Cambodia as early as 1962. Underground fortifications and caves dating back to the time of the Viet Minh were improved and enlarged in order to provide resting areas and depots for weapons, ammunition, and food.[10]

Even with the extensive preparations and the massive economic and material aid from the USSR and the PRC, the VC/NVA logistical support of the war probably would not have been successful except for the unusual method by which the United States fought the conflict. Despite the obvious fact that North Vietnam could not support the war in the South militarily without outside help, and the requirement of the Revolutionary troops in the South to secure much of their arms and supplies from outside the war zone, the United States and the government of South Vietnam did little to impede the continuous logistical stream originating outside North Vietnam.

From the time of the defeat of the French by the Viet Minh in 1954, the port of Haiphong—and the railway from China—were available for the import of Soviet, Eastern-bloc, and other nations' goods. During the first seven years of the conflict, ships transporting the arms and supplies necessary for the North Vietnamese to carry on the war landed unopposed at Haiphong. Even when the United States did bomb the North, the port area was off limits for attacks to prevent any damage to Soviet or other countries' shipping. American pilots flew over the port only to observe helplessly as missiles and other munitions were being off-loaded. Haiphong harbor was left untouched by bombing or mining until Operation Linebacker in 1972.

Just as important, but less known at the time or since, was the landing of Soviet and Eastern-bloc shipping at the Cambodian port of Kompong Son, also known as Sihanoukville.* In 1966 Kompong Son, located fifty miles from islands belonging to South Vietnam and less than one hundred miles from its mainland provinces, began receiving cargoes, which were transported to the VC/NVA by water and overland. (An extension of the Ho Chi Minh Trail—the Sihanouk Trail [*Doung Son Sihanouk*] also delivered supplies by land from the North to the VC/NVA in the southern provinces of South Vietnam.) During the next four years, until 1970, when the overthrow of Prince Sihanouk ended the use of the port, 80 percent of the supplies used by the VC/NVA in the southern half of South Vietnam flowed through Kompong Son.[11]

The only interruption to deliveries at either Kompong Son or Haiphong occurred during the Arab-Israeli war in 1967. Soviet

---

*In 1955 Prince Norodom Sihanouk declared Cambodia neutral and renounced the Southeast Treaty Organization. Cambodia broke off diplomatic relations with South Vietnam in August 1963 and with the United States in May 1965.

shipping to Vietnam nearly all originated from Black Sea ports, and sailed across the Mediterranean Sea and through the Suez Canal. The Six-Day War closed the canal, requiring ships to sail around the Cape of Good Hope to reach Southeast Asia. Even this delay, however, caused only minor problems in the flow of war materials to the VC/NVA.

As the war progressed and the tactical situation changed, the Soviets provided more sophisticated weapons—SA2 and SA3 missiles, and MIG 19s. Larger-caliber rockets and artillery arrived, as did Soviet PT-76 tanks to be used by the NVA against ARVNs and Americans at Lang Vi in February 1968, and at Ben Het in 1969.[12] By the Easter Offensive of 1972, the NVA were equipped with the Soviet T-54 tanks. During the Final Victory Offensive of 1975, the NVA had over six hundred T-54s.

In preparation for these armor operations, the NVA began establishing petroleum pipelines from the North to the South as early as 1968. The first pipeline reached from Vinh to the Mu Gia Pass. In 1969 this line was extended to Muong Nung and on to the A Shau Valley.[13] Prior to the 1975 Victory Offensive, the NVA built two more diesel-fuel pipelines. One crossed the DMZ and extended into Quang Tri, Thua Thien, and Quang Nam—the upper three provinces in South Vietnam containing the cities of Hue and Da Nang. The second pipeline (approximately six inches in diameter) ran inside Laos paralleling the border of South Vietnam until it crossed into Kontum, Pleiku, Darlac, and Quang Duc provinces in the central part of the country.

All the pipelines, their pumping stations, and storage sites were buried or carefully camouflaged—to include the use of water-covered stream beds. Although the pipelines were detected by U.S. long-range patrols and aerial reconnaissance, their impact was not totally understood until the NVA launched their waves of tank attacks. Even when the pipelines were interdicted by ground or air forces, they were rarely out of order for any extended time because repair teams quickly mended any damage.

LOGISTICAL ORGANIZATION

Overall responsibility for moving men and supplies from the North to the war zone belonged to the General Directorate of Rear Services (GDRS). The Directorate's High Command was co-located with the other major sections of the North Vietnamese Army in Hanoi and was responsible for all logistics planning, supply delivery, and war-material production coordination. To execute its decisions and policies, the Logistics Directorate had three subordinate transportation units—the 500th and 559th Groups, and the 603rd Battalion—all of which had been formed in 1959.[14]

The 250-man 603rd Transportation Battalion had the mission of sea infiltration of goods into South Vietnam. Delivery of troops and supplies to departure points within North Vietnam in preparation for their journey south was the responsibility of the 500th Transportation Group.

Charged with the major mission of moving troops and supplies from these depots through Laos and Cambodia and on to South Vietnam was the 559th Transportation Group. The 559th, with an estimated maximum strength of 50,000 soldiers and 100,000 civilian laborers, was divided into subunits with different missions in the logistical system. Operating the twenty way stations along the Ho Chi Minh Trail in Laos was the 70th Transportation Battalion. Other stops along the Trail in North Vietnam, Cambodia, and South Vietnam were manned and administered by commo-liaison battalions responsible for movement, food, quartering, and medical support. At various trail terminuses were the Binh Trams where personnel provided ground and air defense, maintained the trail, and stored supplies. The personnel of each Binh Tram were also responsible for delivery of supplies and replacements from the base areas to the combat units in the military regions of South Vietnam. Various transportation, signal, engineer, antiaircraft, and infantry battalions were assigned to the Binh Trams.

Through 1966, the logistical efforts of the VC/NVA within South Vietnam, like all aspects of the Revolution, were under the overall responsibility of the Central Office for South Vietnam (COSVN). From 1966 to 1968 three additional politico-military-logistic headquarters were formed in preparation for the Tet Offensive of 1968. These four headquarters remained until the end of the war. Under the new, post-1968 organization, COSVN was responsible for the southern half of South Vietnam. Operations in the Central Highland provinces of Kontum, Pleiku, and Darlac were assigned to the B-3 Front while the two hundred miles of coastline from Dan Nang to Cam Ranh Bay, including the hinterlands of Quang Ngai Province, were under Military Region 5 Headquarters. The fourth headquarters was called Military Region Tri-Thien-Hue, which was responsible for the area from the DMZ to the Hai Van Pass.[15]

Attached to the COSVN headquarters was the 90th Straggler Recovery and Replacement Regiment, which had the mission of policing stragglers and deserters, and recruiting, indoctrinating, and training local conscripts. After formation of the additional headquarters, the 90th Regiment was augmented by the 92nd and 94th Straggler Recovery and Replacement regiments, which were formed in July 1969.[16]

The formation of these three new headquarters signaled the NVA takeover of the logistics and other aspects of the war effort from the VC. Each of the new organizations was primarily manned by the NVA. COSVN maintained liaison with the three new headquarters but was not directly responsible for them. Their instruction, like the other headquarters, came directly from Hanoi.

Within each of these headquarters, three agencies were responsible for logistics. These agencies—the Finance and Economic Section, Rear Services, and the Forward Supply Council—were interrelated and either shared or had overlapping functions. This duplication not only produced multiple supply stocks but also insured that all possible sources would be exploited.

The Finance and Economic Section functioned as the chief revenue earner, producer, purchaser, storer, and issuer for the Front. It primarily served the political and civilian portion of the logistics system.

Supporting combat units was the role of the Rear Services organizations. These organizations included a staff agency that worked under the military affairs committee at each political echelon; an operations section organic to each supported combat unit; and a large support unit with area responsibilities. Ranging in size from 300 to 3,000 men, these Rear Services groups were responsible for providing logistical support for NVA and Viet Cong main-force units in their area.

The Forward Supply Council was composed primarily of hard-core cadre divided into two elements and operated at region, province, district, and village levels. A standing section of the Council was responsible for civilian labor recruitment and control as well as provisions. The second element was an amalgam of section chiefs concerned with military affairs, security, public health, information, and the economy. Included in this element, and considered members of the Council, were the chiefs of the Liberation Farmer's Association, the Women and Aged People's Association, the Soldiers' Foster Mothers' Association, and similar groups.[17]

While the Finance and Economic Section was responsible for the flow of supplies from all sources to the Front units in the field, the Forward Supply Council marshaled all resources available in the area. An internal VC/NVA document defined the mission of the council as follows: "Through the direct leadership of the Party Headquarters, all echelons take charge of supplying recruits, civilian laborers, food, money and necessary facilities for main force troops in the battlefield—inspire the people—organize and send all human and material resources contributed by the people to the units and the battlefield—strengthen the people by urging them to increase agricultural production, practice economy to the limit."[18]

Forward Supply councils at the province and village level were further divided into four subsections—recruiting, civilian laborers, food supply, and burial service. The recruiting subsection was responsible for recruiting fighters in the age range of sixteen to thirty-five years for the main-force VC units. They were further charged with indoctrinating and organizing "Youth Volunteer" groups. Attention was given to encouraging recruits and youths to become Party members with the established goal of one third joining the Party. When recruiting subsections at the village or province level were unsuccessful in meeting their recruitment objectives, district cadres were sent to assist. If all else failed, the recruiters were authorized to draft healthy young men to fill in the main-force ranks rather than depend on volunteers.

The civilian laborers subsection was in charge of organizing villagers and farmers into labor platoons and squads. These units were used on an as-needed short-term basis for carrying and construction near their home village or were moved to remote areas to work on special projects for as long as three to six months.

Specializing in procuring food for the main-force units were the food supply subsections. Leaders of a subsection encouraged farmers and villagers to grow additional vegetables for the guerrillas. They also required each household to keep one to three gia* of rice in reserve to supply the troops on an as-needed basis.

The burial services subsection was responsible for burying

---

*A gia contained forty liters—usually equivalent to nineteen kilograms of unmilled rice.

the dead recovered from the battlefield. Membership in this sub-section was considered an honor and Party members of some prestige were selected as were the family members of cadre. A women's organization, known as the Soldiers' Foster Mothers' Association, also assisted the subsection in burials. A cell of three to five people who knew carpentry and had the needed tools to construct caskets was a part of each subsection.[19]

In cases where the bodies of fallen VC soldiers could not be returned to their villages, the main-force units notified the next of kin with as much information as possible.* The notification began "It is with pain and sorrow that we inform you and your family of the death of. . . ." This was followed by the deceased's name, rank, enlistment date, home, parents' name, birth date, death date, Party member status, burial location, and inventory of personal effects returned to the family. Signed by the dead soldier's commander, the notification concluded, "He has completed his glorious mission for the Fatherland and has sacrificed his life heroically. The entire unit is in deep sorrow, because we have lost a comrade in arms and because your family has lost a loved one. In the name of the entire unit, we offer you our condolences."[20]

CIVILIAN LABOR

Although all the subsections of the Forward Supply Council were critical to the logistics of the VC/NVA, the greatest impact on their successes was made by the civilian labor forces. These laborers—who either worked for the Front because of their belief in the cause, because of impressment and threats, or as a means of paying taxes imposed by the Liberation forces—were responsible for recovery and transport of battlefield wounded, transportation of supplies to troops in bivouac, prepositioning of supplies to support combat operations, construction of bunkers and other fortifications, and road building and repair.

---

*Families of the NVA were not likely to receive notification of death of their soldiers. The NVA buried their dead—when they could be recovered—in remote jungle locations to prevent their discovery by the Americans and ARVNs. These burial sites were recorded and some of the remains were removed to North Vietnam or to national cemeteries in the South after the war. However, it was a rare instance during the war that any notification whatsoever was made to families back home. The NVA understood that if they were killed or missing, it would take two to three years for that information to reach the North. It took so long for this information to reach the people at home due to Communist bureaucracy in general, Party obsession with secrecy, and the low priority given to such personal matters in the first place.

Villagers of all ages were included in the civilian laborer force. Typical of this practice was Binh Ba Village in Phuoc Tuy Province. According to a cadre member, "Everyone in the village had to do three months' labor a year. All young men had to do labor in battlefields, carrying wounded and ammunition; seven- to twenty-day missions. Men under forty-five and single females transported rice and goods, but not in battle. Men over forty-five worked on the construction of roads."[21]

Laborers were expected to work from twelve to sixteen hours per day with a day of rest every tenth day. Soldiers worked alongside the construction laborers and also accompanied the porterage forces. This accompaniment not only acted as a security force against attack, but also prevented any of the labor force from escaping to the Allies or back to their villages.

The degree of support by the civilian labor force that could be relied upon depended on the time of the war. During the early development of the Party, the Front, and the Liberation Army in 1960–1963, the rural population was readily available to provide support but was minimally used due to the limited operations of the Viet Cong. By 1965, however, the Liberation Army was forced to form its first light field divisions to combat the arriving U.S. ground forces and an immediate need for an increase in the number of civilian workers resulted. From this point onward, there existed a constant competition for the rural populace—not just for their "hearts and minds" but for their backs and biceps as well.

It was not until 1967 that increased U.S. operations were able to make a major impact in slowing the civilian labor support of the VC/NVA. This lasted only for a short time—until the U.S. began withdrawing combat troops in 1969. With their departure, more and more civilians became available as laborers. By the time all U.S. forces had been withdrawn in 1973, the South Vietnamese government had lost control of the countryside and the VC/NVA had virtually unlimited access to civilian labor support.[22]

Use of civilian workers continued throughout the war and played an important role in the final victory. In a 1976 speech, Senior General Van Tien Dung, the leader of the Victory Offensive of the previous year, stated:

The strategic route east of the Truong Son Range, which was completed in early 1975, was the result of the labor of more than thirty thousand troops and youths. The length of this

route, added to that of the other old and new strategic routes
and routes used during the various campaigns built during the
last war, is more than twenty thousand kilometers. The eight-
meter-wide route of more than one thousand kilometers,
which we could see now, is our pride. With five thousand
kilometers of pipeline laid through deep rivers and streams,
and on mountains more than one thousand meters high, we
were capable of providing enough fuel for various battle-
fronts. More than ten thousand transportation vehicles were
put on the road.[23]

In addition to the various VC/NVA organizations responsible
for logistics between North Vietnam and the war zone in the
South, each combat division, regiment, and battalion had its
own logistical support units. These logistical functions were
under the control of the division rear services, which were
composed of five subsections—quartermaster, medical, transportation, ordnance, supply purchase/accounting, and food production.

The rear services for regiments, while not as large as those
supporting divisions, had much the same organization. For example, according to documents captured in 1967, in one area
the regiment logistical support function was composed of a financial affairs chief; a quartermaster chief with assistants for
food and clothing supply, a warehouseman, and tailors; a medical chief with assistants for drug storage and preventive medicine; an ordnance chief with section leaders for repair, storage,
maintenance, and registration; and a transportation company.

This organization was mirrored in subordinate units with a
battalion rear services composed of a clothing supply section, a
medical officer, an ordnance section, and a transportation platoon. Battalion rear services were under the control of the battalion logistics officer who reported to the battalion adjutant. A
company rear services was made up of a clothing supply sergeant, a medic, and an armorer, who reported directly to the
company commander or his deputy.[24]

In spite of this "layering" of support units, the overall logistical structure of VC/NVA units was austere. Support and headquarters personnel numbered no more than 15 to 20 percent of
the total fighting force. Even those numbers are somewhat de-
ceptive because everyone, regardless of his assigned role, was
armed and prepared to participate in combat if necessary.[25]

* * *

For all practical purposes, both sides supplied their forces from sources outside South Vietnam. While the supply lines of the United States stretched twelve thousand miles, those of the VC/NVA, while shorter, were much more difficult—traversing rugged mountain and jungle, and interdicted on occasion by Allied aircraft. Also, the VC/NVA stockpiles and bases inside the war zone were constantly in danger of discovery and destruction by ground troops.

By contrast, the Americans controlled the air and sea lanes between the United States and South Vietnam and used them with total impunity throughout the war. Under the "Red Ball Express" requisitioning system, the U.S. Army airlifted a total of 66,985 short tons of emergency requisitions to Vietnam from December 1, 1965, to the end of fiscal year 1970. This represented a total of 909,988 Army supply requisitions.

Most of these supplies came by ship. By the end of 1967 the United States was operating ten ports in South Vietnam, seven of which accommodated deep-draft shipping. The development of these facilities almost from scratch is one of the great untold stories of the war. By 1970 the vessels using these ports were being offloaded in an average of less than two days; in 1965, at the beginning of the U.S. buildup, the average per vessel was 20.4 days.

To meet demands, the Americans established huge supply depots in South Vietnam. The depot at Long Binh, just outside Saigon, provided 1,869,000 square feet of black-topped hardstand and 1,458,000 square feet of covered storage. The facilities at Cam Ranh Bay were even more impressive. Built at a cost of over $145 million in an undeveloped area located at one of the finest natural harbors in Southeast Asia, the port-depot complex provided 1.4 million square feet of covered storage, 1.2 million feet of open ammo storage, and facilities for 775,000 barrels (42 gallons each) of petroleum products.

The Army and Navy constructed storage facilities throughout South Vietnam for 1.6 million barrels of petroleum. In 1968 alone, country-wide consumption reached 43,650 barrels (1.8 million gallons). Approximately 140 miles of 6-inch pipe were laid between various strategic points to keep the oil flowing, 126 miles alone on a line connecting Phu Cat, Qui Nhon, An Khe, and Pleiku.

During 1968, an average of 90,000 short tons of ammunition were shipped into Vietnam by the United States every month; in February and March of that year receipts exceeded 100,000 tons each month. That year alone the Army itself consumed $2.2 billion worth of ammunition in Vietnam.

By 1969, of the U.S. Army's 11,000 aircraft (2,200 fixed wing, 9,300 helicopters), 4,228 were deployed in Vietnam. That year Army and Marine helicopters moved more than 1.2 million tons of cargo between points in Vietnam (3.2 million tons January 1967 through December 1969).[26]

To accommodate all these supplies and the troops who used them, the United States armed forces constructed a vast base complex throughout South Vietnam. This complex consisted of 27 major installations that provided cantonment housing for a total of 36,266 officers and 240,834 enlisted men (34,056 officers and men in the Saigon–Tan Son Nhut area alone).

The construction program begun by the U.S. Military Assistance Command, Vietnam (USMACV) in 1966 consisted of 8 jet fighter bases with 10,000-foot runways, 6 new deep-water ports with 28 deep-draft berths, 26 hospitals with 8,280 beds, 280,000 kilowatts of electrical power, 10.4 million square feet of warehousing, 3.1 million barrels of petroleum storage, 5.4 million square feet of ammunition storage, 75 new C-130 airfields, $27.1 million of communication facilities, 39 million cubic meters of dredging, 4,000 kilometers of highway construction, 434,000 acres of land clearing, and 182 water wells.[27]

If anything, the bombing campaigns conducted by the U.S. Air Force in Southeast Asia through August 31, 1973, demonstrate the support capabilities of the U.S. logistic system, which supplied a total of 6.162 million tons of bombs dropped on North Vietnam, Laos, Cambodia, and South Vietnam. As a comparison, during all of World War II, U.S. air forces dropped 2.150 million tons of bombs on Germany and Japan. In addition to the expense of the ordnance, the Air Force lost 2,257 aircraft at a cost to the American taxpayers of $3,129.9 million.[28]

It is estimated that the war in Vietnam cost the United States of America $150 billion in direct costs and twice that amount in indirect expenses. One example of direct costs frequently cited is the expenditure of artillery projectiles—approximately 10,000 fired per day at a cost of $100 per shell.[29]

All the VC/NVA logistical organizations worked together to ensure the proper support of the combat units. Depots were maintained at all levels, but except for those across the border in Cambodia and Laos, they were small. Regiments usually maintained a thirty-day stock of supplies with one third stored in their own depots and two thirds spread out among local villages or in jungle caches. Each soldier was required to carry a seven-day supply of rice in his rucksack as an emergency reserve.

Supplies and logistical support were managed in four primary areas—food, nonfood, ordnance, and transportation. Requirements for food, naturally, remained the most consistent regardless of the level of combat. Each year, the Finance and Economic Section estimated the food requirements for each region over the next twelve months. Quotas for each region, broken down by province, district, and village, were then issued. In each of these areas, the cadre representation of the Finance and Economic Section planned how to secure their food quotas.

FOOD PROCUREMENT

Most food for the VC/NVA was collected from within South Vietnam. Sources included taxation of the local populace payable in food or cash, fund drives payable in food or cash, open purchases in markets in liberated areas, or clandestine purchases in government-controlled areas, and farming or self-sufficiency.[30] The first two of these methods—taxation and fund drives—were often indistinguishable because the tax or gifts were at times not voluntarily contributed but rather were extorted at the end of a gun barrel or by threat of violence.

The amount each farm family was taxed was based on the amount of rice it could produce. Farm taxes were always imposed during the appropriate harvest season while special "fund drives" were held whenever the local Liberation unit was short of money or supplies. Rates varied with the period of the war, the region of the country, and the number of Front soldiers in the area. Typical of a tax was a progressive one levied in the Delta Region which called for 5 percent on farms producing as little as ten bushels up to 25 percent for farms producing more than 146 bushels. Farmers producing fewer than ten bushels were not taxed although they were "encouraged" to give as much as they could.

Another food tax imposed across the board in some areas was a "pot tax," which consisted of a donation of one handful of rice per meal served. Each family set aside these handfuls in a separate pot that was collected monthly by local cadre or village guerrillas.

Money collected by tax or fund-raising from nonfarmers was also a prime source of food procurement. Villagers—usually women who were too old or infirm to be used as laborers—were sent to markets to buy rice and other foodstuffs. Since large purchases would raise the suspicions of government forces, each purchaser bought only what would be reasonable for one family. An entire Liberation unit could be fed by sending all the old women from a village to the market.

In some units, particularly among the guerrillas, each man, or cell, was responsible for procuring his or its own food. They were issued a meager* living allowance of about seven piasters a day to buy food from villagers or in the markets. Some units received an additional allowance of twenty to thirty piasters a month to buy tobacco and other "luxury" items.[31]

For the specific purpose of selling to the VC/NVA, temporary markets were at times established by cadre or agents hired by the Finance and Economic Section in liberated or contested zones. At some locations, the markets were run by profiteers who were more interested in money than either side's cause in the war. There is evidence that military and civilian officials of the South Vietnam government were also not above making a quick profit in selling food to the enemy.

For the most part, however, Saigon officials and officers were aware that depriving the VC/NVA of food was critical to winning the war. With the help of the Americans, entire villages were moved to secure areas so they could not produce or give food to the Front. Other villages were fortified with permanently garrisoned forces to protect the inhabitants and prevent their taxation. The VC/NVA recognized the impact of being denied food and support from local villagers. One local-force squad leader, captured in 1965, stated, "Each person who moves out [of a VC area] will cause one VC to die of hunger."[32]

It is interesting to note that while the RVN and U.S. efforts focused on limiting the availability of rice to the VC/NVA, some American and international agencies worked to increase rice production. An improved variety of rice, IR8, was introduced into Vietnam in 1968 by the International Rice Research Institute in the Philippines. The hardy semidwarf IR8 tripled and quadrupled yields on the farms where officers of the MACV Advisory Team 73 delivered it. Its official name of Lua Than Nong

---

*The description of "meager" is more meaningful when it is understood that the piaster to U.S. dollar exchange ratio varied from 73 to 250 to the dollar during most of the war. In other words, depending on the exchange, a guerrilla was given three to five cents a day for rations.

or "Rice of the Gods" was soon changed to "Lua Honda" because one good crop produced enough profit to buy a motorbike.

Lua Honda and other improved varieties were spread all across the Delta region and other parts of South Vietnam by American advisers. Initially the VC cadres, on instructions from COSVN, spread rumors that the new variety of rice caused leprosy and sterility. However, once they observed the increases in production by IR8 and began to understand that they could extort even higher taxes from the newly successful farmers, they dropped the anti-IR8 campaign. The VC/NVA eventually became such strong supporters of the new rice variety that they gave instructions not to ambush the small MACV teams delivering it to remote villages.[33]

Another means developed to secure food when villagers were no longer available to be taxed or solicited for donations was for the Liberation soldiers to grow their own. In remote jungle fields and vegetable plots, the VC/NVA raised rice, manioc, sweet potatoes, and corn. These crops were supplemented by whatever animal and plant life the soldiers could catch, trap, or gather in the jungle and streams. Depending on the unit, location, and time, units eventually were required to raise enough food to sustain themselves for two to eight months a year.

Some units were so successful in their food-production efforts that they had surpluses to sell to other organizations and to civilians. Profits from these sales went into buying needed nonfood items for the unit. Although it was strictly against Front regulations for any of the excess production to be sold to the RVN government, there were cases where VC/NVA logistic officers were more interested in profit than in rules.[34]

Excesses of food were far more the exception, however, than the norm. Combat soldiers were detailed to grow food not for profit but for survival. The importance of these self-grown crops to the VC/NVA was noted by a patrol of the U.S. Marine Corps' First Force Reconnaissance Company in 1970. According to the patrol's after-action report, "The great importance that the enemy places on these food plots was demonstrated by the fact that when the cultivated plots caught fire due to a fire mission, the enemy could be observed in the open fields trying to stop the fires while the fire missions/air strikes were in progress."[35]

Nonfood items in the VC/NVA logistical system included such diverse items as kerosene, flashlights, batteries, cloth, and typewriters. With the exception of those items worn or carried by replacement soldiers infiltrating down the Ho Chi Minh Trail, most nonfood items were purchased, stolen, or manufactured in the South.

A U.S. Army intelligence report written in April 1967 stated that the Viet Cong, using various fronts and agents, could purchase almost anything they wanted in the Saigon markets. According to the report, purchasing agencies employed by COSVN's Rear Services Group 83 were responsible for buying nonfood goods in Saigon, with most of the purchases taking place in Cholon, the city's Chinese Quarter. Once items were secured, they were moved by pack bicycle within Saigon to the city's waterways, where they were loaded on various types of boats for transport to forward supply bases.

Buyers for the nonfood items included profiteers, South Vietnamese draft dodgers, and VC cadre. Identification cards that gave their holders access to the entire city were produced by several Saigon-based counterfeit shops.

In some of the more remote provinces, it was easier for the VC logisticians to bring the market to the buyers rather than go to the market themselves. In Tay Ninh Province, the VC cadre established jungle markets near the Cambodian border. The location of the market changed each day, but the merchants had no problem finding the new sites as VC guides were plentiful. To make the risk worthwhile for the merchants, the VC paid high prices. Their willingness to pay must have been attractive to the merchants because at a single day's market, over three hundred vendors showed up selling items such as tobacco, salt, wire, and even typewriters and refrigerators.[36]

Ordnance resupply was assisted by internal and external assets. Except for captured weapons and a few crude homemade rifles and pistols, nearly all arms used by the VC/NVA after 1966 had to be moved into country by sea, through Cambodia, or down the Ho Chi Minh Trail. Large-caliber rocket, artillery, and mortar rounds were imported, but much small arms ammunition, mines, and grenades were manufactured in ordnance worksites within the war zone or just across the border in Laos and Cambodia. These worksites were also responsible for the repair of all types of weapons, radios, and mechanical gear.

Workshops varied in size from a single villager working in his hut with hand tools to jungle factories with eighty workers, metal lathes, a foundry, and a twenty-man security force. Typical of such production was that of a twenty-seven-man shop that each month produced 1,400 grenades, 80 mines, and various delay mechanisms for bombs and booby traps in addition to reloading 1,500 rifle cartridges. To accomplish this work load, the shop was organized into four cells consisting of molding, finishing, foundry, and administration and security.

Despite the obvious difficulties in getting ammunition and raw materials to make munitions for the VC/NVA, there is little evidence that any significant shortages occurred. The Front soldiers were taught to conserve their ammo, and their tactic of seldom engaging in sustained combat lessened their requirements. When ammunition was expended, resupply depots or caches were rarely more than a day's march away. When large battles or attacks were anticipated, additional ammunition was brought forward and stockpiled closer to the area of conflict. If at all possible, the soldiers drawing ammunition resupply turned in expended cartridges for reloading. When intensive combat depleted the munition reserves of one district or province, the rear services organization coordinated transport of ammo from other regions.

Since transport of supplies had to be accomplished by foot, with occasional support from animal carts, cargo bicycles, and sampans, each division had a transportation battalion authorized 391 men; each subordinate regiment had a 68-man transportation company—the actual figures on hand greatly varied with the time and place. As with other VC/NVA transportation efforts, the divisions depended on drafted or impressed civilian laborers for assistance. As many as 1,200 civilian laborers were used by the division transportation battalions at any one time. Civilian laborers who were employed as porters to bring supplies out of the cross-border bases often saw double duty because they were required to evacuate wounded men on their return journey.

A fourteen-year-old prisoner captured in 1965 related his experiences as a forced-labor porter the previous year. According to the interview record,

While subject and three other inhabitants of Phuoc Thien village were harvesting their rice, a group of armed Front personnel came and told them to follow them to attend a meeting. Only when they were out of the village did they know that they were captured by the Front and afterwards were forced to transport ammunition. After being captured, they were led to Phuoc Chi. They stayed there for two days. Subject noted the presence of approximately 60 youths from

20 to 30 years old, natives of different districts in Bien Hoa Province. The following day these youths were formed by the Front into six ten-man squads. Squad leaders and assistant squad leaders were Front cadres. In addition to the 60 youths, there were nine girls who did the cooking and a 50-man Front platoon equipped with one machine gun, three automatic rifles and a number of rifles and submachine guns. After one day of movement through the forest the group arrived in Ba Ria and halted for two days. Subject's squad was ordered to transport three 0.80 × 0.50 × 0.50 meter boxes of ammunition of between 24 and 26 kilograms each. Subject was told that other squads transported the same type boxes and they were of a total of 30. Trip of Gioc Moi lasted approximately 12 days since the boxes were heavy and the group moved only at night to avoid airstrikes.[37]

MEDICAL CARE

While the Americans and their ARVN allies fought with the assurance that hospital care was only minutes away by medical evacuation helicopter, the VC/NVA faced austere, often antiquated medical care. Evacuation was strictly by litter, sampan, the occasional vehicle, or on the backs of their fellow soldiers. Hospitals were often hidden underground and staffed with poorly trained doctors operating in near darkness with inadequate medicines. Medical manuals were in such short supply that field medics and even doctors carried hand-reproduced text that they had copied while in school or military training.[38] In addition to the possibility of wounds from a myriad of weapons, bombs, and mines, the VC/NVA were also afflicted with the many illnesses and diseases native to their tropical jungle homes.

Field hospitals were austere due both to a lack of modern facilities and the requirement to be able to move with minimum notice. Treatment facilities were housed underground in tunnels or caves, or in wooden or thatched buildings hidden under thick jungle canopy. Separate wards were maintained for internal diseases, seriously wounded, and surgery with support sections for feeding, housing, and securing the patients and hospital staff. Medicines and other treatment materials were usually stored in hidden sites away from the hospital with the exception of a one-day supply kept on hand.[39]

To care for the sick and wounded, the typical VC/NVA infantry division had eight hundred or so medical personnel, or about

7 percent of its overall strength. A majority of these personnel were assigned to the division medical battalion, which was composed of 546 men. A part of this unit was a field hospital that could treat approximately 150 patients at any one time. Each of the Division's three regiments had a medical company of 50 to 120 men each. The battalions of each combat regiment had no medical personnel assigned to their headquarters, but each of their companies had several medical corpsmen and some platoons had a first-aid man assigned.*

Despite great hardships, frequent shortages, and tremendous challenges in resupply, the VC/NVA logistical system worked—and worked well considering the circumstances. Although food, medicine, ordnance, and other supplies were not always the best, they were sufficient. Their leaders knew that good logistics was a key to ultimate victory and gave this important factor attention from the war's beginning to end.

As with all considerations of the VC/NVA, however, logistics cannot be considered in a vacuum. The attitude and fighting spirit of the men who were being supported was as important a factor in the logistical success as in the actual rice, ammo, and bandages provided. One captured Party member platoon leader reflected that "we weren't in the Front to enjoy life" and that the only purpose of food was "to keep us alive."

The officer best summed up the VC/NVA attitude toward logistics—and the war in general—when he concluded:

All of us lived in the jungles. We all bore the same kinds of hardships and we all ate the same kind of food. When I thought I wasn't alone in bearing these hardships, I felt life wasn't hard at all. When [after being captured] I compared our lives with the outside, or with people in the GVN armed forces, I found we led a much harder life than they did. But in the Front there was no difference between one unit and another; this helped me to bear my hardships. When everyone leads the same kind of life, then you won't have anything to envy others about. You feel you've been cheated by life only

---

*The difference between a medical corpsman and a first-aid man was the amount of training received. Generally a corpsman had formal classroom training while the aid man likely got his in the field. First-aid man at the platoon level was often a "part-time" job with the man so assigned acting as a rifleman until needed as a medic.

when people around you have a better life than yours. If you've been using gas lamps all along, you don't find that the light they give out is weak until someone brings in electricity.[40]

BEFORE THE VC AND THE NVA 156

Our unit stops to rest in an isolated area. My shoes are still covered with dust gathered during the march.

BE DANH OF THE DEMOLITION PLATOON,
514th VC LOCAL-FORCE BATTALION[1]

8

THEIR SILENT TENTS ARE SPREAD: LIFE IN CAMP AND BIVOUAC

Almost the whole battalion had passed right through the place before somebody noticed something interesting and stopped to look and here was this complex of barracks, cookhouses, latrines, bomb shelters, a hospital, everything picture-perfect and spotless but totally invisible from only a few yards away.[2]

The everyday life of the NVA and Viet Cong main-force infantry soldier was spent aboveground, constantly moving between campsites that he fortified with bunkers and trenches constructed or improved with his own hands. The most often voiced complaints about life in VC/NVA were these frequent moves and the heavy labor required to dig defenses at each new campsite.

In addition to aboveground activities, the Viet Cong were especially noted for their ingenuity in creating vast underground complexes. "No one," wrote General William Westmoreland, "has ever demonstrated more ability to hide his installations than did the Viet Cong; they were human moles."[3] While vast underground complexes did exist, they were for the use of headquarters, command and control, hospitals, and logistical activities. Rarely did the common infantryman set foot in them.

LIFE ON THE MOVE*

The Communist ground forces in Vietnam had to be highly mobile—moving frequently to avoid detection and maneuvering extensively during the course of military operations. As previously noted, the NVA came to the South in units, walking all the way from their homeland while carrying their individual equipment and personal possessions on their backs. Once in the South, their lives were defined by endless successions of temporary camps and bivouacs.

"While in the North," confessed an infiltrator captured in Phuoc Long Province in 1966, "I was told that in South Vietnam I would suffer hardships and move with heavy loads . . . in my opinion the hardships were greater than I expected. My comrades said: 'Life is so hard! Can I get through this war?' " When asked which hardships were the greatest to bear, the soldier answered simply, "The moves."[4]

Another NVA soldier, perhaps using understatement, said of life in the South:

> We felt it was a little too exhausting. We lived in tents, sometimes in a cave; we slept in hammocks, or sometimes on the ground; we had hot meals, but we always had to eat quickly; once or twice we had just started eating when the order came to pull up and move again.[5]

This almost constant movement led to problems other than mere fatigue. A squad leader in a Viet Cong main-force battalion noted that the men in his unit suffered poor health (but not degraded morale) because their constant moving caused them to lose so much sleep.[6]

Units that operated in specified areas for any period of time usually had numerous campsites they would occupy and reoccupy, as their mission or the occasion dictated. These camp networks were broad enough to provide many alternative sites and access routes so that unit commanders could maintain flexible movement schedules. The networks included villages as well as isolated bivouac areas. According to a VC platoon leader:

*For a discussion of mobility as an aspect of VC/NVA operational tactics, see Chapter 9, In Battle.

There was no fixed regulation for moving. The short or long marches don't follow any fixed regulations either. Sometimes the battalion reaches a village at night and leaves it for another village at four A.M.[7]

One such organization, the VC 263rd Main-Force Battalion, which operated in the Mekong Delta region, moved sixty-three times throughout its area of operations during a five-month period (June–October) in 1965. During this time, the unit demonstrated a tendency to stay at some places more often than others, visiting one village a total of fourteen times, another nine times. But the average length of stay at any one place was only two and a half days.[8]

New campsites had to be fortified from scratch; old sites could be renovated. Either way, moving into a new camp always involved much labor with pickax and shovel. A platoon leader with a VC main-force unit told his interrogator:

When we camped or we stopped temporarily for four or five hours, we had to spend a half hour digging the combat trenches and the long foxholes, 0.80m deep, 0.30m wide, and 1.20m long . . . if we had to camp for more than one day, we would dig the kind of standing trenches, 0.80m deep, 0.80m wide, and 1.20m long. It would take us two hours to set up camp and dig the trenches.

This soldier claimed these kinds of field fortifications were good for protection from direct hits by projectiles up to 20mm, but offered little defense against bombs, rockets, and artillery. The officer's unit reoccupied its old positions about every two months. He added that the companies in his battalion were deployed about one kilometer apart, platoons at thirty- to forty-meter intervals, and squads and individuals five meters apart.[9] The leader of a VC main-force reconnaissance platoon who rallied in February 1967 recalled camping in War Zone D, northeast of Saigon:

The jungle terrain allowed us to divide the troops up very easily. Each company would give to the individual soldier, according to the terrain, about 6 or 8m of terrain to dig trenches. We would come back to our old positions every month or forty-five days. Every time we camped, it took us from two to three hours to dig trenches and individual shelters.

The field fortifications this recon unit constructed were L-shaped
trenches 1.6 meters deep covered with a layer of earth from .8
to 1 meter thick. "Our unit never sheltered in underground [tun-
nels]," this soldier reported.[10]

VC/NVA field fortifications were much more elaborate and
carefully designed than some of these firsthand descriptions
might indicate. The L-shaped fortification was much preferred
for individual and in-depth defense because it permitted interlocking fields of fire. In some areas the individual foxhole was
connected to a bunker running at a right angle, one meter long
and covered by an earthen roof forty centimeters thick, reinforced by tree trunks.* Unit defensive positions often consisted
of two lines of L-shaped trenches with 50 meters between the
first and second lines. Heavy weapons, if available, were placed
at the intersection of the L in the first line. If forced out of the
first line of trenches by an assault, the troops used the second
line to rally and then mount a counterattack.[11]

Digging in was also required when a unit "camped" in a village or hamlet. According to an NVA sergeant who was captured
in Binh Dinh Province in October 1966, "We were stationed in
the people's houses, but the first things to do were to dig up
trenches and to set up defense positions, and also to dig individual
holes close to where we stayed." His unit's standard operating
procedure called for stationing each company in its own hamlet,
about an hour away from the other companies in the battalion.
This "one-hour" interval was also maintained when the battalion
bivouacked in the jungles, where one hundred to two hundred
meters were allowed between the platoons in a company.[12]

An assistant platoon leader in a VC transportation company
noted a somewhat less stringent routine for his unit:

> As we were always on the move, whenever we came to a
> resting place, we would hang our hammocks between the
> trees and sleep under nylon sheets. Only the Front's agencies
> had fixed stations. They usually built cottages in the midst of
> the forest, near a stream.

These soldiers also had to dig in if they stayed in one place more
than two hours, but their field fortifications were nothing more

---

*In late 1969–early 1970, troops of the U.S. Army's 1st Cavalry Division operating
in Binh Long Province discovered several lines of interlocking defensive fortifications
with bunkers constructed of logs *two feet* in diameter and covered with earth (Tourison).

elaborate than individual foxholes. "We had to dig them because of enemy attacks. In reality, we seldom had to use them,"
he admitted and then added this revealing statement: "The men
were more confident if there were entrenchments where they
stayed."[13]

The length of time a moving unit might spend in any one
location varied with the circumstances. As noted, the 263rd VC
Main-Force Battalion remained in one spot only for an average
of 2.5 days during a five-month period in 1965. Other units
might remain in one location much longer. An NVA private
stated of his unit:

> We moved irregularly. In some places, we stayed one to
> two weeks, but at some others, only one to two days. Some-
> times, we didn't move far, but only from poorly covered area
> to a better-covered area.[14]

CAMP ADMINISTRATION

Camp administration was very strict in theory—although in actual practice the Vietnamese Communist could, and often did,
"goof off" as much as any other soldier. Nevertheless, VC/
NVA leaders wanted their men to pay strict attention to security
regulations, camp administrative procedures, and their respective unit's training schedules. Noise discipline was enforced at
all times; light discipline was followed during the hours of darkness.

Passwords were routinely used. If, for instance, the password
was the number seven, the challenger would give the challenged
a number such as five or three. The countersign had to be any
other number added to the challenge to equal seven.[15]

Each unit established its daily schedule, and commanders
expected it to be followed: "Each thing should be done in its
scheduled hour, in accordance with the time schedule," as one
captured document states.[16] An NVA captain and staff officer
reported his unit's typical daily schedule as follows:

0500 to 0600—reveille and cooking;
0600 to 0700—eat and rest;
0700 to 1130—study session in politics, build combat
       trenches, target shooting and tactics;
1130 to 1330—rest and cleaning;

1330 to 1830—military practice;
1830 to 1930—afternoon meal;
1930 to 2000—rest;
2000 to 2200—practice digging trenches and foxholes. Prac-
        tice digging at night without causing one small sound.
        Build combat trenches without communicating one
        word to the man at his elbow. Complete silence. [17]

The schedule for a VC local-force unit camped in a hamlet
in 1966 started with reveille at four-thirty A.M.:

At five A.M. we finished breakfast. We took position for combat until eight A.M. Then we rested or dug trenches or attended political or cultural courses until ten A.M. We then
went fishing or searching for vegetables to improve our food.
At eleven A.M. we took lunch. We rested between eleven-
thirty A.M. and one-thirty P.M. Then we dug trenches or attended courses as we had done in the morning. Between four
P.M. and four-thirty P.M. we rested and then took dinner. At
five P.M. we began our criticism session which lasted between
ten and thirty minutes. [18]

The daily schedule for the Demolition Platoon of the VC
C646 Company, 514th Local-Force Battalion, was very similar
to those above except that it prescribed ten minutes in the morning (0450–0500) for calisthenics, a specified half-hour daily for
"leisure time" (1830–1900) and "lights out" at 2100. [19]
The daily schedule of a Viet Cong civilian unit operating in
Binh Dinh Province in 1966 provides an interesting comparison
to these "combat units." The informant was a Mr. Huynh
Nghiep, at the time a fifty-nine-year-old purchasing agent for a
depot that supplied rice and other foodstuffs to Viet Cong and
NVA units. Mr. Huynh stated:

All of the days one spends as a Viet Cong follow the same
pattern. I get up every morning around five-thirty. At six
o'clock we listen to a radio program broadcast from Hanoi.
After physical training we wash and eat breakfast. As soon
as breakfast is over we go to work . . . from ten-thirty to
eleven-thirty [we] eat our lunch and relax. At eleven-thirty
we have one hour of study. Those who are uneducated study
and those who are educated teach. During the summer we
have one hour to take a nap before returning to work, and

during the monsoon, only one half hour, as the days are shorter. We then return for work for four more hours and then quit for the day. After we have our supper we again study for two hours . . . the day ends at nine o'clock when everyone must go to bed.[20]

It is worthwhile to note that the schedules for these very different units all include time for a midday "siesta" or noontime rest period—military conditions permitting, of course. This is a common practice in Vietnamese society, which believes in beginning work early and finishing late. This schedule is made easier with a noontime break, when work is hardest because the sun is hottest. The nine-to-five concept of the workday is an American *civilian* standard.

Documents of the 514th Local-Force Battalion also reveal other insights into VC camp administration. The permanent duty sections at battalion and company level were responsible for enforcing camp regulations and controlling the combat-alert or reaction force—a unit that also functioned as a provost guard to "assist the guerrillas in arresting brawlers, gamblers, thieves, robbers, juvenile delinquents, and prostitutes." The "guerrillas" referred to were the local fighters in the hamlet that was hosting the battalion when this order was issued.

Duty section personnel were assigned by roster for a twenty-four-hour period beginning at 1600 hours each day. Men assigned to the "patrol and inspection section" were charged, among other things, with checking "the behavior of all cadres, from the rank of Party Chapter Secretaries down, and their personal appearance." The officer in charge was responsible for filling out a complicated daily report form that was a combination morning (unit strength) report and equipment inventory with observations on unit morale and troop conduct. For instance, the officer in charge of the permanent duty section of a demolition platoon for February 20, 1967, a soldier named Cu, noted:

—The unit members' minds are at ease, and they concentrate their thinking on the struggle.
—They maintain secrecy concerning the unit's movements and the unit's bivouacking area. They take their meals and take cover in the trenches in accordance with the prescribed time schedule. They maintain their equipment well. Only one

comrade did not observe the time schedule strictly* and went
to bed early.[21]

Regardless of what was supposed to occur, large gaps between theory and reality existed. A document entitled "Improving Army Administration" was unsparing in its criticism of
the C646th Company, 514th Battalion, during a march and bivouac in February 1966:

> The unit members talked freely, smoked cigarettes, and
> turned on their radios (even Comrade Phuong, the Deputy
> Company Commander, did so). . . . Orders were shouted
> out loud; or the cadres, instead of going down the column to
> give their orders, just stood in one place . . . on the way, the
> men left the unit to stop by their houses to visit their families
> without permission from their unit commanders . . . when
> the company arrived in its bivouacking area, the men went to
> the shops freely and did not bother to dig fortified trenches;
> those who did . . . lit up their lamps and so did not maintain
> secrecy.[22]

MILITARY DISCIPLINE

"Criticism" was generally the most common discipline administered to soldiers who committed these violations of camp regulations. This reality stands in stark contradiction to basic tenets
of the American mythology about VC/NVA military and Party
discipline. The stereotypical American view of how this discipline was administered has an authoritarian political officer
strutting about the camp and battlefield, waving his pistol, and
summarily executing hapless privates for the slightest infrac-
tions.

Because the Communists in Vietnam consistently used terrorism as a weapon against their enemies and as an intimidation
of the people in contested areas, it is understandable that many
Americans projected this harsh and peremptory method of control onto the Communist military system. In fact, except for

---

*The officer who wrote this report was himself later criticized because "he did not
observe the unit time schedule and regulations strictly." As any soldier knows, observing a strict military time schedule under field conditions—much less in combat—
is difficult at best. Comrade Cu and the man who went to bed early no doubt suc-
cumbed to the universal military malady that at times affects even the best soldiers
confronted with too many regulations.

treason and the most heinous criminal acts such as murder and rape, VC/NVA military discipline was extremely humane. Military crimes, such as falling asleep on guard and even desertion, were leniently treated in many cases, but the VC/NVA military justice system was a highly developed one that was closely related to security. This included corporal punishment, confinement for more serious offenses, or action by the Party security sections—this was the same system in both the North and the South. Asked by an interrogator if anyone in his unit had ever been executed for deserting, a VC local-force private responded:

> Absolutely no. They had a book called *Tam Dac [To Win the Heart]*. The book analyzed the rights and wrongs of our behavior. If the deserter is very stubborn, they'd make him read that book for three days. *[23]

Another local-force soldier described the punishment meted out to two deserters who returned to their farms:

> The VC had them arrested and ordered them back to their units, but they refused. The VC seized them and had them educated for a week in order to make them voluntarily rejoin their forces. But they went on refusing and the VC must have let them go free.

The soldier added, however, that when these men finally returned to their villages in a VC-controlled area "they were despised by their fellow villagers" for having deserted the Viet Cong.[24]

A captain who was deputy commandant of a Viet Cong military training region told of one man—a student at a platoon leader's school—bursting into the commandant's office one day,

> complete with gear and weapons, and after saluting him politely, told him that he was getting tired of fighting and wanted to return to his family, which he had left behind for six or seven years. Then, he turned his back to the commandant and left. All the commandant could do was advise him to stay,

---

*The informant was quite serious. Reading the book was supposed to educate and reform the malefactor; the act of reading the book itself was not intended to be punishment.

arguing that if everyone in the Front forces behaved like that, then there would be no fighters, etc.

The officer then added that when a soldier "spurred by family love and homesickness, decided to leave the army, there was nothing in the world that could stop him."[25]

Another VC soldier, stationed just a short distance from his home, stated that his family took him away from the unit twice, and twice the VC came to take him back to the unit. One day his mother came to visit him in camp and simply took him home with her. The soldier's platoon leader and two privates came after him the next day. "They told me and my mother that it was not possible for me to go home just like that," he recalled. "They told me I couldn't quit without giving notice." The reluctant soldier and his mother argued with the platoon leader for a long time and eventually they left without him. The third time his comrades came looking for him, he wasn't home and they gave up on the attempt to get him to return.[26]

This same soldier, while with his unit before his desertion, was caught asleep on guard duty at least once. While he did not claim to have been punished severely for the offense, he described the punishment given to repeated offenders:

> If you were criticized once, twice and a third time, then the third time you stood the risk of being handed over to the province cadres to decide on the punishment you had to serve, and the worst punishment that you may be given was to be put in isolation away from the unit, under the watch of a guard twenty-four hours a day. In such a case, you couldn't even eat and sleep without a guard watching over you. I heard some fighters say that you couldn't even go to the toilet without a guard taking you there. It is apparently terrible. They shackled you, and worse still, they forced you to urinate into a bamboo tube, and it was therefore very humiliating and painful.*[27]

Sometimes minor offenses resulted in substantial jail sentences ("temporary detention" by the VC/NVA definition)—up

---

*As a contrast, the maximum punishment authorized under the U.S. Uniform Code of Military Justice for "misbehavior of a sentinel or lookout" in a combat zone is a dishonorable discharge, forfeiture of all pay and allowances, and confinement at hard labor for a period not to exceed ten years. (*Manual for Courts-Martial United States 1969, Revised Edition*, Article 113, "Table of Maximum Punishments," p. 25–13.)

to three years' confinement in an isolated camp where malefactors were forced to produce their own food. These prisoners were under continuous supervision during their confinement; however, they were sometimes allowed to bring their families with them. When the prison cadre felt a man had been sufficiently rehabilitated—whether or not the sentence was completed—the prisoner would be returned to his unit.[28]

More serious crimes—illegal abortions, murder, theft, robbery, even pickpocketing—resulted in a sentence of confinement of more than three years and the prisoner was turned over to the mercy of the VC/NVA security services.

Huynh Nghiep, while serving as a VC economic cadreman, was reprimanded and confined in March 1967 for having lost 283,000 piasters. He told his superiors that he left the money behind in a rucksack when he fled his store to escape approaching ARVN infantry. Mr. Nghiep considered the confinement unfair and protested in writing to the central office, but he never received a reply.[29]

Demotion was another method used to discipline soldiers. An officer and Party member stationed in Tay Ninh Province was demoted for "bad leadership." Apparently the district committee and the district security chief charged the officer with responsibility for a feud between the political officer and another man in his unit that resulted in a murder-suicide. "Moreover," he added, "they suspected me of arranging this affair to make the two cadres kill each other." Demoted to the rank of private and transferred to a fighting unit, this man was not, however, purged from the Party.[30]

Even striking a superior was sometimes treated with a surprising degree of leniency—at least when compared to the way such an offense would be handled in the U.S. Army.* A senior lieutenant NVA company commander told of a fight he had had with his political officer, a captain. The incident, which occurred in North Vietnam before infiltration into the South, apparently had a long history that came to a head when the captain upbraided the lieutenant for returning late from a training mission.

I was very angry and shouted out loud, "Comrade, I am a South Vietnamese who came here to serve the Revolu-

---

*Dishonorable discharge, forfeiture of all pay and allowances, and confinement at hard labor not to exceed ten years. (*Manual for Courts-Martial United States 1969, Revised Edition,* Article 90, "Table of Maximum Punishments," p. 25–12.)

tion. . . ." Seeing me talking loudly like this before the soldiers, he threatened me, "Comrade, you belong to the elements that are deviationists or have unsound politics. Your family were servants of the French colonialists. I wonder why the Party accepted you, and I will ask that you be purged from it." I couldn't stand him anymore for having insulted my family. So I grabbed him and beat him very badly.

The lieutenant was punished by being purged from the Party membership for a period of six months.[31]

A deputy company commander of a VC local-force battalion told of a man purged from his company Party chapter for overstaying a home leave by two days and getting married without permission. The entire company was convened and found him guilty. He was sentenced to be discharged from the unit, which resulted in his automatic purge from the Party. "It was very humiliating," the officer later stated. "The local cadres and representatives of local organizations were invited to watch the denouncing session. The women were invited to express their opinions. Of course they all found the guy guilty." According to the VC officer, the "victim" did not take his dismissal very hard. "The man," he concluded, "actually asked to be discharged, to go home with his family, and the Party conveniently purged him."*[32]

As previously noted, public humiliation and isolation from others are the most effective and frequently used methods to enforce discipline. Members of the Communist military leadership exploited this psychology and adapted it to keep the rank and file in line. The effectiveness of a public trial where everyone—Party members and non–Party members alike—participated in passing judgment on the accused reinforced the principle that the Revolution was a democratic process. At the same time, the trials gave all the participants examples of what could happen if they broke the rules. More significantly, as shown in the previous instance, while discipline was administered to both purged soldiers, satisfying the demand for justice, neither was done any permanent harm; the lieutenant was even kept on active duty and eventually readmitted to the Party. This also reflects a reality

---

*It should be noted here that "going home" was for the VC only, not for the NVA soldier.

of the war, which mitigated harsher punishment in view of manpower shortages.

The last case was a slight departure from the rules. Ordinarily a Party member facing purge was allowed to argue his case and if found guilty, appeal that decision to higher echelons of command. Even if the accused did not contest the local committee's decision, the rules required that punishment be approved at the next higher level of command.[33]

Despite these examples of misbehavior, it should not be inferred that military discipline was lax in either the VC or NVA. In some units, particularly small, isolated ones, the degree to which discipline was enforced depended on the initiative of the local commander.* The young soldier quoted earlier, whose mother dragged him away from his local-force unit, explained:

> The discipline was stricter in the district unit. In general, it is known that discipline is stricter in big units than in smaller ones. This is so because since big units have more men, it is necessary to have stricter regulations . . . take for example the district unit in which I served. Everything there was well regulated: For example we were not even allowed to swear, and if anyone did, he would be severely criticized. We couldn't even use the most common swearwords.[34]

In other cases, unit discipline could be transformed either by a Party resolution ordering a general tightening of rule enforcement or by a new commander's policies. The political officer for a VC stevedore unit in the Mekong Delta region noted how discipline changed in his unit in 1965:

> Previously, as morale was good, orders were carried out well and discipline wasn't strict. In 1965 discipline and control were strengthened and became stricter. Previously there had been no punishment, in 1965 there was. The man at fault must stand at attention or do forced labor for some hours. Obeying the Party resolution, the cadres also became stricter. . . . Previously, when a man forgot to tie up the boats at the wharf, he was only reminded to do that. Later, the man at fault might be criticized and examined. . . . I heard that

---

*This is reminiscent of an old U.S. Army adage reflecting a universal truth about the military—life is always better the farther one is from "the flagpole," i.e., headquarters.

once [a company] had lost a boat because of a broken rope and a whole platoon was condemned to eat [only] rice with salt for three days.[35]

A squad leader in a rear-area logistical unit that operated in Tay Ninh Province attributed a disappointing tightening of the regulations to his new company commander:

Take for example the regulation which forbids everyone in the unit to have any informal relations with the weaker sex. Under the former leader—he was a Southerner—although the regulation was also applicable, we could still go over to the woman soldiers' quarters to have a chat with them during the rest days. But since the North Vietnamese leader came, anyone venturing near the women's quarters would be immediately brought up [in front of] the group criticism sessions and criticized and ridiculed in front of everyone.[36]

All these military crimes—breaking the camp regulations, sleeping on guard duty, fighting with one's superiors, even desertion—were one thing, but defecting to the enemy was another, and defecting with a weapon worse still. A soldier caught trying to defect unarmed stood accused of a ''weak standpoint''; defecting with a weapon was treason. ''[For merely defecting] the soldier could expect public criticism, shame, and mild reeducation; [for defecting with a weapon] he can expect severe criticism, detention, and stringent reeducation, and very possibly death.''[*37]

Other incidents of misconduct were so blatantly defiant that the commanders had no choice except to punish the offenders severely. An NVA education cadre told of such an incident that occurred during his unit's march down the Ho Chi Minh Trail. On October 25, 1965, his battalion commander developed a stomach ache so severe that he could no longer continue the march. He asked permission to stay behind at a way station and rejoin the unit later. When the regimental political officer denied his request, the battalion commander lay down and stubbornly refused to get up. The political officer remonstrated, ''We have to move on; I demand that you make an extra effort and show

*Severity of punishment depended on the degree of harm a defector did to the Party. Kit Carson Scouts (ex-VC/NVA who volunteered to work as scouts for U.S. Combat Units), for instance, would have been summarily executed upon apprehension.

that you know how to surmount difficulties and hardships. You have to move immediately with the battalion." Pleading sickness, the battalion commander still refused to get up and continue the march. Again the political officer reasoned with him. "Our duty towards the Party comes first," he reminded him. "Party my ass!" the commander reportedly snapped back. Within three hours the now former battalion commander was expelled from the Party and turned over to the military police.[38]

After constructing or improving the necessary campsite fortifications and establishing camp administration, VC/NVA soldiers faced a succession of training activities. These included cell, squad, platoon, and company meetings; cadre meetings; criticism and self-criticism sessions; political lectures and indoctrination sessions; foraging to supplement the ration issue; food-production activities; and painstaking planning and rehearsals for impending military operations.

When all these tasks had been attended to and when the military operational situation permitted, the soldiers turned their attention to the things of interest to all soldiers—food, money, and recreation.

FOOD*

As with all Vietnamese, the staple food of the VC/NVA was rice. In the South, the allied forces did as much as possible to disrupt rice production and distribution in Communist-controlled areas. During the war, hundreds of thousands of tons of cached rice and other foodstuffs were captured and destroyed by the Allied forces (not to mention that ruined by weather and animals). Crops were also destroyed by aerial spraying of herbicides. As a result, Communist units experienced food shortages and lack of rations. But there exists no evidence that hunger ever played a role in reducing their combat effectiveness. Indeed, it is hard to imagine a more difficult place on earth to starve than South Vietnam, whose tropical climate, luxuriant vegetation, and rich soil provides "one of the most varied diets in the world."[39] In fact, the most common complaint by the VC/NVA was not the amount of food available, but rather the poor quality of their rations.

*For a more general discussion of VC/NVA food production, supply, and procurement, see Chapter 7, Logistics.

As mentioned above, VC/NVA units were supplied with food in a combination of ways: issue from stocks maintained by rear-area logistical units; their own vegetable gardens and paddies; from the local villagers; and hunting, fishing, and foraging. Those units that relied principally upon issued rice and food-stuffs usually supplemented their rations using one or more of these methods.

Each soldier was also given a ration allowance that could be as high as 45VN$ (or piasters) per day—but still only the equivalent of a few U.S. cents—which was usually pooled by the unit and then used to purchase rations from a Front economic agency. The leader of a VC main-force reconnaissance platoon described the process:

> When we arrived in War Zone D, each one of us received one liter of rice and some salt and 3VN$ for the foodstuffs. We used the 3VN$ to buy food from the Management Committee in the battalion, such as dry fish, salted fish and sugar bars. Fish and meat were quite cheap. Sometimes, we could get the fish ourselves by angling or by bailing out water from the fish pond. Rice from the daily ration distributed by the Front was sometimes good, sometimes bad.[40]

The political officer in the stevedore unit quoted previously gave a graphic picture of how his unit subsisted in the Mekong Delta area:

> For food, each month each soldier—no matter whether he was a fighter or a cadre—received 30 liters of rice and 45 piasters for supplementary food and condiments. We caught the fish we ate. We never had pork or beef. Once every month the battalion had the rice bought for us. Each company had condiments, cigarettes, and other goods bought once every month for the whole unit. Usually our men bought all the food and goods at the places where the traders' junks came from the GVN areas. We didn't raise pigs or poultry. We couldn't plant vegetables because of the salty water. For game, there were wild boars, monkeys, and iguanas. We ate only iguanas because we weren't allowed to hunt with firearms.[41]

One hunter, who supplied his unit with meat, fancied himself a sort of Viet Cong Nimrod. When asked if he was afraid of the "wild beasts in the jungle" he smiled and replied:

Not at all. I want to tell you that I was an excellent hunter and a sharpshooter of my unit. While in the Front, I killed 2 tigers, 4 elephants, 6 deers [sic], 20 wild boars [per year] of 100 kg each, and more than 50 white-haired monkeys per year. I liked to hunt for this kind of game and each time my platoon leader gave me carbine or Garand bullets, I might at least bring back 8 [white-haired monkeys].[42]

Storage of food and supplies once provided was also important. A squad leader in a rear-area logistical unit described how his unit built and maintained food warehousing in Tay Ninh Province:

The storehouses were built above the ground so as to protect the food from humidity. They were built at some 0.80 meters from the ground; they had a black-painted iron roof; the walls were made of medium-size wood logs. Inside, bamboo rattan provided a container for the rice. Most of the stores contained rice, but our unit had also built two or three storehouses to keep such commodities as dried fish, sugar, milk, etc.

Barbed wire protected these storehouses from wild pigs and elephants. They were also sometimes booby-trapped, especially when enemy troops were known to be operating in the vicinity, but usually they were left unguarded. The VC placed padlocks on the more pilferable stores such as sugar, milk, and dried fish, but otherwise the storage facilities were only inspected about once a week. Losses were unavoidable:

Once, wild pigs succeeded in passing through the barbed wire fence and getting to the rice stock. . . . Another time elephants going by the stores leaned against one of the storehouses, making it collapse. The elephants trampled on the rice, and when our financial cadre went by to inspect the stores, it was already too late. The rice had [turned moldy] and had to be thrown away.[43]

What the VC/NVA routinely ate might sound unappetizing to Westerners but it was judged to be adequate by the Communist soldiers. An NVA squad leader stated that in the morning his unit ate boiled sweet potatoes or manioc mixed with rice and salt; sometimes lunch and supper rice rations were supplemented with potatoes and manioc, vegetables, or wild meat if they had it. In the five months he was with his unit in the South, his squad was issued only one can of pepper, a can of nuts, two cans of salt, and a can of sugar. "But we never went hungry," he added.[44]

"Our food in South Vietnam was not so good as the food in North Vietnam," an NVA corporal reported. "In the South even vegetables were scarce. The rice was sometimes good, sometimes bad."[45] Regardless of the food's adequacy or inadequacy, the VC/NVA, like soldiers of all armies, commonly complained about their rations.

An NVA platoon leader who rallied to the GVN in June 1966 said his men "lived like animals" and lacked just about everything:

> Once, as we were on our way to rejoin our unit, we found a heap of empty food cans left behind by the ARVN or the Allied troops, all of us seemed to show signs of craving for foods. One of the soldiers said loudly in the presence of the cadres, "The GVN soldiers are so well supplied, while our troops are unable to find even a grain of salt to eat."

The cadres made no reply to this outspoken remark.[46]

An NVA sergeant remarked that the rice in his unit mess was "mixed with the manioc, very little rice, so little that once cooked, it couldn't be seen anywhere!"[47]

Complaints about rations, again as in other armies, rarely did any good. "They were, of course, very unhappy," a VC local-force assistant squad leader said of the men in his unit. "They felt that it was their right to demand higher food rations, and that was why they expressed their demand, but it was turned down. They made the demand several times, and each time it was turned down. After a while, they just gave up."[48]

"There were comrades who complained about the lack of supplementary foods," a VC local-force private reported, "but the cadres said that while carrying out a revolution one had to bear hardships, that we were all volunteers. Moreover, our predecessors in the Resistance days had eaten potatoes and manioc, now we had rice and therefore must not complain." When asked how the troops received this explanation, he replied, "Some comrades said: 'We don't know what the situation in other times had been, but now we are facing hardships and we say so.' "[49]

Comparing the worse hardships of their "predecessors" to their own was an approach the VC/NVA cadres often used to help their men bear up. Another very effective argument, one hard to refute in a small infantry unit, was "We are all in this together"; the cadres obviously endured the same hardships as their men. This may not have been true in all VC/NVA units, however, especially the rear-area logistical units. An assistant platoon leader in a finance-economy section claimed that while the high-ranking cadres in his unit "ate the same kind of food as we did," he had "heard" that they received a higher food allowance and that sometimes they were "supplied with beer and sweet cakes." However, this soldier admitted that the men in his unit were not above a little cheating themselves, confirming the suspicions frontline soldiers everywhere have of rear-echelon troops*: "We were in charge of buying rice, so we used to choose good rice for ourselves. The bad rice was distributed to men of other units."[50]

Despite claims of brotherhood and common enemies, incidents of outright stealing were not uncommon. An NVA captain reported that some soldiers in his unit "took advantage of weighing and transporting the rice to their units to steal a few handfuls of rice and hide it in their pockets for later use." This occurred so often that his political officers made it a topic for warnings during unit study sessions. The captain further reported that the pilfering often reduced his unit's five-day rice supply to only a four-day supply. "There were other incidents in which the soldiers stole rice from the cadres who used to keep their rice in their beds since they ate their meals separately," he stated. The culprits did not always escape undetected:

After the battle of Tuy An [July 1966] a company found twelve squad leaders guilty of stealing rice. They were brought out to be criticized and to receive disciplinary punishment. After being insulted mercilessly, the twelve not only didn't plead guilty, they answered boldly that "We were too hungry and we were afraid that we might not have the strength for fighting. We did steal rice. It is up to you to apply discipline."[51]

Despite the complaints, not everyone in the VC/NVA camps was dissatisfied with the rations. More common were remarks like that of a squad leader in a VC main-force battalion, who

---

*There is no evidence that the VC/NVA combat soldiers referred to the support troops as REMFs (rear-echelon motherfuckers) in the way their American counterparts did. However, regardless of the language used, the feelings were evidently the same on both sides.

admitted that while he ate better at home, he "thought the food allowances as established by the Front were fairly adequate" and the rice his unit received always good.[52]

Because the Communist forces in Vietnam had no refrigeration at their disposal and did not rely on canned or prepackaged rations from their own sources, almost all the food consumed by the VC/NVA was freshly prepared daily. On marches the soldiers carried precooked cold rice, dried fish or meat to eat, but in camp they cooked their food as needed.

In most VC/NVA units, squads or cells messed together. Meals were eaten two or three times a day, depending upon circumstances. If the unit schedule called for only two cooked meals a day, some soldiers would eat half their breakfast ration in the morning and the other half at noon, so they would not be too hungry by the time for the evening meal. In combat units, the full ration might be held back during nonoperational periods and then given to the troops to build up their strength in preparation for battle.

There was a constant danger that smoke and flame from cooking fires might give away unit positions to ARVN or American forces. The soldiers coped with this problem in many ingenious ways. An assistant platoon leader in a VC main-force unit said that often his men would prepare enough rice in the morning to last all day. "Our cook had a very good technique which enabled him to cook with just a little smoke. However, when we cooked in the afternoon we tried to cover the flames as much as possible. If an airplane approached in our direction, we put our utensils away."[53]

The cook's "good technique" that allowed him to prepare meals with a minimum of smoke was called the Hoang Cam (after its inventor) or "golden guitar" stove (after its shape). This was an ingenious device that consisted of a fire pit about two meters deep connected to an exhaust trench that allowed the smoke to seep gradually to a point some distance from the fire. What was not absorbed into the earth rose a few inches above the surface and dissipated virtually without any visible trace.

Smoke could also be controlled by burning different kinds of fuel that gave off little smoke during combustion.[54] To kindle their fires, cooks were issued cigarette lighters.[55]

PAY

If the rations the VC/NVA soldiers ate were sometimes insufficient, or of poor quality, their pay—at least by Western soldiers' standards—was infinitely worse.

As noted, the VC and NVA paid their men a cash food allowance. They were also paid a salary in South Vietnamese piasters graduated by rank, but it is significant that when speaking about this stipend, the soldiers frequently referred to it as "spending money" or "pocket money."

The amount paid varied widely from unit to unit: In the Viet Cong, local-force troops were not paid as much as main-force personnel. A main-force platoon leader stated that in 1967, privates and squad leaders received 20VN$ per month; platoon leaders 40VN$; company cadres 80VN$; and battalion cadres 100VN$ per month.[56] The deputy company commander of a VC local-force unit said that in October 1967 his pay amounted to only 20 piasters a month, "Just enough for a haircut—back there [in the countryside], not in Saigon."[57] The rate of exchange at that time was 72VN$ to $1 U.S.

A VC company commander, who rallied in February 1967, said that he received "two hundred piasters per month as spending money."[58] But a VC political officer, who was captured in August 1966 and who also claimed the rank of captain, stated he was paid only eighty piasters a month—sixty for his food ration and "the other twenty piasters were for pocket money."[59]

An assistant platoon leader in a VC transportation company reported that in 1965–1966 his pay was only 40VN$ per month while the company cadres received 100VN$. He explained the difference was necessary because the company cadres "needed the money to buy more food or tea, because they had to work hard and stay up late at night."[60]

A sixteen-year-old VC main-force private who rallied in September 1966 noted bitterly that his pay of 20VN$ per month "wasn't enough for cigarettes."[61] But another main-force private, also a rallier, said in January 1965 that after 1963, his monthly pay had been increased to 170 piasters per month.[62]

There is some reason to believe that the Party had ample money to finance its activities in South Vietnam—with some of it being counterfeit. A regroupee platoon leader reported that before infiltrating to South Vietnam in 1961:

I went with the [adjutant] of the unit to the financial affairs section of the division to get some spending money for the unit on its way south. I have seen the place where 500VN$ bills were stored. They were stacked helter-skelter in a square room of 4m x 4m. The height [of the stacks], rounded up, would be 0.50m. We thought, at that time, that the North had printed GVN money to use because the bills were brand-new and hadn't been folded yet.[63]

FEMALE COMPANIONSHIP

The average VC/NVA soldier never saw any of those 500-piaster notes. Even if he did, there was not very much to spend it on in the jungles or the NLF-controlled villages he passed through. Compared to the leisure activities available to most Americans in South Vietnam—clubs, libraries, movies, professional entertainers—the life of the Communist soldier was Spartan indeed. He was not even paid enough to have a few bottles of beer in the village market place, much less avail himself of professional female companionship.

There is some evidence that the sexual needs of the VC/NVA troops were satisfied by groups of "official" prostitutes whose duty was to solace the fighters in their camps at no cost. One organization was known as the *Ho Ly,* or "Satisfaction Support Unit." These women were reported to have serviced only the high-ranking cadres and their existence is said to have been kept a secret. A "sister service" *(can bo ho ly)* was reported to have been in existence for the support and consolation of the ordinary soldiers. Of course the existence of such an organization was totally contrary to Liberation Army and Party rules and Vietnamese social practices. The Party constantly railed against immoral conduct of all sorts.

Women served in Communist military units as cooks, clerks, and medical orderlies. "Frequently they are pretty," one soldier commented, "and have a nice manner about them," so it was inevitable that relationships sprang up.[64]

The rear-area logistical unit squad leader quoted earlier admitted that there had been at least two marriages between couples in his organization "before the arrival of the North Vietnamese company leader," who took a dim view of such fraternization.[65] He added that there were twenty-three women in his unit, the unmarried ones ranging in age from about eighteen to twenty-one. According to this soldier:

Before the North Vietnamese company leader came to the unit, the soldiers used to be able to visit the women soldiers, although they could not stay too long. Some of my friends even arranged to date the girls, and they met one another at night, without the cadres knowing anything about that. When the North Vietnamese cadre came, relations between the women and men became absolutely forbidden, and anyone found guilty of breaking the discipline by either dating or courting the girls was severely criticized and if he persisted, he might be put into jail or sent to a reeducation course.[66]

While the North Vietnamese commander's attitude toward fraternization might seem harsh, it was perfectly consonant with the puritanical policy of the NLF, which was the rule rather than the exception. The existence of the *Ho Ly* girls, if there really was such an organization, had to be kept secret because if the Party leadership ever found out about them, the cadres responsible would have been punished. In fact, when a Party member got into trouble with his superiors, it was usually over sexual indiscretions. The VC finance-economy section assistant platoon leader quoted earlier related an incident involving a high-ranking cadreman in his unit. Somehow it had been discovered that this man was a bigamist with four wives, two of whom were pregnant. The assistant platoon leader stated:

According to the Front's rules, this man had committed a very serious sin.* This case was called to the attention of the provincial Front organizations for judgment. . . . According to the results of this meeting, the offender was sentenced to death. A circular on this case was sent out to many other units in order to advise other men to avoid doing things like this man did.

In due time the offender was conducted to a spot in the jungle where his execution was to be carried out. His escort, after tying him to a tree, decided to have a bite of lunch before killing him. Believing the prisoner was securely fastened, they adjourned some distance to eat. "One thing that made me laugh," the

---

*The choice of words used in these transcripts was up to the translator, who often picked the most convenient he or she could find to express the interviewee's meaning in a context readily understandable to their American supervisors. There were Catholics among the VC/NVA, but "sin" as it is understood in the West is not in the official NLF or Lao Dong Party vocabulary.

officer recalled, was that when they returned to carry out the execution "everyone was surprised because the offender was already gone! No one knows what way he could take off the rope."

About six months after this incident, the man's unit commander, realizing that he had been "one of the backbone elements of the unit," decided to offer him amnesty. He had several letters posted at various crossroads in liberated areas announcing that if he would return to his unit all would be forgiven. Eventually the bigamist did return, but was purged from the Party and demoted.[67] Of course, that was better than being shot, but it can also be questioned just how serious anyone was about carrying out the original sentence in the first place.

Not every soldier in the NLF felt constrained to abstain from relationships with women. Nguyen Van Be, known as "Be Danh," a soldier in the demolition platoon of the 514th VC Local-Force Battalion, not only found time to get himself engaged, but actively corresponded with thirty-four women and girls throughout My Tho Province, South Vietnam.[68] When not writing to his female friends, Be Danh wrote love poems and addressed them to himself:

> My dearest! Here's all my love to you!
> This letter, written on paper from your own village,
> I send to you and sweetly say
> Tomorrow, when victory is achieved, come and see me![69]

POSTAL SERVICES[70]

The VC/NVA had an elaborate postal system to support personal and official correspondence.[71] This system mirrored the one in use in the North. It was simple, effective, and seemed to apply stringent security practices to help ensure secrecy. Be Danh, during the time he wrote the captured letters—some of which have been quoted here—used at least two addresses, Letter Box 11-207/FOT12 and Letter Box 7809.

A VC private (the demoted officer who was held responsible for the murder-suicide incident described earlier) explained how the military postal service operated in Ben Cau District, Tay Ninh Province, in 1967. The service was composed of six sections staffed by approximately forty personnel. The command committee included the chief of the service, his assistant, a political officer, and two liaison agents; the mail section, composed of three persons; the "[postal route] section," which had from ten to fifteen persons (runners), including a "[security guard] squad"; the flash (urgent) message section, which employed from nine to ten people; a food-production section, which had three persons; and the "medic and foster sister section," which was composed of four women.*

The Ben Cau service was one of many "[mail] distribution lines" that composed the Tay Ninh provincial military postal service. These lines ran from province down to the districts with a mail-handling station at each. The district station, in charge of mail distribution, received mail from the postal route section couriers, sorted it out, and forwarded it, either through the postal route section as ordinary mail or the flash message section as urgent mail. The provincial mail-service headquarters for Tay Ninh Province was located in the jungle; some of its subordinate sections were located in villages throughout the province.[72]

There were separate systems for and under the control of the Liberation Army, the People's Revolutionary Party, and the National Liberation Front. Each system interfaced with the other at each echelon but normally at only one point. For example, a provincial military headquarters postal communications office would be aware of and routinely route mail through military channels to higher and lower headquarters. Mail to and from Party and Front offices went laterally to a central distribution point for those addressees that would then make further specific distribution.

Mail was hand-carried between distribution points by individuals known as *giao lien*, or "commo-liaison persons," a term roughly equating to "courier." These individuals transported mail along trails and other lines of communications that were at times separate from the routes used to move supplies. The operation of this system was one of the more secure and highly sensitive of all aspects of the VC/NVA organization.

An NVA lieutenant who served as assistant chief of a financial affairs section on the rear services staff described the postal system as follows:

---

*The terms *chi nuoi* (female) and *chi anh* (male) are literally translated "foster sister" or "foster brother," but in actual usage, neither signified anything more intimate nor emotional than "cook." This illustrates one of the problems encountered when using texts translated by researchers not familiar with the actual language used by the Communist soldier.

In the South, the hamlets would send the letters to the villages, then the village to the district; the district would send them from one station to another and the letters were very liable to be mislaid or lost. The letters we sent back to our family were in the same situation, going from the unit to the regiment, then from the regiment to the division, then they would be sent back to the hamlets or the villages where our families stay. To send letters to the North, we, Northerners as well as Southerners who had some acquaintances in the North, had to send our letters according to a special fixed route, for example to Kontum, from Kontum to Quang Ngai, from Quang Ngai to Quang Nam, to Thua Thien, then to Laos.

This officer claimed it took letters traveling the route described above "three or four months" to reach an addressee in North Vietnam but he admitted that there were men in his unit who hadn't heard from home for three years. A regroupee himself, he claimed to have received only one letter from home during the two-year period before he rallied to the GVN.[73]

An NVA infiltrator, a corporal in a VC main-force unit, claimed never to have written home because he was worried about censorship "and I was afraid I would be blamed if I wrote about our life in South Vietnam. No one in my company wrote to his family."[74] An NVA sergeant serving in the South stated that while many of the men in his unit did write home, "they never got any letters or news about their families at all after they left the North."[75]

Postal communications were addressed between individuals and/or agents through the use of *hom tho*, or "letter box numbers." Letter box numbers were normally assigned for units down to individual company level and to major staff elements. The numbers were numerical or alphanumeric and changed frequently when the postal communications office believed a document showing the existing allocation had been compromised.

Official directives and related documents were sent from one headquarters to the next lower subordinate headquarters for further distribution. Cadre routinely wrote to one another through this system in what amounted to semi-official communications. Letters were normally written on a small piece of paper. The paper slips were folded over onto themselves and a blank part of the backside became the "envelope" on which the sender's name and recipient's name and letter box number were placed.

At times there were either unit or agency designations written in place of the individuals' names.

The letter box system, for all its security, was still highly vulnerable. U.S. intelligence agencies routinely noted these numbers and were able to determine the allocations quite soon after a change had taken place. Personal letters that contained only a letter box number could often be correlated to specific units within hours of their capture. When VC/NVA soldiers complained of their poor mail service, in many instances it was because their mail had been captured by Allied forces.

In theory, all letters written by military personnel in Communist units were subject to censorship. But the pace of the war often limited this practice. "If I write everything down here, those guys will object," Be Danh informed his brother in a letter written at My Tho on November 12, 1966. A correspondent writing to Be Danh's unit noted in a postscript: "Your letter to me was completely torn up when it reached me; the comrades in the village censored it again. What a nuisance!"[76]

Some soldiers felt that these censors sometimes destroyed their letters instead of forwarding them. The assistant political officer of a VC local-force company said of his mail:

> [I] sent them through my superiors. I guessed that the Front cadre in my sisters' village were afraid that my morale might be affected by news about my family. So they didn't send my letters to my sisters or give me news about my family.[77]

HOMESICKNESS AND HOME LEAVE

For the "ethnic" North Vietnamese—those men who were born in the North—the occasional letter from home was the only news they received from friends and family while in the South. For men raised in the Vietnamese family tradition, this separation was extremely hard to endure. A university graduate sent South as an education cadre did not understand, during indoctrination before infiltrating, why the men in his group "were constantly warned by North Vietnamese cadres against all family sentiments. We were told that 'family should come next to the State,' and that 'family-minded cadres are poor cadres, requiring thought correction—otherwise they would be punished.' "

But once on the trail, this man, far better educated than most who infiltrated south, "experienced an unsurmountable feeling":

Homesickness usually came to me during rainy and sleepless nights. My mind would wander from one thing to another, from my innocent childhood days to my parents and family. I would wonder whether my parents knew that I was being tortured by starvation and solitude in the middle of a remote jungle. These were the thoughts that kept recurring in my mind.[78]

Thoughts of home occupied the minds of the men in the Viet Cong as well, with one major difference: They were already home. Sometimes, in fact, the VC found themselves quite close to their home villages. However, the VC practice of a "highly restrictive leave policy" seldom allowed any homecomings.[79] A private in a regional main-force unit put it simply: "No one in my unit was allowed to see his family because the cadres were afraid they would desert."[80]

A VC assistant platoon leader noted that the VC policy on home leave became more restrictive as time went on so that in his unit, by 1966, only cadres were occasionally allowed to go home on visits. The men were told "that since the unit was always busy carrying out operations, no one should leave the unit to go home. The men would be given permission to visit their families when the situation became better."[81] A local-force assistant squad leader who did manage several visits home said that he was never able to stay long; "I just dropped by, and had to go away almost at once."[82] A regional-force lieutenant stated that his visits with family members had to take place at prearranged locations. "It had to be far from my village and far from my area of operation. I went to such a place and waited for the liaison agent to bring my family there to meet me."[83]

Apparently service in the Viet Cong did not entitle families to any special treatment: They paid their taxes like everyone else, and the VC soldiers were often quite concerned with the treatment their families received despite assurances from their cadre that their dependents would be looked after during their absence. One main-force squad leader, upset at the way he felt the Front was treating his family, went home, shot up the village committee, and then defected.[84]

A physician's assistant assigned to a main-force unit said that he went for two years without once seeing his family. One reason was that they lived in a GVN-controlled area and he did not want to cause them any trouble by visiting them. He said that his understanding of the VC's policy on home leave was·that:

It depended on whether or not you operated near or far from your family. If you operated near your family, you were allowed to visit them as often as you could. According to the zone cadres, we were allowed fifteen days to visit our families. But for many Front people, fifteen days weren't enough to make the trip back and forth, and so they didn't make the trip at all.[85]

The VC leadership realized, as did the officer quoted earlier in a different context, that once a soldier "spurred by family love and homesickness decided to leave the army, there was nothing in the world that could stop him."[86]

RECREATION

Countless meetings and criticism sessions were used by the VC/NVA leadership as a means of building morale and assisting the soldiers in coping with the general hardships of living in the jungles, constantly moving, eating a reduced diet, suffering homesickness and fighting the war. During these sessions the men often spoke frankly about the things that bothered them and the cadres patiently explained the reasons why they were required to make sacrifices for the Revolution and reunification of their country. Often, of course, this was not enough. Another way of helping them to cope was to keep them occupied—as the crowded daily schedules testify. The VC/NVA leaders, like commanders from time immemorial, realized that if they could keep their soldiers' hands and minds busy, hardship and boredom were more easily endured.

Still another way to assist the soldiers in enduring their hardships was by providing various forms of entertainment and leisure-time activities. Formal entertainment was provided by troupes of singers, actors, and musicians who toured the jungle hideaways and the villages in the Communist-controlled zones, putting on musical shows and plays for the enjoyment of the troops and people.* Heavily laced with Communist Party propaganda, these shows did provide badly needed diversion for the soldiers. A civilian regroupee who came south with a Front Entertainment Group and was later captured in Binh Dinh Prov-

---

*These shows were not unlike the USO shows that visited U.S. personnel all across South Vietnam.

ince in September 1966, said there were twenty men in his group.
According to the entertainer:

> We were composed of musicians, singers, and actors. We
> played folk music to entertain the troops and people of Binh
> Dinh. I reached the South in April and was ordered to rest
> and practice my guitar. We didn't begin to play in Binh Dinh
> until August.[87]

A VC main-force captain attested to the propaganda content
of these shows: "There was no artist group in the liberated area
that did not have a propaganda mission attached to it." Nevertheless, the people liked these shows, he added, because "people in the countryside always love shows and singing." As a
rule, his unit (a training center) was visited once a month by
one of these groups.[88] An acting platoon leader in a VC main-
force unit described the entertainment groups that visited his
village about twice a year:

> Besides singing, dancing, and a stage show, this group also
> read war news to the audience, [and] told stories about the
> atrocities of the GVN and its killing of innocent people. . . .
> The villagers and I were fond of the singing and performances
> of the artists in this entertainment group, but paid little atten-
> tion to the propaganda talks.[89]

The physician's assistant quoted earlier told of how the students at his medical school in the jungle managed to entertain
themselves during class breaks:

> [T]here was solo singing by some male or female students,
> or by those with good voices, so that others might enjoy their
> golden voices. Sometimes, we sang in groups, other times
> someone would tell jokes for others to laugh at . . . we could
> play volleyball and the female students played badminton.
> Besides that, we organized races, put on shows, collected
> money from all the students, and then made a party out of it,
> eating chickens or ducks and drinking beer.[90]

There were also holiday celebrations to break up the monot-
ony, such as the annual observance of Ho Chi Minh's birthday
on May 19:

On that day we killed pigs and cows, we made soybean pudding, cakes, and all kinds of food. We considered Ho Chi Minh's birthday a very important, happy day. Sometimes the entertainment group came to our area on that day to perform plays for the jubilee.[91]

Reading newspapers and listening to radio broadcasts were other ways to relieve the boredom of camp life. The NLF-produced newspapers and periodicals might have been seen as rudimentary, but almost every provincial committee had one, usually entitled *Giai Phong (Liberation)*. The troops read them "avidly," according to one study. Occasionally the troops picked up and read copies of the Saigon papers, usually obtained in the local market places in NLF-controlled villages, where they were used to wrap food sold to the soldiers.[92]

An NVA political officer captured in the summer of 1966 was encouraged to read the GVN newspapers freely in his POW camp. His comments offer an interesting contrast to the kind of news he was used to reading while with his unit:

I noticed that the press here [Saigon] has too much freedom. They criticize even the government and the National Assembly. I enjoy reading them even though they like to fill up the empty space with too many knight-errant stories and advertising. In the North, if they talked so freely, they would be suspended.*[93]

Also available from time to time in some Communist military units were North Vietnamese newspapers such as *Quan Doi Nhan Dan (The People's Army)*, *Nhan Dan (People's Daily)* and *Tien Phong (Advance)*. Another paper, *Van Hoc (Literature)*, was a Communist literary magazine. Still another, entitled *Phu Nu (Women)*, was published especially for women. All these papers were distributed free to the troops. In many units newspaper-reading time was included as part of the daily schedule.[94]

Another source of entertainment and information was the unit "wall newspaper," a large wooden board on which soldiers

---

*The NVA in South Vietnam in the 1960s were shocked by Southern society's comparative openness. The extent of social and political criticism in South Vietnam would not have been acceptable in the North. "Freedom of expression" in North Vietnam consisted of criticizing people who did not adhere to the Party line.

were encouraged to pin up articles, sketches, and poetry of their own composition. Articles, written by the soldiers themselves, consisted of reflections on their daily activities as well as criticism and praise. Unit political officers encouraged their men to write personal pieces in which they promised to excel in the performance of their duties, or autobiographical essays detailing their personal contributions to the Revolution or some specific military operation. The best of these kinds of essays took the tone of a kind of written self-criticism session.[95] The poetry posted on the wall newspaper was in the heroic, ideological-romantic vein best exemplified in the verses composed by "Be Danh" of the 514th VC Local-Force Battalion:

"From the Rear Area to the Front Line"
Here is all my love, offered to you.
I hear marching music echoing from somewhere,
I miss you and send you my love, my dearest.
I am proud to know a fighter
Who has unsheathed his sacred sword to relieve the
      country of its burden,
Whose shoulders are bent under the weight of his love
      for the country and his family,
Who has girded himself for combat, and cherishes
      his adventurous life.[96]

Radio was another source of news and entertainment for the Communist forces in the jungles. Individual soldiers did not usually own radio receivers, so in some units the platoon radio would be circulated among the squads on a rotational basis, so the troops could listen to authorized (Radio Hanoi, Liberation Radio) broadcasts. These sessions were usually monitored by a unit cadre.[97]

The cadres themselves had more freedom to tune in to whatever stations their sets could receive and apparently used them whenever they wished. "They have the radio habit," one analysis concluded.[98] One NVA training cadre admitted that he listened to the BBC "every day, between seven-thirty P.M. to eight P.M. Sometimes, two comrades in my team were with me."[99] The BBC appears to have been the most popular non-Communist radio broadcast because it was thought to have been neutral in its news reporting and therefore unbiased.*[100]

---

*Most Vietnamese, Communist and non-Communist, also thought so.

Other programming aside, by far the most popular "radio habit" among the VC/NVA troops was listening to Radio Saigon's *cai luong,* or "reformed theater" broadcasts. *Cai luong* has been described as a "comedy of manners" consisting of dialogue interspersed with songs (Oriental and Western). The plots were highly sentimental and dealt with characters who expressed—volubly—all the basic human emotions.[101] A VC main-force captain stated:

> *Cai luong* is the most popular thing in the liberation area. Everyone listened to it. Even soldiers of the Front forces were fond of *cai luong.* As a result, the Front repeatedly conducted anti-*cai luong* campaigns to discourage the people from listening to it. Front cadres would say that *cai luong* was as harmful to the minds of people as poison was to their bodies. It will sap their energy and soften their will-power. Its romantic wording will corrupt young people and lead them to debauchery and finally to self-destruction, etc.[102]

Listening to the radio, especially some of the propaganda broadcast by Radio Hanoi, sometimes had an unexpectedly adverse effect on the morale of soldiers in the South. This was particularly serious in the case of the NVA education cadreman quoted earlier, who eventually defected to the GVN:

> Toward the end of July 1966, I contracted malaria and was unable to sleep at night. It was during these moments that I felt mostly homesick and resentful of the lying propaganda I heard over Radio Hanoi about the great happy life of the North Vietnamese people. To make things worse, it repeatedly announced the names of students being sent to Poland, Korea, [and] Red China for advanced study. This certainly was an injustice I could not tolerate. How could these privileged students be blessed with advanced study abroad while I was dying, in this strange land, unnoticed. . . .[103]

The usual punishment for anyone caught reading banned newspapers or listening to forbidden radio broadcasts was a warning or criticism the first time. Confiscation of the radio or reeducation was the punishment for repeated acts of such disobedience.

AWARDS AND DECORATIONS

As in all armies, the VC/NVA had a system of decorations and awards that could be bestowed on individuals and units in recognition of deeds of valor or exceptionally meritorious service. The Viet Minh awarded several different medals for heroic and meritorious service during the First Indochina War. Medals given to North Vietnamese soldiers during the Second Indochina War included at least six different decorations for combat achievement. In order of precedence they were the Gold Star Medal, the Ho Chi Minh Medal, the Independence Medal, the Resistance Medal, the Military Exploit Medal, and the Combat Medal. The Army Hero Medal, the Patriotic Soldier's Contest Medal, and a "joint service" award for noncombat achievement known as the Illustrious Soldier Decoration and authorized for all three components of the armed forces, were added in 1962. Citations were also given to NVA units for outstanding achievement in combat, training, and labor projects.[104]

What agency or headquarters actually issued these decorations to NVA soldiers fighting in South Vietnam is not clear. An NVA sergeant, captured in Binh Dinh Province in October 1966, when asked who was running the war in South Vietnam, answered the National Liberation Front "because all the medals and certificates of commendation received by the fighters in the unit were issued by the Front." He stated that the letters of commendation accompanying the award of the Military Victory Medal to his battalion were signed by Nguyen Huu Tho, chairman of the NLF.[105] That the NLF decorated NVA soldiers makes sense if one remembers that North Vietnam consistently maintained, to the end of the war, that it had no troops in the South.

The National Liberation Front, like the NVA, also had its "pyramid of honor," consisting of medals, citations, and commendations. Decorations included the 1st, 2nd, and 3rd Class Brass Fortress Medals; the Iron Fort Medal in three classes; and three degrees of the Liberation Military Medal (1st, 2nd, and 3rd). On February 13, 1968, the Liberation Military Merit Medal 2nd Class was awarded to units that attacked various points in the city of Saigon during Tet 1968: Independence Palace; the U.S. Embassy; the RVNAF Joint General Staff at Tan Son Nhut Airbase; and the Saigon radio station.*[106]

---

*The majority of these medals were awarded posthumously inasmuch as the VC attacks on these points, though they gained much publicity in the Western press at the time, were utter military failures.

On February 28, 1968, the Liberation Radio announced the award of the Military Medal 3rd Class to units in Bien Hoa Province for an attack on February 17 and 18 against the 199th Light Infantry Brigade, which resulted in the destruction of seventy tanks and armored personnel carriers, and nine 155- and 105mm howitzers, and killed two hundred men of the brigade.*[107]

Commendations consisted of "Determination to Win Brass Fortress" and "Commendations Bearing Dead Heroes' Names." The Determination to Win Brass Fortress was awarded annually to company-, battalion-, and regimental-size units "having scored outstanding performances in all fields." The Commendations Bearing Dead Heroes' Names was awarded to recognize the achievements of small infantry units and consisted of four categories: *Dong Quoc Que*, awarded to squads and platoons of the regular forces; *Chau Thi Huyen*, awarded to female guerrilla squads and platoons in hamlets and villages; *Pham Van Coi*, awarded to male guerrilla squads and platoons in hamlets; and *Nguyen Van Be*, awarded to transportation and liaison squads and platoons.[108]

Other kinds of awards were also given by local jurisdictions and unit commanders. For instance, the deputy commander of a VC local-force unit described a flag trophy awarded to battalions several times a year: "On various holidays, the province military section would review the achievements of each battalion and, as a result, the one which scored the best achievements won the flag."[109]

The assistant chief of the financial affairs section of a rear-area services staff quoted earlier regarding the postal system, also mentioned a valor award given on the basis of how many Americans the men in a unit might have killed in combat:

A man who could kill three Americans or more would be decorated as "valiant American killer"; a battalion† of nine people [*sic*] who succeeded in killing twenty-five or twenty

*Perhaps one reason the VC gave the lowest degree of this particular medal for this spectacular battlefield victory is because it never happened. When this report was shown to veterans of the 199th LIB at their annual association dinner in 1988, it caused many of the "dead" who were there to erupt in howls of derisive laughter. It is also notable that the figure of "seventy tanks and armored personnel carriers" is more than double the total number assigned to the entire brigade at the time.

†This is either a translator's mistake or the informant did not know the difference between a battalion and a squad.

Americans would be called "valiant American killer battalion"; each platoon and each company that could kill three
quarters of the number of soldiers in the unit would be classified as good.[110]

Some Viet Cong units also had what might be called "impact" awards, or awards given on the spot in recognition of
specific deeds or achievements. The huntsman quoted earlier,
while denying he had ever received a commendation, mentioned
a comrade who got one for "his high fighting spirit." The man
was rewarded by his platoon leader, who gave him a fountain
pen and a notebook.[111]

Promotion was another method for recognizing sustained and
meritorious service. With the pay so uniformly small for all
ranks in the VC/NVA, men did not vie for promotion for the
extra money, but for the recognition, trust, and privilege associated with higher rank. Some men, denied promotions they
thought they deserved, felt so strongly that they defected.[112]

A captain in the Viet Cong, the deputy commander of a training center, said that he was "deeply depressed and dissatisfied
over my slow promotion." He was frustrated and angered because "individuals who joined the Front at the same time as I
were promoted to the rank of company commander or even
battalion executive officer, while I was still a lieutenant." This
man's superiors recognized the injustice of his situation and
arranged for his appointment as deputy to the school commandant, a position relatively equal to that of battalion executive
officer in a main-force unit.[113]

For an enlisted man to be promoted to the rank of cell leader
in a VC main-force unit required that he serve at least six months
and during that time display courage in battle. Assistant squad
leaders were required to have served two years in the unit before
they were eligible for promotion. Asked if he thought the men
promoted to these grades in his unit deserved their promotions,
a squad leader, who defected to the GVN in May 1967, replied,
"I thought so because they all had at least two years of fighting
experience, excellent behavior, and great tenacity in times of
hardship."[114]

MEDICAL TREATMENT*

An extremely important morale factor in any military unit is adequate medical treatment. Because they spent so much time in the jungles, exposed to tropical diseases such as malaria, there was much sickness among the VC/NVA. With their penchant for comparing everything to their own standards, many Americans in Vietnam thought the Communist medical system was shockingly primitive. This was not always correct. "The tendency to downgrade the extent and effectiveness of the Viet Cong medical operation should be avoided," a U.S. Army doctor wrote in 1966. While admitting that "in many aspects Viet Cong medicine is at a level parallel with American medicine during our Civil War," he concluded that "if the full truth were known, all would be amazed at the quality of medical care they are able to give their sick and wounded."[115]

A VC medic described the Front's medical service credo:

> The assistant physicians were "like mothers." It meant that while the fighters were away from their parents, the physicians had to take the place of the fighters' parents. The medical men lessened the pain where there was pain, gave solace where there was unhappiness, and acted as the men's confidants.[116]

The first-aid men could dispense a wide variety of drugs from their medical kits, including antibiotics such as tetracycline; also available were vitamins C, B-1 and B-12, aspirin, and herbal remedies. When a patient failed to respond to treatment, his case would be discussed among all the unit's medical personnel. "My patient came down with this or that sickness," a platoon medic might inform his colleagues at one of these conferences. "I have given him such and such a medicine but his condition has remained the same. Do you have any suggestions?" and the others would make recommendations based on their own training and experience.[117]

Men who did not respond to these ministrations and those wounded in combat were evacuated to a hospital. Some of these hospitals were quite elaborate, such as the one in Cambodia at a station along the Ho Chi Minh Trail known as "Dat Ong Cu." An NVA cook described the hospital:

*A more general discussion of VC/NVA medical practices and capabilities is to be found in Chapter 7, Logistics.

Inside the hospital there were operation rooms underground. There were doctors, military medics, male and female nurses. There was plenty of medicine. The hospital was built on a piece of land about one acre large. Under the hospital were underground tunnels . . . on a very big scale, two meters deep, from twenty to twenty-five meters long and about fifteen meters wide. Inside the tunnels one could even hang hammocks.[118]

A main-force acting platoon leader who spent three months in hospital because of wounds said that his complex was built above ground, the three patient wards situated at one hundred– to two hundred–meter intervals, and consisting of seventy to eighty beds each. This hospital had an X-ray machine and at least four medical doctors as well as "many medical assistants. I heard that they could treat all types of diseases and wounds, including surgery and amputation."[119]

Evacuating battlefield casualties was difficult at best. A main-force squad leader who sustained a broken arm during a battle in October 1965 said it took a day and a half to transport him and his wounded comrades to the province hospital by boat, where he spent more than two months recuperating. Once there, the treatment he received was quite good. "The food at the hospital was highly nutritive. Every day, I got milk, lemonade, and a lot of meat, including beef, pork, and chicken." There were about one hundred other patients at this facility. The chief surgeon was highly respected by his patients because he "only resorted to amputation as a last alternative, and he always tried to save the patient from disability."[120]

Having a limb amputated was a very real and disturbing possibility for the VC/NVA soldier—it was "the treatment of choice," according to an American surgeon who studied their medical system.[121] Soldiers crippled by amputation were returned to their native villages, where the local Party committee assumed responsibility for their support and rehabilitation, even to the extent of assisting them in finding wives among the villagers. Some of these men, however, had a difficult time adjusting to their new status. According to the medic quoted earlier:

In 1964, I went to visit two crippled soldiers who had been fighters in my unit. Some of these cried when they saw us, their former fighting comrades. As far as I can make out, they cried for their future. Though they had been told that the country owed them a debt, they knew that they were crippled and no longer able to do anything.*

The medic, a humane and decent man by any standard, went on to describe the affecting story of a crippled soldier who returned home to a less-than-heartwarming welcome. Neither his wife nor his parents could accept his condition. "His wife cried and cried. Some time later, his wife left him and married another man." Unable to live with his parents because their home was in a GVN-controlled area, this man moved to another village where the people took him in and found him a wife. "She told others," the medic continued, "that not only did she felt [sic] sorry for his physical condition and that his wife had left him, but that she loved him because he was a good person. The local villagers helped them celebrate their wedding."[122]

BOMBING ATTACKS

No matter how remote, well-constructed and organized, and fortified the VC/NVA camps were, none was more than a few minutes from the war. Residents lived under the constant threat of attack and nothing was more frightening than the Allied air raids, especially the B-52 bombings. Survivors of these bombings describe them in apocalyptical terms. "We were all very scared," one survivor admitted. "Whenever the B-52s dropped bombs, ten or fifteen minutes after the planes had left, the bombs could still be heard exploding. Their explosion is something terrifying. It shatters the atmosphere of the whole area, and sitting in the trenches, we could feel the ground trembling although the explosion occurred some kilometers away."[123]

"Oh, yes, I was scared to death. Everyone was," an NVA sergeant said of his reaction during a B-52 raid. "Lying in the trench, I prayed and prayed for the bombs not to walk into it." The sergeant, who was convalescing in a hospital when the raid took place about three A.M., recalled:

As soon as I got into the trench, I saw two big fireballs in the sky. A short moment later the bombs started to fall down; each time there were more than one hundred bombs, and there were three times altogether. I was in a deep trench and

---

*The crippled NVA soldier was also sent home, although his route was far more arduous and uncertain than that of his Viet Cong counterpart.

the trench was covered, and it felt as if the ground was trembling all over; there were times I was nearly bounced up out of the trench. The explosion was uninterrupted for some time and was so big that I became deaf for three whole days. When the bombs exploded they brightened up one whole part of the forest. My own trench was laying [sic] in the bombed area, but I was unscathed. What luck![124]

Fear of the B-52s was not limited to the VC/NVA. At least one Soviet delegation to the NLF was caught in such a raid. After it was over they were embarrassed to discover that in their terror they had involuntarily emptied their bladders on themselves.[125]

During the course of the long war, more than two million American military personnel served in Vietnam. Most of them spent their one-year tour in vast base complexes or in the cities and towns of South Vietnam. Even the infantrymen, who spent weeks living in the jungles, could look forward to stand-downs in base areas and temporary relief from the war through an out-of-country R&R program in which every single soldier, marine, sailor, and airman was guaranteed participation. Every American soldier who served in Vietnam, whether an infantryman or a clerk in General Westmoreland's headquarters, drew combat pay; enlisted personnel paid no income tax for the year they were in Vietnam; and everyone had free mailing privileges. The American PX system in Vietnam was bursting with all the trappings of a rich consumer society—at prices even the lowest private could afford. The U.S. government's spending in Vietnam*
plus hundreds of thousands of American servicemen, their wallets jammed with cash and unleashed upon South Vietnam's towns and cities, stimulated the service sectors of the country's economy that catered to Americans and contributed to the disruption of Vietnamese society. But the pay of the U.S. serviceman's Communist counterpart was barely sufficient to afford a haircut and not enough to buy cigarettes.

Every American who went to Vietnam knew that if he survived after no more than a year in the country (thirteen months

---

*In 1967 alone military construction in South Vietnam cost the United States more than $200 million plus another $26 million for real estate leases. Cumulative construction costs, 1964–1970, totaled over $1.8 billion with another $100 million paid to the Vietnamese over that same period under leasing agreements (Heiser, p. 192).

for marines), he would step aboard an air-conditioned jet liner and be home again within twenty-four hours. A letter sent home by a North Vietnamese soldier serving the war's duration in South Vietnam took months to reach its destination, if it got there at all.

The Americans in Vietnam were literally ten thousand miles from home, but the VC/NVA soldier, while geographically much closer to his native village, might just as well have been on another planet for all he got to see of home during his military service. In every aspect the VC/NVA made do with far less than any Western soldier would consider the bare minimum. Ultimately, not only did the VC/NVA survive, but also he frequently managed to enjoy his life in the jungles and rural villages of South Vietnam.

9

IN BATTLE

STRATEGY

The long-term objectives of the VC/NVA in Southeast Asia were defined by the Lao Dong Party during the early 1950s. In the spring of 1952, the French Expeditionary Corps captured a secret Party document that stated, ''The ultimate aim of the Vietnamese Communist leadership is to install Communist regimes in the whole of Vietnam, in Laos, and in Cambodia.''[1]

To accomplish this ambitious aim, the government of North Vietnam intended to continue the same strategy that the Viet Minh had used to topple the French. This procedure followed a three-phase methodology originally developed by Mao Tse-tung, leader of the Chinese Communists. Vo Nguyen Giap, a former Vietnamese school teacher and architect of the Viet Minh victory at Dien Bien Phu, would lead the fight as minister of defense and commander-in-chief of North Vietnam's army.

General William C. Westmoreland describes the three-phase offensive in his book *A Soldier Reports*. According to the former Military Assistance Command, Vietnam (MACV) commander, ''In Phase One the insurgents remain on the defensive but work to establish control of the population and conduct terrorist and guerrilla operations. In Phase Two, regular military forces are formed, guerrilla attacks increase, and isolated government forces engaged. In the climactic Phase Three, large insurgent military units go on the offensive to defeat the government's large units and to establish full control of the population. A peculiarly Vietnamese aspect of the final stage is the 'khoi nghai,' the general uprising, wherein the people theoretically arise and overthrow the government."[2]

Giap, in his own writings, elaborates on the type of warfare required in the three phases by stating, "The long-term people's war in Vietnam also called for appropriate forms of fighting: appropriate to the revolutionary nature of the war as well as to the balance of forces which revealed at that time an overwhelming superiority of the enemy over the still very weak material and technical bases of the People's Army. The adopted form of warfare was guerrilla warfare. It can be said that the war of liberation of the Vietnamese people was a long and vast guerrilla war proceeding from simple to complex then to mobile war in the last years of the resistance."[3]

This guerrilla-war philosophy Giap followed while leading the Viet Minh against the French did not hold completely true in the war against South Vietnam and its American ally. Instead of allowing the Viet Cong to conduct the war in South Vietnam by themselves, North Vietnam began sending cadre to assist in 1963 and regular NVA forces in the summer of 1964. According to Brigadier General Dave Palmer in his book *Summons of the Trumpet*, "By committing its regular forces to a cause which had previously been cloaked in the guise of an internal war, Hanoi dramatically altered the entire thrust of the conflict."[4]

Thus the Vietnam War in which the Americans became involved was different from the conflict between the French and the Viet Minh. Rather than a true guerrilla movement that had led to success at Dien Bien Phu, the forces that would eventually defeat Saigon were regular NVA units instead of Viet Cong organizations.

Despite this alteration, the pathway for victory for the VC/NVA did follow the Three Phase Plan fairly closely. Although the general uprising of the people of South Vietnam never occurred, the VC/NVA were able consistently to accomplish the first two stages. The most difficult phase of the plan was attempting to escalate to Phase Three and conduct offensive operations against large ARVN and Allied units. First efforts of taking the war to the Americans were conducted by the NVA 32nd, 33rd, and 66th Regiments in November 1965, when they attempted to stand against units of the 1st Calvary Division, which had just arrived in Vietnam. Despite the fact that the battle took place in the area selected and prepared by the NVA—the Ia Drang Valley—they were defeated by the "skytroopers" and within ten days were in full retreat.[5]

The next effort by the VC/NVA to conduct extensive offensive operations was during the Tet of 1968. Although the battle ultimately proved to be a strategic victory by further eroding American support for the war, the fighting itself was disastrous for the Liberation Army. Losses were so severe that the Viet Cong virtually ceased to be an effective fighting force, leaving the remainder of the war in the hands of the NVA.

With the American ground forces almost totally withdrawn from the war zone, the NVA's chances for a successful offensive in the spring of 1972 seemed much better. Attacking south with division-size forces supported by tanks and artillery in what became known as the Easter Offensive, the NVA misjudged the resolve of the ARVNs and the strength of American air support. Once again the NVA were defeated and had to retreat to their jungle and cross-border hideaways.*

LEADERSHIP

Regardless of the philosophy, or the plans and strategy of the leaders of North Vietnam and the Viet Cong, the primary burdens and hardships of the Vietnam War, like all conflicts, fell not on the shoulders of the political leaders, but on the backs of the soldiers in the field. Fortunately for the Revolution, the responsibility for victory was in the hands of worthy men. Brian Michael Jenkins, in an unofficial staff paper written for the RAND Corporation in March 1972, best sums up the fighting spirit of the North Vietnamese and the surviving Viet Cong. According to Jenkins, "The genius of the North Vietnamese people is their tenacity. It is also their most terrible weapon. Hanoi's apparent determination to go on fighting reflects convictions that in their eyes seem correct—so correct that the alternative of not fighting may be inconceivable. Confucian

---

*The Easter Offensive resulted in 100,000 battlefield casualties and the loss of one half of all the NVA's tanks and large-caliber artillery. The operation was considered in Hanoi to be so disastrous that Giap, who had planned the offensive, was removed as commander of the North Vietnamese Army. Giap's replacement, General Van Tien Dung, had led a division under Giap's overall command at Dien Bien Phu. It would be Dung, not Giap, who would ultimately lead the NVA to the fall of Saigon and victory in 1975.

doctrine imported from China centuries ago permeates the arguments put forth by the Vietnamese Communist. Terms such as 'just cause,' and 'legitimate government,' dominate the speech of their leaders. Vietnamese Communists firmly believe that they possess the 'Mandate of Heaven' to rule all of Vietnam and therefore must emerge victorious eventually.''[6]

Along with tenacity, Jenkins could have easily added one more word of description that typified the Liberation fighter—patience. Ho Chi Minh promised from the beginning of the war that the Vietnamese would continue fighting for fifteen years, twenty years or as long as necessary to achieve victory. When he died in 1969 a portion of Ho's will again charged the Vietnamese fight on for as long as required.*[7] In a 1967 interview published in a German magazine, Ho is credited with further explaining his resolve when he said, "Everything depends on the Americans. If they want to make war for twenty years, we shall make war for twenty years. If they want to make peace, we shall make peace, and even invite them for tea afterwards.''[8]

Patience and tenacity were apt characteristics of the Viet Cong and NVA soldier, as well as resignation. The Revolution soldier accepted his role in the "twenty-year war" with various degrees of enthusiasm, but accept it he did. In August 1965, one VC rallier said of his training, "The instructor taught us that the Revolution is not a short-term business." A main-force private added in the summer of 1969, "I only knew that as long as I lived, I would have to fight the war. The cadres said that if we didn't win the war, our sons would, and if they didn't our grandsons would.'' An NVA sergeant who served as a platoon leader in 1966 added, "The cadres did nothing but repeat what had been said by the national leaders, that the war might last five,

---

*The complete contents of Ho's will were not revealed until August 31, 1989, when Vietnamese Communist Party Chief Nguyen Van Linh issued a communiqué admitting a number of discrepancies with the will and even the date of Ho's death. According to the communiqué, Ho actually died on Vietnam's National Day of September 2, 1969, but it was announced that he died on the following day "to prevent the date of Uncle Ho's death from coinciding with a day of great national rejoicing." It was also reported that contrary to Ho's wishes outlined in his will (to be cremated and his ashes be placed in three earthen pots for burial in the northern, central, and southern parts of the country), he was embalmed and placed in a glass-covered coffin for public display in Hanoi. The involvement of the Americans in the war was also changed from Ho's original writings. Ho's "the anti-U.S. war for national salvation may last for a few years" was changed to "the anti-U.S. resistance is likely to drag on."

ten, or twenty years. As for me, I thought I would be sacrificing myself for the people."[9]

Other comments from the men who actually fought the battles are marked by a lack of hope; others spoke sarcastically. One main-force private, captured in 1966, reported, "While in the unit we just lived from day to day, and one day lived was one day gained. That was all." A fellow private, captured during the same time period, stated, "The new recruits who weren't married heard President Ho declare that we would go on fighting for another five, ten, or even twenty years, from this generation to the next, lost confidence because how could their children continue the fight if they didn't even have time to get married."[10]

Despite the various strategies employed by the VC/NVA, the end result of the Vietnam War was not a direct outcome of what occurred on the battlefield. Retired Colonel Harry G. Summers, Jr., military historian and former chief of U.S. Negotiations Division, Four Party Joint Military Team, best sums up this situation at the beginning of his masterful *On Strategy: The Vietnam War in Context*. According to his book, Summers remarked to the chief of the North Vietnamese delegation at negotiations in Hanoi in April 1975, "You know you never defeated us on the battlefield." The North Vietnamese colonel, after a brief pause, responded, "That may be so, but it is also irrelevant."[11]

The colonel's answer was, of course, correct in that although the United States did not lose the war on the battlefield, it did lose its national will to sustain the fight.* What the colonel could have also said to be irrelevant was the knowledge and opinion of the common VC/NVA soldier in the field of the overall war strategy. For the most part, the Liberation soldier knew of Ho's promise that the war would be long and sacrifices many. While he could parrot these philosophies when asked, the VC/NVA in reality was much like soldiers of every other army in every other war—he neither knew nor cared about the overall "big picture" but rather was primarily concerned with his small portion of the conflict. Information on the war as a whole was sparse at best to the soldiers in the jungle, with accurate information even

---

*The purpose of this book is not to dwell on the overall strategies of either side in the war beyond how it affected the VC/NVA soldier in the field. Excellent books that offer in-depth studies on the national strategies of the United States and North Vietnam—including their strengths and weaknesses—are offered in *On Strategy: The Vietnam War in Context* by Harry G. Summers, Jr., and in *Summons of the Trumpet* by Dave Richard Palmer.

more elusive. The VC/NVA were told by their leaders, "The war is going well, we are winning, but it will be a long time before final victory is achieved."

TACTICS

Rather than national goals and theater strategies, the Liberation fighters concerned themselves with the tactics they employed to accomplish these objectives. Tenacity and patience emphasized in the VC/NVA strategy dominated tactics as well with one important addition—survivability. Tactical doctrine was explicit and can be summarized in four words: Four fast, one slow. This meant fast advance, fast assault, fast clearance of the battlefield, and fast withdrawal—all based on slow preparation.[12]

Although this "four fast, one slow" doctrine is worded primarily for offensive actions, it was also the basis for the defensive tactics that dominated VC/NVA operations. In a war where patience was the key, defense was the most expeditious tactic. Moreover, the Liberation forces learned in 1965, 1968, and again in 1972 that their large offensive operations were not only unsuccessful, but also were disastrous in terms of lives and equipment lost.

The objective of the VC/NVA in avoiding contact with ARVN and U.S. forces was achieved by constant mobility and elaborate information-denial procedures.[13] These procedures were developed primarily for use in populated areas where units moved from village to village, but were also effective in the remote jungle sanctuaries in the highlands, War Zone D, and other jungle strongholds.

To accomplish this requirement for constant mobility, the Front units often moved daily and never stayed in one location more than four days.* Denial of information of intelligence value to the enemy was a continuing process and was accomplished through detailed camouflage procedures, picking up or covering any evidence of the unit's passage, and most important, preventing villagers from departing the area to inform government or American forces of its presence.

Camp sites had to meet three main criteria. If at all possible,

---

*In remote jungle sites, far from villages and/or Allied operations, camps might take on a semipermanent nature with some soldiers occupying the fortifications full time, others coming and going as required by missions and operations. Some of the semipermanent stations nearer population centers or in areas of frequent Allied sweeps were underground in elaborate tunnel systems.

they were to be established under dense foliage to deny observation from the air. The distance between campsites had to be a single night's march or less. Finally, the sites had to have some minimum potential for defensive works.

While the first and third criteria are easy to define and were fairly consistent from location to location, the second factor of camps being a *single night's march** apart had the greatest variability. Distances that could be covered in one night depended upon type of terrain, the number of roads and waterways that had to be crossed, and the presence of enemy camps or patrols in the area.

Movement methods followed the same general procedures regardless of the size of the unit. Although movement doctrine was designed for battalion-size forces, it was easily adapted to units as small as a squad or as large as a division. The day prior to the move, reconnaissance elements from the moving unit (if the unit was as large as a battalion, representatives of each company also came along) made contact with district or village cadre to arrange guides and provisions and to familiarize themselves with the movement route.

Recon elements returned to their parent units to brief their commanders on terrain, enemy activities, and natural obstacles along the proposed route. Beyond this planning by leaders and reconnaissance forces, the remainder of the unit was not informed of the move. Information denial, although designed to deprive the enemy of any intelligence, began in the unit itself. Secrecy was preserved at all levels with only those having a "need to know" informed during the planning phase. Typically, soldiers were not told of a move until one to two hours before departure. This amount of warning would itself have been avoided except for the requirement to sanitize the bivouac area and to prepare men and equipment for movement. Foxholes, fortifications, and trenches were not filled in but rather were camouflaged for use on future visits.

During the actual movement, a reconnaissance-intelligence team preceded the formation at a distance of two hundred to three hundred meters depending on terrain and weather. Local guides accompanied the recon element if it was unfamiliar with the area. This point element was followed by two combat units,

---

*A night's march might begin several hours before sundown and extend to as much as two hours after sunrise. Whatever the schedule, a night's march never exceeded fourteen hours.

the unit headquarters and heavy weapons section, combat support elements, and another combat unit. Following the formation at an interval of one hundred to two hundred meters was a rearguard detachment from the trailing combat unit. This basic formation was consistent from squad through battalion with the only difference being the number of men in each element.

In territory where enemy contact was likely, individuals walked in file at intervals of five to ten meters during both day and night movements. In liberated or friendly areas, this interval was also used during day moves while the distance was shortened to two to four meters for night movement. In larger formations, platoons traveled at fifty-meter intervals between each other with companies one hundred meters apart. Using these standard figures, a battalion-size force was spread out over 4,000 to 7,500 meters.

Security was most important during movement. To minimize detection, units maintained radio silence and conducted communications by voice or runner. Although most moves were made at night, the soldiers had strict concealment procedures to follow in day movements. They camouflaged their uniforms and equipment with vegetation typical of the area and followed routes covered by overhead canopy. When aircraft approached, the troops hid themselves and remained as still as possible. Special care was taken when crossing roads and streams, with recon elements checking far to both flanks and across the obstacle before the main elements crossed.

DEFENSIVE TACTICS

When a unit arrived at its destination, it began immediately to prepare defensive positions. If in a village, squads were assigned houses and sectors of the perimeter. Various teams were responsible to see that no villagers left the area while recon elements and local guerrillas established outposts along avenues of approach. Communications between outposts and the perimeter were established by laying telephone wires. Coordination was continued with local and district Revolutionary officials to tie together defensive efforts and share intelligence matter.

Selection of villages or jungle positions for camp sites was regulated by strict criteria. The site had to provide good defensive terrain for the defenders while at the same time offering little protection for an attacker. Dense overhead cover to hide the fortifications from aerial observation was critical as was an absence of obstacles such as rivers or large open areas that would prevent a quick, safe withdrawal.

Under the dense canopy of vegetation, two lines or belts of fortifications were constructed fifty to two hundred meters apart, depending on the density of the ground cover and the slope of the terrain. These belts of defensive positions followed the outline of an L, U, or V so as to offer the possibility of a crossfire. Trenches deep enough to conceal and protect a crouching man were dug to connect individual positions with combined fighting holes and bunkers. Individual positions were L-shaped with an open trench on one end 1.2 meters long, 1.2 meters deep and 0.4 meters wide. Dirt from the trench was piled in front of the position with an embrasure left as a firing port. At a right angle to the trench was a bunker one meter long by half that wide with a roof of tree trunks and earth up to a half-meter thick.

Digging was a way of life to the Front soldier and he could quickly prepare his defensive positions. Fighting holes, bunkers, and connecting trenches were prepared in as little as one to two hours. If the unit moved into an area that they had previously occupied, this time was reduced considerably as old positions were improved rather than new ones dug.

According to the men who built and used them, the fortifications worked well. A VC main-force fighter in 1967 explained, ''The Front soldiers can shoot at the advancing column of attackers and force them to withdraw, and when the enemy withdraws to shell the defenders, the latter can take refuge in the covered portion of the trench and therefore remain unharmed. If the enemy stops shelling to launch a new assault, the Front's soldiers once again move to the embrasure of the trench to fight.''[14]

The distance between the first and second lines of fortifications was dictated primarily by the consideration that the second line not be visible from the first. This second line of defense provided the defenders a protected position to which to withdraw if pushed out of the first belt. From there they could further withdraw from the contact area or counterattack to regain the first belt. The main-force fighter who explained the purpose of the bunker design also was a firm believer in the two-belt system. According to this soldier:

The second line of trenches has great utility. If the Front soldiers are driven out of the first line of trenches they can withdraw to the second line and once again take advantage of

Many of the following photographs were captured from the VC/NVA and bear slogans and/or captions in Vietnamese. Translations of the original captions are included in quotation marks. Since the original captions were intended to boost morale within the VC/NVA forces or to serve as positive propaganda in the world press, their accuracy may well be in question.

An NVA unit prepared for inspection. Note the mixture of uniforms and weapons. *(Indochina Archive)*

An NVA platoon with honor flag for distinguished service. Note the individual medals and decorations. Caption on flag states "Strive to fight, strive to win. Trophy flag of President Ho." Ca. 1967. *(Indochina Archive)*

"Our strength is the strength of youth. Our mission is to stand on the head of our enemy." Trung Lap Thuong village guerrillas stand before an M-118 they destroyed on April 4, 1966. *(Indochina Archive)*

« Sức ta là sức thanh niên,
Thề ta là thề đứng trên đầu thù ».
— Đội du kích Trung-lập-thượng
bên xác chiếc xe M.118 bị họ diệt
ngày 4-4-66.

"Our forces grow stronger and stronger day by day." Viet Cong leaders receive a briefing and map orientation prior to an attack. Ca. 1966. *(Indochina Archive)*

"Even as the enemy increases in strength, our children hurry to the battlefield." A Viet Cong unit moving to new positions. Ca. 1965. *(Indochina Archive)*

"Trung Lap Ha guerrillas on an operation to encircle the enemy and kill Americans." Note the rice-stalk camouflage. Ca. 1966. *(Indochina Archive)*

"Youth is in arms now! They follow their fathers' footsteps to kill Americans for revenge." Ca. 1968. *(Indochina Archive)*

"The deeper our hostility toward the enemy, the higher our struggle. The fire is on! Look for puppet soldiers to fight! That is the oath of Fia Dinh's people!" Gia Dinh Main Force Guerrillas on patrol. Ca. 1966. *(Indochina Archive)*

"The more sweat on digging defensive positions, the less blood in fighting." Trung Cap Ha guerrillas digging in. Ca. 1966. *(Indochina Archive)*

"There is no way the Americans can escape our ambush." VC/NVA prepare an ambush position. Ca. 1967. *(Indochina Archive)*

"Nhuan Duc guerrilla forces strengthen their perimeter." During the four-day period March 28-April 1, 1966, these forces killed 275 American soldiers. *(Indochina Archive)*

"An Phu village guerrillas practice antiaircraft defense." Ca. 1967. *(Indochina Archive)*

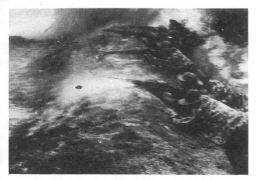

"American bombs can never interrupt the stride of the Duc Hiep guerrillas fighting day and night to destroy Americans and protect our homeland." The "bombs" are, likely, artillery shells. This appears to be one of the few photos of VC/NVA forces in actual combat. Ca. 1967. *(Indochina Archive)*

"A trophy moves to base." Viet Cong remove a .50-cal. machine gun from a destroyed U.S. M-113 personnel carrier. Ca. 1966. *(Indochina Archive)*

"Transport Team No. 806 of the Road Transport Service. One of the nine newly decorated units. It has worked for eight years at dangerous places, subjected to 2864 U.S. air raids." North Vietnamese trucks head south on the Ho Chi Minh Trail. June 1972. Photo was released by Hanoi to East German news media. *(Indochina Archive)*

Viet Cong troops armed with recoilless rifles are surprised by an Air Force reconnaissance aircraft in a rice paddy. Ca. 1965. *(U.S. Air Force)*

North Vietnamese infiltrators in the Plain of Reeds. Ca. 1967. *(Indochina Archive)*

An old man and a child assist a Local Force Viet Cong in preparing a punji pit. Ca. 1965. *(Indochina Archive)*

"This American bomb will soon be dropped back on them." Ordnance soldiers saw apart a dud bomb to secure explosives for a booby-trap factory. Ca. 1966. *(Indochina Archive)*

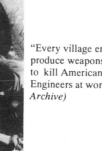

"Every village engineer section strives to produce weapons to support the guerrillas to kill Americans. Duc Hiep village Field Engineers at work." Ca. 1965. *(Indochina Archive)*

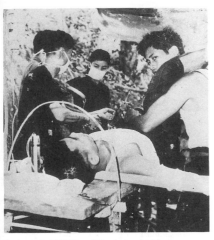

A wounded NVA soldier is treated in a jungle hospital. Ca. 1969. *(Indochina Archive)*

The main entrance to a Viet Cong underground tunnel system. Ca. 1966. *(U.S. Army)*

Viet Cong training area and barrack. Note that much of the camouflage has been stripped away by the U.S. Marines who found the camp. *(U.S. Marine Corps)*

Bamboo slats and sturdy limbs are used on muddy trails that connect bunkers, sheds, and training facilities at a jungle base. Ca. 1970. *(Indochina Archive)*

AK-47 assault rifle on the right,
SKS semiautomatic rifle on
the left. *(U.S. Army)*

Type 56 Chicom RPD light machine gun.
(U.S. Army)

RPG-2 rocket-propelled grenade
launcher. *(U.S. Army)*

Chicom 82mm mortar. *(U.S. Army)*

RPG-7 rocket-propelled grenade
launcher. *(U.S. Army)*

Soviet 122mm rocket with field-expedient launcher. *(U.S. Army)*

Handmade aircraft identification manuals captured from the Viet Cong in 1968. *(U.S. Army)*

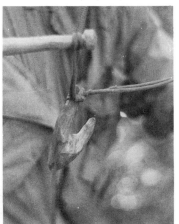

Surgical instruments captured from the Viet Cong in 1968. *(U.S. Army)*

Homemade "body hook" used by the NVA to remove dead from contested battlefield (captured near Hill 1338 in 1967). *(U.S. Army)*

prepared fortifications to continue the fight. Since the GVN soldiers do not have any fortifications to their advantage, they could be pushed back after their first effort, and immediately after the withdrawal of the enemy, the Front soldiers would be ordered to come back to the first line of trenches. We call this tactic of countering sweep operations the 'rubber-band tactic.' This tactic helps the platoon leaders to keep control and command the fighters during the battle, and prevents the Front soldiers from being disbanded by the first successful assault from the ARVN. It also helps us to resist until darkness comes and, at that time, we can withdraw from the battlefield in safety.[15]

To further confuse the attackers, several variations of the two-belt defensive system were used. Frequently, when the camp sites were in villages, the outer defensive belt was dug in outside the hamlet's boundaries. The second belt was formed inside the village, often using bunkers and protective positions typically already a part of houses in the war zone. This method not only saved time and labor in preparing positions but also theoretically deterred the attackers from using artillery and air strikes so as not to destroy the village and inflict civilian casualties.

Another deception method was to construct dummy positions to draw artillery and air attacks. These fortifications were dug to resemble real positions but were not well camouflaged and could be seen by aerial observers. Dummy positions were constructed in proximity to Front fortifications to draw fire away from the fighters. They were also built in remote areas the Front had no plans to occupy so that Allied ammunition and ground sweeps were expended with no results.

In remote jungle bases, which were usually out of artillery range and where Allied sweeps seldom ventured, more permanent defensive positions were developed. These positions, occupied more or less full time, were known as base camps because of their permanence and their use as depots for resupply of ammunition and rations. Base camps followed the same two-belt design as the temporary bivouac sites with two primary differences—a third belt was added in the larger camps and fighting positions/bunkers were larger and better protected. Base-camp bunkers typically were eight feet long by five feet wide. Dug out to a depth of three to four feet, the bunkers were covered with two feet of logs and dirt. Small entrance ways at each end of the bunker doubled as firing ports. Trenches connected bunkers in each belt as well as offering protected withdrawal avenues to the next line of defense.[16]

ARVN and U.S. commanders discovered that the VC/NVA were quite difficult to dislodge from both temporary and base-camp defensive positions. After unsuccessful attacks that cost them many casualties, Allied commanders learned that the best way to destroy the enemy in their defensive camps was to surround them and then lay on artillery fire, helicopter-gunship attacks, and tactical air strikes. One American officer summarized:

> I have talked to small-unit commanders all over Vietnam since the first of the year [1967], who have slugged it out with a fanatical enemy in these positions. From these detailed after-combat interviews, I have concluded that it is impossible to penetrate, flank, or envelop these fortifications without taking extremely heavy casualties. To fight the enemy in these positions is analogous to cornering a tiger in his lair and then trying to stalk him with only a Bowie knife. The smart hunter will trap the tiger and then stand back and blow his brains out with a Weatherbee Magnum.[17]

One tactic developed by the VC/NVA to counter this "surround and pound with fire support" technique was to "hug the enemy" rather than fall back to the second belt of defenses.* This involved following the attackers as they pulled back to put in artillery and air. "Hugging" the enemy prevented the air and artillery from doing any damage because to hit the enemy required the attackers to bring in the fire support so close that they would risk becoming casualties as well.

Another technique employed was to attack the attackers. These counterattacks were especially effective if the attacking force was inferior to the defending force in numbers and/or training and motivation. Regardless of their success, however, the counterattack was merely a measure to assist the VC/NVA unit in breaking contact and withdrawing.

Whether the VC/NVA unit defended their camp by moving from belt to belt, by "hugging" the enemy, or by counterattacking, their objective was to take minimum casualties while waiting for darkness and the opportunity to withdraw. Interest-

---

*Regardless of the amount of digging and overhead cover, direct hits by artillery and bombs and indirect hits by napalm were lethal to the defenders.

ingly, neither captured documents nor former VC/NVA make any reference to "retreat." All doctrine referred to this portion of defensive warfare as the "withdrawal phase." Part of this was strictly rhetorical while a larger portion was practical reality. VC/NVA units had no plans to retreat because they never had any plans to hold any village or territory to begin with. Campsites, although built up as defensive positions, were merely places to spend the night before continuing movement. The best action for the VC/NVA was no action at all, for time was on their side. When they did happen to be discovered, they expended only minimum effort to ensure the unit's safe withdrawal.

OFFENSIVE TACTICS

Although VC and NVA units remained primarily in a defensive posture except for the brief offensives of 1965, 1968, 1972, and the final assault on Saigon in 1975, they did conduct limited offensive actions throughout the war. Offensive operations included attacks on fixed installations (posts, fire bases, airfields), ambushes, and indirect fire with weapons such as mortars, artillery, and rockets.

The same close attention to detail that characterized defensive operations highlighted offensive activities. As with all operations, the "four quicks, one slow" doctrine prevailed with the "quick attack" portion being emphasized with the aid of the "three strongs"—strong fight, strong assault, strong pursuit.

The "four quicks, one slow" and "three strongs" doctrine arranged in sequence of occurrence for offensive operations were:

—Slow plan (as long as six months including rehearsals)
—Quick advance (up to forty kilometers in as little as six hours)
—Quick attack (measured in minutes)
—Strong fight (surprise)
—Strong assault (concentration and mass)
—Strong pursuit (including displacement of mortars)
—Quick clearance (preplanned to prevent confusion on the objective)
—Quick withdrawal (calculated to create an aura of doubt over the enemy because of speed of execution and lack of evidence of ever having been in the area)[18]

Attacks on fixed installations by the VC/NVA began in the early years of the war as assaults on government outposts and police stations. The attacks then graduated to ARVN and U.S. fire-support bases. In keeping with the patience of the Front soldiers—as well as being good basic tactics—planning for these attacks was detailed and long-term. From conception to execution might take as much as six months, with cancellation of the mission a constant possibility. Each phase of the operation was broken down into the smallest tasks, and each was rehearsed in detail. Only after each portion proved to be practical did the unit conduct the attack.

While the attacking unit itself was responsible for planning, preparation, and execution of the operation, it was assisted by its senior headquarters. The higher command also exercised complete authority over whether or not the attack could take place at all. During the early years, when the VC were the primary aggressors, initial requests to conduct attacks went to the appropriate province military affairs committee.* The plan was then studied by the head of the committee to determine the political effects of the plan and the capabilities of the friendly and enemy units involved. If the military committee chief approved the plan, he forwarded it to the secretary of the provincial Party committee. If the secretary decided the plan was sound he called for a combined meeting of the entire province committee to study, discuss, and ultimately to approve or disapprove the plan.

ATTACK PLANNING

Procedures for approving attack plans by the Front were as well known by the Americans as by the VC/NVA themselves. A study conducted by the MACV intelligence section recorded how the province committee continued planning after initial approval. According to the study,

> Once the proposal is approved by the Province Committee, the Military Affairs Committee divides the preliminary tasks among its three staffs. The Military Staff sends a reconnaissance unit to study the objective from a military point of view,

*After the Tet Offensive of 1968, when VC units were decimated, this process of approval for attacks was adjusted more to the military chain of command of the NVA. However, it should be noted that VC and NVA forces were so badly mauled in the offensive that it was over a year before they could mount any offensive operations of significance.

and to prepare a sand table mock-up. The Political Staff sends a cadre to contact the civilians in the area, to learn their reaction to the proposed attack. It also studies the morale of the troops to see if they are mentally and emotionally prepared. If they are not, the Political Staff must take the necessary measures to prepare them. The Rear Services Staff determines whether civilians can furnish food and labor, including that needed for removal of the dead and the booty.[19]

Reconnaissance efforts during the planning phase were directed to gather information on the terrain, enemy troop strength, weapons, morale, and the operating procedures of the enemy commander. In addition to on-the-ground recons, local guerrillas and cadre were questioned about any information they had on the objective. Teams observed the target day and night as they recorded the layout of the base, location of crew-served weapons, possible routes of approach, and the general routine of the camp. This information was recorded on charts that eventually provided a detailed diagram of the enemy post.

When adequate information could not be gathered from reconnaissance outside the enemy camp, teams were prepared to go inside to gather the needed information. A member of the recon unit for the 261st VC Battalion, operating in the Delta in 1965, recalls:

Once I got into the middle of Cai Be post where the district chief's office was. It was fifteen days prior to the attack and takeover of the post by our battalion. I was accompanied by two comrades armed with submachine guns to protect me in case my presence was discovered while I was nearing the post entrance. I was then wearing pants only and had in my belt a pair of pincers, a knife, and a grenade. At one hundred meters from the post I started crawling and quietly approached the post entrance with the two comrades following me. At twenty meters from the post, my comrades halted while I crawled on. At the post entrance there was a barbed-wire barricade on which hung two grenades. Behind the barricade stood a guard. I made my way between the barricade and the stakes holding up the barbed-wire fence. I waited in the dark for the moment when the guard lit his cigarette. I passed two meters away from him and sneaked through the entrance. On that occasion I was unable to find out where the munitions depot was but I did discover the positions of two machine guns and the radio room. I got out at the back of the post by cutting my way through the barbed wire.[20]

Information gathered by the recon teams was supplemented by civilians who worked at or visited the post to be attacked. Interestingly, attacks were on occasion called off because the civilians surrounding a post felt they were being treated well by the ARVNs and/or Americans and would give no information to the Front intelligence gatherers.

At the same time information was being gathered about the proposed target, an analysis of possible support that could be mustered to assist in the defense of the base was determined. Reaction time of Allied artillery and air support was calculated, as was the time it would take reinforcements to reach the base. In conjunction with the latter, routes to the base were reconned to see how quickly reinforcements could move and to determine the best locations for ambushes to slow or stop their advance.

When the study and reconnaissance of the objective was completed, the military affairs committee held another meeting. In attendance were the leaders of all the units that were to be involved in the attack. If these commanders agreed that the attack should be made, the military affairs committee reported to the province committee with their recommendation. The province committee again reviewed the political, military, and logistic aspects of the proposed attack, and, if satisfied, approved the plan.

The criteria for approval of an attack were further explained by a cadre member of a VC unit in 1966. According to the soldier, "We usually carried out an attack operation only when we had obtained reliable information as to the number of enemy troops, their weapons, and their position. And we always ensured that we were absolutely superior in numbers before starting the attack. If not, we preferred to avoid contact with the enemy."[21]

Approval for the attack was only the beginning of the preparation for the assault. Rehearsals for the operation began on sand tables and progressed to practices on stake-and-string replicas of the target. Depending upon the difficulty of the objective, this phase lasted from three days to well over a month. While the assault forces were practicing their attack, local guerrilla guides and laborers were recruited or drafted to carry supplies before the fight and to remove the wounded and the dead and captured materials after the battle. Facilities for evacuation and treatment of the wounded were prepared and coffins for burying the anticipated dead were built. Ammunition and provisions for the attack and resupply afterward were procured and stockpiled.

Secrecy about the exact attack objective was maintained as close as possible all the way up to the actual date of the assault. Normally, only leaders—squad leaders for a company mission or platoon leaders for a battalion attack—knew the specific target. If for any reason—such as one of the unit's troops rallying to the ARVNs—it was felt that the attack plan had been compromised, it was called off. Cancellation was much more typical than attack for the patient VC/NVA. For every assault that actually took place, over a hundred were proposed and developed to some stage of planning before being terminated prior to the actual attack.

One of the priorities in determining if the operation was to take place was that the VC/NVA had to be superior in numbers to the defenders. The more the VC/NVA outnumbered the defenders, the more favorable the plan was considered. Numbers were so important to the planners that the most popular maxim for the attack was "pit ten against one." Americans and ARVNs more commonly referred to this outnumber tactic of the VC/NVA as "if it appears that it may be a fair fight, bug out instead."

When an attack plan and practice met all the requirements to indicate maximum chance of success, the attacking unit began its move to the objective after sundown. The attacking force was divided into sappers, heavy weapons section, and the main assault unit. Although a diversionary force might make a feint to draw the defenders to another part of the target, the actual assault was concentrated on one main axis of advance. To maintain surprise, preparatory fires were normally not used and the attack usually began between midnight and two A.M. Approach was made from the best-concealed or the least-defended direction. Frequently this was the same location as the post's garbage dump.[22]

The sappers led the attack by approaching the objective as slowly as necessary to avoid detection. In addition to clearing approaches through barbed wire and mines, the sappers initiated the attack by blowing up important targets within the base. Once the sappers were detected by the defenders, the heavy weapons began firing from protected positions outside the camp to cover the main attack force. An additional unit or units might also be positioned in ambush along routes where reinforcements would approach. The first priority target of the sappers, heavy weapons, and the main attack was the defender's communications position. Knocking it out early in the fight might prevent or at least slow reinforcements, air and/or artillery support. Other priority targets were artillery and mortar positions, automatic weapons, command posts, and ammunition dumps.

Alternate plans were made and rehearsed in case the sappers were unable to penetrate the defenses without being detected. A platoon leader in the 514th VC Regiment recalled an attack in 1965: "We crawled toward the post silently. When we reached the first barbed-wire fence, the first sapper destroyed it with a mine. The second sapper jumped ahead immediately after the first blast and destroyed the second barbed-wire fence by exploding a second mine. The third sapper did the same after the second blast; then, a sort of wooden bridge was thrown down over the ditch and the fourth sapper rushed ahead to blow up the blockhouse wall. All this was done so quickly that the soldier who manned the blockhouse did not react in time and got killed, while the four sappers were still alive."[23]

Despite the dangers, most sappers welcomed their role as the leaders of attacks. According to a sapper platoon leader captured in 1967, "We have the responsibility of being the forward group in any attack, of opening the way for the other elements, and of removing obstacles, erected by the enemy to stop our advance, with explosives. Since we are the fighters who have to carry out our attacks with explosives, we should always be brave and heroic."[24]

AMBUSH TACTICS

In addition to assaults on fixed installations, the VC/NVA conducted ambushes as a part of their offense. The ambush was a preferred method of offensive operation because it was a "poor man's tactic" in that the element of surprise compensated for the lack of sophisticated weaponry. Types of ambushes covered a broad spectrum of operations and varied from a hasty hit-and-run—the result of a meeting engagement in the jungle—to carefully planned regimental-size traps that included maneuver forces to encircle the enemy to prevent his escape from the kill zone.

The successful conduct of an ambush began with a complete understanding of the enemy situation regarding movement patterns, strength, reaction time of supporting fires and units, and degree of training and morale. Much of this was determined by the direct observation of trail watchers and recon units. Information was supplemented by local guerrillas, civilians, and agents within the South Vietnamese government.

Preparation for planned ambushes was as detailed as that for attacks on fixed installations. A thorough reconnaissance of the proposed ambush site was conducted to see if its terrain met the following criteria:

—provided concealment to prevent detection from the ground or air of ambushing troops
—enabled ambushing troops to deploy, encircle, and divide the enemy
—allowed for heavy weapons emplacements to provide sustained fire from beginning to end
—enabled a unit to set up observation posts for early detection of the enemy
—permitted the secret movement of troops to ambush positions and the dispersal of troops during withdrawal

In addition to these requirements, recon elements studied the terrain to determine if it was advantageous in slowing the enemy and causing them to "pile up" after being attacked, preventing them ease of withdrawal from the kill zone, and obstructing use of his heavy weapons and supporting fires. Areas surrounding the ambush site that were not favorable to the attackers and that might provide protection or escape for the enemy were covered with mines, booby traps, or indirect fires.

Once an ambush site was selected and approved, planning was broken into three phases—actions prior to opening fire, actions upon opening fire, and actions during withdrawal. Each phase was carefully rehearsed repeatedly on a sand-table model and on terrain similar to the actual ambush site. Throughout the planning process a checklist was followed that required each question to be answered before execution of the ambush. Questions included "How strong is the enemy? How do we fight him? Where? When? What means and measures do we have at our disposal to knock down the enemy opposition? How is secrecy maintained? How would the enemy oppose us? How would we react? What will we do when the enemy is destroyed—should we advance or pull out, where and how?"[25]

Oftentimes the enemy, weather, and terrain were not conducive to the VC/NVA ambush plans without overt action by the ambushers. The best time for ambushes was just before dark because this limited the enemy's use of air support and the rapid arrival of reinforcements. To delay the unit to be ambushed, the VC/NVA would deploy small patrols or snipers to harass it. Roads and bridges might also be sabotaged or mined to slow the enemy so that they would reach the ambush zone at the correct time.

Ambush formations used by the VC/NVA were composed of a lead-blocking element, main-assault element, rear-blocking element, and observation and command posts.* The lead-blocking element's mission was to use surprise and firepower to halt or to concentrate the enemy. Once the lead-blocking unit had accomplished its mission, the main assault force moved in to encircle, split, and/or destroy the enemy by use of recoilless rifles, rocket-propelled grenades, heavy automatic weapons, antipersonnel and antitank mines, and individual weapons. During the attack by the main assault force, the rear-blocking force attacked the rear elements of the enemy formation to prevent a retreat as well as to engage any reinforcements. The rear-blocking force was sometimes supplemented by 60mm and 82mm mortars to put fire on the ambushed unit and to protect the flanks of the ambushers.

The command post for the operation was situated in a central location overlooking the ambush position. In addition to the lead-blocking, rear-blocking, and main-assault elements, the command post controlled one or more observation posts (OPs). These were responsible for reporting initial sighting of the unit to be ambushed, the formation it was using, and any unanticipated conditions observed. The OPs remained in position during the actual ambush in order to report routes used by the enemy in its withdrawal, location of pockets of resistance, and the approach of reinforcements. OPs made their reports to the command post by wire communications and/or runners.

Various other offensive tactics typical of guerrilla warfare were used by the VC and NVA. All were designed to inflict maximum damage on the enemy with minimum danger to themselves. These tactics included the use of sniper fire, mortar or rocket

---

*U.S. ambush terminology is similar but somewhat simpler with its two elements of assault and security. The security element is responsible for both front and rear security while the assault unit makes the main attack. Depending on the type of ambush, U.S. doctrine may call for the assault unit to be supplemented by search teams who look for documents, weapons, etc., once the ambush is completed, and by snatch teams that attempt to take live prisoners.

attacks on fixed installations, and various attended and unattended mines and booby traps. In each case the objective was
hit-and-run. If all worked as planned, the VC/NVA inflicted
casualties and withdrew before effective fire could be returned.

TERRORISM

The final tactic used by the VC/NVA was terrorism. Although
much more a political weapon than a military one, it nonethe-
less was an integral part of Front operations. According to writer
Douglas Pike:

> To the communist, terror has utility and is beneficial to his
> cause, while to the other side [the United States] the identical
> act is self-defeating . . . terror is integral in all the communist
> tactics and programs and the communists could not rid them-
> selves of it if they wanted to. Meanwhile, the other side firmly
> believes, even though its members do not always behave ac-
> cordingly, that there is a vested interest in abstaining from
> such acts.[26]

At the time Pike was writing this analysis, apologists for the
VC/NVA were busily justifying the Communists' use of political terrorism. One wrote:

> The NLF has occasionally attacked, but more frequently
> provoked "Allied" assaults on, South Vietnamese villages.
> Assaults could not be provoked, of course, without the exis-
> tence of a U.S.-ARVN policy of virtually unrestrained use of
> firepower on villages that are in enemy hands or are "sus-
> pect." This has made it possible for the NLF to enlist the
> cooperation of ARVN and the United States military in rad-
> icalizing these elements of the population still adhering to the
> Saigon cause.[27]

Interviews with Vietnamese villagers conducted by the RAND
Corporation in 1965, while they uncovered understandable resentment over air and artillery bombardment, also revealed that
the victims put the blame for the attacks squarely on the Viet
Cong. "The guerrillas always fired one or two shots to provoke
the GVN, which brought bombers or artillery on the village,
and then ran away letting the people bear the consequences,"
one interviewee commented.[28]

VC main-force cadres, when interviewed regarding the use of terror, consistently and defensively denied any knowledge of (or at least responsibility for) terrorism that claimed the lives of innocent civilians. They blamed these deeds on the guerrillas, insisting that main-force units were "too disciplined to have engaged in terrorism or sabotage."[29]

The question of who used terrorism more frequently—the VC or the NVA—is valid. Pike concluded that the most horrendous example of Communist terrorism during the war, the massacre at Hue during Tet of 1968, was carried out by "local communist cadres and not by the PAVN troops or Northerners or other outside communists."[30] Again, it was the VC who, on December 5, 1967, at the village of Dak Son in Phuoc Long province, committed an act of terrorism Pike says "should be remembered as long as Lidice,"* when, using sixty flame throwers, they incinerated 252 Montagnard tribesmen—mostly women and children.[31] But it was the NVA who were responsible for the massacre which took place at the village of Phu Than, eighteen miles south of Da Nang, on the night of June 14, 1970, when they methodically dropped grenades and satchel charges into the villagers' bunkers, killing an estimated one hundred civilians "with the precision of a deadly corps de ballet."[32] When the U.S. Army's leadership learned early in 1969 that troops from the Americal Division operating in Quang Ngai Province, had murdered an estimated four hundred civilians in the hamlet of My Lai on March 16, 1968, the secretary of the army and the army Chief of Staff, General William C. Westmoreland, appointed a commission headed by Lt. Gen. W. R. Peers to investigate the allegations. At the height of its investigation, the so-called Peers Commission consisted of thirty-two officers, forty-four enlisted men, and ten civilians.[33]

Between November 1969 and March 1970, the commission took hundreds of pages of evidence and testimony and traveled thousands of miles.[†34] The commission recommended actions be taken against thirty individuals, including the major general who commanded the division at the time of the incident. Charges were actually brought against sixteen individuals and of the four

---

*A village in Czechoslovakia eleven miles northwest of Prague destroyed by the Germans on June 10, 1942, in reprisal for the assassination of Nazi leader Reinhard Heydrich. All males over the age of sixteen were shot and women and children sent to concentration camps. Afterward, the entire village was destroyed.
†Not to be left out, the House Armed Services Committee took another 893 pages of testimony between April 15 and June 22, 1970.

who went to trial, one, Lt. William Calley, was convicted of murdering twenty-two Vietnamese villagers. Eight other soldiers, including two generals, were punished administratively.[35]

The My Lai massacre was given sensational media coverage in the United States and, justified or not, has become a lasting stain on the record of the United States Army in Vietnam. On the other hand, the Communist Vietnamese leadership has never admitted that its troops ever committed any atrocities whatsoever during the war.

Terrorism, admitted or not, as practiced by the VC/NVA was aimed at three important goals:

—Intimidation of the people: The VC/NVA assassinated, abducted, threatened, and harassed the population of South Vietnam in order to force their cooperation, to obtain laborers and porters, to collect taxes, food, and other supplies, and to prevent the local inhabitants from giving intelligence to the Allied forces.

—Elimination of enemies: Individuals, particularly South Vietnamese officials (such as hamlet and village chiefs), National Police, school teachers, and other citizens who defied VC/NVA threats, were marked for execution. If the individual was unpopular with the local populace it was so much the better because the assassination squads could claim credit for removing an "enemy" of the people.

—Propaganda: Terrorism in the countryside and in the cities provided a sign of strength and presence of the VC/NVA to the South Vietnamese. Attacks provided a boost to the morale of the Front soldiers as well as providing publicity for their cause.[36]

Terrorism was a prime tactic of the VC/NVA from the beginning of the conflict and was another useful means of economy of manpower and resources. Assassination squads or single hit men could enter village or city and kill or kidnap South Vietnamese officials. Those kidnapped were indoctrinated by way of lectures, beatings, and starvation before being returned to their homes with warnings that if they did not stop supporting the government, they would be executed. Not only were key leaders lost to the government, but confidence of the people was eroded and troops who otherwise could have been searching for the Front camps in the jungle were required to stay behind and secure the villages and hamlets.

Although isolated incidents of terrorism by Allied troops received much more attention in the world media, the fact remains that murder, torture, and intimidation were routine tactics of the VC/NVA. This was formally outlined in their COSVN Resolution Number 9, published in July 1969. The resolution, which detailed the military, diplomatic, and political strategy of the Revolution, included that "Integral to the political struggle would be the liberal use of terrorism to weaken and destroy local government, strengthen the party apparatus, proselyte among the populace, erode the control and influence of the Government of Vietnam, and weaken the RVNAF [Republic of Vietnam Armed Forces]."[37]

Although the use of terror by the VC/NVA was not a formal part of their published doctrine until the summer of 1969, it was a part of their field operations from the beginning of the war. Months before Resolution Number 9, VC and NVA murder squads played an important role in the Tet Offensive. In Hue City alone, the VC/NVA assassins killed more than 2,800 unarmed government officials, school teachers, and intellectuals. By war's end, the VC/NVA terror units accounted for more than 33,000 murders and nearly 58,000 kidnappings.[38] (For additional information on terrorism statistics, see Appendix I.)

Killing and kidnappings varied from simple murders to elaborate plots. One VC private in Long An Province explained why a village council member was killed: "It was the policy of the Front to destroy all Government organizations, and to destroy those who did not want to resign. They killed this man to make an example for others."[39]

In 1966, two VC cadres and a civilian village chief explained how terrorism could be used against individuals as well as entire villages. According to the first cadre member, "I myself have carried out orders to kill innocent people who were not able to pay contributions to the Front." The second cadre member added, "I worked in the security section. I know how the Viet Cong treated people. Outwardly they said that they did not torture but only interrogated them, but I have witnessed many sessions where the poor guy was being tortured and beaten mercilessly."

A former village chief's story relates how killing one could influence many. According to the chief,

Armed Viet Cong went from house to house in my hamlet and forced everyone to go and meet in my hamlet. When I arrived there, I saw at least three thousand people, most of whom were from my village. There were some thirty Viet Cong, half of whom were armed with rifles. One Viet Cong stood on a table and harangued the inhabitants. He said this in essence: "I call on you all to draw up in lines and go to the district chief's town [Song Cau] to ask the government authorities never to shell your village and kill innocent people [and the VC who would be living there]. It's in your interest that I ask you to do this. We people of the Front ask nothing from you. Those who refuse to take part in the demonstration will be counted as traitors opposing the people's interests, and will be executed." Then the Viet Cong brought forward a man and tied him two hundred meters from the spot and killed him with gunshot before the crowd's terrified eyes. As a result, everyone neatly put himself in line, and marched in the direction of Song Cau. The Viet Cong marched outside the lines on either side of the road.[40]

Another Front soldier described a more subtle but just as effective method used by his superior in the Delta in 1967. According to the cadre member, "He has done several cruel things and terrorist acts. For example, one time he taxed people and the people didn't want to pay the tax for two or three times, so he took them to an unsecure place and let them stay there for the bombing of the GVN, so the people were killed."[41] Another advantage of this method was that the ARVNs or Americans received credit for the "atrocity."

COMBAT INTENSITY*

While the tactics of the VC/NVA remained fairly consistent, the entire war rhythm, timing, and concentration of fighting varied. Combat intensity in Vietnam grew each year from 1964 until the Tet Offensive of 1968. After Tet, fighting steadily decreased until the Easter Offensive of 1972 when NVA forces attempted to gain territory before the peace agreement of 1973. Following this offensive, fighting again decreased until the final Victory Offensive of 1975.

Within the "big picture" of combat, periods of combat varied within each year. This cycle remained seasonally consistent regardless of the time period of the war. The heaviest fighting on

*For a comparison with U.S./Allied forces, see Chapter 3, Recruiting and Training.

a countrywide basis always occurred during the period from February through June. On the average, the month of May had the most combat, which produced the highest number of casualties on both sides. July was a month of relative lull. Combat intensity again rose in August and September. The period of October through January was again comparatively quiet, with October producing the lowest number of casualties each year.[42]

The cause of this cycle of combat was quite simple. In the southern part of South Vietnam the rainy monsoon season extends from May through September; in the northern part of the country the rains last from September through January. This extended period of bad weather slowed movement on the Ho Chi Minh Trail to the point where replacement soldiers and supplies were reduced to a trickle. Fighting by VC/NVA forces already in the war zone was further affected by the rains because many regions in the Delta were under water during the monsoon season. In areas of higher elevation, flooding was not as much of a problem as were the health and comfort difficulties related to the constant damp.

This cycle of combat was not limited to the period of American involvement during the Vietnam War. Similar campaign seasons were followed by both the Viet Minh and the French during the late 1940s and the early 1950s. It is no surprise that the battle of Dien Bien Phu occurred from March 13 to May 7, 1954, during the peak period of the cycle of combat.[43]

Combat was not evenly distributed across South Vietnam but rather tended to be highly localized. Over half of the combat casualties inflicted and received by the VC/NVA occurred in ten of the country's forty-four provinces. These provinces included the five nearest the DMZ in Military Region 1: Quang Tri, Thua Then, Quang Nam, Quang Tin, and Quang Ngai; two in Military Region 2: Kontum, and Dinh Dinh; and three near Saigon in Military Region 3: Tay Ninh, Dinh Tuong, and Kien Hoa. The reasons for the concentration of fighting in these regions were their accessibility to infiltration routes, their importance to the defense and morale of the South, and the advantages offered by the terrain of the provinces. It is worthwhile to note that while most of the fighting by the French against the Viet Minh occurred in North Vietnam, the part of the war that took place in the South was concentrated in the same ten provinces.[44]

Regardless of the tactics, timing, or location of VC/NVA operations, the dominant characteristic of their fighting was its spasmodic nature. On the whole, operations by the Front were typified by frequent moves and infrequent fights. With the exception of the previously mentioned offensives, the VC/NVA were content to remain undetected, inflict damage sporadically, interfere with American pacification efforts, and keep control—primarily by presence alone—over the liberated regions and a minimum grip over those areas still contested. If cornered, the Liberation fighters strived to give a good account of themselves, inflict maximum casualties with minimum risks, and withdraw as soon as possible. This "evade-and-hold" strategy was marked by defensive actions with offensive operations limited to ambushes and hit-and-run attacks on fixed installations.

Interviews with POWs and ralliers in 1969 revealed that the average Front soldier was engaged in a full-scale fight only a few times a year. For a period of over two years prior to the study, the majority of soldiers interviewed claimed to have been in two or three fights per year.[45]

Infrequent fighting and thorough preparation and practice before the sporadic engagements had several purposes. In addition to preserving limited manpower and supplies, the long intervals between fights were good for the morale of the Liberation solders. More important, however, was that by fighting only when conditions and planning were favorable to the VC/NVA, they were able to create an illusion of invincibility to their enemies, the local populace, and themselves.[46]

Despite extensive preparation and few engagements, not all Front soldiers were ready for battle. A twenty-three-year-old main-force private in 1966 stated, "During engagements some of the fighters were scared and remained in their communications trenches, while some were very enthusiastic and fought with ardor. Of every ten fighters, about three or four were too scared to fight."[47]

Regardless of the bravery of the Front soldiers, the tactics used, or the frequency of battle, the Liberation fighters were resigned to a lengthy war where their best virtues were tenacity and patience. Victory was not to be easily or quickly attained and battles were fought to extend the war rather than bring it to a conclusive result. In January 1969, a twenty-one-year-old main-force deputy squad leader best explained this wait-and-see attitude by stating, "Sincerely speaking, I was never disappointed with the result of any battle. Fighting the war we always think that there will be times when we lose and there will be times when we win, and we should not be too optimistic when we win or too disappointed when we lose. When we lose we must find out what caused us to lose and gain experience for the next time."[48]

10

VOICES FROM THE OTHER SIDE: THE GENERALS

Perhaps one of the best assessments of what soldiers think of their enemies is attributed to the Roman emperor Alus Vitellius, who after his victory over the troops of Otho at Bedricum in A.D. 69, is supposed to have said, "*Optime olere hostem occisum* [A dead enemy always smells good]." After a reign of only five months, poor Vitellius himself was stinking up the streets of Rome, the victim of assassins' knives, perhaps an object lesson to professional soldiers who coin deathless dictums.

While Vitellius' remark is undoubtedly true of some combatants' opinions of each other in every age, other, more respectful relationships have always existed between men on opposite sides of the battlefield. In the days of chivalry, knights were reputed to have saluted each other before engaging in mortal combat. During the American Civil War, Johnny Reb traded tobacco for Billy Yank's coffee during cease-fires, and relatives in uniforms of blue or gray often met between the lines to inquire of family news. On at least one Christmas during World War I, French and German soldiers laid down their weapons to serenade each other with holiday carols. Downed aviators in the same war were often treated to a hot meal and drinks in their enemy's officer mess before being transported to POW camps.

Despite these accounts of civilized behavior on the battlefield and of respect among enemies, the general opinion of men who face each other in combat is closer to that of Vitellius—hatred mixed with fear and occasionally a bit of grudging mutual respect. It is only after the passage of time, seasoned in a calm world and a long peace, that soldiers begin to remember their erstwhile enemies with something akin to respect or at least tolerance.

The civilized exchange between enemies of earlier wars was rare or nonexistent between opponents in Vietnam. No quarter was expected by the men of either side and usually it was not given. One of the few known instances of interaction on the battlefield occurred in the Central Highlands, near Pleiku, in 1967.[1] Even this incident, although it resulted in the saving, not the destruction of lives, appears to have been more an example of war weariness and spontaneity than an example of mutual respect or civility. On a steep mountainside a company of the U.S. 25th Infantry Division had a meeting engagement with an NVA unit of similar size and strength. Heavy clouds and a driving monsoon rain prevented the Americans from calling in air support. After more than three hours of intense fighting and heavy casualties on both sides, a brief moment of relative calm descended as the soldiers regrouped and prepared for the next attack. Suddenly one of the Americans shouted, "Hey, you sons of bitches, you quit fucking with us and we'll quit fucking with you!"

Someone on the other side apparently understood English and shouted a quick translation to his comrades. Without a further word or even a laugh, the few guns still firing became quiet. Both sides gathered their dead and wounded and withdrew.

Vietnam was a war different from others fought by the United States. Perhaps no aspect was as confusing, however, as the American public's opinion of its own military and of the enemy it faced. In previous wars, those in the uniforms of the U.S. armed forces were hailed as heroes and defenders of the greatest way of life in the world. Enemies were ridiculed and despised. During World War II, for example, newspapers and radio commonly referred to the enemy as "Japs," "Nips," and "Krauts," ethnic slurs that, if uttered today, would generate a storm of public indignation and cast severe opprobrium upon the head of any newscaster insensitive enough to use them.

During World War II Americans loved their President and respected the flag. Novelties were produced like the jackass with Hitler's head imposed on its body and ashtrays that encouraged smokers (there were a lot of them in those years) to "Put their butt out on the red meatball sphere symbol of Japan."

Not so during the Vietnam War. Flags of the VC/NVA flew defiantly at antiwar demonstrations on college campuses; all across the United States students burned the Stars and Stripes; movie actors, church leaders, newsmen, and politicians visited North Vietnam and returned with praise for the Revolution and disdain for the American soldier; Ho Chi Minh was compared favorably to George Washington while President Lyndon Johnson was damned in the same breath as Adolf Hitler.

While the VC/NVA, who used ambush, booby traps, torture, assassination, and terrorism as his way of making war, was praised as a hero by some Americans, the U.S. soldiers who referred to him as a "gook," "slant-eye," or "slope," were called racists and babykillers by those same righteous citizens. It should come as no surprise to anyone that during those dark years many American servicemen developed an antipathy for their own countrymen that sometimes exceeded the outrage they harbored for their Communist enemy.

Regardless of where their feelings were directed, the men who faced the Viet Cong and the NVA developed strong resentment and downright hatred for an enemy who killed their comrades and was a constant threat to their own survival. Nevertheless, soldiering then, as always, was a business where there was still room for respect toward a worthy opponent.

Although "gook" was the most common term used for the VC/NVA (indeed for the Vietnamese people as a whole), it was also common to call the VC "Victor Charles," or "Victor Charlie," using the letters V and C of the NATO phonetic alphabet. "Mr. Charles" or "Mr. Chuck," profoundly respectful terms, were also frequently used. Equal, indeed greater, respect was given to the troops from the North.

Soldiers must eventually give their enemy his due, if for no other reason than to justify the losses he inflicted on the battlefield. It is also natural for winners as well as losers to give their enemies credit for being worthy opponents.

Despite the passage of time, there is still no consensus by U.S. commanders and soldiers about the fighting ability, morale, discipline, and tactics of the Viet Cong and the NVA. Variety in the opinions of the leaders and men who fought the VC/NVA is as diverse as the attitudes about the war itself. Some comments are still tainted with the agony of spilled blood and bitter memories of lost comrades, but most reflect deep thinking and study of a war that is as perplexing and controversial as any ever fought by the United States.

The comments that follow are in many ways paradoxical. Some are at complete variance with others. But the sincerity of the remarks is beyond question, for they are accurate reflections of how these men saw their enemy during their time in the combat zone.

This is not the first survey of its kind. In September 1974, Brigadier General Douglas Kinnard circulated 173 questionnaires to U.S. Army general officers who had held command positions in Vietnam during 1965–1972. Sixty-four percent of the officers he queried returned completed questionnaires. It is interesting to note that General Kinnard's respondents rated the Viet Cong higher as a fighting force than the NVA; 23 percent thought the NVA "a force that left something to be desired," while only 6 percent rated the VC in those terms. Ninety percent of Kinnard's generals rated the VC (prior to Tet 1968) "adequate" to "skilled and tough fighters," while only 76 percent so rated the North Vietnamese Army.[2]

The following two chapters are taken from personal and telephone interviews or from correspondence with the commanders and the soldiers of U.S. units that participated in the war. One retired four-star general, writing in a shaky hand from his hospital bed, exerted great effort to respond in what proved to be his final days.

Still other responses served as a reminder that the war has indeed been over for a long time. Notes from families and executors reported that several of the high-ranking leaders during the war are now dead. One widow took the time to write shortly after her husband's death, not to tell of her personal loss, but to offer assurance of how much he would have liked to have participated had he lived.

The sad fact remains that despite the controversy surrounding the Vietnam War, many of those responsible for making the policy and leading the armies are dying in silence. Some former U.S. commanders apparently prefer not to take a role in the study of the war. Perhaps that reveals they were part of the problem at the time and feel it is best for their reputations to keep quiet. Several retired generals failed to respond to repeated written requests and even refused to return telephone calls. One, who commanded at the four-star level during the war, and who did briefly respond, stated, "At this point in time I don't have any insights that would be a useful contribution on this subject." Another, who commanded at the two-star level and was later promoted to full general, explained that he had several requests for comments about different aspects of the war and that "Since I am still fully employed I find I do not have the time to do these requests justice."

Fortunately, many former leaders and fighters of the war did share their experiences and insights on the war and the VC/NVA. Their responses follow.

GEN. (RET.) W. B. ROSSON

General Rosson served a total of six years in Vietnam, with his first tour in 1954–1955. During the primary years of U.S. involvement in the war, Rosson served as Chief of Staff, MACV; Commanding General, Task Force Oregon (later the Americal Division); Commanding General, I Field Force; Commanding General, Provisional Corps, Vietnam (later XXIV Corps); Acting Commander, III Marine Amphibious Force; and Deputy Commander, USMACV.

Rosson goes into far more detail than the average respondent. His remarks are so poignant, however, that they are included in their virtual entirety. According to Rosson:[3]

Strategy

The ultimate objective, to which both the VC and NVA subscribed, was to establish control over all of Indochina. This translated into the strategic offensive.

The heart of the strategy was Mao Tse-tung's concept, dating to the 1930s, of protracted war. As articulated by General Vo Nguyen Giap in his 1961 book, *People's War, People's Army*, protracted war involved three phases:

    1. Contention—the weaker force is on the strategic defensive, tactical offensive.

    2. Equilibrium—both sides contend equally.

    3. General counteroffensive—The weaker power gains superiority and launches a counteroffensive that forces the stronger side onto the strategic defensive and tactical defensive.

The NVA achieved phase three during the First Indochina War, 1946–1954, culminating in victory over the French at Dien Binh Phu. In contrast the VC were in phases one and two from 1954 until the early 1960s, even later in some areas.

As seen by the Vietnamese Communists, again reflecting

Maoist dogma, the people comprise an instrument of war. They must be organized and motivated to engage in a "struggle" (*dau tranh*). The latter is composed of two inseparable parts: "political struggle" (*dau tranh chinh tri*) and "armed struggle" (*dau tranh va trang*). The first part commands highest priority and is regarded as the key to victory.

Returning to the three phases of protracted war strategy:

In phase one, guerrilla warfare is emphasized. Guerrillas attack only when superiority is assured.

In phase two, larger units are formed. They add to guerrilla activity and attack as units when superiority is assured. During this phase Giap calls for initiation of "mobile warfare" by the larger units—wider-ranging operations that retain a guerrilla character.

In phase three, mobile warfare is conducted by increasingly larger units until it assumes conventional-warfare dimensions. Guerrilla warfare continues.

In 1965 and again in 1966, Giap described his strategy for South Vietnam as being one of "strategic mobility." Also in 1966, he spoke of an "offensive-defensive" version of strategic mobility wherein major NVA and VC forces were positioned in South Vietnam near border sanctuaries. These forces would attempt to attract friendly forces into previously prepared killing zones.

Interestingly, Giap also stated in 1965 that he was employing a "regular force strategy," but this was interpreted on the U.S. side to signify types of tactical operations, e.g., numerous small, simultaneous attacks; carefully planned and executed battalion and regimental attacks.

Both in 1972 (Easter Offensive) and 1975 (Spring Victory Offensive), Hanoi's strategy was called "high-technology armed struggle." Apparently this denoted use of major amounts of Soviet armor, artillery, motor transport, other weapons/equipment and ammunition, coupled with the POL pipeline and depot assets of the Ho Chi Minh Trail.

Political struggle made full use of psychological warfare. In the First Indochina War it was used effectively to turn French opinion in the Métropole against continuation of the war. In the Second Indochina War it was used effectively to fuel antiwar sentiment in the United States. Although U.S. authorities claimed that Hanoi was pursuing a strategy of attrition, Hanoi never acknowledged this to be the case. On the other hand, the North Vietnamese leadership believed that the United States was not prepared to accept a long war of attrition. For this reason they exploited the psychological theme that they were determined to fight on indefinitely. At the same time, they indoctrinated the people, as part of political struggle, to accept heavy sacrifices while "waiting the Americans out."

During the latter part of 1967, Hanoi elected to change the offensive-defensive version of Giap's strategic mobility to a new formulation calling for creation of a general uprising through simultaneous attack of major cities and key provincial capitals. The result was the Tet Offensive launched early in 1968. Struggle dogma held that a general uprising by the people would mark the culmination of successful political and armed struggle, but the significant thing about the 1967 change is that it followed not from success, but from a gamble aimed at reversing the losses through surprise and psychological impact. Although the new strategy failed militarily, it produced a political struggle (psychological) victory for Hanoi.

Tactics

In the realm of tactics, I do not propose to do more than acknowledge enemy expertise in terrorist tactics. Developed by the Viet Minh and carried out later in South Vietnam by local-force guerrillas, those tactics embraced a careful blend of psychological and physical coercion. A basic tenet—whether for assembling villagers for a propaganda lecture, conducting a people's trial, assassinating a local official, attacking a police station or a Popular Forces post, recruiting by force, or operating a tax-collecting post on a road or canal—was to hit, run, and hide. For armed attacks, complete superiority was a prerequisite. Beheading of officials was a standard technique.

My experience [based on field duty with ARVNs and Americans in all four regions of South Vietnam] armed me with an appreciation for the place and importance within the Mao/Giap doctrine of need for secure base areas and for the organization of forces at three levels—local, regional, and national. In the case of the base areas, these were essential to the marshaling, training, indoctrination, administration, supply, and refitting of regional and national (formally called regular) forces. They also equipped local forces with arms, ammunition, and explosives as required. A number of these bases were located in remote, sparsely inhabited areas within South Vietnam; others were situated in sanctuaries in Laos, Cambodia, and southern North Vietnam. All came to be "fed" primarily by the Ho Chi Minh

Trail. (Seaborne infiltration of supplies and infiltration through the Cambodian port of Sihanoukville had been used earlier.)

With respect to the three-tier force structure, local (hamlet, village, district) units operated only near their homes—some as guerrillas. Normally they were of platoon size, and were composed largely of VC. Regional (provincial and regional) units theoretically could be used anywhere in their region, but customarily operated in a single area. Originally VC, they absorbed so many NVA replacements as to become VC in name only. These units were of company, battalion, and regimental size, although prior to Tet 1968 there had been two VC divisions, the 7th (Region IV) and the 9th (Region III). The regular forces, largely NVA as the war progressed, could be and were used anywhere in South Vietnam. They were regiments, divisions, and appropriate supporting elements.

As in the case of guerrillas, larger enemy units employed the doctrine of hit, run, and hide. Major operations normally were initiated from a secure base, with forces returning to the base upon conclusion of the operation. Prior to "hitting," VC and NVA units placed major emphasis on obtaining and exploiting intelligence on all aspects of the target area. Weeks, even months, might be devoted to satisfying intelligence requirements. Heavy reliance was placed on ground reconnaissance, but of equal—if not greater—importance was reliance upon agent networks within the South Vietnamese Armed Forces and within various categories of Vietnamese civilians employed by U.S. forces. The agents or informants probably were of greatest use in providing the VC and NVA with information on our operations, but there can be no doubt that they facilitated the enemy's target-analysis tasks.

An important characteristic of VC and NVA tactics is found in Mao/Giap emphasis on the "set-piece battle." It was this fetish, of course, that required the strong accent on intelligence. By the same token, it required methodical, time-consuming preparation.

To round out my overview of VC and NVA tactics, I consider that the enemy must be credited with expert employment of mines and booby traps, with advancing use of tunnels and underground shelters to a level of effectiveness that approached if not exceeded that of the Japanese in World War II, and with making the hours of darkness a valued ally in preparing for and in conducting tactical operations. When one considers that for most of the war they were limited in the main to foot mobility (and sampans to some extent), that they enjoyed limited direct fire support, telecommunications and logistic wherewithal, and were under extensive air surveillance, one must acknowledge that their tactics necessarily had to be simple and within their capabilities. An increasingly difficult problem for them revolved around the "hide" portion of their hit, run, and hide triad. The potential devastating effect of massed artillery fire and aerial attack by B-52s and fighters required them to keep on the move and to have recourse to well-protected positions in the base areas.

Morale

Not infrequently during the American involvement in Vietnam, U.S. intelligence estimates erred with respect to assessment of the VC and NVA morale. The reason, in my estimation, lay in a tendency to judge enemy morale by Western, especially American, standards. This was true of the off-hand views on the subject held by our officers and enlisted men. We found it difficult to accept that the VC and NVA soldier could be content under conditions of jungle living, limited rations, few creature comforts, and the ever-present danger of artillery and air attack. We were certain that his knowledge that he was in the war for the duration—in contrast to our one-year tour—was demoralizing.

What we failed to appreciate for a considerable period was that the typical VC and NVA soldier was a peasant whose premilitary life-style was one of hardship and privation that helped to prepare him for the rigors of field service. Moreover, we found it hard to visualize the pivotal influence on morale of the enemy's system of indoctrination and control.

Indoctrination, as we came to know (and I should have remembered more clearly from my discussions with former Viet Minh in 1955), was based not on force-feeding the recruit with Communist dogma, but on the theme of nationhood for all of Vietnam. Vietnamese nationalism, easily explained and understood, was held to be a sacred, virtuous cause to which every Vietnamese was duty-bound to sacrifice himself should that be required, i.e., country before self. Victory in the struggle for nationhood for all of Vietnam was proclaimed as being inevitable.

VC and NVA morale, it is fair to say, appears to have been sustained under conditions of dire stress by belief in the rightness of the cause, the requirement for sacrifice, and the inevitability of victory. It was sustained as well by the individual soldier's identification with a small group (the cell) that met his social needs and with which he shared the good and the bad. My own experience, stemming from direct observation, discussion, interrogation of prisoners, and study of documents, led me to conclude that VC and NVA morale was subject to ups and downs that had some parallels within our own armed forces. Examples:

—Success in battle and/or membership in a unit that had amassed a record of success enhanced individual pride and exerted a positive effect on morale. From the time of introduction of NVA units (as opposed to cadre) into South Vietnam beginning in 1964 until the end of the third Tet wave in 1968, NVA personnel were imbued with confidence—even with a sense of superiority—born of earlier Viet Minh success fighting the French.

—Poor leadership could lead to low morale, as could extended periods of inadequate food, shortages of supplies, illness and wounds (especially under circumstances in which medical care was limited), unfavorable weather, and the shock imposed by B-52 strikes and napalm attacks.

—Some prisoners expressed disillusionment over the length of time involved in achieving inevitable victory. Others chafed under forced recruitment.

—Although both VC and NVA emphasized bestowal of awards following important actions, failure to receive recognition produced low morale on the part of some.

—Humiliation brought on by the standard Communist practice of requiring self-confession and self-criticism before one's comrades had a decidedly bad effect on morale.

All things considered, I regard VC and NVA morale as having been remarkable. Significantly, several of my senior South Vietnamese military associates praised their adversary's morale. Almost without exception, however, they maintained that it was the product of propaganda, iron discipline, and fear of punishment for dereliction of duty. They attributed the small number of VC and NVA deserters to these same factors, and to the fact that both the VC and North Vietnamese authorities threatened reprisals against the families of deserters. I personally believed the low desertion rate was attributable to sound morale—primarily belief in the cause and the willingness to sacrifice for it—and to fear of what would happen to one who fell into enemy hands.

Discipline

No one familiar with VC and NVA combat performance during the years of U.S. involvement would argue that battlefield discipline was not one of their strongest suits. The example possibly cited most often in support of this contention pertains to the prompt and thorough manner in which enemy units removed dead, wounded, and weapons—usually under fire—when disengaging from an action. I was familiar with many instances of this indicator of discipline, but noted that during the 1968–1972 period, when NVA replacements became progressively younger, their "policing" of the battlefield was less complete, sometimes nonexistent.

In my view, the system of indoctrination and control (prominently the three-man cell and the close relationship between leaders and the led at the small-unit level) undergirded VC and NVA discipline. Additionally, the emphasis on meticulous preparation for operations unquestionably enhanced cohesion, confidence, and sense of purpose. While I cannot deny that fear of punishment played a part, I regard it as having been a secondary factor.

As mentioned earlier, some of my senior South Vietnam military associates maintained that VC and NVA discipline depended in strong measure on fear of punishment for dereliction of duty. A good many on the U.S. side held this view as well. Implicit in this position was the belief that liberal use was made by the enemy of on-the-spot or early follow-on execution of those who ran from the enemy, failed to press an attack, malingered, etc. While interrogation and documents produced reports of such action, I interpreted them to apply only to flagrant cases.

In the domain of fear, I am persuaded that the VC and NVA soldiers were not unlike our own in encountering fear of fear, fear of violent death, and fear of punishment, notably that of self-confession and self-criticism. Their system and ours provided means for enabling the individual to cope with these problems.

As a further point on discipline, one recalls that for centuries the structure of Vietnamese society has been such that the vast majority of the people has been subject to authoritative rule. Although revolts have occurred, obedience to authority is more the norm than the exception. One of the more thought-provoking questions of the war has to do with how North Vietnam was able to exploit this characteristic—a key element of discipline—to its advantage whereas South Vietnam was less successful in doing so.

Fighting ability

Generally speaking, I found the VC and NVA soldier to be tough, courageous, well-motivated, dedicated, and competent. His overall quality diminished during the U.S. involvement due primarily to heavy combat losses. Units on the whole were well led, well trained, reliable. Commanders displayed considerable ingenuity in making do with little and in overcoming the harshness of jungle camp life. Unit effectiveness also diminished as the war progressed and as casualties took their toll. The VC and NVA excelled in the guerrilla role, and were able to surmount the challenge of operating and surviving in difficult terrain—jungle, mountain, and delta. The VC, for obvious reasons, operated more easily among the people in populated areas than did the NVA, but once NVA personnel became acquainted with an area they blended in effectively.

One came to admire, possibly envy, the VC and NVA for their stealth, mastery of camouflage, ability to move and operate at night, noise and light discipline, and removal of bodies and weapons from the battlefield. They were impressive at times in breaching wire obstacles by stealth, demolition, or wave assault. Conduct of ambushes became a specialty.

Some have contended that the VC and NVA soldier's fighting ability was bolstered by his Oriental stoicism and patience. While I agree with this view, I cannot recall its having been applied to the South Vietnamese fighting man with the same degree of conviction. In any case, the VC and NVA demonstrated convincingly their ability to withstand the physical and psychological hardships of campaigning "for the duration" in an environment of uncommon severity and danger.

GEN. (RET.) WILLIAM E. DEPUY

General Depuy was the J-3 (Operations Officer) of MACV in 1964–1965 and commanded the 1st Infantry Division in 1966–1967. Depuy states:[4]

The VC had the high motivation of guerrillas fighting in their own communities, on their own ground among their own fully supportive families, friends, and compatriots. Each engagement was planned, prepared, and executed in minute, careful detail in such a manner that almost always guaranteed success and safe disengagement. The guerrilla had almost total knowledge of the local situation and local morale including penetrations of government forces—particularly the Regional Forces/Popular Forces.

They also knew through the village, district, and sometimes the province level agent penetrators all about the most likely reaction and reinforcement plans. Thus they could use district companies and even provincial battalions (such as the Phu Loi Battalion in Binh Doung north of Saigon) to ambush relief forces.

The VC main-force regiments and divisions (the best example of which was the 9th VC Division north of Saigon) fought large engagements but in the same patterns as the local guerrillas insofar as intelligence and local support are concerned. The NVA tried to emulate the VC main forces but didn't have the same local connections and thus were launched into operations with less intelligence and more conventional logistical support. The NVA fought well (as bravely) but were less effective than the VC main forces.

Interestingly, VC penetrations of perimeter defenses of Special Forces camps, district headquarters or U.S. infantry night defensive positions used suppression followed by single-point penetration by sapper parties—all exactly as Erwin Rommel did against Italians and Rumanians in infantry attacks in World War I.

Of course, eventually the VC were reduced in strength by the attrition (dirty word) of a decade of combat and were progressively replaced by NVA fillers down to local level. By 1972—the Easter Offensive—the VC and NVA were indistinguishable.

Both VC and NVA were motivated patriots fighting for their country against "colonialist" forces. Individual VC/NVA motivation was enhanced and enforced by the three-man cell system and the practice of self-criticism.

The NVA "strategy" was to win the war at whatever cost in time, lives, and effort. The presence of seventeen VC/NVA divisions in the final battle for Saigon attests to this determination. We (the Americans) still had a guerrilla-war mentality long after the NVA turned it into a main-force war—Tet-68, Easter-72, etc.

The only antidote available to carefully planned surprise attacks was quick reaction via airmobility. We eventually defeated (destroyed) the VC this way and did much damage to NVA as well. But their system of refusing combat—returning to sanctuaries—permitted them to regulate their losses to a tolerable level. Even so these amounted to over 800,000 by their own tacit admission. Because they metered their losses, we could not win a war of attrition in any reasonable time. Our military proposal to cut the Ho Chi Minh Trail physically was the only alternative operational concept that might have won the war short of an invasion of North Vietnam.

LT. GEN. (RET.) JULIAN J. EWELL

General Ewell was the commander of the 9th Infantry Division in 1968–1969 and commanded the II Field Force in 1969–1970. He is also the author of *Sharpening the Combat Edge*. Ewell writes:[5]

To write about the VC/NVA is quite an ambitious task. I don't consider myself an expert on the subjects, which are quite different. We (the United States) saw them both very dimly. Combat is a very confused situation at best and the Vietnam experience more so.

The VC were essentially local. Each province was different due to terrain, the people, the opposing forces, etc. In addition, the VC varied from cocks of the walk to trying to stay alive, so their postures varied widely. For example, Xuan Loc [northeast of Saigon] was very complicated. The mixture of real jungle, scrub jungle, villages, North Vietnamese Catholic refugees, rubber plantations, and the lack of strong Allied pressure made it possible for the VC to be fairly aggressive.

Long An, south of Saigon, was quite different. The VC there had been under attack for years. As a result in '68–'69 they laid low and it was easy to skate over them. Eventually we broke their "armor plate" and tore them up.

Dinh Thuong was entirely different. The SVN (RF/PF) and the VC evidently struck a bargain and it was ostensibly "peaceful."

Kien Hoa was unique. The VC ruled the roost for some years and were quite cocky and overconfident. Once we put the pressure on them it was like shooting ducks in a barrel. At their peak the U.S. forces reached an elimination ratio of 158 to 1.

Another factor that made for variability was the effect of attrition on the VC. If they suffered heavy losses they began to come apart at the seams. If they were successful their combat effectiveness improved.

So, in summary, the VC varied from place to place, from time to time and from situation to situation.

Their organization was a pyramid of hamlet and village guerrillas, district companies, provincial battalions, and in some places main-force battalions and in some areas NVA units. The infrastructure also played a role—in some areas they displaced the government, in others they were forced underground. The peasants were in the middle and supported whoever could deliver or could force them to do so. If a lower unit couldn't handle the local situation, a higher and larger unit was brought in to rectify it.

Tactically, the VC would lie out in the countryside, reconnoiter and retrain, and periodically mount a night attack. If located ('68–'69) they would attempt to evade, fighting a rearguard action. They were good at moving at night and in the use of booby traps. They had plenty of modern weapons (AK-47s, etc.); however, they were not very good shots.

Once we got a handle on the VC, which was not easy, they were no problem. We used good night ambushes, good daylight patrolling, etc., etc., which produced kill ratios of 50 to 80 to 1. The ARVNs were not able to keep up the pressure but were fairly good in a head-to-head fight. The best ARVN division, the 25th, achieved a kill ratio of 25 to 1—pretty good. SVN airborne was not bad and their marines were fair plus but fought like U.S. Marines.

The national mobilization in 1968 also had an effect on the VC by cutting their supply of young recruits. Also, heavy pressure generated lots of ralliers (Chieu Hois), which reduced their support.

One factor that is often overlooked was the pervasive Communist intelligence organization. Some U.S. units coordinated their offensive operations in detail with the ARVN and/or local GVN. Due to agent penetration, their plans sooner or later got to the targeted units who could then try to evade. The alternative was to very carefully conduct minimum essential coordination so that the actual plan was not disclosed.

In some areas the Communists had primitive but adequate SIGINT [signal intelligence] monitoring units that could monitor Allied radio nets. If radio discipline was poor, these units could pick up useful tactical information.

Now to the NVA. Around Saigon (mostly in Cambodia) there were three NVA divisions (two of which were called VC) and several independent regiments. As you would expect, they were more homogeneous than the VC. While not as elusive as the VC, they were tougher. Their original strategy, if you could call it that, was to lay down supplies near their objectives, then to march down [from Cambodia], resupply, and attack. This was the so-called "high-point" concept—Tet, February 1968 mini-Tet, May–June 1968 campaign, and so on.

After this approach petered out, they would refit in Cambodia and make sorties into SVN. Some units attempted to maintain themselves in forward positions. The best tactic was to interdict their LOCs [lines of communications] with automatic ambushes [unattended claymore mines rigged in a series much like a booby trap] and patrol them out of their bases. Most of the NVA units were in jungle areas (scrub jungles in the main) as they could no longer maintain themselves in the open.

By the '69–'70 period they were beginning to run short of experienced officers and NCOs and did not fight as well as before. Of course, by then, many VC units were receiving NVA fillers and, as a result, began to react like NVA units.

NVA morale was quite high; few if any rallied. VC morale was good but if under heavy pressure they reverted to a passive evasion role. Their deserters generally just disappeared into the countryside. Of course, hard-core VC could only be converted six feet under.

MAJ. GEN. (RET.) ELLIS W. WILLIAMSON

General Williamson commanded the 173rd Airborne Brigade for two years while it trained in Okinawa and led it into Vietnam in May 1965. He left the brigade in 1966 only to return to Vietnam in 1968 to command the 25th Infantry Division. Williamson states:[6]

The VC and NVA were both very lousy, pitifully stupid fighters—period.

We of the United States, principally through our own news media, played them up as something different. A few thoughts to back that up will confirm what I believe.

First, let's give them credit where it is due. Some of them, but damned few, really believed. Very early in the game we picked up a diary in which a soldier had written, "The Americans have been so overpowering we have had to stay down in this cold, damp tunnel for over two weeks without even seeing the sunlight once. We cannot cook our rice. All we have had is cold uncooked food. I have not been dry the entire time. I am so uncomfortable, but at least I am free.''

The enemy was often given credit for ''fading away into the jungle'' when he wanted to. We had an operation close to Vung Tau. A group of American correspondents came up and reported that when flying in they had seen large groups of enemy just a few hundred yards to the north of us. We changed our plans and swung over there to check out the area. There was no enemy in the area. The next day there were several big articles in our papers about how the enemy evaded us and slipped away into the jungle. We could not confirm that there ever was an enemy force in the area.

We had a pitched battle in which we literally mauled the enemy force. The only way he saved any of his men was by driving women and children between us and his fleeing cowards. They even dropped their weapons and ammunition. The press again gave them credit for ''evading us by fading away into the jungle''—at their will.

An entire enemy battalion came down to the Cu Chi area to conduct ''tunnel warfare.'' A book [*The Tunnels of Cu Chi* by Tom Mangold and John Penycate, Random House, 1985] was written about how brave they were, fighting quote ''to the last four men.'' The two British authors failed to mention that at one time we had over 60 percent of their entire strength in our POW cages and that most of them were deserters— some of whom volunteered and showed us the locations of their comrades. Some even tried to join our side. The same book tells of the tunnel fighters who threw a bomb into one of our recreation centers, when just a little research would have shown that it was a hand grenade from an American escapee from a psycho ward of the hospital who was trying to kill himself. He did blow his legs off. He put the hand grenade under his own chair.

During their big bust in July and August 1968 in the Tay Ninh area we destroyed an entire battalion that refused to surrender or to move. It turned out that they were told to assemble at a specific map coordinate. Whoever issued the order did not know that we had Rome-Plowed* the woods away and what he thought was a wooded area in which they could hide was then an open

---

*The Caterpillar D7E tractor fitted with a 4,600-lb. blade used in land-clearing operations. So called because it was manufactured by the Rome Caterpillar Company of Rome, Georgia.

field. They could have had reasonable concealment just a few yards away.

Their communications were awful. As shown above, they would issue orders and start off without the capability of changing if the situation turned out to be different.

In the daylight we could fight the VC and NVA with a casualty ratio in our favor of about 30 to 1, sometimes even better; however, the press continued to say that the night belonged to the enemy. He could not afford to operate except at night and it was so much to our advantage to fight him in daylight that we often waited for light when we had him bottled up.

We were so wrong in not admitting that many of the local people were supporting the other side. In one instance, after a small engagement, the local civilians came running out repeating that American gunfire had killed the local Catholic priest. His body was there with a bullet hole that entered his chest and went out his back. Our men checked him and found that there was no hole in his shirt or cloak. Local authorities checked and found that he was the commander of a VC unit and had been murdered by his own men.

Once we got a report that our helicopters were diving just to terrorize local civilians and had dived so low that the skids of one of the helicopters had actually cut a lady's head off. Investigation showed that no helicopter had even been in that area all day.

One night an enemy column walked right into the position of one of my machine guns. The entire column continued walking to their deaths out of sheer ignorance. It was dark and nobody told them to change directions.

As you can see it was sickening to fight such an inept enemy. In my two and a half years in command of large units that were fighting this enemy, not one single small unit of mine was ever forced off a position and not once did the enemy prevent our going to any location that we started toward.

I realize full well that an individual rifleman or even a platoon leader viewing the situation from his level may see it somewhat differently from the way I have described it. I have personally been wounded by enemy gunfire five different times. I believe I know what I am talking about.

BRIG. GEN. (RET.) JAMES S. TIMOTHY

General Timothy commanded the 1st Brigade, 101st Airborne Division (Separate) during the last six months of 1965. During the first half of 1966 he was the Senior Adviser II Corps (ARVN) in Pleiku. He returned to Vietnam in June 1968 and was the Assistant Division Commander of the 9th Infantry Division, followed again by being the Senior Adviser II Corps (ARVN) until January 1970. According to Timothy:[7]

I wish to elaborate on my highly favorable assessment of the VC and NVA that follows. Certain clear advantages were held by the enemy that contributed to their success. The government of North Vietnam:

—Faced an alliance whose commands were independent, whose cooperation was weak, and with one force, the ARVN, manifestly deficient in fighting ability.

—The people of Vietnam had a long history of opposing any conquerors; first Imperial China—from whom they won their independence—then the French, whom they finally defeated despite our material support of the French army. The NVN government, through the VC, were highly successful in portraying the United States as another "colonial" power and the Mandarin-controlled GVN and ARVN as mere puppets. The result, as later borne out, was that the GVN could never win the support of the majority of their own people.

—Confronted a U.S. government whose resources in manpower, material, and trained armed forces were overwhelming, yet, paradoxically, never gave its armed forces the mission of winning the war. The results of this policy led to our disgraceful abandonment of the SVN people and to their overwhelming defeat—without our promised material and air support. In my view, if the U.S. government was not prepared to defeat the NVA (possibly because of fear of the Chicoms supported by the USSR) then not one U.S. fighting unit should ever have been sent to SVN. Once committing our troops to the mission of preventing NVA to invade and conquer SVN, our gutless President and his gutless advisers in State, DoD, and NSC proceeded to mandate restrictions on our forces that prevented even the accomplishment of that mission: the vacillating air missions vs. NVN, failure to bomb military targets in Hanoi and Haiphong (until the end!), their key bridges, and the dikes of the Red River; prohibition of "hot pursuit" into NVN, Laos, and

Cambodia; failure until the last days of our participation in the fighting to send ground forces to cut the Ho Chi Minh Trail, etc.

The morale, discipline and fighting ability of the VC were excellent. They admirably fashioned their tactics to take advantage of ARVN weaknesses—poor leadership, poor morale, and generally poor fighting ability of the SVN Army (with few exceptions, e.g. airborne troops, 1st Infantry Division, and a few armor units) and their "home guard" troops. Conversely, the tactics of the VC were restricted to guerrilla warfare to minimize weaknesses—no air cover, little artillery or rocket support, and no motor transport.

The strategy of the VC, presumably directed by the NVA, was also excellent. They successfully maintained control of most of the population outside the cities, held key supply routes, supply dumps, etc., and controlled most harvests.

The morale, discipline, and fighting ability of the NVA were superior. Against the ARVN there was generally no contest because of ARVN weaknesses cited above. Despite ARVN and U.S. air superiority, the NVA generally won close-fought battles against the ARVN, thus leading the U.S. command to take over the majority role in opposing NVA main-force units—in retrospect, I believe an unfortunate decision. Against U.S. forces, the NVA regulars performed admirably—considering their lack of air support and inferiority in armor, artillery, and motor transport. Again, in retrospect, their decisive superiority vs. both the United States and the ARVN was their strategy in accurately assessing the opposing political leaders.

As an example of the items discussed above, I cite one incident, which, according to Army records, constituted the first conquest of a VC main-force unit by U.S. Army elements during the VN conflict. In mid-September 1965, the 1st Brigade, 101st Airborne Division, while charged with the mission of protecting the movement of the 1st Cavalry Division by road from Qui Nhon through the An Khe Pass to An Khe, conducted Operation GIBRALTAR. Based on intelligence reports, we sent the 2nd Battalion, 502nd Airborne Infantry, on an air-assault mission beyond the river at the foot of the An Khe Pass. We landed on a VC main-force battalion that was in training. U.S. forces were completely surrounded and, as but one and one-half companies were successfully landed with the first and only airlift, we spent the remainder of the day reinforcing their artillery support and obtaining massive air support. Not until the following day were supporting infantry, advancing by ground and airlift, able to relieve elements of the 2/502nd. When the enemy finally withdrew on the third day of battle, they left 226 KIA [killed in action] on the field. U.S. casualties were around 65 including 28 KIA.

I can express great admiration for the fighting ability and leadership of that VC battalion. Despite massive artillery support and overwhelming air support furnished by the brigade, the 1st Cav Division, and air units from not only the USAF but also U.S. Navy offshore carriers (luckily we were the only "show" in country during this battle), the VC hung in there for three days with no artillery support and little rocket support.

It is because of the massive and prompt-reacting U.S. artillery and air support that, in my opinion, U.S. ground forces never lost a "battalion-size" fight against the VC or the NVA. In larger-scale battles against the NVA, I cite the 1st Air Cav Division's victory over an NVA division in the Ia Drang Valley in November 1965 and the USMC/1st Cav victory over NVA divisions at Khe Sanh near the Laotian/NVN border in I Corps in early 1968.

A second incident occurred in spring 1970 at an ARVN fire-support base west of Kontum defended by a reinforced company. During a stormy night VC and/or NVA, estimated to be around twenty men, sneaked undetected through the wire, spiked four 105mm howitzers, and killed or wounded thirty-five ARVN soldiers. Only three enemy bodies were found after the fight.

A third incident involved highly trained and courageous NVN underwater demolition teams that blew a critically important bridge over a wide estuary of the Mekong between Saigon and My Tho one night in November 1968. Anyone who has served in the Mekong Delta region knows of its vicious tides. The bridge was defended by an ARVN company who employed nets in the river and searchlights, and shot or grenaded anything suspicious. In the face of the tides and the defenses, the UDT was able to reach the understructure and plant explosives that completely destroyed the bridge—thus cutting the main artery to the Delta for over two months before the bridge could be replaced.

LT. GEN. (RET.) WILLIAM J. MCCAFFREY

General McCaffrey was the Deputy Commanding General of
the U.S. Army Vietnam (USARV) in 1970–1972. McCaffrey
states:[8]

I arrived in Vietnam in April of 1970. The VC was a dimin-
ishing force at that time. The ranks of units that were serious
military threats were filled with North Vietnamese. I can't remember a major threat by any VC unit. They were still capable
of assassinations, small-scale raids, and so forth but the military
threat was the NVA.

My opinion of the NVA was that they reflected the revolutionary zeal of the great independence movements of the past.
They were convinced that they fought for the freedom of the
people and that no sacrifice that could be asked of them was too
great. They maintained adequate morale through tactical defeat
after defeat, relying on the righteousness of their cause and the
inevitable lack of commitment on the part of their opponents to
give them the ultimate victory. Considering the state of technical
competence of the society from which they came, they fought
very well against a technologically superior society. They rapidly adopted tactics and techniques designed to diminish the
effectiveness of their opponent's weaponry. They exploited the
advantage they possessed and hung in there until they won. They
were especially effective off of the battlefield. They convinced
the American electorate, or at least large parts of it, that a to-
talitarian government was preferable to a democratic one.

The political skill of the Communist government of North
Vietnam in portraying their cause in terms that would elicit the
support of liberal Americans must be judged one of the most
successful in history. They oppressed the Catholic Church and
somehow secured the support of a large number of American
Roman Catholic clergy. They savagely suppressed any movement that seemed to diverge from the official party line and were
supported by large numbers of academics, students, and clergy
in the United States and around the world. They were good
soldiers but they were world-class propagandists. They won in
the media that which they could not win on the battlefield. Having won the right to govern they are now demonstrating that an
authoritarian government, however effective it may be to wage
war, fails miserably to meet the needs of its people in times of
peace.

LT. GEN. (RET.) ELVY B. ROBERTS

General Roberts commanded the 1st Cavalry Division in 1969–1970. Roberts writes:[9]

In 1965–1966 the morale of the VC seemed high. However, the morale, discipline, tactics, and fighting ability were progressively eroded and seemed lacking in purpose and direction through succeeding years. By late 1969 the VC as such was not a force to be reckoned with.

The same appraisal is generally true concerning the NVA; however, this varied considerably between units with which the 1st Cav and ARVN units were confronted in War Zones C and D. By the summer of 1968 through 1970, there seemed to be little direction and purpose to their operations above company or perhaps battalion level. It always mystified me how small units seemed to be laced together in senseless attacks against our fire bases.

When captured prisoners were interviewed they had no idea what they were doing except that being in a strange country they felt the option of sticking together gave them the only hope of ever getting back to the North. By the fall of 1969 through the spring of 1970, neither the NVA nor VC could mount an effective military operation worthy of the name. In fact our intercept of the letter carriers coming down the various trails dealt with instructions not to get involved in a fight with U.S. units, as they were winning their objectives at the conference table in Paris. This is not to say, however, that there were not some low-level attacks against our well-fortified fire bases that caused painful results on both sides.

LT. GEN. (RET.) WILLARD PEARSON

General Pearson, a combat veteran of World War II and Korea, commanded a brigade in the 101st Airborne Division in 1966 and organized the MACV command post in I Corps during Tet of 1968.

In 1974, as a part of the Department of the Army's *Vietnam Studies*, Pearson wrote, "The enemy was tough, versatile, tenacious, and cunning. He possessed strong entrenchments in villages, mountain hideouts, and jungle redoubts. He was difficult to find and identify. At one end of the spectrum he merged into the civilian population as an agent or guerrilla or civil official wearing no uniform, unarmed, and supported by a military political organization. At the other end of the spectrum he was a uniformed member of the regular North Vietnamese Army. The North Vietnamese and Viet Cong fighters possessed as much courage and motivation as any foe to face the American soldier. They proved a formidable adversary."[10]

More recently, Pearson adds:

The morale and discipline of the VC was very high. Reason: They were fighting for their country. The NVA were excellent for the same reasons. Nationalism is a great factor in a war where the goal is to unite a country. Ho Chi Minh was their George Washington. He provided a source of inspiration, protected by a sanctuary, to carry on the war to unite their country.[11]

GEN. (RET.) WILLIAM C. WESTMORELAND

General Westmoreland commanded MACV from 1964 to 1968 and USARV from 1965 to 1968. Concerning the VC/NVA Westmoreland states, "I refer you to my book *A Soldier Reports*."[12] Of particular note in Westmoreland's biography concerning the enemy is the following description:

As part of the tendency to deprecate allies, many Americans also tend to see our enemy as twelve feet tall. The VC and the North Vietnamese were wily, tenacious, persevering, and courageous to the point of fanaticism—the way he supplied himself, for example, through the most primitive methods: cargo bicycle, ox cart, corvée labor, elephant, sampan, floating supplies down rivers. Yet they were also human. They too blundered; they sacrificed themselves needlessly and often foolishly. Any American commander who took the same vast losses as General Giap would have been sacked overnight.

In evaluating the performance of the North Vietnamese soldier, Americans should ask, "What choice did he have?" Many a North Vietnamese prisoner trembled in the conviction that his murder at the hands of his captors was inevitable, for that he had been taught to expect. Many captured soldiers had tattoos on their bodies bearing the slogan, "Born in the North to die in the South." They told of funeral ceremonies in their honor before they left their home villages.[13]

MAJ. GEN. (RET.) PAUL F. SMITH

General Smith commanded the 173rd Airborne Brigade in 1966. Smith recalls:[14]

In the context in which we consider morale as a factor affecting the performance of our soldiers, I do not believe morale to have been important in measuring performance of the VC soldier. I believe indoctrination and discipline induced subjugation of all personal feelings.

Discipline within the VC was outstanding until a situation arose that had not been covered in instructions or indoctrination—then it broke down.

VC small-unit tactics lacked the element of fire and maneuver. This was probably so because the VC units were not designed for confrontational warfare nor were they structured or trained to engage organized, aggressive, well-controlled and supplied enemy forces. Their hit-and-run, ambush, infiltration, and harassing tactics were outstanding—particularly against the impatient American. Their lack of small-unit commo equipment had a lot to do with their tactics and lack of flexibility.

I cannot comment on the NVA as I don't recall that my unit had sufficient contact with NVA forces to allow me to develop opinions firsthand.

MAJ. GEN. (RET.) GEORGE S. ECKHARDT

General Eckhardt commanded the 9th Infantry Division in 1966–1967 and was the Senior U.S. Adviser in IV Corps from 1967 to 1969. Eckhardt states:[15]

In 1966 in III Corps, I thought the VC were well trained, highly motivated, and well disciplined. After the 1968 Tet Offensive, morale, discipline, and tactics deteriorated as the VC were replaced by recruits from North Vietnam. As a result the pacification efforts in IV Corps succeeded more rapidly even after the 9th Division was inactivated (August 1969) and the fighting was being done almost entirely by the ARVN.

I had little direct experience with NVA during my first two tours. My last tour was as a special assistant in Saigon and was mainly concerned with local security—police, RF, and PF. They were terrified of the NVA.

Before Tet '68, when I traveled in III Corps to inspect civic action projects or visit my battalions, I always went by chopper. Before leaving IV Corps to become commandant of the Army War College in '69, John Vann* and I toured many of our bridge and road projects in IV Corps by jeep without an incident. That's progress.

LT. GEN. (RET.) FILLMORE K. MEARNS

General Mearns commanded the 25th Infantry Division in 1967–1968. Mearns writes:[16]

VC units varied widely but were more effective than NVA units. Their replacement system was very effective.

Combat units of the NVA, whenever [they] could be located, suffered such high losses that they were unacceptable by U.S. standards. They fought bravely during Tet and afterward but were unable to achieve significant success.

GEN. (RET.) GEORGE S. BLANCHARD

General Blanchard was the Assistant Division Commander (ADC) of the 1st Cavalry Division in 1967. Blanchard states:[17]

In general, the VC capabilities were spotty compared with the NVA. They could be excellent fighting men depending upon their leadership, support, training, etc. Tactics were rudimentary and strategy basic. I was always surprised at how well they maintained morale under adverse conditions.

Generally, the NVA had high morale, good discipline (under fire, for example) and fair tactics (ambushes, etc.).

As ADC of the 1st Cavalry Division in 1967 I participated in a considerable number of combat actions in Binh Dinh Province (Bong Son). The cav squadron (in aircraft) found the NVA and we piled battalions on. The enemy was almost all NVA in these situations and we would fight until they were destroyed. Few ran away, few surrendered.

---

*John Paul Vann, U.S. Army adviser to ARVN in 1961–62, resigned from the Army in 1963 and returned to Vietnam as a civilian working for the Agency for International Development. He was killed in a helicopter crash in 1972. An outspoken critic of U.S. military policy in Vietnam, Vann is the subject of Neil Sheehan's controversial book, *A Bright Shining Lie*.

GEN. (RET.) FREDERICK J. KROESEN, JR.

General Kroesen commanded the 196th Light Infantry Brigade in 1968–1969, was Commanding General of the 23rd (Americal) Infantry Division in 1971, and was Senior U.S. Army Adviser in I Corps in 1972. Kroesen recalls:[18]

The VC were characterized by typical terrorist operations—daring, resourceful but dependent on finding undefended or poorly defended targets. They fought well when cornered, but did so because they had no alternative. Success bred confidence and high morale, but it wore thin and setbacks reduced the VC to ineffectiveness by Tet '68. Terrorism became their last resort as well as their first.

The NVA were formidable primarily because their officers held life-and-death authority over subordinates. For that reason discipline was excellent, morale was incidental, and fighting ability was automatic. NVA also fought well when cornered and they responded well to initiatives demanded of them. Nevertheless, their principal successes were against poorly prepared or weakly defended positions. They were no match for Americans in routine combat.

LT. GEN. (RET.) WILLIAM K. JONES, USMC[19]

Former commander of the Marine 3rd Division, Jones writes:

The morale, discipline, tactics, strategy, and fighting ability of the VC were excellent in every way. As for the NVA, they were very good, particularly their morale, discipline, and fighting ability. They were very good on their tactics; just fair on strategy.

I served twice in Vietnam. First in 1966 as a brigadier general, USMC, on Westmoreland's staff and director of his Combat Operations Center. Each day he would visit two corps areas and I the other two, reporting to him in the evening. The second tour I was a major general, CG of the 3rd Marine Division in 1969, in Quang Tri Province. Both tours provided me with excellent opportunities to study both the VC and NVA, also to become convinced that the USMC solution to stay in the lowlands protecting the South Vietnamese from both the VC and NVA was better than chasing them all over the heavily wooded, mountainous and inland areas. It was far superior to the MACV strategy mentioned above, which, of course, III Marine Amphibious Force was ordered to follow.

Our Marine close-support air was far superior to that of the USAF. In fact, the U.S. Army always pleaded to have Marine air provide them close-air support. The Vietnamese Marine Corps, though small, was also far superior to the South Vietnamese Army.

GEN. (RET.) MICHAEL S. DAVISON

General Davison commanded the II Field Force in 1970–1971. Davison states:[20]

The morale, discipline, and fighting ability of the VC were very poor after the Cambodian operation of May–June 1970. A number of high-ranking cadre defected. The eleven provinces in the II Corps sector became quite peaceful and calm. They became self-sufficient in rice and the lumbering industry came to life and thrived. What was left of the VC was ineffective.

As I recall, only two understrength NVA regiments remained in the II Corps sector. They took no offensive action, avoiding combat as much as possible. U.S. Army units continued to make contact from time to time but the NVA seldom stood and fought. Contacts by ARVN units in cross-border operations found stronger NVA units more able to fight and inflict damage—especially so after the death of Do Cao Tri, the ARVN II Corps commander, who was an outstanding leader and tactician.

11

VOICES FROM THE OTHER SIDE: THE GRUNTS

Soldiers and Marines who actually fought the VC/NVA on the field of battle also have strong opinions about their adversaries.

JAMES H. WEBB, JR.

Jim Webb served as a platoon commander, battalion intelligence officer and a company commander with the 5th Marine Regiment, 1st Marine Division, in 1969–1970. Webb is the author of *Fields of Fire* (Prentice Hall, 1978), and other successful novels. He served as Assistant Secretary of Defense and Secretary of the Navy from 1984 to 1988. According to Webb[1]:

I interrogated a lot of NVA prisoners. Many referred to the VC in the same contemptuous way that a lot of Americans talked about the ARVN. The political discipline of the VC was very strong but their military capabilities varied from unit to unit. The VC units in my area "connected" a lot with the NVA—particularly as transport units and guides for night infiltration. During my time in Quang Nam Province—most of 1969—I'd estimate that 75 percent of the soldiers in VC main-force units were NVA. They had crew-served weapons and used conventional tactics. The Q-83rd Main-Force Battalion and the 1st VC Regiment had excellent reputations, as good as most NVA units.

The VC were capable guerrillas as well. They constructed highly sophisticated booby traps from captured U.S. ordnance.

Some of these booby traps were so well concealed that they were like plastic surgery on the earth. Twenty-five to thirty percent of my unit's casualties were from booby traps. In a booby-trapped region our morale often sagged, knowing they could hurt us like that and we couldn't hit back. Booby traps create within you an emotional uneasiness with the earth.

However, I'd say the morale of the VC was low in '69 because by then we'd beaten the crap out of them and they knew it. VC soldiers seemed less dedicated than those in the NVA. They often seemed happy to be captured while the NVA were scared to death of us at first—they'd been told we'd kill them when we got hold of them.

Their political strategy was aimed at their own people. They used assassination as a disciplinary tool. The main element of their political strategy was ruthlessness—a carrot with a very big stick. The South Vietnamese officials literally could not remain in the villages and hamlets they were responsible for administering because of the terrorism the VC used against them and their families.

Probably the bloodiest scene I viewed while in Vietnam was inside a small hootch where we had persuaded thirty people from nearby villages to come to a "town meeting." Our commanders convinced the District Chief to come out along with the morning convoy from Da Nang—the VC/NVA totally controlled the roads in the An Hoa basin except when protected convoys ran. Although a squad from our company was providing security for the meeting, a small VC assassination team infiltrated in broad daylight. I was coming back from a patrol. I heard three automatic rifle bursts and three grenade explosions. A few seconds later one of the assassins ran right into my point man. By the time we got to the hootch, nineteen people were lying dead in a lake of blood, and the other eleven were hideously wounded—for the crime of meeting with the RVN District Chief, who also had died. That was the VC version of "hearts and minds."

During my time in Vietnam, I'd estimate that 90 percent of the villages in the An Hoa basin were under VC political control, 100 percent in the Arizona* region. Militarily, it depended on who was there at any moment. VC/NVA hit-and-run tactics were

*The Marines' name for the An Hoa Valley area, 30 km southwest of Da Nang, whose inhabitants were noted for their sympathy with the VC/NVA. While the etymology of this term is uncertain, it may refer to the Arizona "badlands" of the Old West.

effective until you caught on. When I began to think like they did I was able to preempt them. Eventually, my company had one of the highest kill ratios in the entire 1st Marine Division. We had succeeded in figuring out their patterns. The VC and NVA became very predictable.

The NVA were good soldiers but so were we—my Marines were super. We beat the socks off them most of the time. And I think this needs to be said, because too often it's forgotten—so were the better ARVN units, like the Rangers. I particularly remember the 51st ARVN Regiment, which operated with good success in the Arizona Valley.

The NVA had great fire discipline and good marksmanship skills. They built excellent fortifications, incredibly impressive trenches and emplacements. They used a "grab and hold" tactic: Their ideal scenario was to wait until we were so close to them that we couldn't use supporting fires for fear of hitting our own men. That required tremendous fire discipline on their part—to hold off until we were so close. They were able to spring very effective and sizeable daytime ambushes in the trenches and treelines adjacent to wide rice paddies by using the "grab and hold" tactic.

When the NVA could control the terrain or when we stayed too long in one spot, they were deadly; when we could use maneuver and fire support, we did a number on them. In one daylight ambush a company in my regiment took eighteen KIA in the first ten seconds. Another company was so badly mauled it took three months to reconstitute them. But when we caught the 90th NVA Regiment unprepared after a night infiltration "sweep and block" by several rifle companies, we killed more than two hundred in a few hours.

We had very little helicopter support so usually we would walk all night to get into position for a "first-light" engagement. This was often effective in surprising the enemy. But when we moved at night, especially in battalion force, we'd be spread out for miles so that night contact bogged us all down. But the NVA moved in eight- or nine-man cells* to a collection point, and then massed for an attack. If one cell got ambushed on the move the men in the killing zone knew they'd be okay if they just ran

---

*This may be a question of semantics—the Marines called these groups "cells," and we certainly do not question Mr. Webb's figures. While this seems a contradiction to the basic organizational structure of the VC/NVA forces—the three-man cell concept—the enemy, just like our forces, often had to compromise between organizational doctrine and reality when manpower was short.

back the way they'd come. They knew no Marine would ever let eight or nine enemy soldiers pass by his ambush site without opening up on them. By contrast, Marines would usually lie down in the kill zone when they were ambushed, because they were unsure where other enemy soldiers were. When I was a company commander I worked both ends of this—teaching my men to lay more complex ambushes, and also to assault their way out of an enemy kill zone.

I'll never forget the letter we took off the body of an NVA sergeant we killed in one engagement. He'd been shot through the waist before we found him and he was obviously bleeding to death at the time, but his last act was to try and grease my point man. He fired an automatic burst from his AK and somehow missed, and we killed him.

We found an unfinished letter on his body. Our Vietnamese interpreter translated it on the spot. He told us it was a letter to the guy's "congressman" back in North Vietnam. That's just how the interpreter translated whatever this official's title happened to be. In the letter this sergeant wrote that he'd been in the army in 1949–54, fighting the French with the Viet Minh, and then again since 1964. Here he was in the South, still fighting. He said he had teenaged children back in the North. He was complaining that he'd had too much war and now he just wanted to go home.

MAJ. GEN. BERNARD O. LOEFFKE

General Loeffke first served in Southeast Asia as a lieutenant in the early 1960s in Laos. He later was an adviser to a South Vietnamese airborne battalion and in 1969 commanded the 2nd Battalion, 3rd Infantry, of the 199th Light Infantry Brigade as a major and a lieutenant colonel. At this writing, Loeffke is still on active duty. Loeffke states:[2]

The morale and discipline of the VC were excellent. As for their tactics, they were in the most part better trained than we were. There was a great contrast in the experience of the guerrilla fighter and the ordinary soldier he faced. They surprised us in their ability to fight with little medical support and indirect fires.

The NVA were better equipped than the VC. Their fighting in units required them to fight in larger formations and use more complex tactics. The morale of the NVA units that had been in the South for a long time tended to be lower than those who had arrived recently.

I fought three different wars in Vietnam. My first tour as a lieutenant in Laos was with a Special Forces team with the "Meo" tribesmen trying to stop the enemy from taking over the country. My next tour as a captain was as an adviser to a Vietnamese airborne battalion. I learned to fight by watching my Vietnamese counterparts do it. Then the third tour I commanded one of our own forces. In all three tours, I never met an enemy with low morale. This means their indoctrination was good, their tactics simple, their discipline strong.

CARLTON SHERWOOD

Carlton Sherwood was a corporal and scout-sniper with G Company, 2nd Battalion, 4th Marine Regiment, in 1967–1968. Today he is a journalist with a Pulitzer Prize to his credit. Sherwood recalls:[3]

On my second day in country I was sent on an ambush at a site about twenty miles southwest of Da Nang. We set up in a graveyard, on a grave mound. At about two A.M. here came this string of guys, chatting, walking along—a VC mortar platoon we found out afterwards. It was a turkey shoot, a piece of cake, easy. We wiped them out. I thought, if this is what war is like, it's okay! That was my immediate impression but later, after it was light, we found this one guy, whose leg had been blown off, trying to drag his dead buddy out of the kill zone. Now that scared me.

When we operated in the VC-controlled areas, we had a sort of "accommodation" with the people there. They didn't fuck with us and we didn't fuck with them. They knew that if we hit mines or booby traps going through their villages we'd take it out on them, so they made sure we didn't. In our turn, we wouldn't search their hooches. Unless we had provocation, we never searched their homes. These were VC villages.

Then there was "Teatime Charlie," a VC sniper who'd fire four or five rounds into our positions every day exactly at 1600. He was so regular that we knew to get ready for chow at 1700 whenever he'd open up. He never hit anybody. I'm convinced that was his only mission in the war—pop four or five rounds our way each day and then he was off duty until the next time. When we operated in VC territory it was mostly minor harassment like snipers and booby traps. My overall impression of the VC is that they were sneaky little fuckers, ill-disciplined, but that guy with no leg, dragging his dead buddy away from the ambush, that was scary.

The NVA were different. Once, on an operation in Quang Tri Province, in heavy bush, thirty clicks [kilometers] off Highway 1, the whole battalion, out twenty-eight days, no resupply, lost, clothes rotting off our bodies, everybody had jungle rot, suddenly we came across this trail—it ran for miles! It had handrails along it, like you'd see in somebody's back yard. It was six to eight feet wide, steps carved into it, clean as a whistle. We followed it for two days. We left a trail of litter and shit the whole way. We followed it right through a base camp complex and almost never knew it. Almost the whole battalion had passed right through the place before somebody noticed something interesting and stopped to look and here was this complex of barracks, cookhouses, latrines, bomb shelters, a hospital, everything picture-perfect and spotless but totally invisible from only a few yards away.

They'd built the place with natural products completely, not even a nail was used. The only man-made building material I saw was some wire. It was as if a master carpenter had designed and built everything to exactly the same proportions. The walls of the buildings were of packed earth with leakproof roofs, bamboo flooring, drains, each with a bomb shelter underneath it, but this place would have been totally undetected from the air. It was evidently an R&R center that had just recently been evacuated.

We made so much noise approaching the place they had plenty of time to get out, but we did find some NVA packs. We opened them up and each was neatly packed, clean, perfectly organized. There was no smell to anything inside. I even took a pair of gook shorts and exchanged them for the ones I had on. These were the cleanest, most disciplined guys. This place both impressed me and it scared me.

Eventually we started using their packs. They were smaller and lighter than ours and dried out quicker when wet. We also began carrying AKs. Remember, when I was there we were having a lot of problems with the M-16s, so we would hump both the AK and the M-16 but use the AK. We began looking like NVA after a while.

We noticed after a while that if we ate their food and used their soap the leeches seemed to leave us alone. The ones I saw never seemed to show any jungle rot, trench foot, leech bites; their skin was clear, they had no body odor and their bodies were well manicured, no dirt under their nails. These guys had been in the bush for years and you should have seen 'em! They got big fucking balls. No choppers, no tanks, they were there for the duration. It was literally do or die for them.

When we did fight with the NVA they almost always had the initiative—except once, when we ran into a bunch of guys out jogging in blue sweatshirts. Where they got them I'll never know. Maybe the Quakers sent in a shipment of the things. They were unarmed, at a real R&R center. Even so, they didn't panic and we never got all of them. The NVA were fanatical about carrying off their dead and wounded. Rarely did we ever find any bodies after an ambush unless we managed to kill them all.

We didn't always get away with all our own dead and wounded. The single worst day of my life was September 19, 1967, on the DMZ, just above Con Thien. There were three divisions of NVA operating in that area and it was SOP never to go out in anything less than battalion strength, but that day, our battalion commander, a rookie, sent out a company-size patrol. They were ambushed by a regimental-size force, well dug in. The NVA had excellent mortar and artillery support on the DMZ. The battalion commander sent in his other companies piecemeal to relieve the first company. I have never seen so many machine guns in my life. They just mowed us down. It was like Custer's Last Stand. We lost two companies that day. We left dead and wounded behind—the official history of the event says fifteen "dead," but I know some of those guys were alive when we pulled out. There was no way we could have gotten to them. That area was so hot we couldn't get back in to recover the dead until twenty days later.

At Khe Sanh there were 40,000 NVA dug in around us. We used ARCLIGHT [B-52] strikes as close air support at Khe Sanh. I got nosebleeds from the concussions, the bombs were falling so close to our positions. Observing an ARCLIGHT from that close up is like watching the end of the world—it's unbelievable how destructive those B-52s were. They pounded the NVA every night. But the next morning those guys got up and started fighting again. How did they survive that constant pounding?

Let me tell you another sniper story. This was in Quang Tri Province. The whole battalion was walking in the bush just off Route 1. It was rolling hill country. We got a sniper who knew how to shoot. This guy was about a half mile away. Each shot got a guy right between the eyes. He got about five men. We had no idea where he was shooting from. The whole battalion went to ground. This one sniper held us up the whole day. Next day, same thing. Nobody wanted to stand up anymore. The battalion commander called in air strikes—bombs, napalm, 20mm cannon for one sniper! They laid it on the ridge line where we thought he was. After the air strike we walked for about an hour when "bang!" another guy went down. At that point we'd made about a mile and a half in two days. Then we tried flanking him with two platoons, which is what the battalion CO should have done in the first place. Night came on and do you know he actually took pot shots at us in the dark! The CO called in another air strike and do you know what? When the jets came in I could hear "ping, ping, ping," that motherfucker was shooting at the goddamned jets!

We never found him. Eleven hundred guys, the meanest fighting force in the world, held up by one man armed probably with an SKS. He took napalm, bombs, 20mm, grenades—we even fired LAWs [light antitank weapons] at him. He was great!

We respected the NVA. They were a challenge to us. The only time I ever took anything they did personally was when we discovered that they'd mutilated the bodies of guys we left behind during the fight on September 19, 1967. They skinned one guy, took the USMC tattoo he had on his chest and displayed it on a tree trunk. There was no call for that sort of thing. We never did it to them. We didn't even collect ears from NVA corpses. That was just sheer meanness.

AL SANTOLI

Al Santoli served with C Company, 2nd Battalion, 22nd Infantry of the 25th Infantry Division, and the CRIP Platoon (Combined Recon and Intelligence) of the Division's 3rd Brigade in 1968–1969. Santoli is the author of several nonfiction books about the Vietnam War including *Everything We Had* (Random House, 1981). Santoli states:[4]

The VC had a good intelligence network that worked to their strategic advantage. In the rubber plantations the VC were skillful in tactics of using the terrain to their advantage for ambushes along roads and camouflaging tunnels and base camps. In the forests of the Loc Ninh area they also used terrain well and the advantage of nearby Cambodia for tactical retreat and resupply.

Their morale varied from fighting to certain death in attacks on fire bases to the number of Chieu Hois who surrendered. They weren't very successful in frontal attacks on U.S. fire bases, where they received massive casualties. Booby traps were their most successful ploy along with hit-and-run ambushes.

The NVA were tenacious but not very successful against U.S. forces in III Corps. They suffered needless mass casualties attempting frontal assaults on U.S. positions and, in most cases where they used concealment of terrain for ambush, were unable to sustain initiative beyond immediate surprise against U.S. infantry. They had better luck against truck-supply convoys in roads through rubber plantations until Rome Plows cut back the foliage. Rocket and mortar attacks were their most successful tactic. The NVA were definitely unloved and unwanted by the South Vietnamese villagers.

BILL JAYNE

Bill Jayne served as a rifleman and a fire team leader with B Company, 1st Battalion, 26th Marine Regiment in 1967–1968. Jayne recalls:[5]

When my Marine unit left Hill 55 near Da Nang another Marine battalion unfamiliar with the area took our place. A few of us remained behind to provide security for a truck convoy that was to take some of our equipment north. The VC attacked a bridge near the foot of the hill. The attack seemed to be staged from a nearby ville that had been quiet all the time I had been in the area. The new unit now in defense of the hill opened up with everything possible to defend the bridge position, doing considerable damage to the ville. It appeared that the VC had husbanded their resources waiting for such an opportunity. The attack seemed designed more to turn the Vietnamese against us than to damage us directly.

After Hill 55, in the spring of 1967, my battalion moved north to Khe Sanh. It was after the Hill Fights and the area was very quiet. When we did encounter NVA they were loaded for bear. I could not discern any pattern to the infrequent firefights (which, in retrospect, seem more like pitched battles rather than meeting engagements). Through 1967 these events seemed designed to wear us out, keep us off balance. There was never any serious attempt to take a position except once when they overran a small hilltop radio-relay station defended by a platoon from another company in our battalion.

Their morale, discipline, and fighting ability seemed excellent. Their engagements must have been well planned since we seldom saw or heard of them carrying large loads. Ammunition and supplies evidently were cached ahead of time.

In January 1968 that began to change. We began meeting more NVA as, evidently, more of them were moving around getting ready for the "siege." Their strategy at Khe Sanh is still a mystery to me. It's difficult to believe they accepted the punishment they took simply to affect American public opinion. In late February they seemed to be in good shape to try a serious attack on the combat base itself but supporting arms, including B-52 ARCLIGHTs, apparently stopped them. (I was in the battalion aid station that night with a piece of shrapnel in my foot. From that position—lying on a cot in a tent with a four-foot wall of sandbags around it and unable to walk normally—it was a most unpleasant night.) I'm not sure their strategy of affecting American public opinion was not something they cooked up later to justify the battle. They did, of course, claim a traditional military victory that summer when we abandoned the base.

TOM CARHART

Tom Carhart served as a platoon leader in the 1st Brigade, 101st Airborne Division, and as an adviser to the ARVNs in Go Cong Province and in the 44th Special Tactical Zone along the Cambodian border in 1967–1968. His personal experiences in the war zone are related in his book, *The Offering* (Morrow, 1987). Carhart states:[6]

The VC had high motivation on an ethnic/racial basis. They were largely unschooled in formal tactics, but heavy political dominance in some regions facilitated their preparation of the terrain—booby traps, support of populace, etc. (particularly in the Delta in 1968).

As for the NVA, they were a highly worthy adversary. Their performance varied by unit, no doubt, but those I faced with the 101st performed superbly in Phan Thiet, Song Be, and approaches to the A Shau Valley in I Corps in 1968.

DAVID SHERMAN

David Sherman served with a Marine Combined Action Program (CAP) unit in 1966. He is the author of *The Night Fighters* series of Vietnam novels (Ivy Books). According to Sherman:[7]

I only fought VC, never NVA. They were sneaky little bastards whose booby traps and hit-and-run tactics could be very frightening and demoralizing. For the most part, when I was in the 1st Marines we never wanted to fight them. But when we did we wanted them to stand and fight so we could kick ass on them.

When I joined a CAP, we turned the tables on Charlie and wound up beating him at his own game.

My only other comment is that combat commanders should make strong efforts to keep the troops honestly informed of the results of what they do. Rarely, during my time in the war anyway, did we have any idea of why we did what we did or what it accomplished other than getting some of us crippled or wasted. In the CAP it was different, most of us understood what we were doing there.

LT. COL. WILLIAM J. MORROW, JR.

Bill Morrow served as a pathfinder with the 25th Infantry Division in 1970 and as an adviser with Team 162 to the ARVN airborne in 1971. Morrow is still on active duty. He states:[8]

My experiences with VC were limited. Most actions were faceless terrorist acts such as mines or single mortar rounds. Morale is difficult to assess because I did not witness the VC as a cohesive fighting unit. Individually, the VC were courageous and well disciplined. I did not perceive an integrated strategy nor did they appear to have cohesive tactics in the traditional sense of tactical warfare. They avoided fights and pitched battles. They were tough—but I would classify them as terrorists/criminals.

The NVA were tough, well disciplined, and motivated. My experiences included engagements with NVA regulars in the triborder area near Dak To, near Khe Sanh in I Corps, and Tay Ninh Province in III Corps. They were fierce fighters! They maneuvered, controlled fires, used cover and concealment, etc. Tactics were excellent. Results of each engagement, when subjected to intelligence analysis, usually confirmed a strategic thrust or a part of a strategic move. Morale is difficult to assess because I never talked to any NVA. But they fought as a cohesive team and my perception was that morale was relatively high and getting better.

My tour began the day U.S. forces returned from Cambodia in June 1970. Being stationed at Cu Chi, most of my operations were in War Zone C–Tay Ninh Province. The six months after Cambodia were quiet—very few encounters with NVA regulars, only small, squad-sized elements who quickly disappeared—never stood and fought. Viet Cong activity was light but significant. The command-detonated mine or stray mortar round struck terror into many U.S. soldiers. We found numerous instances of arms caches in villages or arms being smuggled or hidden in farm produce.

The end of November 1970, the 25th Infantry Division was formally returned to Hawaii and U.S. presence in War Zone C and Tay Ninh Province was significantly reduced. I was transferred to a MACV team that advised ARVN soldiers working the old 25th Division area of operations. Almost immediately NVA contacts increased. In December, my unit made contact three times with NVA units from squad to platoon size. In January, we had three more contacts, all platoon size. They inflicted more casualties on the ARVN than we inflicted on them. We found base camps for company-sized elements that indicated a high level of training and discipline.

My unit was moved to the Dak To area where NVA regulars ruled the jungle. Battalion-sized units maneuvered at will. Prior to our arrival an ARVN brigade had been decimated and two fire bases overrun by NVA regulars. Our encounters were with troops who were tenacious, fierce, and well disciplined. Our success was only because we brought superior fire power—air and artillery—to bear on NVA positions. We literally bombed them into retreat.

My last experience with NVA was Lam Son 719 into Laos. The results of that excursion speak for themselves. My personal observation—the NVA would have defeated any army that tried that invasion. They exhibited all the traits that a successful army has. Very tough!

LT. COL. (RET.) VIC RESTON

Vic Reston served as an infantry platoon commander and staff officer with the 1st Battalion, 4th Marine Regiment, 3rd Marine Division, in 1969–1970. Reston is presently the Minority Counsel of the U.S. Senate Veterans Affairs Committee. According to Reston:[9]

I fought in northern I Corps and had no experience with the VC, ours being restricted to the NVA. As much as I respected the NVA for their willingness to fight without close air support, with long logistical lines, and only rudimentary hospitals and medical equipment for their wounded, I must temper that respect with the fact that our political leaders hampered and restricted our abilities to fight the NVA soldier in a way to defeat them. It was like playing football in which the officials only allowed the ball to be played inside our fifty-yard line but never to be taken into their area of the field or to cross their goal line.

During the spring of 1969, our company was operating alone in the corner of northern I Corps where the borders of Laos and the DMZ meet. At night we could see torches on the far mountains, and the torches stretched for miles as the NVA headed south with supplies, equipment, and personnel. We would call in artillery strikes and, as the distant booming picked up, the torches would be extinguished. In the darkness the artillery fire could not be adjusted because we didn't know where the targets were. When the barrage lifted, the torches would be relighted and the marchers would continue. When we made any attempt to seal off any of the approaches to the South, the NVA would use a different one. Had we been able to destroy their supply depots and staging areas on the other side of the Ben Hai River, we would not have had such trouble finding these supplies and soldiers in a piecemeal way as they headed south on hidden trails.

LT. COL. CLARENCE D. LONG, III

Lt. Col. Long served as rifle platoon leader, C Company, 2nd Battalion, 502nd Infantry, and reconnaissance platoon leader, 2nd Battalion, 502nd Infantry, 101st Airborne Division, July 1966–July 1967.[10] According to Long:

Tactics of the VC generally were well suited for the environment. They avoided contact with superior U.S. forces whenever possible. Morale for the most part appeared to be high, but could be degraded by long-term patrolling of a given area—some defected under those circumstances. Strategy is hard to assess. Certainly, the "overall strategy," to wear down the U.S. forces, ultimately succeeded. The most successful tactic (against U.S. forces) was the booby trap. Most other tactics failed or were counterproductive. Fighting ability was good, but for the most part the VC were very poor shots, probably due to inadequate training/practice. I had the impression that individual weapons were not sighted-in. The VC placed heavy emphasis on "preparing the battlefield."

Morale of the NVA was generally high, although fifty soldiers from the 95th NVA Regiment did surrender in October 1966 to the 2/502. Discipline for the most part appeared extremely high. Strategy was to lure U.S. forces into situations where superior firepower could not be brought to bear. Fighting ability was good, but the NVA generally had poor marksmanship. I do not believe most NVA had fired their weapons prior to entering combat. Most successful NVA tactic was the surprise attack against a recently occupied night position in territory they were familiar with and we were not. The NVA were fully prepared, under those conditions, to take extremely heavy casualties if they had a chance to overrun a U.S. unit.

My worst experience against an NVA unit occurred in July 1967. One of my platoons was sent to attempt recapture of a prisoner who had escaped after convincing the S-5 he was a Chieu Hoi. I felt it necessary to immediately move the other recon section because the prisoner had seen our position after being returned from battalion. Our new location, unfortunately, was right in the middle of an NVA weapons company, and they attacked at 0200 with a shower of grenades. Had it not been for the superior power of U.S. grenades, we would all have been killed and overrun. The NVA attempted to bring mortars and 75mm recoilless rifles to bear, but could not do so because of the closeness of the fighting and our artillery. One concerted rush would have taken us, but they were unable to form an assault line—probably because they were unable to obtain complete fire superiority. A muzzle flash from either [side] immediately drew a grenade.

LT. CDR. F. C. BROWN

F. C. Brown served as a Navy petty officer third class medic with Advisory Team 64 in Chau Doc Province in 1969–1970. He returned for a second tour as a petty officer second class in 1971–1972 as a medic with the Naval Advisory Group, Vietnam, and was present for the Communist Easter Offensive of 1972. Brown currently is a lieutenant commander and is the director, Branch Medical Clinic, Cubi Point, and contingency planning officer for U.S. Naval Hospital, Subic Bay, Philippines. Brown recalls:[11]

Generally, the VC were good, but not quite the supermen they were often made out to be. The generally accepted image of a black pajama-clad guerrilla with an antiquated weapon, defending his paddy against a huge mechanized American force, is simply not true. Many VC units were well armed and well supplied; it was not unusual to find VC with AK-47s against ARVN armed with M-1 carbines (prior to 1969). VC security service personnel were their best—dedicated, incredibly brave, and well indoctrinated; usually preferred death to capture.

U.S. and ARVN forces actually won the guerrilla war. The Communist victory in 1975 was due to regular—vice guerrilla—forces of the North Viets.

There was much animosity between the VC and NVA, particularly in VC units partially fleshed out with NVA "fillers." The NVA had a superiority complex over the VC and usually kept the better weapons for themselves. A spirit of "war weariness" was evident among NVA POWs from 1970 on—many claimed they were forcibly drafted and complained of the months they spent on the trail moving south.

The best NVA troops were sappers; engineers were also good. NVA tactics were frequently flawed—they often suffered needless casualties attacking objectives they had no hope of holding. They were particularly adept at small-unit ambushes—quickly vanished into the bush after policing up ambush site. However, in 1972, they used armor poorly—no infantry support.

KENN MILLER

Kenn Miller served with a long-range reconnaissance patrol unit in Vietnam from 1967 to 1969. He is author of *Tiger the Lurp Dog* (Ballantine Books, 1986).[12]

One of the things I found most fascinating about recon work was trying to figure out what daily life must be like for the guys on the other side. Although they were nowhere near as wasteful and materially extravagant as conventional American troops, we found sign of them more often than we found them—sleeping positions, fighting positions, caches, night halt positions cleared by trails, trails of various kinds, latrines, and occasionally even lost or abandoned equipment (mess kits, ammo, an occasional ground cloth, or even cigarette butts), etc. One thing I always wondered was how they protected themselves against leeches and insects. Judging from bodies, they valued American bug juice, when they could get it.

For a while in the spring of 1969, we pulled numerous ambushes in an area of rolling, grassy, savannahlike ground near the edge of the jungle and foothills, about twenty klicks south of Hue, where foraging parties would come and go at dawn and dusk, heading for visits to the populated area near the coast. Once, we hunkered down while thirty-seven of them passed— in motley uniform, but all armed—but usually we found ambushable elements of three to seven. And we were springing these ambushes so successfully and regularly, we came to call the area the "Game Preserve." I remember our general delight when we discovered a little "cowboy" VC hoodlum with an RPG in our kill zone, for here was someone we could tell we didn't like, on a personal basis. But usually, they were just soldiers—so skinny they didn't bleed much, but basically normal guys. I still have the plastic Bic wallet I took off one guy, with a picture of his wife or girlfriend. It seemed a matter of moral obligation to keep the picture, look at it from time to time. I killed the guy (with help from another guy who opened up at the same time), and I still look at the picture, still remember that it wasn't just a gook, but someone with loved ones that we killed.

It is hard to comment specifically about VC—at least on my experience. I saw part-time guerrillas, who impressed me not at all, live or dead, and people who had to be main force. I can say, however, that their standards of marksmanship seemed very low—always firing way high or way wide, even on semiautomatic. But they did not waste ammo, spraying blindly as often as American troops, for obvious reasons.

When it comes to NVA, I was not all that impressed. But then, we usually saw them at our advantage, not theirs. We were moving much more carefully than they were, in the areas I saw most of them, and I remember thinking how slack and lacka-daisical they looked. But that was unfair, to them, and to people who had to deal with them when the advantage was theirs.

As far as I can determine, the VC and NVA had a strategy, and we never did. Tactically, it is easy to both praise and fault the VC and NVA. At the time, I was appalled at their commanders' willingness to take unacceptable casualties for minor gains. I remember sitting on a hilltop with ten other guys, radio relay, and having to fight off maybe a platoon (who knows? it was night), because they wanted our radios and codebooks and bug juice, etc., or so we imagined. Our claymores did keep them distant, and they had nothing for indirect fire. I have no idea if they were VC or NVA, but the only reason we could figure they bothered with us was for our equipment—not some brilliant plan to leave the teams without radio relay. Since then, living in Asia for ten years after the war, I discovered that this willingness to expend lives is not some evil Commie lack of humanity. It is Asian military tradition.

When it comes to basic infantry equipment, the NVA seemed as well supplied as we were—except for their grenades, which, fortunately, weren't that reliable, or as devastating as ours. (But then, they had a lot of ours.) We often would kill three or four enemy, and take only one or two weapons, but this, like slackness, was probably a function of us being in their rear. Guys in line companies and people who had to fight when the enemy initiated probably weren't so lucky.

In general, I think morale must have been excellent. And discipline was probably better than the ARVN average—and the later American average. Those guys had an incredibly tough life, and still drove on. That says something about morale and discipline.

When I see something like that draft-dodger Stallone taking on whole companies of NVA with his napalm arrows, I get very angry at the insult offered to my enemies and those of us who actually fought them. It is a symbiotic relationship. If the VC and NVA were no good, then neither were we. If we were good (and with the exception of a few units in the last stages of the war, we were), then they must've been good too. A couple of years ago, I talked to a triple Combat Infantryman Badge [one for each war] man, who jumped into Sicily, fought in Korea, and did two tours in Vietnam, with Special Forces in the early '60s, against local VC, then later as adviser to some ARVN unit, fighting NVA. He had more respect for the Vietnamese we fought than the Germans, North Koreans, or Chinese.

I never bought into this bullshit mystique of the superhuman VC, and I figure they were as scared and human as the rest of us. But I suppose they were good soldiers, for the most part. And except for the murderous bastards responsible for the massacres like Hue (who weren't really soldiers, but Commie politicos, I guess), I don't have anything against them.

SERGEANT MAJOR OF THE ARMY (RET.) WILLIAM G. BAINBRIDGE

SMA Bainbridge served in Vietnam first as the battalion command sergeant major, 1st Battalion, 28th Infantry, 1st Infantry Division, and later as II Field Force command sergeant major. Bainbridge was serving with the 423rd Infantry Regiment, 106th Infantry Division, when he was captured by the Germans at the Battle of the Bulge in December 1944. Later he was appointed Sergeant Major of the Army and served in that office from July 1, 1975, to July 1, 1979. Today he is director, Member Services, U.S. Soldiers' and Airmen's Home, Washington, DC.[13]

During my August 1965–August 1966 tour in Vietnam, I participated in several operations against the VC. Their tactics and fighting ability were, for the most part, excellent. I believe that their morale and discipline were very good. In order for a soldier to be good in combat he must have good morale and discipline.

Although my units had fewer encounters with the NVA troops, in my view, their organization, morale, discipline, and fighting ability were generally superior to those of the Viet Cong.

My unit was part of the early-1965 combat operation in the vicinity of Cu Chi to secure the area for the arrival of the 25th Infantry Division from Hawaii. We were able to secure the area to assist the 25th in establishing their base; however, we had not evicted the VC. They continued to be a viable force in the backyard of the 25th Division base camp for a considerable period of time.

CAPT. (RET.) LAWRENCE J. DE MEO, JR.

Larry De Meo served with 1st Battalion, 50th Infantry, 173rd Airborne Brigade from April to October 1969, when he was wounded and medically evacuated to the United States. In July 1969 he took over command of A Company, 1/50, which operated in Phu My District, Binh Dinh Province, South Vietnam. Today Mr. De Meo works as an analyst for the Department of Veterans Affairs in Washington, DC. De Meo writes:[14]

Our mission was to secure the villages [in Phu My District], destroying any local control the enemy (exclusively Viet Cong) may have had over their inhabitants; support the local rural/ popular forces; and help train the villagers to defend themselves. Enemy contact at that time was light; they were too few in number and too ill-equipped to challenge us directly, and movement was difficult for them in the daytime because there was very little cover within our area of operations.

These VC were skilled and effective in conducting harassment operations against us. Their intelligence was very good, perhaps even better than ours. They conducted enough harassing operations to keep us from going inland to the foothills, where we knew they were infiltrating men and supplies southward through our area.

I never saw an NVA soldier in our area, and it was quite obvious that the Tet '68 Offensive had decimated the local VC units. There were very few military-age males in our area; those that were here were definitely VC, but mostly teenaged kids complemented by a few middle-aged veterans. They were obedient to their orders and highly skilled at carrying them out. They were courageous to a fault, knowing that their chances of surviving contact with us were slim. The first VC I ever saw was a kid no older than thirteen or fourteen who had been killed by one of our patrols. He had been carrying the decrepit remains of a Thompson submachine gun that looked like it had lain in a rice paddy since World War II.

But they were the meanest SOBs around when it came to constructing booby traps, emplacing mines, planning and initiating ambushes, intelligence infiltration, and conducting terrorist acts. They knew what they had to do and they did it well, exploiting our inability to maneuver and fight. They kept us alert for ambushes and our nerves continually on edge with their booby traps and mines. All of the casualties we took while I was with the brigade were from these ambushes and mines.

Our rules of engagement provided the enemy an advantage. We were forbidden from using artillery or air strikes within one thousand meters of any village, occupied or not, and a village was defined as a single hut. We found huts constructed all through the area; consequently, I never could use artillery, and only saw one air strike: two F-100s from Phu Cat bombing some sappers trying to infiltrate LZ Uplift at dusk. They were spotted within a few hundred yards of the perimeter and were dragging a .51-caliber machine gun with them. They fired it at each plane after it was pulling up out of its dive—we could see the green tracers following the planes. They had only a few seconds to fire before the next aircraft rolled in to strafe them. Courageous and determined to a fault!

In the end, the Phu My VC were successful in their mission: preventing us from interrupting their supply lines to the south and ultimately demonstrating that we could not prevent them from operation in our assigned area. They accomplished this with minimum resources and maximum resourcefulness, skill and hard-bitten bravery. The net result was a stalemate characterized by grudging mutual respect.

CHIEF WARRANT OFFICER (RET.) SEDGWICK ("WICK") TOURISON, JR.*

Wick Tourison is both a fluent Vietnamese linguist and a trained interrogator. While in Vietnam Mr. Tourison conducted extensive interviews with enemy defectors and prisoners of war, including the deputy chief of staff of the 5th Viet Cong Infantry Division. These "conversations" with Viet Cong and North Vietnamese soldiers gave Mr. Tourison a view into the enemy camp seldom vouchsafed to any other American. After a twenty-year career in the U.S. Army, Mr. Tourison worked as an intelligence officer and expert analyst for the Defense Intelligence Agency. Mr. Tourison's memoir of his time as an interrogator for the Military Assistance Command, Vietnam, *Talking with*

---

*The authors would like to take this opportunity to thank Mr. Tourison (and the wonderful folks at Reno's—Aldridge, Rea, Carolyn, and Ronda—who kept "the Wickster's" coffee cup full during our marathon interview sessions) for the insights, advice, and criticism he gave them during their review of this manuscript. Without his help certain parts of this book would have lacked valuable perspective and essential accuracy.

Victor Charlie, was published in February 1991 by Ivy Books. His second book, a history of the U.S. covert operations into North Vietnam, is presently in press. Mr. Tourison writes:[15]

I am aware we distinguished between the VC and the NVA during the war, but I felt at the time that this was wrong to do. Both groups are essentially Vietnamese with a common history and culture that predates the modern and transitory Communist movement in Vietnam.

The emergence of the terms "VC" and "NVA" is a reflection of a flaw in our (U.S.) policy. We sought to emphasize the legitimacy of the Republic of Vietnam and illegitimacy of the North. It didn't work. The terms, rather than helping Americans understand the single-mindedness of the North's activities, supported the North's claim that there was a viable and significant group against President Ngo Dinh Diem within the South who were independent of control by the Communist North. Nothing was further from the truth.

The armed forces of the Communist movement in the South, the VC or "Liberation Army," were a creation of the Democratic Republic of Vietnam (DRV)—the North. The DRV denied this during the war. Their heir, the Socialist Republic of Vietnam (SRV), now admits it. The NVA, or "People's Army of Vietnam" (PAVN), was the military force of the North, the army directed by the DRV Lao Dong Party Politburo to fully support the "liberation of the South." The National Liberation Front was a smoke screen that served the DRV well in the international arena because many in the West found it a convenient justification for their own support of the North over the South. As one example of this, the original "National Liberation Front" entertainment group formed in Hanoi in 1966 to perform internationally was composed of members drawn from the DRV National Song and Dance Troupe.

Recent military writings published openly in Hanoi by the SRV's People's Army Publishing House have now openly acknowledged and described both candidly and in some detail the role of the DRV in the external manipulation of the "struggle" in the South. These writings have acknowledged for the first time the details of the assassination squads in the South, the attack on the U.S. B-52 base in Thailand in 1972, the sabotage of a U.S. airliner timed to explode upon landing back in Hawaii, and other details that will keep military historians busy for decades.

Former SRV military and political cadre who have left Vietnam over the past decade have also spoken of the extensive Soviet military intelligence support to the SRV/PAVN during the war years. Their revelations include descriptions of Soviet trawler operations from Haiphong, the passing of communications intelligence from trawler-based intercepts to the PAVN General Staff, and the failed Soviet recruitment of PAVN senior officers studying in Moscow (who were later labeled "revisionists" to disguise the nature of the Soviet espionage attempt against a "fraternal brother"). More fascinating details can be expected to emerge in other areas to help document the history of the last Indochina war.

For my second tour in Vietnam during 1965–1967, as well as my time in Laos during 1970–1974, a period which included duties in Vietnam, Cambodia, and Thailand, I dealt with the survivors of the Liberation Army and the People's Army who came into U.S. hands as prisoners, defectors, and suspects. My interests at the time were in "enemy" military forces that our commanders faced, whether in Binh Duong Province in southern Vietnam or those in transit on the Ho Chi Minh Trail in Laos. At times what I learned came from face-to-face discussions with them and at times from interpreters.

During the war, time was a precious commodity. And there was little of it during which to explore aspects of the history and culture of Southeast Asia that were fundamental to an understanding of those whom we faced on the battlefield. What I learned and applied in my craft came more from my Vietnamese counterparts—intelligence officers—than anything I ever learned from our own military intelligence system. This was not a fault of our system. It was merely the way things worked out.

The strategy I saw applied during and after 1965 was always in strict response to the instructions received from the Lao Dong Party Politburo in Hanoi. It was interpreted and massaged in both the North and the South to attain the objective of a united Vietnam under the direction of the Politburo.

The earliest cadre were often those who had fought with the Viet Minh against the French and had been "regrouped" to the North by 1955, in accordance with the Geneva Accords. These cadre were the "VC" of the early 1960s. But nearly all were members of the NVA by the time they infiltrated into the South and were classified as VC. It was the beginning of the paradox. Those whose infiltration became the very foundation of the "insurgents" eventually became an inconsequential force in contrast to the maneuver battalions General Westmoreland contended were his primary threats. Those first several thousand who returned to the South by 1961 formed the nucleus of cadre and staffs for the Liberation Army and People's Revolutionary Party in the South.

The National Liberation Front was not a large group of citizens organized to counter the Diem government. It was formed, directed, and managed by the Lao Dong Party through the People's Revolutionary Party in the South. It was then acknowledged—and has been generally acknowledged since—by Hanoi as being that mechanism the Party led to organize different sectors of the population to support "the revolution." It never was a force independent of the Party's control and direction. Its passing into extinction by 1976 makes any other argument superfluous. The ability of the Front to pass itself off as an offspring of popular discontent to President Diem and devoid of Party direction is a reflection of the political ignorance of those who accepted such statements at face value. It is history, not this writer, who has made such a judgment.

The military aspects of "VC/NVA" strategy were managed on the ground in the South until circa 1963 by a small group of key political cadre who either "stayed behind" in 1955 or who were infiltrated back into the South and included such individuals as General Tran Van Tra, Le Trong Tan, and Tran Do. In 1964 General Nguyen Chi Thanh became the architect, at least for the southern half of South Vietnam, until his death in 1967.

Returning to Vietnam in 1965, I encountered an enemy armed force that was significantly larger and better organized than that which I had only heard about vaguely in 1963. By that fall I was facing regular troops of the PAVN for the first time, at the battle of Plei Me. The early 1965 U.S. Department of State White Paper documenting aggression from the North based on evidence of infiltrators of several years earlier had been overtaken by events as the army of the North began its inexorable and massive march south.

Morale and discipline within the NVA ranks was reflective of the more austere and conservative North and was not simply a reflection of Communist ideology. These were regular army forces who went into combat on command. They were also the first generation of the North that had been educated and raised under Communism. They were well equipped for their mission and followed orders. They were nominally the troops of the "Liberation Army" only insofar as they were fighting in the

South. Those recruited into the fold in the South had less training and lacked the single-minded purpose of their northern
cousins. Since many of the southern-born forces served in units
that were more closely linked to their native areas, they often
maintained a tie to the perceived injustices of their local area.
Thus, those from the North might be seen as fighting for a more
long-range goal that the Party had instilled for a decade before
the arrival of the first major U.S. ground forces in 1965. Those
who joined in the South viewed it as a more personal war, at
least at first.

After the start of the U.S. bombing in August 1964, there
were many from the North to whom the war did take on a very
personal character. Some viewed their duty in the South as a
"historical duty" to liberate the South and reunify the country.
After 1965 it was not uncommon for NVA POWs to speak of
revenge for friends and relatives who had been killed in the
North.

The field tactics employed during the war were evolutionary.
They developed from a body of knowledge that included a
thousand-year history of campaigns against various forces and
in a variety of settings, all in the same geographic area. As U.S.
forces increased in size and complexity, the tactics and forces
employed were modified accordingly. The tactics of the early
1960s, a slow and careful management of the meager resources,
were modified during and after 1965 when large U.S. units went
on the offensive to relieve the Army of the Republic of Vietnam
and to secure major population centers. For the next three years,
the Liberation Army maneuvered its elements in the face of a
growing U.S. combined arms presence.

The continuity in the infiltration corridor through Cambodia
and Laos mitigated against the forces being stopped. Unlike
Greece, fifteen years earlier, which had been able to seal its
borders with the help of neighbors, South Vietnam could not
count on such aid. Cambodia's port of Sihanoukville made possible the flooding of the southern South Vietnam battlefield with
a family of Sino-Soviet equipment that was completely compat-
ible with that used by VC/NVA forces in the rest of Vietnam.
The overthrow of Sihanouk and the closing of the Sihanoukville
port in early 1970 were too little too late. Laos was still a wide-
open corridor, and U.S. forces were withdrawing. It was never
a question of victory for the North. It was only a matter of
timing.

Even as early as 1968 the war had taken on a new character.

The United States committed to a withdrawal of U.S. forces and the North knew the end was a matter of time. The Tet Offensive had decimated the "Liberation Army," but those losses had come primarily to local force units assigned to conduct the initial assault, which often had not been reinforced by NVA forces kept in reserve. This was done to convince observers that the war was one of the Southerners against Southerners. Thus, when the Tet Offensive became a disaster, it indirectly purged the Southern strength and character of the Liberation Army; internal North-South squabbling was thereby resolved on the battlefield in the favor of the NVA reserves, a reality that permitted the Northerners to rise to power on the graves of their southern-born comrades.

From that point on, there appears to have been little Southern prominence in the conflict. This may account for the relatively easy transition from the nominally Southern Provisional Revolutionary Government in 1976 to a Northern-mandated Socialist republic. It was reinforced by the passing into retirement of those who "had served the revolution in the South during the war" and in the 1980s became the basis for claims of injustice by former combat veterans in the South. As the Party would have explained it, it is to the Party that the spoils of war are destined, not those who participated in the final offensive of the Ho Chi Minh Campaign of early 1975.

The individual northern and southern Vietnamese I interrogated were a relatively homogeneous group. All were ethnic Vietnamese. It was only in northern Laos that minorities such as the Black T'ai from northwestern North Vietnam saw any extensive combat; the North generally excluded its ethnic minorities from much of the fighting and it became by and large a war between ethnic lowlanders.

As to the fighting ability of the VC/NVA soldier, that is a commentary I leave to those who faced them in direct combat. It was not unusual to ask the survivors with whom I talked why they were fighting. Their response was simply that their commanders had assigned them a mission and they set about to carry it out to the best of their ability. Based on all available records, most of them never lived to accomplish their mission.

Most Vietnamese POWs with whom I spoke during 1965–1967 viewed their conflict as one that should have been resolved by large groups of opposing soldiers. They had little appreciation for combined arms and little understanding of other than small-unit tactics. They felt that man-to-man they were more than a match for Americans, at least as far as being individual soldiers and demonstrating both courage and perseverance. Most felt frustration at not being able to close with American forces they faced in the field. To them it was a contest between soldiers. The tremendous casualties caused by air and artillery made them both frustrated and angry. In one sense, it made them try just that much harder to close with the American fighting man, whom they viewed as an elusive enemy. They knew he was there, but every time they got close, he pulled back and let the air and artillery fire pound the battlefield.

The soldiers from the North eventually did develop the maxim that they were "born in the North to die in the South." The great majority followed the orders of their commanders. For them the war was open ended. They were there "for the duration." They fought a war to which only victory could bring an end. It was a powerful motive that Americans, who generally served a one-year combat tour, simply could not match psychologically. The enemy's motivating force was thus sufficiently strong to almost guarantee that U.S. forces would not be able to prevail, given the domestic and international constraints imposed by Washington. These constraints prevented the accomplishment of the objective of the war in ways in which Clauswitz would have said guaranteed failure.

The Liberation Army won the war only to lose the peace in its own Vietnam War in Cambodia. Their victory in 1975 was not a clear-cut victory. It was by default. To them, that may have been the more frustrating reality.

Suddenly we were over Saigon, but I couldn't recognize it. There were several fires throughout the town. I glanced north toward Bien Hoa just eighteen miles away where I had spent a year, and where the VC now, presumably, slept in my old hooch. I got sad on me. I mean some jaw-breaking, teary-eyed sad. When 45,000 good men do the big PCS bit [U. S. combat deaths], something permanent is supposed to come of it.

—A USAF A-7 PILOT, APRIL 29, 1975[1]

12

LOSERS AND LOSERS: VIETNAM AFTER THE FALL OF SAIGON

THE DEATH OF THE ARVN

Hanoi planned well for the final conquest of South Vietnam. Although the Paris Peace Accords, signed in January 1973, specifically prohibited the "introduction of troops, military advisers, and military personnel including technical military personnel, armaments, munitions and war material into South Vietnam," these restrictions applied only to the ARVN and the Viet Cong, not to the North Vietnamese. As a result, during 1973 more than 75,000 replacements infiltrated into South Vietnam from the North. While the VC and ARVN were permitted to replace weapons and munitions on a piece-by-piece basis for material "destroyed, damaged, worn out or used up after the cease-fire," no similar restriction applied to resupply of the NVA by the Soviet Union or Red China. In fact, the accords were silent on any presence at all of North Vietnamese troops in South Vietnam.[2]

At the time the accords were signed in January 1973, the government of South Vietnam had at its disposal an estimated 700,000 troops, 200,000 of which were organized into 13 divisions and 500,000 of which served in the Regional and Popular Forces or in administrative and support units. By contrast, the VC/NVA in the South numbered 220,000 personnel organized into 16 divisions consisting of approximately 123,000 NVA and 25,000 Viet Cong. These divisions were backed by an es-

279

timated in-country 71,000 administrative and support troops as well as the entire military structure of the North Vietnamese Army.

With American military aid dwindling, all American ground combat troops withdrawn from Vietnam by January 1973, and a restriction on the employment of American air power in support of the ARVN, the Paris "Peace" Accords were a green light for Hanoi to lay its final plans for the conquest of the South. Despite these advantages, ultimate victory was not easily attained by the Communists.

Immediately after the cease-fire, Hanoi began building up its armor and artillery in the South. By the end of April 1973 the NVA had close to 500 tanks and more than 250 pieces of 122- and 130mm artillery in the South. They also had a complete arsenal of antiaircraft weapons including 100mm cannon, 12.7- and 14.5mm machine guns, SA-7 "Strela" hand-held heat-seeking missiles, and at least one regiment equipped with surface-to-air missiles (SAMs)—the 263rd, deployed in Quang Tri Province near Khe Sanh.[3]

Moreover, by 1974 the NVA had organized its forces in the South into corps-sized formations,* abandoning the independent or combined divisions that they had used in the past for larger, more mobile combined-arms forces deployed in strategic areas.[4] Following their three-phase plan of warfare, the Communist forces were elevating from a guerrilla to a conventional warfare strategy, applied now on a national level.

Hanoi's plan called for widespread, large surprise attacks beginning in 1975, which were designed to prepare the way for a general offensive and uprising in 1976. The timetable was not inflexible, however. If opportunities for victory should arise early or late in 1975, the plan permitted taking full advantage. As it turned out, the offensive succeeded beyond anyone's—on either side—wildest expectations.[5]

By March 24, 1975, it was apparent to Hanoi that the South could be taken before the beginning of the rainy season in May.[6] Subsequently, what had started out as simply "Campaign 275," became the "Ho Chi Minh Campaign" of final victory.

---

*Patterned after Front 70B, which operated in the DMZ area in 1970. It should be noted that according to North Vietnamese sources, with the withdrawal of U.S. forces, the VC/NVA were then on a parity with the ARVN, whom the North Vietnamese considered vulnerable to an all-out assault (Tourison).

As in the earlier years of the war, the Ho Chi Minh Trail was essential to the success of the spring campaign. Beginning in 1973, enormous effort was expended in upgrading the route. Thousands of workers—engineers, troops, youths, civilian laborers—toiled day and night upgrading roads and bridges. Soon what had once been a series of trails and way stations interdictable by U.S. airpower was transformed into 20,000 kilometers of strategic communications lines including a 1,000-kilometer, 8-meter-wide, all-weather road that accommodated 10,000 vehicles traveling two ways around the clock, and supported by 5,000 kilometers of pipelines.[7] With the advent of Khmer Rouge/ NVA control in northeast Cambodia, an expanded supply line to troops in South Vietnam was also available.

The trip down this trail, which had once required three to six months and was so arduous that many who started out died along the way, could, by early 1974, be made by jeep in only eleven nights at an average speed of thirty kilometers per hour. It was estimated that the number of administrative and support personnel and workers needed to maintain the trail and its logistical facilities in 1974 was nearly 100,000. One official who traveled it at that time remembers that he "drove along this marvel of construction . . . amidst a continual flow of traffic not much different from what I would later experience heading into the suburbs of an American city during rush hour."[8]

The first objective of the spring campaign was the II Corps area where, oddly, the ARVN was weakest, with only about 30,000 men deployed against an estimated 42,000 enemy.[9] While control of the area had historically been the key to domination of the country, the government of South Vietnam and ARVN high command were taken by surprise when the NVA struck.* Successfully concealing their objective and strength from the ARVN, the NVA began the final campaign at 0200, March 10, 1975, with the assault against the town of Ban Me Thuot, capital of Darlac Province, South Vietnam. The NVA outnumbered the ARVN defenders 5.5:1; in tanks and armored vehicles, the ratio in favor of the attackers was 1.2:1; in artillery, 2.1:1.[10] By mid-morning, March 10, elements of the 320th NVA Division were in the city and by nightfall they held the city center.[11] "Basically, the battle was over by 1030 on 11 March

---

*This despite the fact that in early 1967 Maj. Huynh Cu, chief of military training for VC Military Region 5 Headquarters, described in detail to U.S./ARVN intelligence precisely how this attack would eventually unfold! (Tourison)

1975,'' wrote NVA Senior General Van Tien Dung, who had overall command of the Great Spring Offensive.[12]

With Ban Me Thuot in their hands, the NVA attacked Pleiku and other points throughout South Vietnam. Severing supply routes, making ARVN reinforcement and withdrawal extremely difficult, if not impossible, Saigon's control in the Central Highlands instantly began to weaken.

The decision to write off the northern half of South Vietnam in order to consolidate a resistance in the remaining two military regions (Military Regions III and IV) was made at Cam Ranh Bay on March 14, 1975. According to William Le Gro:

> The disastrous turn of events in Military Region 2 led to the turning point in the long and bitter war, compelling President Thieu to make a decision regarding the conduct of the defense which would create chaos for the RVNAF and opportunities for the enemy.[13]

The strategy might have had a chance of success had it been made sooner, but in the face of determined NVA pressure in the Central Highlands and elsewhere in South Vietnam, the plan to retake certain strategic points and commence an orderly withdrawal from the Central Highlands was made too late.* It turned into a rout. Once the civilian population learned of the pullout, a panicked mass exodus ensued. With 60,000 headed for Nha Trang and 400,000 fleeing to Da Nang, the refugees intermingled with military formations impeding the soldiers' movement and ability to deploy and fight.[14] Writers Cao and Dong state:

> The rapid collapse of South Vietnam stunned almost everybody, to include every segment of South Vietnamese society. No one, even our enemy, could imagine that the one-million-man RVNAF could have disintegrated so tragically in only forty-five days. This resulted from a near-total morale collapse which engulfed the population and armed forces of South Vietnam beginning in mid-March 1975.[15]

And collapse South Vietnam did: Pleiku was taken March 17; Quang Tri the 19th; Quang Ngai the 24th; Hue the next day; Da

---

*In fact, there had been *no* contingency planning by ARVN to cover a withdrawal because that would have been planning for defeat, which was contrary to ARVN doctrine.

Nang the 29th; Nha Trang April 1; Dalat the 3rd; Phan Thiet the 19th.*

On April 6, during an interview on *Face the Nation,* United States Secretary of Defense Schlesinger said, "It is plain that the great offensive is a phrase that probably should be in quotation marks. What we have had here is a partial collapse of South Vietnamese Forces, so that there has been very little major fighting since the battle of Ban Me Thuot, and that was an exception in itself."[16]

The NVA/VC continued their almost unimpeded march south. In the final and climactic battle of the campaign, ARVN units held out valiantly against far superior NVA forces at Xuan Loc, twenty-five miles from Saigon. The siege of Xuan Loc lasted eleven days, from April 10 to 21, 1975. The actual fighting began on the night of April 9 with an assault by the 341st NVA Division preceded by a four-thousand-round artillery bombardment against the ARVN 18th Division positions.†

The fighting ended the night of April 16 with a furious assault against the 3rd Battalion, 52nd ARVN Infantry Regiment, during which one thousand rounds of artillery fell into their positions.[17] It was the ARVN's finest moment; it was also their last. By April 21, all ARVN troops at Xuan Loc were withdrawn to Vung Tau or Bien Hoa.

"The road to Saigon," Senior General Dung wrote, "was very good."[18] He was referring specifically to the Saigon–Bien Hoa Highway, but he could have meant the entire spring campaign. The NVA planned and executed the final campaign superbly. They proved their ability to supply and maneuver large conventional combined-arms (infantry, artillery, armor) forces against a numerically superior enemy and, when local advan-

---

*The South Vietnamese Navy, which had the only lift capability to evacuate troops from the cities along the beleaguered coast, was found woefully inadequate for this task.

†Many other ARVN units distinguished themselves during the war, in particular the 18th ARVN Division, whose valorous last stand at Xuan Loc surprised everyone. Originally named the 10th Division, it had the reputation of being the weakest, most ineffective unit in the ARVN. Its numerical designation did nothing to dispel its reputation because "Number 10" was the ultimate insult to quality for Americans and Vietnamese alike. In 1969, the 10th was renamed the 18th and the U.S. 199th Light Infantry Brigade was given the mission of training and upgrading the division. By the time the 199th went home in late 1970, the 18th ARVN was a motivated and capable unit. Unfortunately, the proof of their worth came only in the final days and there were few left to appreciate their new-found proficiency. While Saigon was falling, the last units of the 18th were still fighting the invaders from the North. Several of the division's regiments fought to the last man and never formally surrendered.

tages presented themselves on a very fluid battlefield, they were able to exploit them.

Working also in their favor was the fact that by 1975 the morale of the ARVN had been shattered. The U.S. Army, by saddling them with a logistical tail comparable to its own, and the U.S. Congress, by cutting that tail off, denied them their own "Ho Chi Minh Trail." As a result, the Republic of South Vietnam died under the treads of Vietnamese-manned Soviet tanks backed by conventional infantry and artillery units of the North Vietnamese Army. The myth of a "civil war" executed by indigenous guerrilla forces supported by the bulk of South Vietnam's population was dispelled forever in the hail of NVA fire and steel that descended upon the South in March and April 1975.

THE DEATH OF THE VIET CONG

On April 30, 1975, at twelve-fifteen P.M. Saigon time,* a Viet Cong soldier named Bui Quang Than unfurled the flag of the National Liberation Front on the roof of Doc Lap ("Independence") Palace, former seat of the government of the Republic of South Vietnam.[19] So ended the Vietnamese Communists' thirty-year struggle to unify their country. Shortly afterward, in the first of many place-name changes, Saigon became Ho Chi Minh City in honor of the man whose leadership and vision had made their revolution a success.†[20]

Another visitor to Doc Lap Palace that eventful day was Col. Bui Tin, deputy editor of *Quan Doi Nhan Dan (People's Army),* the North Vietnamese Army newspaper. Wandering through the sumptuous halls, Bui, a veteran of Dien Bien Phu, asserted that he encountered General Doung Van Minh, provisional head of the Saigon government, who was looking for someone to surrender to. "You have nothing to fear," Bui claims to have told the old general. "Between Vietnamese, there are no victors and no vanquished. Only the Americans have been beaten. If you are patriots, consider this a moment of joy. The war for our country is over."[21]

---

*Van Tien Dung, *Our Great Spring Victory,* says eleven-thirty A.M. (p. 120).

†Other changes: The Hotel Caravelle became the Doc Lap (Independence), and Tu Do (Freedom) Street (Rue Catinat in the 1950s) was changed to Dong Khoi (Uprising). But the Saigonese are *still* calling it Catinat.

Outside the palace the "Cadre of the 30th"* welcomed their VC/NVA "liberators" with open arms. One eyewitness recalls thousands of allegedly happy citizens mingling with the soldiers. "I saw nothing but smiles—smiles and waving hands. Homes blossomed with flags—the red and blue banner of the National Liberation Front."[22] Despite the NLF flags, the majority of the troops who entered Saigon that day were NVA rather than VC. Tiziano Terzani, an Italian Communist who witnessed the liberation, gushed enthusiastically over the "reunification" of the two Vietnams and the merger of the Viet Cong into the mainstream of Vietnamese life after years of hiding in the jungles. He wrote, "From that day on people no longer spoke of the 'Vietcong.' "[23]

Only days later Terzani's naïve statement was to prove a bitter prophecy. The morning of May 15, 1975, dawned clear and bright over Ho Chi Minh City. It would be a fine day for the great victory parade. The crowds that began forming in Independence Palace Square long before dawn that morning eventually swelled to several hundred thousand people. Military and political leaders of a reunified Vietnam, their guests and children, filed into the reviewing stands. Some, overcome by the emotion of the historic moment, were in tears.

President of the Democratic Republic of Vietnam Ton Duc Thang spoke of a new era and a new happiness for the whole Vietnamese people; Pham Hung of the Worker's Party reminded the throng that "Only the American imperialists have been defeated. All Vietnamese are the victors."

In the march past that followed, every unit of the North Vietnamese Army, all spruced up and well equipped, seemed represented. Standing with the other notables, Truong Nhu Tang, former minister of justice in the National Liberation Front, began wondering impatiently when the Viet Cong units would appear. At last they did come into sight, "several straggling companies, looking unkempt and ragtag" compared to the NVA, marching under the banner not of the NLF, but of the Democratic Republic of North Vietnam.

Truong asserts he was shocked and bewildered. He turned to Senior General Van Tien Dung, architect of the "Great Spring Victory." Where were the Viet Cong divisions? Truong asked.

---

*Can Bo Ngai 30, in Vietnamese, which became a derogatory term the South Vietnamese used to describe opportunists who became "instant" VC on April 30, 1975, in order to take advantage of the change in their country's leadership (Tourison).

He remembers that Dung stared at him for a long moment and then, lips curved upward in a slight smile, simply replied, ''The army has already been unified.''[24]

Truong subsequently wrote:

> The PRG and the National Liberation Front, whose programs had embodied the desire of so many South Vietnamese to achieve a political solution to their troubles . . . this movement the Northern Party had considered all along as simply the last linkup it needed to achieve its own imperialistic revolution. After the 1975 victory, the Front and the PRG not only had no further role to play; they became a positive obstacle to the rapid consolidation of power.[25]

What happened to the Viet Cong after April 30, 1975, should have come as no surprise to anyone familiar with Hanoi's methods. That high-ranking officials of the NLF, willing architects of the ''big lie,'' want the world to believe now that they entertained any hope of their autonomy in 1975, following the North's almost total takeover of the war after 1968, strains credulity too far.

Truong's justification notwithstanding, thousands of other people chose to cast their lot with the government of the Republic of South Vietnam rather than the NLF. The majority of these people were every bit as devoted to their cause as Truong was to his. They were loyal to the Saigon government. If there is any consolation to be found in these events, it is that the Viet Cong and former members of the Saigon regime are now equally miserable.

Mr. Truong, who currently lives in France, departed from Vietnam by boat in August 1978. He was not the first and certainly not the last person to ''wind up inside a tiger he thought he could ride.''

Another official, one who participated in two sessions of the National Assembly of the Socialist Republic of Vietnam held in Hanoi in 1976 and 1977, told author Al Santoli that by 1976 open dissension had begun to appear among NLF officials because the Northerners had given them so little responsibility in the new government. He added that by 1977 this dissent had begun landing them in jail and he estimated at that time that the Communist authorities had placed 300,000 Vietnamese into prison cells.[26]

After the fall of Saigon, all the National Liberation Front

organizations were either merged with North Vietnamese organizations or simply dissolved. They had served their purpose and were no longer needed. The Central Office for South Vietnam (COSVN), which U.S. and ARVN forces had tried unsuccessfully to find and destroy for years, was officially and quietly dissolved in December 1976 by the Fourth Party Congress in Hanoi. The People's Revolutionary Government (PRG) had already been replaced in June 1975, its ranking officials relegated to secondary appointments in the new, DRV-dominated government. When the ex-PRG officials hosted a farewell party on July 18, 1975, at the Rex Dance Hall in Saigon, none of the Communist Party leaders bothered to show up.[27]

THE THIRD VIETNAM WAR

> *Go to the front, get sacrificed*
> *For a bunch of Central Committee pigs*
> *For a bunch of Central Committee pigs!*
> —*Nguyen Chi Thien*[28]

Wars do not begin in vacuums. Vietnam's invasion of Cambodia on Christmas Day 1978 and China's invasion of Vietnam the following February had antecedents. Before April 30, 1975, these events would have seemed wildly impossible unless one remembered Vietnam's ancient hostility toward China and long-standing Cambodian-Vietnamese animosities, all of which were greatly aggravated by a series of more recent events.

Bui Diem, writing in 1979, pointed out that "the Vietnamese Communists never forgot" that Chou En-lai supported the partition of Vietnam at the 1954 Geneva Conference "and forced them to accept a settlement that fell far short of their expectations." Chou also welcomed President Richard Nixon to Beijing in 1971 "as if the war in Vietnam did not exist."[29]

After 1969, Vietnam began to tilt more and more toward Moscow and away from Beijing. In June 1978, Hanoi joined Moscow's trade alliance, the Council for Mutual Economic Assistance (COMECON). About that same time, the Vietnamese Communists began a purge of the ethnic Chinese in their ranks. There were many arrests and forced deportations—estimated between 70,000 and 90,000.*[30] It is estimated that between

---

*Known as the *Hoa*, there were an estimated 860,000 ethnic Chinese in Vietnam in 1978—700,000 in the fifth and sixth districts of Ho Chi Minh City (previously Cho

1977 and 1979, 263,000 ethnic Chinese fled to China.[31] China, which had supplied the Vietnamese with an estimated $14 billion (and 350,000 troops) from 1954 to 1974, cut off all aid following this repression.

Other evidence that Hanoi was placing itself within the Soviet sphere of influence became more apparent in March 1978 when three Russian warships—a guided-missile cruiser, a frigate, and a minesweeper—visited Cam Ranh Bay. Western intelligence sources also noted the presence in Vietnam of at least two Soviet TU-95D reconnaissance planes. Hanoi denied it had granted the Soviet Union permanent base facilities in its country, but the strategic importance to the Soviet Far Eastern Fleet of the huge U.S.-built port complex at Cam Ranh was not missed by analysts.[32]

Finally, in November 1978, Hanoi made the relationship official by signing a treaty of friendship and cooperation with Moscow, placing itself firmly within the Russian orbit. One more spark and the tinder-box relations between China and Vietnam would burst into flame.

Not content with merely slaughtering an estimated one million of their own people after the fall of Phnom Penh in April 1975, the Khmer Rouge (Cambodian Communists) under Pol Pot* initiated a campaign of "senselessly dangerous provocations" of Vietnam.[33] These provocations included reprisals against, and persecution of, ethnic Vietnamese living in the Cambodia-Vietnam border region as well as armed incursions into Vietnamese territory. The most blatant cross-border attack, resulting in 2,000 casualties, occurred in Tay Ninh Province in December 1977.[34] Another penetration occurred in June 1978 when Khmer Rouge forces, using Chinese tanks and heavy artillery, pushed ten miles into Vietnamese territory. The Vietnamese responded by besieging the Cambodian towns of Mimot and Karek. Throughout the rest of the summer and into the fall of 1978, these border clashes continued until a de facto state of war prevailed between the two Communist states.[35] Vietnamese forces were deployed along the border and former ARVN officers undergoing "reeducation" in the area were quickly moved farther

Lon when the city was known as Saigon) and another 160,000 in Quang Ninh Province, bordering China.
*Pseudonym of Saloth Sar, a follower of Ho Chi Minh in the 1940s.

east, to prevent the possibility they might have been recruited by the Khmer Rouge into a fifth column.[36]

It seems sheer madness that the Cambodians attacked Vietnam, considering that the Vietnamese then had the largest, best-equipped, and most experienced army in Southeast Asia, second in size only to China. But the Pol Pot regime, never a rational government by any standard, was reacting to a well-founded historical imperative that considered Vietnam an ''alien enemy civilization.''[37]

Both sides issued formal justifications for their actions. The Cambodian statement, *Livre Noir (The Black Book),* and the two-volume Vietnamese response, *Kampuchea Dossier,* are full of the familiar denunciations that characterize the rhetoric of Communist powers in conflict. Writer Nayan Chanda commented that ''few could have foreseen . . . that the conflict would generate such primeval hatred and pure racism.'' Chanda's naïve comments notwithstanding, the Cambodians referred to the Vietnamese as ''savages'' while the Vietnamese insinuated that both Pol Pot and Foreign Minister Ieng Sary have Chinese blood in their backgrounds.[38] To the Vietnamese, the insinuation of mixed racial ancestry is a deadly insult.

The Vietnamese/Cambodian conflict is another of those anomalies of in-fighting so common in the history of this region. In 1954, when the Viet Minh were obliged to withdraw their forces from Cambodia following the Geneva Peace Accords, they took with them 4,000 Cambodian boys aged ten to fifteen years. These youths were educated in Hanoi and married Vietnamese women. When General Lon Nol ousted Prince Norodom Sihanouk in March 1970, many of these young expatriates returned to participate in the Khmer Rouge insurgency that eventually toppled Lon Nol's government.[39] In 1989 thirteen of the original twenty-three Khmer Peoples Republic (PRK) Central Committee members had spent more years in Hanoi than in their own country.[40]

Vietnamese troops crossed into Cambodia in force early in December 1978. By December 11 they had pushed to within twenty-five miles of the Mekong River port of Kratie. Farther south they had penetrated seventy miles into Cambodian territory by December 14, putting them in position to cut Highway 4 linking Phnom Penh and the port city of Kompong Son on the Gulf of Siam. During this fighting the Kampuchean United Front for National Salvation (KNUFNS—Vietnamese-supported rebels) reported killing or wounding over five hundred of Pol Pot's soldiers.[41]

The Vietnamese then paused their advance inside Cambodia as they consolidated their positions and brought up troop reinforcements. By December 25, 1978, they had an estimated 135,000 troops near the border. On Christmas Day, an estimated 100,000 Vietnamese troops—as many as 13 divisions—supported by Soviet-made aircraft renewed the offensive and the incursion became an invasion.[42]

This conventional two-prong wartime operation used the "blooming lotus" tactic of attacking the enemy's main forces directly while outflanking him to destroy the remnants. The Vietnamese main elements to the northwest seized the Mekong River port of Kratie by December 30 and then wheeled southwest down the Mekong toward Kompong Cham to cut the road to Phnom Penh. Meanwhile, farther south, motorized units supported by air cover and artillery took the town of Takeo and then moved directly north to Phnom Penh along Cambodia's major highways.

The forces of Pol Pot were caught off guard. Anticipating a thrust along Highway 7 in the vicinity of the Parrot's Beak, they concentrated the main body of their army there and found themselves quickly outflanked by the Vietnamese forces. On January 2 the Pol Pot government advised all foreigners to leave the country. "Several thousand" Chinese railway workers, maintenance personnel, technicians and military personnel were evacuated from Kompot Som by two Chinese freighters.[43]

Phnom Penh fell on January 7, 1979. On January 8 the Vietnamese installed Heng Samrin, a dissident Khmer Rouge military commander, as the president of an eight-man People's Revolutionary Council, as the People's Republic of Kampuchea had been renamed.[44] On the same day more than seven hundred foreigners who had been serving as advisers and diplomats to the Pol Pot regime crossed into Thailand at the border town of Aranyaprathet. About 650 of these were Chinese technicians and military advisers.[45]

Meanwhile, the Vietnamese forces pushed steadily on to the Thai border, mopping up what was left of the Khmer Rouge forces. By January 12 there was heavy fighting near Battambang. Pol Pot's forces made a stand at Siem Reap, near the Angkor Wat temple ruins. Heavy fighting was also reported in the towns of Kompong Speu, Kompong Cham, and Svay Rieng, south and east of Phnom Penh.

While there was never any doubt about the final outcome of this invasion, the Vietnamese did encounter some problems and temporary reverses. As they pushed farther into Cambodia their lines of communications and supply became attenuated, causing their forces to bog down because of logistical and transportation problems. This afforded the Khmer Rouge local tactical opportunities that they quickly seized. On January 15 the Cambodians managed to recapture Kompong Som and the provincial capital of Takeo, but the Vietnamese forces quickly retook those positions with the assistance of air support.[46]

Pol Pot's field headquarters at Tasanh, southwest of Battambang, only six miles from the Thai border, was finally overrun in an operation that began March 27. Radio Hanoi reported killing one thousand Khmer Rouge and driving another eight hundred over the border "in panic." It was reported at the time that the Vietnamese used Soviet aircraft to ferry troops into Battambang and Siem Reap.[47]

As in their Great Spring Offensive of 1975, the Vietnamese proved again in Cambodia that they could mount a well-coordinated ground offensive, but this time with the added dimension of effective air power.

The Vietnamese success in these initial operations is not surprising. At that time Hanoi had at least 600,000 men in its active army, 200,000 of whom were stationed in South Vietnam, with another 50,000 in Laos. These men were well armed and supported by Soviet and captured American tanks, artillery, and aircraft. In addition, Hanoi could call upon an estimated 70,000 paramilitary forces and a militia of over a million men. The Cambodians, according to one observer, faced the invasion with an army of only 200,000 poorly equipped troops who lacked experienced and dedicated commanders.[48] This comment notwithstanding, the Khmer Rouge forces were combat-hardened themselves after five years of fighting against the Lon Nol government, from whose army they had captured all the modern equipment furnished it by the United States.

Why the Vietnamese launched a major attack against Cambodia seems obvious enough, given the provocations initiated by the Pol Pot regime, but why they pushed onward to occupy the entire country is less clear. When the Pol Pot government rejected a three-point Vietnamese proposal for negotiation of their differences in February 1978, Hanoi might have felt that invasion was the only course to rid itself of an obstreperous thorn in its side. No doubt the Fourth Plenum of the Vietnamese Communist Party convened in Hanoi in mid-February 1978 had Cambodia high on its list of topics for discussion. The Russians may have recommended a quick, surgical strike and it is possible that this was the limit of the Vietnamese intent.[49] Then, finding the road to Phnom Penh open, they apparently decided to go all the way.

The Vietnamese could have been encouraged in this escalation by divisions within the Khmer Rouge itself, most notably by the apparent success of Heng Samrin's United Front for the National Salvation of Kampuchea (KNUFNS). However, in view of the fact that Heng had obtained Vietnamese support for KNUFNS in October 1978, it may be that the Vietnamese were already laying groundwork for local support of more than just a cross-border punitive operation.[50] That possibility is lent further support by the fact that shortly after the invasion, the Vietnamese began to settle thousands of their own people in Cambodia, reportedly 400,000 to 600,000 between 1979 and 1984.[51] Knowing the Vietnamese Communists' penchant for the long view and thorough planning, it is difficult to believe anything spontaneous of them.

"It was a deliberate attack," Bui Diem, former South Vietnamese ambassador to the United States, wrote, "masterminded by a small group of hard-core revolutionaries in Hanoi, who took advantage of what they called 'historic circumstances' to fulfill their decades-old dream of domination."[52] Bui Diem's denunciation directly contradicts Hanoi's claim that one of the reasons it moved into Cambodia was for humanitarian concerns. The fact is, Pol Pot had long since wreaked his ghastly "reforms" before the Vietnamese invaded. And since many of the men in the invading army were young South Vietnamese, sending them into Cambodia was a good way to get rid of potential dissenters while Hanoi worked its own revenge upon the former Republic of South Vietnam.

One thing is certain—neither Hanoi nor Phnom Penh acted as the unwilling pawns of either Russia or China; the great powers were drawn into the fray solely by the actions of the two belligerents. Hanoi must have known, as its forces hammered their way across Cambodia, that sooner or later China would react. In their swift move through Cambodia, the Vietnamese forces left behind small pockets of resistance, apparently forgetting what experienced Communist guerrillas should have known all along: "that in an unfriendly country, territory, highways, and cities mean very little if rural guerrillas are permitted to survive.''[53] The Khmer Rouge guerrillas were desperate but they had one important ally. On February 17, 1979, China struck hard at the SRV's northern borders to ease the pressure on the Khmer Rouge. The Vietnamese were not caught unprepared, but now they were in a two-front war and the one in the north against the Chinese required immediate attention.

Like a dormant volcano about to erupt, China gave ample warning before the February 17 attacks. These ''warnings'' consisted of numerous violations of the China-Vietnam border—873 recorded by the Vietnamese in 1977 alone. In 1978 the Vietnamese claimed 584 ''outright violations'' of their frontier ''going from infantry rifles to machine guns and mortars.'' They also counted 100 violations of their air space and ''481 provocations in our territorial waters.''[54]

For their part, the Chinese alleged more than 1,100 disputes from August 1978 to the eve of their ''counterattack.'' The Chinese accused the Vietnamese of carrying out 705 ''armed provocations,'' and 162 armed incursions into China resulting in the killing and wounding of 300 frontier guards and civilians.[55]

In countering some of these Chinese-initiated border incidents in 1977, it was alleged that the Vietnamese did poorly due to lack of discipline among the troops and poor leadership. Much of the problem was blamed on the presence of ethnic South Vietnamese units. Subsequently, some commanders were removed and army discipline tightened. As a result, General Hoang Cam, a rising star (he had commanded the NVA IV Corps during the Ho Chi Minh Campaign in April 1975), was given increased command responsibilities. It was he who led the Cambodian invasion.[56]

Meanwhile, various Chinese officials were making unequivocal public statements. Deng Xiao-Peng said in January 1979, ''If we don't give the Vietnamese a necessary lesson, then we might as well sit with folded arms. We cannot allow Vietnam to run everywhere. We may be forced to do what we do not like to do.'' Li Hsien-nien, vice premier, stated in February, ''We must warn Vietnam against turning a deaf ear to our words.''[57]

Rhetoric aside, one thing is certain: The Chinese prepared well for their invasion. In their planning, they were faced with three major considerations—how well the Vietnamese would fight, what Russia's reaction would be, and the weather.

The rainy season begins in North Vietnam in April, with the spring thaw on the Amur and Ussuri rivers in the northeast along the China-USSR border beginning at about the same time. The Chinese had to accomplish their objectives in Vietnam before their forces got bogged down in the monsoon while at the same time allowing the Russians minimal weather advantage if they launched punitive ground attacks against them. The break-even point in this weather gamble was mid-February.[58]

The Chinese wagered, quite correctly, that the Soviet Union was not prepared to go to war to aid the SRV. Besides the weather, which would not be to their advantage, the Russians at that time were deeply engaged in the SALT II talks with the United States. Beijing assumed they would not endanger the talks by going to war with China.

Another factor to China's advantage was that in late 1978 the Chinese had cut off oil exports to Vietnam, depriving the SRV of half its supply. Thus a mid-February invasion would catch the Vietnamese, who were still heavily engaged in Cambodia, with low-level reserves.[59]

All these factors indicate that the Chinese planned for a quick incursion with limited military objectives. During the first week of the invasion they described it as a "self-defense counterattack" and denied any desire to occupy Vietnamese territory. Despite these protests, the Chinese wisely kept everyone in doubt as to just how far they were willing to go.

Having played their cards perfectly up to this point, the Chinese, according to some observers, then made a strategic mistake. When the People's Liberation Army (PLA) forces had not yet achieved the lightning victory expected after a week of fighting, Vice Premier Wang Chen announced they would not push on into the Red River Delta.[60] Henceforth, according to this view, the Vietnamese knew just how to respond and seen in this light, their refusal to divert troops from the Cambodian front or to commit reserves in the North seems perfectly reasonable.

But another view is that China's invasion of North Vietnam was intended only to send Hanoi and Moscow a clear message: Watch your step, comrades. The blunt truth is that if China had wanted to, it could have rolled the Vietnamese up like a rug.

No one, except of course the Chinese leaders—and they are not talking—is quite sure when China decided to attack Vietnam. That the Chinese had been massing forces along the China-Vietnam border for weeks before the invasion, however, seems proof that the decision was made some time in advance. One analyst believes it likely the decision was approved at the Third Plenum of the Chinese Communist Party Central Committee in

December 1978.[61] Another reason is that contingency planning for an invasion of Vietnam had probably been going on for a number of years, although large-scale movement of troops into the border regions was not detected until January 1979.[62]

China's reasons for launching the attack were manifold—to "punish" Vietnam for its recent ties with the Soviet Union, for its repression of the *Hoa,* to assert its hegemony in the area, to prove the Soviets an unreliable ally, and to relieve the pressure on its Cambodian ally.

Equally important, in light of the beginning of the reduction of Soviet assistance to Vietnam in the late 1980s, is a compelling argument that the Chinese action was *intended* to draw the Soviets into an inconclusive war in an area traditionally influenced by China. The Soviets did indeed tire of the "drain" imposed on them by Hanoi's war in Cambodia and, as they began to withdraw that support, the Vietnamese were left holding the bag. The PAVN had become like the ARVN ten years earlier and Hanoi is still trying to come to grips with this turn of events.

The Chinese committed 8 army corps (20 divisions) numbering 300,000 men supported by 1,000 tanks and 1,500 heavy artillery pieces to the Vietnam invasion. The total strength of the Chinese army at the time was estimated at 121 infantry, 40 artillery, and 3 airborne divisions supported by about 5,000 aircraft.[63] Most of the tanks and infantry were held in reserve, however, and never committed, including an estimated 700 to 1,000 aircraft. At the maximum extent of the invasion, the PLA is estimated to have had only 80,000 troops inside Vietnam, with most of those engaged in the battle for Lang Son.[64] To counter these forces the Vietnamese had between 75,000 and 100,000 border troops and militia.

The invasion was launched along two main axes, from Yunnan Province in the northwest, southeast toward the Vietnamese provincial capital of Lao Cai across the Red River from China (and farther south against Lai Chau, where the Chinese forces penetrated fifty miles into Vietnamese territory); and from Kwangsi Province, southwest toward the provincial capital of Lang Son, along the main rail and road artery connecting China and Vietnam. Although the initial invasion penetrated the border in twenty-six different places, the main objectives appear to have been the provincial capitals.

Sources differ on the tactics used by the Chinese. The Vietnamese claim the Chinese used frontal assaults preceded by heavy artillery bombardments combined with attacks in the rear by "montagnard commandos."[65] Western sources, however, deny the Chinese used direct assault, but rather employed a more cautious method of infiltrating sapper forces to weaken Vietnamese positions while main forces advanced along the roads to exploit their successes—the same so-called "exploding lotus" tactic used by the NVA during the 1975 spring campaign in the South and in 1978 against the Cambodians. What is known for sure is that when the main assault commenced at 0500, February 17, thousands of Chinese soldiers were already inside Vietnam, securing crossing sites and destroying installations and communications links.[66]

The fighting in some areas was extremely heavy, particularly around the provincial capitals of Lao Cai and Lang Son. Lao Cai was taken by the Chinese on February 19. They then advanced down the Red River, where they encountered stiff resistance and were thrown back upon the city with heavy losses.

Lang Son was not occupied until March 5 and then only after the Chinese had laid siege to the city for three days. The attack began February 27 with a tank-infantry assault preceded by intense artillery-preparation fires against Vietnamese positions situated on the high ground north of the city. The attack against the city itself did not get under way until March 2. On March 5 at 1440 local time the city finally fell when PLA forces succeeded in capturing the high ground to the southwest.[67] Less than four hours after the fall of Lang Son the Chinese announced they had reached their objectives and would withdraw from the occupied territories.

The Vietnamese border troops and local forces fought outnumbered at least two to one in the frontier areas and still inflicted substantial losses on the invaders—estimated by some sources as high as 50,000. Vietnamese losses are estimated at about the same number.[68] Other estimates for Chinese losses are lower, at 20,000 casualties and 1,000 prisoners.[69] Perhaps as many as 30,000 men died on both sides between February 17 and March 15 with another 45,000 civilian and military personnel wounded.[70] However, considering the intensity of the fighting, which was terrific in some places, the higher casualty figures for both sides are probably more accurate. One Western observer is reported to have said that in one attack the Chinese fired almost one artillery shell every second.[71] Wu Xiuquan, the PLA's deputy chief of General Staff, told a French delegation on May 2, 1979, that his forces had sustained 20,000 casualties, the Vietnamese 50,000.[72]

The Vietnamese did not seem to panic. After China announced their forces would not go into the Red River Delta, Hanoi's high command had little reason to consider the Chinese invasion as anything more than a limited incursion. Drew Middleton, writing in *The New York Times* on March 6, 1979, characterized the Vietnamese reaction as "surprisingly lethargic."[73] While Hanoi did reinforce the embattled border units with troops brought in from Laos and the South (ferried in by Soviet-built aircraft),[74] they had no reason to commit their best divisions to a war whose objectives, they must have realized by late February at the latest, were limited from the start. All Hanoi had to do was check the invaders. By refusing to commit either their air or naval forces, and holding the bulk of their invasion army in reserve, the February admission as to objectives notwithstanding, the Chinese clearly telegraphed their punch—or delivered their message—to Hanoi. Knowing this, Hanoi was justified holding back the commitment of its own excellent air forces. The Vietnamese knew they did not have to fight the entire Chinese army.

By their own account, the Vietnamese used the terrain to the best advantage while the Chinese suffered from poor coordination between their infantry, artillery, and armor.[75] This is substantiated by Western observers.[76] Under the circumstances, however, their border and frontier forces fought extremely well.

Regardless of the results, though, the Chinese certainly succeeded in getting Hanoi's attention with their February invasion and proved that their threats should never be taken lightly. In 1987 an estimated 700,000 men of the Vietnamese army were deployed along the Chinese border, 60 percent of the active army and three times the troop strength thought sufficient to secure the area before the border war.[77]

If the border war was intended by the Chinese to relieve pressure on the Khmer Rouge, it was a total failure. No troops were diverted from the Cambodian front, and fighting there actually increased in intensity in April 1979, proving that Vietnam had lost neither the will nor the military capacity to continue that war. Also, the Chinese invasion only forced Vietnam more firmly into its alliance with the Soviet Union. But alternately, the Chinese may have *wanted* the Vietnamese to get bogged down in Cambodia, with Soviet assistance—Vietnam's own "Vietnam," in a way. If so, the plan worked perfectly because a decade later Vietnam was still slugging away at the Khmer Rouge, to the great detriment of its own economy and international prestige. Even with the return of Prince Sihanouk from his twenty-year exile in China, and the beginning of peace talks between the rival factions, true peace is still elusive in Cambodia and the horrors of war loom as menacingly as ever over its long-suffering people.

Today, the borders between China and Vietnam are still not quiet and the unrest has spread to the common border between China and Laos. Despite the reported final pull-out of PLA forces from Cambodia in the early fall of 1989, a bitter guerrilla war still raged there. After nearly forty-five years of uninterrupted warfare, the Vietnamese Communists seem to avoid peace and seek further conflict. They now possess one of the most combat-hardened armies in the world and their leaders are as determined as ever to use it.

VIETNAM TODAY

> *Mortifying this one great mistake*
> *Forever marked in history!*
> *O formerly, life was suffering*
> *But it now is worse than hell!*
> —*Nguyen Chi Thien*[78]

As remarkably successful as Hanoi has been in waging war, it has never learned how to wage peace. Today Hanoi spends an estimated 25 percent of its gross national product on the military budget. It maintains a regular force estimated at 1,260,000 men: 1,100,000 in the army, 40,000 in the navy, and 120,000 in its air force. Another 3,000,000 men are in the reserve forces.[79]

Cam Ranh Bay became "the only jewel in the Soviet Union's Pacific crown."[80] The Russians quadrupled the size of the facility after the departure of the Americans. In March 1987, Admiral James A. Lyons, commander in chief of the U.S. Pacific Fleet, produced photographs showing a frigate, a destroyer, a diesel attack submarine, and a nuclear submarine as well as five TU-95 long-range reconnaissance planes and fifteen TU-16 bombers using the port and its airfield.*[81] When the Soviet em-

---

*In late 1990, it was widely reported in the Western press that the Soviet Union "as part of its policy of economic retrenchment and political accommodation with the West" had begun pulling its naval and air forces out of Cam Ranh. In the wake of this event, Nguyen Van Linh, Communist Party chief of the SRV, offered the United States and Japan the use of the complex! "Vietnam is ready to overcome all obstacles on the path to normalization" with the United States, Linh is quoted as having stated,

pire collapsed in 1991, Vietnam was well on its way to becoming another Cuba. So long as unreconstructed Marxists rule in Hanoi, the question is not whether but to what extent Vietnam will turn to Red China for support. Before the Soviet drawdown in the 1990s, it was estimated that 2,500 Soviet military personnel were now permanently stationed at the Cam Ranh naval/air complex and at an airbase located near Da Nang.[82]

During the 1980s, Moscow gave the Vietnamese MiG-23 Flogger jets, Mi-24 Hind attack helicopters and *Petya II*–class frigates. An estimated 68 percent of Vietnam's total imports came from the Soviet Union.[83]

The Vietnamese withdrawal from Cambodia, once it began, moved quickly. In May 1988, Hanoi pledged to withdraw 50,000 of the 120,000 troops by the end of the year.[84] By December 1988 the U.S. State Department estimated that the Vietnamese had withdrawn 20,000 to 30,000. In the same pledge, Vietnam promised to remove all of its troops from Cambodia by 1990. As of March 1989, 80,000 were still there[85] but according to wide coverage in the Western press, all of these troops were withdrawn by the fall of 1989.*[86] If in fact Vietnam has entirely removed its combat forces from Cambodia, it is a rare example of Hanoi honoring a promise—and ahead of schedule at that.

In the spring of 1989 the number of Khmer Rouge guerrillas active in Cambodia were estimated at 35,000 men, including logistical and support personnel. This force is actively backed by China. The non-Communist resistance forces, the Khmer People's National Liberation Front (KPNLF) and the Sihanoukist National Army (SNA) were estimated to have in the field 2,000 and 9,000 men respectively.[87] The People's Republic of Kampuchea (PRK) forces are estimated to number about 60,000. This force has been trained, armed, and backed by the Vietnamese and despite their withdrawal from Cambodia, Hanoi will probably continue to support the PRK forces as long as China continues to back the Khmer Rouge. It is estimated that between

adding that "some American officials still have reservations." (*The Washington Times*, "Vietnam offering Japan, U.S. use of Cam Ranh Bay Facilities," November 12, 1990, p. A7.)

*On October 1, 1989, Thailand's Deputy Foreign Minister Prapas Limpabhandu reported that despite Hanoi's claim to have withdrawn its forces by September 27, "tens of thousands of Vietnamese troops" were still in Cambodia and that "tens of thousands of Vietnamese settlers have been recruited and trained to be soldiers replacing the withdrawn troops." (*Asian Defence Journal*, "Thailand Says Vietnamese Troops Still in Cambodia," November 1989, p. 94.)

50 and 60 percent of Hanoi's budget now goes to propping up this surrogate government in Phnom Penh.[88] With these forces poised in the wings, the peace negotiations begun in 1991 are nothing if not tenuous.

The Vietnamese military forces have also paid a heavy price for Hanoi's Cambodian war. Since 1980 at least one thousand Vietnamese troops, most of them ethnic Southerners drafted into the army, have deserted to Thailand. Significantly, most of these men admitted to no special training or indoctrination before they were sent to Cambodia and their greatest fear while there was from enemy booby traps.[89]

Neither war nor peace has brought prosperity to Vietnam. In 1966 North Vietnam was classified among the poorest nations in the world with a per capita income of under $100 per year.[90] In 1987 the per capita income of the Socialist Republic of Vietnam (whose fiscal mismanagement was now extended to the South by right of conquest) was estimated at only $180 with an annual estimated inflation rate of 700 percent.[91]

Other sources estimated the inflation rate as running at levels over 1,000 percent annually, with severe food shortages throughout the country and a breakdown in the rationing system for state workers. In June 1988 it was reported that there had been no rice ration distribution in the North since February while the free-market price of rice had risen to 1,000 dong per kilogram. At that time the U.S. dollar exchange for the Vietnamese dong was running at 3,000 to 1, while the basic wage of a state employee remained at between 5,000 to 10,000 dong per month.*[92] The economy seemed to have collapsed totally in 1988 after the central bank decided in February to print large-denomination notes of 1,000, 2,000, and 5,000 dong. By year's end the dollar was selling at a rate of 5,000 to 1 against the Vietnamese dong.[93]

It was also estimated in mid-1988 that the staples output per person for all of the SRV was then "well below" 300 kilograms. UNICEF estimates that 350 kilograms are required for an adequate diet, but the Vietnamese "rule of thumb" is "around 300."[94] These shortages are at least partly due to poor harvests because of bad weather, but the stark reality of life in Vietnam today is that after more than a dozen years under Communist

---

*In 1966 a common laborer in the Republic of South Vietnam earned between 60 and 100 dong a day. At that time the rate of exchange between the dong (South Vietnamese piaster) and the U.S. dollar was 73.5 to 1.

misrule, the country in 1988 had to seek emergency food aid abroad. The SRV today is among the twenty poorest nations in the world. It has the sixth largest army—after China, the former USSR, the United States, India, and North Korea.[95] The breakup of the Soviet Union and the loss of its support will undoubtedly make matters even worse.

Adding to economic hardships, the Vietnamese currently living in the South have been the victims of harsh political repression. Every person in the country feels the long arm of the Communist government through rigid controls placed over their every movement. Control is enforced by the Ministry of Interior through the SRV Public Security Service. "You gradually realize," one refugee has written of life in the new socialist republic, "that you have no life of your own."[96]

In 1975 as many as 300,000 former officials and military personnel of the South Vietnamese government were ordered to report to "reeducation" centers—which turned out to be nothing more than concentration camps where thousands died and thousands more still languish as political prisoners. It is difficult to estimate how many are still in captivity.[97]

The South Vietnamese have responded to this oppression with characteristic forbearance and humor. For instance, the abbreviation for "socialism," XHCN (xa hoi chu nghia), which appears prominently in posters and banners throughout the country, is often rendered as xao het cho noi, "so deceitful you can't tell the difference."

Another way of getting back at the Communist regime is by creating cynical versions of popular patriotic songs such as the one every child learns in school:

> Last night I dreamed of meeting Uncle Ho.
> His beard was long, his hair was gray.
> I kissed him tenderly on both cheeks . . .

and changing it to

> Last night I dreamed of meeting a lost wallet.
> In the wallet I found 4,400 dong.
> I was so happy I ran and showed it to Uncle Ho.
> He smiled at me. "Let's split it," he said.[98]

Unfortunately, humor and forbearance are not enough to make life bearable for everyone in today's unified Socialist Republic of Vietnam. Between 1975 and as of this writing in late 1990, 660,000 people have fled Vietnam by boat. While the number of people arriving in neighboring countries from the sea has dropped off since the spring of 1979, when an estimated 60,000 were leaving Vietnam each month, 18,168 boat people were given asylum in various Southeast Asian countries during the first nine months of fiscal year 1987. It is estimated that at least 100,000 have perished at sea during this fourteen-year exodus to freedom.[99]

Between April 30, 1975, and September 30, 1988, a total of 1,739,189 people have fled Indochina, 837,160 of whom (including 528,000 Vietnamese through October 1987) have been admitted into the United States. Another 167,892 remained in various refugee camps awaiting resettlement. This figure does not include an estimated 300,000 Cambodians classified as displaced persons who are languishing on the Thai-Cambodian border, victims of the long guerrilla war in their country. Also omitted from most statistical tables are the 672,000 whose names are in the Orderly Departure Program computer file at the U.S. Embassy in Bangkok. These are Vietnamese who have applied for official permission to leave their country to be reunited with family members who have fled previously.[100]

Many of these people are "permitted" to flee by boat with the collusion of local authorities. The usual bribe is one to two taels (a tael is equivalent to 1.21 ounces) of gold per person. The SRV government is said to have made $115 million or 2.5 percent of its GNP in 1978 from this traffic in human misery.[101]

The cost of the Vietnam War in human terms was staggering. The South Vietnamese lost between 183,000 and 250,000 men killed in action and almost 500,000 wounded; between 300,000 and 400,000 civilians were killed and from 900,000 to 1,000,000 wounded. The VC/NVA lost, by various estimates, between 666,000 and 924,000 killed; 65,000 North Vietnamese civilians are estimated to have been killed.[12] If one accepts the usual ratio of 3:1 for wounded to killed, then the Communist forces suffered between 1.9 and 2.7 million wounded during the war.

The VC/NVA veterans of the war, especially those who were severely wounded, have paid an inestimable price for the victory. The SRV is said to be operating nine major centers and a number of smaller provincial facilities to take care of the disabled vets. "I don't feel any regret that I took part in the war, even now that I am paralyzed,'' one vet wounded by a mine explosion in the Central Highlands in 1975 told a Western reporter recently, ''but sometimes I do have nightmares—not because I have psychological problems, but because some memories come back at night.'' That is just as well because the state officially denies any of its veterans suffer from war-related psychological problems.

Another paraplegic said of his life in a government hospital, ''We wait until night, and at night we wait until day. And it just goes on that way, like a circle.'' A fellow inmate, wounded near Hue in the 1972 Easter Offensive, complained of the lack of social life at the hospital. ''Society, that's what we need. I always dream of the war. The war still comes back every night. I also dream of being normal again. I dream of the time when I was healthy. I dream that I can run, I can jump, I can dance.''[103] While this man speaks for the war wounded everywhere, he is fortunate, compared to the lot of the ex-ARVN amputees who, because they fought against the Communists, do not even have veteran status in their new socialist republic and must therefore *pay* for prostheses. Most of them are destitute.[104]

The final irony of the Vietnam War is that of all the belligerents, only the United States of America emerged with its power undiminished, its institutions sound, its people free and prosperous, and still a shining beacon of democracy and freedom for the ''world's huddled masses yearning to breathe free.''

AFTERWORD

Writing this book was no easy task. While both of us have rather lengthy lists of previous publications, we have been professional soldiers far longer than we have been writers. From the beginning of this book we have done our best to be as unbiased as possible. This was difficult at times as we wrote of men who had killed and maimed soldiers we had proudly called friends. Memories did not just return while we were researching or working at the keys of our word processors. They crept back in the middle of the night in dreams we thought had been at peace for years.

We began this book with our deepest feelings about the VC/NVA a memory of regret that we had not killed more of them when we had the chance—and a sincere desire to learn more about the enemy who had played such an important role in our lives. As the writing of these pages progressed, we became uneasy with the grudging admiration, respect, and even twinges of sympathy we began to feel for our former enemies. We questioned each other and ourselves about whether we were "going soft" on the VC/NVA who were dedicated to the deaths of our friends and the enslavement of our South Vietnamese allies. Yet the more we researched and wrote, the more we learned that the majority of the VC/NVA did their duty as they saw it—not unlike ourselves and our fellow soldiers. Ultimately, we came to realize that if by fate of birth we had been thrust into their

sandals, we cannot honestly say to which side—North or South—
we would have given our allegiance.

Slowly, and despite our efforts to do otherwise, we began to
feel more kinship with the soldiers of the VC/NVA than we did
with many of our fellow Americans, those who had protested
the war on campuses and in the streets—or worse, avoided altogether any concern with the conflict that otherwise might have
disturbed their placid lives. Even more sobering to us was the
moment when we finally realized that we had more in common
with our former enemies than with the politicians who had sent
us to war.

While we still harbor regrets about America's lack of commitment to victory in Vietnam and its treatment of Vietnam
veterans, we have finally accepted that the VC/NVA who fought
America and our allies earned their place in history. They sacrificed in the belief that their cause was just and that someday
they would return home to enjoy peace with their families. Unfortunately, the Marxist ideologues who rule the reunified Vietnam from Hanoi—men with much innocent blood on their
hands—have not allowed the peace to be enjoyed. Today, war
and economic turmoil continue to be the life-style of the Vietnamese—North and South. The best and brightest are still in the
military or have been driven into exile. The only Vietnamese
who have real peace today are the dead—and the only ones who
have any future are those who have fled to the West.

Since the war it has become fashionable for some American
veterans to claim that they were "betrayed" in Vietnam by their
own government and the American people. But it was Hanoi
who betrayed its own men, for truly, they have become the
"bamboozled" soldiers.

Hopefully, this book has made the individual soldiers of the
Viet Cong and the North Vietnamese Army a little easier to
understand and perhaps more human—or a bit less superhuman,
depending on preconceptions. Some issues, of course, cannot
be resolved. In war can any side claim honor and justice in its
cause? Can the indiscriminate killing of noncombatants ever be
fully justified, no matter what the circumstances? Can good men
serving an evil cause—for whatever reasons—still be good men?

We readily admit that we have neither the wisdom nor the
presumption to venture answers to these age-old questions. What
we can say is this: To Nguyen Van Be Danh—he of the 514th
Local-Force Battalion with the thirty-four girlfriends—and to

the anonymous Viet Cong medic who "lessened pain where there was pain, gave solace where there was unhappiness," and finally to all the VC/NVA who did their duty as they saw it and kept their hands clean, many of whom we faced with no formal introductions on the battlegrounds nearly two decades ago, if we should ever meet (hopefully not all at once), the first drinks are on us.

APPENDIX A ———————————

VC MAIN-FORCE/NVA
COMBAT FORCES ORDER OF BATTLE

Any enemy order of battle study must be used with care. This is not presented as a definitive listing of enemy units, strengths, or locations during the 1966/1967 period. While it was prepared by intelligence professionals relying on a variety of sources, it is at best only an estimate.

1967*
I Corps Tactical Zone

Unit	Strength	Location
2d NVA Division	6,450†	Quang Ngai
1st VC Inf Regt	2,000	Quang Ngai/Quang Tin/Quang Nam
40th, 60th, 70th 90th Bns		
3d NVA Inf Regt	1,300	Quang Tin/Quang Nam
1st, 2d, 3d Bns		
21st NVA Inf Regt	1,500	Quang Tin/Quang Nam
1st, 2d, 3d Bns		
2d VC Inf Regt	1,650	Quang Ngai/Binh Dinh
1st, 2d, 3d Bns		
324B NVA Division	7,800	
803d NVA Inf Regt	2,600	Quang Tri
1st, 2d, 3d Bns		
812 NVA Inf Regt	2,600	Quang Tri
4th, 5th, 6th Bns		

*Source: *MACV Order of Battle Summary*, May–June 1967.
†Totals do not include headquarters and support units.

90th NVA Inf Regt	2,600	Quang Tri
7th, 8th, 9th Bns		
325th NVA Division	7,790	
101 D NVA Inf Regt	1,800	Quang Tri
1st, 2d, 3d Bns		
95C NVA Inf Regt	1,550	Quang Tri
4th, 5th, 6th Bns		
18C NVA Inf Regt	1,650	Quang Tri
7th, 8th, 9th Bns		
5th NVA Inf Regt	1,390	Quang Tri
814th Sapper Bn		
416th Bn		Thua Thien
6th NVA Inf Regt	1,400	Thua Thien
800 VC, 806th		Thua Thien
NVA Bns		
802d VC Bn		Quang Tri

NONDIVISIONAL UNITS (3,200)
1st NVA Bn, 31st Inf Regt, 341st NVA Div, Quang Tri/DMZ
2d NVA Bn, 31st Inf Regt, 341st NVA Div, Quang Tri/DMZ
402d VC Sapper Bn, Quang Nam
120th VC Montagnard Inf Bn, Quang Ngai
409th VC Sapper Bn, Quang Ngai
804th VC Inf Bn, Thua Thien
808th NVA Inf Bn, Thua Thien
810th NVA Inf Bn, Thua Thien

Il Corps Tactical Zone

Unit	Strength	Location
1st NVA Division	9,525	
32d NVA Inf Regt	1,760	Pleiku
334th, 635th, 966th Bns		
66th NVA Inf Regt	1,700	Kontum
7th, 8th, 9th Bns		
88th NVA Inf Regt	1,880	Pleiku
K4, K5, K6 Bns		
24th NVA Inf Regt	1,500	Kontum
4th, 5th, 6th Bns		
33d NVA Inf Regt	860	Darlac
K1, K3 Bns		

Unit	Strength	Location
95B NVA Inf Regt 4th, 5th, 6th Bns	1,825	Pleiku
3d NVA Infantry Division	2,870	
18th NVA Inf Regt 7th, 8th, 9th Bns	1,170	Binh Dinh
22d NVA Inf Regt 7th, 8th, 9th Bns	1,700	Binh Dinh
5th NVA Infantry Division	3,620	
95th NVA Inf Regt 4th, 5th 6th Bns	1,700	Phu Yen
18th NVA Inf Regt 7th, 8th, 9th Bns	1,920	Khanh Hoa

NONDIVISIONAL UNITS (2,290)
30th VC Inf Bn, Phu Yen
95th NVA Arty Bn, Phu Yen
145th VC Arty Bn, Lam Dong
186th VC Inf Bn, Lam Dong
407th VC Sapper Bn, Pleiku
840th VC Inf Bn, Binh Thuan

III Corps Tactical Zone

Unit	Strength	Location
5th VC Infantry Division	3,300	
27th VC Inf Regt 1st, 2d, 3d Bns	1,650	Phuoc Tuy
275th VC Inf Regt 1st, 2d, 3d Bns	1,650	Phouc Tuy
7th NVA Infantry Division	5,250	
141st NVA Inf Regt 1st, 2d, 3d Bns	1,800	Tay Ninh
165th NVA Inf Regt 1st, 2d, 3d Bns	1,950	Tay Ninh
52d NVA Inf Regt 3 Unidentified Bns	1,500	Tay Ninh

9th VC Infantry Division	10,260	
271st VC Inf Regt 1st, 2d, 3d Bns	1,300	Phuoc Long
272d VC Inf Regt 1st, 2d, 3d Bns	1,070	Binh Long
273d VC Inf Regt 1st, 2d, 3d Bns	1,100	Long Khanh
2d VC Inf Regt 267th, 269th Bns	1,200	Hau Nghia
69th VC Arty Regt 52d, 58th Arty, 56th AD Bns	1,700	Tay Ninh
70th VC Inf Regt D1, D2, D3 Bns	1,450	Tay Ninh
84th NVA Arty Regt 1st, 2d, 3d Rocket Bns	1,200	Long Khanh
101st NVA Inf Regt 1st, 2d, 3d Bns	1,240	Tay Ninh

NONDIVISIONAL UNITS (2,380)
C10 VC Sapper Bn, Binh Duong
Dong Nai VC Inf Bn, Long Khanh
1st VC Inf Bn, Hau Nghia
8th VC Arty Bn, Binh Duong
46th VC Recon Bn, Tay Ninh
725 NVA Sniper Bn, Tay Ninh

IV Corps Tactical Zone (5,700)

D 509th VC Inf Bn, Vinh Binh
D857th VC Inf Bn, Sa Dec
D7164 VC Inf Bn, Bac Lieu
Tay Do VC Inf Bn, Phong Dinh
U Minh 2 VC Inf Bn, An Xuyen
U Minh 10 VC Inf Bn, Kien Giang
501st VC Inf Bn, Vinh Binh
503rd VC Inf Bn, Kien Phong
504th VC Inf Bn, Kien Tuong
512th VC Inf Bn, Chau Doc

514th VC Inf Bn, Dinh Tuong
516th VC Inf Bn, Kien Hoa

**Recapitulation, VC Main Force/NVA Combat Forces: 70,355
All Other Units: 52,236**

1973 (January)*

I Corps Tactical Zone

Unit	Strength
325th NVA Infantry Division	5,000
18th, 95th, 101st Regts	
320B NVA Infantry Division	3,500
48B, 64B Regts	
312th NVA Infantry Division	6,000
141st, 165th, 209th Inf Regts	
304th NVA Infantry Division	5,000
9th, 24B, 66th Rets	
324B NVA Infantry Division	5,000
29th, 803d, 812th Regts	
2d NVA Infantry Division	4,000
1st, 52d, 141st Regts	
711th NVA Infantry Division	3,500
3rd, 35th, 270th Regts	

*Source: William E. Le Gro, *Vietnam from Cease-Fire to Capitulation*, pp. 29–30.

NONDIVISIONAL REGIMENTAL UNITS (15,250)
Infantry and Sapper
**27B, 31st, 126th Naval Gp, 270B, DMZ Sapper Group
5th Inf, 6th Inf
45th, 5th Sapper**
Armor
202d, 203d, 572d Tank/Arty Gp
Artillery
45th, 58th, 68th, 84th, 164th, 166th, 675B
Miscellaneous
15th Sapper, 47th Inf, 75th AAA

II Corps Tactical Zone

Unit	Strength
320th NVA Infantry Division	3,000
48th, 64th Regts	
10th NVA Infantry Division	3,800
28th, 66th, 95B Regts	
3d NVA Infantry Division	3,500
2d, 12th, 21st Regts	

NONDIVISIONAL REGIMENTAL UNITS (2,700)
Infantry, Sapper
24C Inf, 400th Sapper
Artillery
40th

III Corps Tactical Zone
(All Under Control of COSVN*)

Unit	Strength
7th Infantry Division	4,100
141st, 165th, 209th Regts	
9th Infantry Division	4,100
95C, 271st, 272d	

---

*Total VC Combat troops in III Corps Tactical Zone: 5,000 out of 24,600.

NONDIVISIONAL REGIMENTAL UNITS (6,200)
Infantry and Sapper
29th Sapper, 33d Inf, 101st Inf, 201st Inf, 205th Inf, 271st Inf,
274th Inf

IV Corps Tactical Zone (All Under Control of COSVN*)

Unit	Strength
1st Infantry Division	3,400
44th Sapper, 52d Inf, 101D Inf Regts	
6th Infantry Division	2,300
24th, 207th Regts	
5th Infantry Division	3,900
6th, 174th, 275th Regts	

*Includes 11,000 VC combat troops out of 27,000 in IV Corps Tactical Zone.

NONDIVISIONAL REGIMENTAL UNITS (1,600)
Infantry
Z-15, Z-18

Total Combat Troops (Including Separate Battalions): 148,000
All Other Units (Administrative & Service): 71,000

APPENDIX B

RANKS AND INSIGNIA OF THE NORTH VIETNAMESE ARMED FORCES

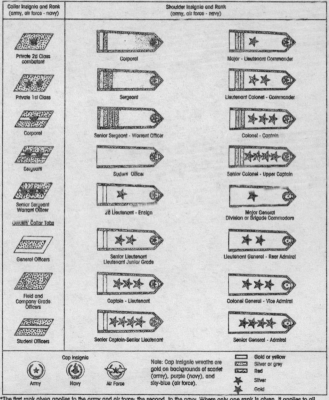

Collar Insignia and Rank (army, air force - navy)	Shoulder Insignia and Rank (army, air force - navy)	
Private 2d Class combatant	Corporal	Major - Lieutenant Commander
Private 1st Class	Sergeant	Lieutenant Colonel - Commander
Corporal	Senior Sergeant - Warrant Officer	Colonel - Captain
Sergeant	Student Officer	Senior Colonel - Upper Captain
Senior Sergeant Warrant Officer	2d Lieutenant - Ensign	Major General Division or Brigade Commodore
Officers' Collar Tabs		
General Officers	Senior Lieutenant Lieutenant Junior Grade	Lieutenant General - Rear Admiral
Field and Company Grade Officers	Captain - Lieutenant	Colonel General - Vice Admiral
Student Officers	Senior Captain-Senior Lieutenant	Senior General - Admiral

Cap Insignia

Army   Navy   Air Force

Note: Cap insignia wreaths are gold on backgrounds of scarlet (army), purple (navy), and sky-blue (air force).

Gold or yellow
Silver or gray
Red
Silver
Gold

*The first rank given applies to the army and air force; the second, to the navy. Where only one rank is given, it applies to all three services.

Source: Smith, et al., *Area Handbook for North Vietnam*, U.S. Government Printing Office, 1967.

APPENDIX C —————

SOVIET 7.62MM ASSAULT RIFLE AK-47 (CHINESE COMMUNIST 7.62MM ASSAULT RIFLE TYPE 56)

Two basic types exist: a model with a conventional wooden buttstock and one with a folding metal stock. Both types of AKs are easily recognized by high front sights, long receivers, large selector/safety on the right side, and long, curved "banana" magazines.

Characteristics

Caliber	7.62mm
Operation	Gas, selective fire
Weight, loaded	10.58 pounds
Length: Stock folded	25.4 inches
Stock extended	34.25 inches
Sight	Front: protected post; rear: adjustable V notch
Feeding device	30-round detachable box magazine
Effective range:	
Semiautomatic	400 meters
Fully automatic	300 meters
Rate of fire: Semiautomatic	40 rounds per minute

  Fully automatic ....   90–100 rounds per minute
  Ammunition...................   Soviet 7.62mm M43 or
                                  Chicom Type 56 rimless car-
                                  tridges

SOVIET 7.62MM SEMIAUTOMATIC CARBINE MODEL SKS (CHINESE COMMUNIST 7.62MM CARBINE MODEL 56)

Recognition factors consist of a permanently attached folding
bayonet, a protruding magazine, a high front sight, and a top-
mounted gas cylinder. The Chicom version differs from the SKS
primarily in manufacturer's markings only.

Characteristics

Caliber 7.62mm
Operation ....   Gas, semiautomatic
Weight, loaded...............   8.8 pounds
Length.........................   40.2 inches
Sight ....   Front: hooded post; rear:
                                  adjustable tangent leaf
Feeding device................   10-round integral magazine
Effective range ....   400 meters
Rate of fire ....   30–35 rounds per meter
Ammunition type.............   Soviet 7.62mm M43 or Chi-
                                  com Type 56 cartridges

SOVIET 7.62MM LIGHT MACHINE GUN RPD (CHINESE COMMUNIST LIGHT MACHINE GUN TYPE 56)

Recognition features of the RPD are a long, exposed barrel and
gas cylinder, with a dumbbell-shaped handguard mounted over
them, and a belt drum that is positioned below the receiver when
it is in place. Minor changes in the gas mechanism and operating
handle are found in various models and copies.

Characteristics

Caliber 7.62mm
Operation ....   Gas, automatic fire, air-
                                  cooled
Weight, loaded................   19.4 pounds
Length.........................   40.8 inches

Sight	Front: hooded post; rear: adjustable V notch
Feeding device	100-round metallic-belt drum
Effective range	800 meters
Rate of fire	150 rounds per minute
Ammunition type	Soviet 7.62mm M43 or Chicom Type 56 cartridges

SOVIET TOKAREV TT33 7.62MM PISTOL (CHINESE COMMUNIST 7.62MM PISTOL TYPES 51 AND 54)

Production of the Soviet TT33 Pistol ceased in 1954, but Communist China continued to make copies. Neither the Soviet nor the Chicom version has a safety device beyond the option of locking the hammer in a half-cock position. If a round was carried in the chamber, there was a distinct chance of accidental discharge.

Characteristics

Caliber	7.62mm
Operation	Recoil, single action
Weight, loaded	2.2 pounds
Length	7.7 inches
Feeding device	8-round box magazine
Ammunition type	7.62mm × 25 Type P pistol cartridge

FRENCH 60MM MORTAR M1935 (U.S. 60MM MORTAR M2) (CHINESE NATIONALIST 60MM MORTAR TYPE 31)

All three versions have a square base plate, a handcrank on the end of the elevating screw housing, and a cross-leveling mechanism of two-piece construction. Each is smoothbore, muzzle-loaded, and drop-fired.

Characteristics

Caliber	60mm
Length of tube: M1935	27.5 inches
M2	28.6 inches
Type 31	26.5 inches

Weight: M1935	38.78 pounds
M2	42 pounds
Type 31	44.5 pounds
Muzzle velocity...............	158 meters per second
Maximum range: M1935....	1,760 meters
M2	1,820 meters
Type 31	1,530 meters
Rate of fire	20–35 rounds per minute
Ammunition type.............	High explosive (HE), smoke, illumination

SOVIET 82MM MORTAR M1937 (1942–1943 VERSION) (CHINESE COMMUNIST 82MM MORTAR TYPE 53)

Both models are muzzle-loaded, drop-fired, smoothbore consisting of three components—tube, base plate, and bipod. The distinguishing features are the baseplate, which is circular with a flat surface across the back edge, and the bipod, which has a turnbuckle type of cross-levelling mechanism between the right leg and the elevating-screw housing.

Characteristics

Caliber	82mm
Length of tube	48 inches
Weight..........................	123 pounds
Muzzle velocity...............	210 meters per second
Maximum range	3,040 meters
Rate of fire	25 rounds per minute
Ammunition type.............	High explosive (HE), smoke

SOVIET ANTITANK GRENADE LAUNCHER RPG-2 AND RPG-7 (CHINESE COMMUNIST ANTITANK GRENADE LAUNCHER TYPES 56 AND 69)

Both the RPG-2 and the RPG-7, as well as their Chicom copies, are muzzle-loaded, shoulder-fired, smoothbore, and recoilless. Recognition features include a gas escape hole on the right side of all models restricting operation to right-handed gunners only, tube insulation on the RPG-2, and a funnel-shaped rear-tube opening to spread the back blast on the RPG-7.

Characteristics

Caliber 40mm
Weight, loaded............... 10.3 pounds
Length.......................... 47 inches
Muzzle velocity............... 84 meters per second
Effective range:
   RPG-2/Type 56 .... 100 meters
   RPG-7/Type 69 .... 500 meters
Rate of fire .... 4–6 rounds per minute
Ammunition.................... High explosive antitank
                                        (HEAT)
Armor penetration............ 6–10 meters

APPENDIX D ─────

VIET CONG
CODE OF DISCIPLINE

1. I will obey the orders from my superiors under all circumstances.
2. I will never take anything from the people, not even a needle or thread.
3. I will not put group property to my own use.
4. I will return that which is borrowed, make restitution for things damaged.
5. I will be polite to people, respect and love them.
6. I will be fair and just in buying and selling.
7. When staying in people's houses I will treat them as I would my own house.
8. I will follow the slogan: All things of the people and for the people.
9. I will keep unit secrets absolutely and will never disclose information even to closest friends or relatives.
10. I will encourage the people to struggle and support the Revolution.
11. I will be alert to spies and will report all suspicious persons to my superiors.
12. I will remain close to the people and maintain their affection and love.

Source: *Know Your Enemy: The Viet Cong*, DoD Gen-20, Washington, DC: U.S. Government Printing Office, 1966, p. 16.

APPENDIX E ──────────

VIET CONG OATH OF HONOR

1. I swear I am prepared to sacrifice all for Vietnam. I will fight to my last breath against imperialism, colonialism, Vietnamese traitors, and aggression in order to make Vietnam independent, democratic and united.
2. I swear to obey absolutely all orders from my commanders, executing them wholeheartedly, promptly, and accurately.
3. I swear to fight firmly for the people without complaint and without becoming discouraged even if life is hard or dangerous. I will go forward in combat without fear, will never retreat regardless of suffering involved.
4. I swear to learn to fight better and shape myself into a true revolutionary soldier battling the invading American imperialists and their servants, seeking to make Vietnam democratic, wealthy and strong.
5. I swear to preserve organizational secrecy, and to keep secret my unit's plans, the name of my unit commander, and all secrets of other revolutionary units.
6. I swear if taken by the enemy I will not reveal any information even under inhuman torture. I will remain faithful to the Revolution and not be bribed by the enemy.
7. I swear in the name of unity to love my friends in my unit

Source: *Know Your Enemy: The Viet Cong*, p. 15.

as myself, to work cooperatively with them in combat and at all other times.

8. I swear to maintain and protect my weapons, ensuring they are never damaged or captured by the enemy.

9. I swear that in my relationships with the people I will do three things and eschew three things. I will respect, protect, and help the people; I will not steal from, threaten, nor inconvenience the people. I will do all things to win their confidence.

10. I swear to indulge in self-criticism, to be a model soldier of the Revolution, and never to harm either the Liberation Army or Vietnam.

APPENDIX F ———————————

THE TEN OATHS
OF THE SOLDIER

1. Defend the Fatherland, fight and sacrifice myself for the people's Revolution.
2. Obey the orders received and carry out the mission of the soldier.
3. Strive to improve the virtues of a Revolutionary soldier.
4. Study to improve myself and build up a powerful Revolutionary Army.
5. Carry out other missions of the Army.
6. Be vigilant, preserve secrecy, heighten the Revolutionary soldier's honor.
7. Help consolidate the internal unity.
8. Preserve and save public properties.
9. Work for the solidarity between the Army and the People.
10. Maintain the Quality and Honor of the Revolutionary soldier.

Source: Michael Charles Conley. *The Communist Insurgent Infrastructure in South Vietnam: A Study of Organization and Strategy.* Washington, DC: The American University, 1967, p. 154.

APPENDIX G ———————
THREE MAIN RULES OF DISCIPLINE
EIGHT POINTS OF ATTENTION

The Three Main Rules of Discipline are as follows:
   (1) Obey orders in all your actions.
   (2) Do not take a single needle or piece of thread from the masses.
   (3) Turn in everything captured.

The Eight Points of Attention are as follows:
   (1) Speak politely.
   (2) Pay fairly for what you buy.
   (3) Return everything you borrow.
   (4) Pay for everything you damage.
   (5) Do not hit or swear at people.
   (6) Do not damage crops.
   (7) Do not take liberties with women.
   (8) Do not ill-treat captives.

Source: Conley, op. cit., p. 154.

APPENDIX H

RULES OF SECRECY

1. Be always vigilant against enemy sabotage plots.
2. Never disclose unit's designation, strength, weapons and commander's name and rank.
3. Never disclose the policy and place for the struggle and use of friendly forces.
4. Never disclose friendly locations and installations.
5. Never disclose the operation route and the roads leading to bases.
6. Do not take the unauthorized persons to the bases, units and agencies.
7. Unauthorized persons will not be allowed to enter bases, units and agencies.
8. Never disclose your name, rank and mission to anyone except to your commander.
9. Report to your commander upon completion of mission.
10. Never disclose the secrets and internal organization of your unit or friendly units to relatives or friends.
11. When living in civilian houses, educate the people on preservation of secrecy according to the "Three NO's motto: no hear, no see, no know."
12. Papers and documents should be carefully protected. They should not be carried along in missions and combat if they are not necessary. When they are no longer needed, they should be burned.

Source: Conley, op. cit., p. 155.

13. The mail should be censored by the command section.
14. Personnel should be permanently educated to observe the regulations on preservation of secrecy.
15. Uncover and punish the violations of these regulations.

APPENDIX I

VC TERRORISM, 1965–1972*

	1965	1966	1967	1968†	1969	1970	1971	1972	Total
Officals									
Killed	209	168	285	362	342	464	352	518	2700
Kidnapped	323	176	192	172	119	160	67	134	1343
Other Civilians									
Killed	1691	1564	3421	5027	5860	5483	3419	3887	30352
Kidnapped	7992	3634	5177	8587	6170	6771	5322	12985	56638
Total Killed	1900	1732	3706	5389	6202	5947	3771	4405	33052
Total Kidnapped	8315	3810	5369	8759	6289	6931	5389	13119	57981

Source: *Southeast Asia Statistical Summary*, Office of the Assistant Secretary of Defense (Comptroller), April 11, 1973, pp. 1–9.

*A. J. Tachmindji, *Journal of Defense Research, Series B: Tactical Warfare*, Vol. 7B, No. 3, Fall 1975. Washington DC: Battelle Columbus Labs, 1975. Table 25, p. 805.

†Prior to August 1968, includes terrorist incidents reported by the SVN National Police. Beginning August 1968, includes additionally those incidents reported through military channels.

APPENDIX J

COMMAND STRUCTURE FOR THE PROSECUTION OF INSURGENCY IN THE SOUTH

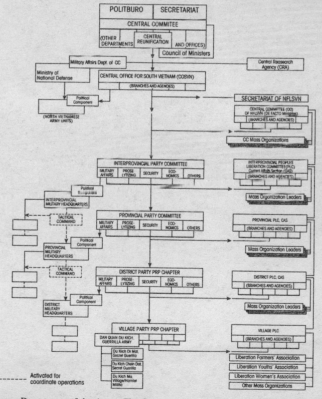

-------- Activated for coordinate operations

Source: Department of the Army. *The Communist Insurgent Infrastructure in South Vietnam: A Study of Organization and Strategy*, DA Pamphlet 550–106. March 1967, p. 22.

APPENDIX K ───────────

TYPICAL VIET CONG
INFANTRY BATTALION ORGANIZATION

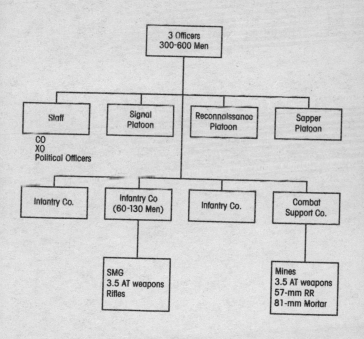

Source: M. Anderson, et al. *Insurgent Organization and Operations: A Case Study of the Viet Cong in the Delta, 1964–1966.* Santa Monica, CA: RAND Corporation Study RM-5239-1-ISA/ARPA, August 1967, p. 82.

APPENDIX L

ORGANIZATION OF THE VIET CONG 514 LOCAL-FORCE BATTALION

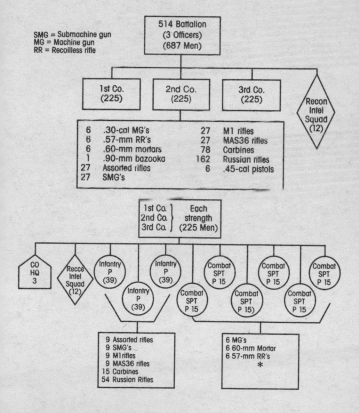

SMG = Submachine gun
MG = Machine gun
RR = Recoilless rifle

514 Battalion
(3 Officers)
(687 Men)

1st Co. (225)   2nd Co. (225)   3rd Co. (225)   Recon Intel Squad (12)

6	.30-cal MG's	27	M1 rifles
6	.57-mm RR's	27	MAS36 rifles
6	.60-mm mortars	78	Carbines
1	.90-mm bazooka	162	Russian rifles
27	Assorted rifles	6	.45-cal pistols
27	SMG's		

1st Co.
2nd Co.   Each strength
3rd Co.   (225 Men)

CO HQ 3   Recce Intel Squad (12)   Infantry P (39)   Infantry P (39)   Infantry P (39)   Combat SPT P 15   Combat SPT P 15   Combat SPT P 15   Combat SPT P 15   Combat SPT P 15   Combat SPT P 15

9 Assorted rifles
9 SMG's
9 M1 rifles
9 MAS36 rifles
15 Carbines
54 Russian Rifles

6 MG's
6 60-mm Mortar
6 57-mm RR's
*

Source: Anderson, et al., op. cit., p. 24.
*1st Company has Bazooka

341

APPENDIX M

NLF LETTER OF COMMENDATION

Considering Regulations concerning Awards and Punishment prescribed "R" (COSVN) Military Affairs Committee for SVN Liberation Army.

Based upon the authority and responsibility of the Commanders at all levels in the SVN Liberation Army.

Considering recommendations of————Commander, and the outstanding performance of duty of Comrade T————, First Aid Man during the attack on enemy boats at K————X———— on————1964, the following is recorded:

This individual performed his first-aid duty in a good manner, and participated in the engagement as a courageous soldier. Met with a hard-to-handle situation, this individual insisted on remaining in his position, killing 3 of the enemy, and seizing 1 TSMG [Thompson submachine gun] and 200 rounds.

In order to encourage distinguished personnel, "D" Commander

Decides:

ART. 1: Grant Letter of Commendation to Comrade I————
 V——T——First Aid Man, a group member of————.

ART. 2: This decision has been disseminated throughout "D":
 as subject for indoctrination class, and one copy to the
 family of individual concerned.

Source: Conley, op. cit., p. 155.

343

ART. 3: Political and Staff Sections,——— and Comrade
T——— will comply with this decision as outlined.

1964
For the Commander of "D"
B——H———
P——V——H———

SOURCE NOTES

1. IN THEIR OWN WORDS

1. Joint United States Public Affairs Office, Saigon. "Diary of a Viet Cong Infiltrator," *Vietnam Documents and Research Notes*, Document No. 1, October 1967, pp. 1–6.

2. Joint United States Public Affairs Office, Saigon. "Out of Rice, Ammunition and Bandages: Notes of a VC Veteran," *Vietnam Documents and Research Notes*, Document No. 13, January 1968, pp. 1–7.

3. David W. P. Elliott and Mai Elliott. *Documents of an Elite Viet Cong Delta Unit: The Demolition Platoon of the 514th Battalion—Part Five: Personal Letters*, Santa Monica, CA: RAND Corporation Study RM-5852-ISA/ARPA, May 1969, pp. 13–14, 29–31.

4. Ibid., pp. 52–54.

5. Document Exploitation Report, 199th Light Infantry Brigade, RVN, "Diary of Nguyen Van Nhuong," August 1969, pp. 1–3.

6. United States Department of State, *A Threat to the Peace: North Vietnam's Effort to Conquer South Vietnam*, Washington DC: U.S. Government Printing Office, 1961, pp. 64–67.

2. THE VIETNAM ENIGMA

1. The account of the Roman mission is in Bernard B. Fall, *The Two Viet-Nams*, New York: Frederick A. Praeger, 1963, p. 19; the discovery of the Roman medal at Oc Eo is noted in Peter T. White, "Mosaic of Cultures," *National Geographic*, March 1971, pp. 301–2; and the source for the meaning of "Giao-chi" was explained by Sedgwick Tourison in an interview at Crofton, MD, June 23, 1990.

2. Ellen J. Hammer, *A Death in November*, New York: E. P. Dutton, 1987, pp. 3–5; the observation on the Vietnamese fear of failure as a contributing factor to their inability to arrive at quick decisions is from Tourison.

3. Ibid., p. 6.

4. Nguyen Van Thai and Nguyen Van Mung, *A Short History of Viet-Nam* (Saigon: The Times Publishing Co., 1958, p. 6).

5. Harvey Smith, et al., *Area Handbook for North Vietnam*, Washington, DC: U.S. Government Printing Office, 1967, p. 399.

6. Harvey H. Smith, et al., *Area Handbook for South Vietnam*, Washington, DC: U.S. Government Printing Office, 1967, p. 36.

7. R. Ernest and Trevor N. Dupuy, *The Encyclopedia of Military History*, New York: Harper & Row, 1970, p. 397; Nguyen and Nguyen, op. cit., pp. 119–21.

8. Nguyen and Nguyen, op. cit., pp. 149–53.

9. Ibid., p. 252.

10. Smith, et al., op. cit., p. 45.

11. Ibid., p. 44.

12. Nguyen and Nguyen, op. cit., p. 299.

13. The information that the Viet Minh renamed Saigon Ho Chi Minh City in 1945/46 comes via Sedgwick Tourison from Archimedes Patti, author of *Why Vietnam*? (Berkeley: University of California Press, 1980).

14. Bernard B. Fall, *Hell in a Very Small Place*, New York: J. B. Lippincott Co., 1967, p. vii.

15. Ibid., p. 487.

16. Stanley Karnow, "Giap Remembers," *The New York Times Magazine*, June 24, 1990, p. 36.

17. Thomas C. Thayer, "How to Analyze a War Without Fronts, Vietnam 1965–1972," *Journal of Defense Research, Series B: Tactical Warfare*, Alexandria, VA: Defense Technical Information Center, DDCOO4262, pp. 846–47.

18. Paul Berman, *Revolutionary Organization, Institution-Building Within the People's Liberation Armed Forces*, Lexington, MA: Lexington Books, 1974, p. 38.

19. Bernard B. Fall, *Viet-Nam Witness*, New York: Frederick A. Praeger, 1966, pp. 244–45.

20. *The Tale of Kieu*, trans. Huynh Sanh Thong, New Haven: Yale University Press, 1983, 2517–518, 56.

21. *Area Handbook for South Vietnam; Area Handbook for North Vietnam; Encyclopedia Americana*; Armed Forces Information Service, "Capsule Facts for the Armed Forces, North Vietnam," July 1970; *The U.S. and Asia: A Statistical Handbook*, Washington, DC: The Heritage Foundation, July 1988.

22. Allan H. Brodrick, *Little China*, London, Oxford University Press, 1942, p. 260.

23. Ibid., p. 262.

24. Nguyen and Nguyen, op. cit., pp. 300–301.

25. The Simulmatics Corporation, *Improving the Effectiveness of the Chieu Hoi Program, Vol. II, The Viet Cong—Organizational, Political and Psychological Strengths and Weaknesses* (AD827204), Cambridge, MA: September 1967, pp. 164–65.

26. *RAND Vietnam Interviews*, Series AG, No. 507, p. 19.

27. Davison and Zasloff, *A Profile of Viet Cong Cadres* (RM-4983-1-ISA/ARPA, ADA032416), Santa Monica, CA: The RAND Corporation, June 1966, pp. 48–49.

28. *RAND Vietnam Interviews*, Series AG, No. 533, pp. 22–23.

29. Ibid., No. 460, p. 26.

30. Ibid., No. 174, p. 8.

31. The Simulmatics Corporation, op. cit., pp. 167–68.

32. *RAND Vietnam Interviews*, op. cit., pp. 26–29.

33. W. Phillips Davison, *User's Guide to the RAND Interviews in Vietnam*, RAND Corporation Report R-1024-ARPA, Santa Monica, CA, 1972, p. 15.

34. Richard Holmes, *Acts of War*, New York: The Free Press, 1988, p. 132.

35. Frances FitzGerald, *Fire in the Lake*, Boston: Little, Brown & Co., 1972, pp. 42–43.

36. Gerald C. Hickey, *Village in Vietnam*, New Haven: Yale University Press, 1964, p. 285.

37. Ibid.

38. *Analects*, XIII, 1.

39. Berman, op. cit., p. 33.

40. Ibid., p. 285.

41. Ibid., pp. 9–11.

42. Nguyen Du, *Tale of Kieu*, lines 2655–657.

43. Berman, op. cit., pp. 35, 36.

44. Personal observation of Dan Cragg.

45. Bui Diem, *In the Jaws of History*, Boston: Houghton Mifflin, 1987, p. 329.

46. Hoang Van Chi, *From Colonialism to Communism*, New York: Praeger, 1968, p. 33.

47. Truong Nhu Tang, *A Viet Cong Memoir*, New York: Vintage Books, 1986, p. 12.

48. Hoang Van Chi, op. cit., p. 18.

49. Nguyen Chi Thien (supposed author), *Prison Songs*, trans. Nguyen Ngoc Bich, Hoi Van-hoa VN tai Bac-My, 1982, Song No. 3.

50. BDM Corporation, *A Study of the Strategic Lessons Learned in Vietnam*, vol. I, *The Enemy*, McLean, VA: November 30, 1979 (BDM/W-768-1208-TR), p. 2–19.

51. Hoang Van Chi, op. cit., pp. 39–40.

52. Brian Michael Jenkins, "Why the North Vietnamese Will Keep Fighting," Santa Monica, CA: RAND Corporation, March 1972 (RAND Paper P-4395-1), p. 2.

53. Bui Diem, op. cit., p. 31.

54. John S. Bowman, *The World Almanac of the Vietnam War*, New York: Bison Books, 1985, p. 341.

3. RECRUITING AND TRAINING

1. Personal reminiscence of Dan Cragg.

2. A. J. Tachmindji, *Journal of Defense Research, Series B: Tactical Warfare*, Vol. 7, No. 3, Washington, DC: Government Printing Office, pp. 846–47.

3. The Simulmatics Corporation, *Improving the Effectiveness of the Chieu Hoi Program, Vol. II, Appendix A, The Viet Cong—Organizational, Political and Psychological Strengths and Weaknesses* (AD827204), Cambridge, MA: September 1967, p. 151.

4. Harvey H. Smith, et al., *Area Handbook for North Vietnam*, Washington, DC: U.S. Government Printing Office, 1967, p. 409.

5. William C. Westmoreland, *Report on the War in Vietnam*, Washington, DC: U.S. Government Printing Office, June 1968, pp. 114, 194–95.

6. *The Washington Times*, "Chinese Troops Fought U.S. in Vietnam," June 17, 1989, p. A10.

7. *RAND Vietnam Interviews, Infiltration Routes and Methods*, Series SX, Santa Monica, CA: RAND Corporation, March 1972, No. 40, p. 1.

8. *RAND Vietnam Interviews, Active Influence Within the Viet Cong and North Vietnamese Army*, Series AG (R-1024-ARPA-AD741301), Santa Monica, CA: RAND Corporation, March 1972, No. 612, p. 10.

9. Harvey H. Smith, et al., *Area Handbook for North Vietnam*, Washington, DC: U.S. Government Printing Office, 1967, pp. 409–10.

10. David Chanoff and Doan Van Toai, *Portrait of the Enemy*, New York: Random House, 1986, p. 48.

11. *RAND Vietnam Interviews*, Series SX, No. 19, p. 1.

12. Ibid., No. 25, p. 1.

13. Chanoff and Doan Van Toai, op. cit., p. 44.

14. *RAND Vietnam Interviews*, Series SX, No. 40, p. 1.

15. Chanoff and Doan Van Toai, op. cit., p. 47.

16. *Area Handbook for North Vietnam*, op. cit., p. 410.

17. *RAND Vietnam Interviews*, Series SX, No. 13, pp. 1–2.

18. Ibid., No. 16, p. 2; SX No. 33, p. 9.

19. *RAND Vietnam Interviews*, Series AG, *Active Influence Within the Viet Cong and North Vietnamese Armed Forces*, Santa Monica, CA: RAND Corporation, March 1972 (R-1024-ARPA-AD 741301), No. 176, p. 9.

20. *RAND Vietnam Interviews*, Series SX, No. 16, p. 2.

21. The Simulmatics Corporation, op. cit., p. 157.

22. *RAND Vietnam Interviews*, Series SX, No. 47, p. 2.

23. Ibid., No. 2, p. 1.

24. Ibid., No. 5, p. 1.

25. Anders Sweetland, *Rallying Potential Among the North Vietnamese Armed Forces*, Santa Monica, CA: RAND Corporation (RM-6375-1-ARPA), p. 2.

26. *RAND Vietnam Interviews*, Series SX, No. 13, p. 1.

27. Konrad Kellen, *A Profile of the PAVN Soldier in South Vietnam*, Santa Monica, CA: RAND Corporation (RM-5013-1-ISA/ARPA), June 1966, p. 17.

28. Ibid., p. 5.

29. *RAND Vietnam Interviews*, Series SX, No. 52, p. 2.

30. Ibid., No. 2, p. 1.

31. Ibid., No. 8, p. 1.

32. Ibid., No. 4, p. 1.

33. Ibid., No. 3, p. 1.

34. Ibid., No. 6, p. 1.

35. Ibid., No. 32, p. 1.

36. Ibid., No. 37, p. 1.

37. Ibid., No. 45, p. 2.

38. Ibid., No. 43, p. 2.

39. Ibid., No. 24, p. 2.

40. Ibid., No. 44, p. 1.

41. Ibid., No. 19, pp. 1–3.

42. Ibid., No. 50, p. 1.

43. *RAND Vietnam Interviews*, Series AG, No. 176, p. 9.

44. Sweetland, op. cit., pp. 7–8; illiteracy among the Viet Cong, especially after 1967, was a significant problem that had a deleterious effect on their training programs (Tourison).

45. Ibid., p. 13.

46. Ibid., p. 2.

47. Kellen, op. cit., p. 22.

48. Harvey H. Smith, et al. *Area Handbook for South Vietnam*, Washington, DC: U.S. Government Printing Office, 1967, pp. 430, 442. The South Vietnamese authorities did, however, have their own recruiting problems. Many people belonging to South Vietnam's ethnic minorities (Chinese, Cambodians, etc.) and politically dissident Buddhist sects were not only unwilling to serve in the ARVN, but were looked upon as poor security risks by the military services (Tourison).

49. *MACV Order of Battle Summary*, June 1966, Part IV, RG 472, Box 39, ''Westmoreland vs. CBS Litigation Collection,'' Washington National Records Center, Suitland, MD.

50. Westmoreland, op. cit., p. 194.

51. William E. Le Gro, *Vietnam from Cease-Fire to Capitulation*, Washington, DC: U.S. Army Center of Military History, 1981, p. 28.

52. Tachmindji, op. cit., p. 788.

53. John C. Donnell, *Viet Cong Recruitment: Why and How Men Join*, Santa Monica, CA: The RAND Corporation (RM-5486-1-ISA/ARPA), December 1967, p. 97.

54. The Simulmatics Corporation, op. cit., pp. 87–88.

55. Ibid., pp. 110–11.

56. Frank Denton, *Volunteers for the Viet Cong*, Santa Monica, CA:

RAND Corporation (RM-5647-ISA/ARPA), September 1968, pp. xi–xii, 19–20.

57. Donnell, op. cit., pp. 8–9.

58. Per Tourison.

59. Leon Goure and C.A.H. Thomson, *Some Impressions of Viet Cong Vulnerabilities: An Interim Report*, Santa Monica, CA: RAND Corporation (RM-4699-1-ISA/ARPA), August 1965, pp. 51–52.

60. The Simulmatics Corporation, op. cit., p. 109.

61. Donnell, op. cit., p. 114.

62. Donnell, op. cit., pp. 13–14.

63. *RAND Vietnam Interviews*, Series AG, No. 623, p. 18.

64. Per Tourison.

65. *RAND Vietnam Interviews*, Series AG, No. 116, p. 4.

66. Ibid., No. 152, p. 2.

67. Ibid., No. 118, p. 4.

68. Ibid., No. 644, p. 18.

69. M. Anderson, M. Arnsten, and H. Averich, *Insurgent Organization and Operations: A Case Study of the Viet Cong in the Delta, 1964–1966* (RM-5239-1-ISA/ARPA, AD A032420), Santa Monica, CA: RAND Corporation, August 1967, pp. 155–65.

70. *RAND Vietnam Interviews*, Series AG, No. 566, p. 2.

71. Ibid., No. 633, pp. 12–13.

72. Ibid., No. 634, pp. 27–28.

73. Ibid., No. 625, pp. 11–12.

74. Ibid., No. 584, pp. 5, 16, 30, 33.

75. Ibid., No. 579, p. 41.

76. Ibid., p. 67.

77. Ibid., p. 81. It should be noted that this kind of capitalist enterprise would have been strictly prohibited by the NLF, and cadres found engaging in it would have been subjected to harsh disciplinary measures.

78. Ibid.

79. Ibid., p. 107.

80. Ibid., No. 571, pp. 4–5.

81. Sweetland, op. cit., p. 6.

82. Michael Charles Conley, *The Communist Insurgent Infrastructure in South Vietnam: A Study of Organization and Strategy* (DA Pam 550–106), Washington, DC: The American University, March 1967, p. 151.

83. David W. P. Elliott and Mai Elliott, *Documents of an Elite Viet Cong Delta Unit: The Demolition Platoon of the 514th Battalion—Part Three: Military Organization and Activities* (RM-5850-ISA/ARPA (AD691717), Santa Monica, CA: RAND Corporation, May 1969, p. 123.

84. *RAND Vietnam Interviews*, Series AG, No. 634, p. 28.

85. The Simulmatics Corporation, op. cit., pp. 94–95.

86. *RAND Vietnam Interviews*, Series AG, No. 74, pp. 7–9.

87. Donnell, op. cit., p. 109.

88. Joseph Browning, "Women of the Viet Cong," *The National Guardsman*, August 1968, p. 5.

89. *RAND Vietnam Interviews*, Series AG, No. 579, p. 55.
90. Ibid., No. 595, pp. 5, 7, 8–9, 30–31.
91. Donnell, op. cit., p. 109.
92. *RAND Vietnam Interviews*, Series AG, No. 579, p. 14.

4. THE INFILTRATION SOUTH

1. David W. P. Elliott and Mai Elliott, *Documents of an Elite Viet Cong Delta Unit: The Demolition Platoon of the 514th Battalion—Part Five: Personal Letters*, Santa Monica, CA: RAND Corporation Study (RM 5852-ISA/ARPA), May 1969, p. 29.
2. Department of State, *A Threat to the Peace: North Vietnam's Effort to Conquer South Vietnam*, Washington, DC: U.S. Government Printing Office, 1961, p. 4.
3. Ibid., pp. 22–26.
4. Ibid., pp. 13–17.
5. *Nan Dan (The Party Daily)*, Hanoi, November 22, 1984, p. 4.
6. Department of Defense, *Journal of Defense Research, Series B: Tactical Warfare*, Volume 7B, Number 3, Washington DC: U.S. Government Printing Office, 1975, p. 788.
7. Konrad Killen, *A Profile of the PAVN Soldier in South Vietnam*, RAND Corporation Study (RM 5013-1-ISA/ARPA): RAND Corporation: Santa Monica, CA, 1966, p. 11.
8. Ibid.
9. Ibid.
10. Ibid., p. 13.
11. Ibid.
12. Ibid., p. 14.
13. Ibid., p. 15.
14. Ibid.
15. Ibid., p. 17.
16. Ibid.
17. The Simulmatics Corporation, *Improving the Effectiveness of the Chieu Hoi Program, Vol. II, The Viet Cong—Organizational, Political and Psychological Strengths and Weaknesses*, Cambridge, MA: The Simulmatics Corporation, September 1967, p. 163.
18. "An Anatomy of the Enemy and Why He Is Hurting," *Army*, October 1967, pp. 124–25.
19. The Simulmatics Corporation, op. cit., pp. 178–179.
20. Killen, op. cit., p. 19.
21. Ibid., p. 18.
22. Department of State, *Aggression from the North: The Record of North Vietnam's Campaign to Conquer South Vietnam*, Washington DC: U.S. Government Printing Office, 1965, p. 5.
23. Ibid. Also per Tourison interview.
24. Document Exploitation Report, 199th Light Infantry Brigade, RVN,

"Diary of Nguyen Van Nhuong," August 1969, pp. 1–2; Tourison interview.

25. *Intelligence Collection Guide*, "Identification of Viet-Cong and North Vietnam Army Documents." Saigon: Combined Document Exploitation Center, U.S. Military Assistance Command, Vietnam, MACJ214, August 1966, p. 116.

26. The Simulmatics Corporation, op. cit., p. 164.

27. Department of State, op. cit., p. 10.

28. Document Exploitation Report, 199th Light Infantry Brigade, op. cit., p. 1–2.

29. J. M. Carrier and C. A. H. Thomson, *Viet Cong Motivation and Morale: The Special Case of Chieu Hoi*, RAND Corporation Study (RM 4830-2-ISA/ARPA), Santa Monica, CA: RAND Corporation, 1966, p. 100.

30. Anders Sweetland, *Rallying Potential Among the North Vietnamese Armed Forces*, RAND Corporation Study (RM 6375-1-ARPA), Santa Monica, CA: RAND Corporation, 1970, p. 22.

5. ORGANIZATION

1. *A Study of Strategic Lessons Learned in Vietnam*, Volume I, "The Enemy," McLean, VA: The BDM Corporation, 1979, pp. 3-1, 3-2.

2. Per Tourison.

3. Department of Defense GEN-20, *Know Your Enemy: The Viet Cong*, Washington DC: Armed Forces Information and Education Service, 1966, pp. 10–14; Department of Defense, *North Vietnam*, Washington DC: Armed Forces Information Service, 1970, p. 9.

4. Department of State Publication 7839, *Aggression from the North: The Record of North Vietnam's Campaign to Conquer South Vietnam*, Washington DC: American Forces Information and Education Service, 1965, pp. 59–60.

5. *A Study of Lessons Learned in Vietnam*, op. cit., pp. 3-28–3-35.

6. Department of Defense GEN-20, op. cit., p. 13.

7. Battelle Columbus Laboratories, *Journal of Defense Research*, Series B: *Tactical Warfare Analysis of Vietnam Data*, Volume 7B, Number 3, Washington DC: U.S. Government Printing Office, Fall 1975, p. 788.

8. Frederick P. Peterkin, "The Sapper," *Infantry*, November–December, 1969, pp. 51–53.

9. Konrad Kellen, *Conversations with Enemy Soldiers in Late 1968/Early 1969: A Study of Motivation and Morale*, RAND Corporation Study RM-6131-1-ISP/ARPA, Santa Monica, CA: RAND Corporation, 1970, pp. 28–30.

10. Department of Defense GEN-20, op. cit., pp. 16–17.

11. David W. P. Elliott and Mai Elliott, *Documents of an Elite Viet Cong Delta Unit*, RAND Corporation Study RM-5850-ISA/ARPA, Santa Monica, CA: RAND Corporation, 1969, p. 2.

12. Kellen, op. cit., pp. 30–33.

13. J. M. Carrier and C. A. H. Thomson, *Viet Cong Motivation and Morale: The Special Case of the Chieu Hoi*, RAND Corporation Study RM-4830-2-ISA/ARPA, Santa Monica, CA: RAND Corporation, 1966, p. 99.

14. Kellen, op. cit., pp. 34–35.

15. Anders Sweetland, *Rallying Potential Among the North Vietnamese Armed Forces*, RAND Corporation Study RM-6375-1-ARPA, Santa Monica, CA: RAND Corporation, 1970, p. 7.

16. Elliott and Elliott, op. cit., pp. 8–10, 82.

17. W. P. Davison and J. J. Zasloff, *A Profile of Viet Cong Cadres*, RAND Corporation Study RM-4983-1-ISA/ARPA, Santa Monica, CA: RAND Corporation, 1966, pp. 11–12.

18. Douglas Pike, *Viet Cong: The Organization and Techniques of The National Liberation Front of South Vietnam*, Cambridge, MA: M.I.T. Press, 1966, p. 150.

19. M. Anderson, M. Arnsten, and H. Averich, *Insurgent Organization and Operations: A Case Study of the Viet Cong in the Delta, 1964–1966*, RAND Corporation Study RM-5239-1-ISA/ARPA, Santa Monica, CA: RAND Corporation, 1967, pp. 20–23.

20. Melvin Gurtov, *Viet Cong Cadres and the Cadre System: A Study of the Main and Local Forces*, RAND Corporation Study RM-5414-1-ISA/ARPA, Santa Monica, CA: RAND Corporation, 1967, pp. 15–17, 46.

21. Ibid., pp. 11–12.

22. The Simulmatics Corporation, *Improving Effectiveness of the Chieu Hoi Program, Vol. II, The Viet Cong—Organizational, Political and Psychological Strengths and Weaknesses*, New York: The Simulmatics Corporation, September 1967, pp. 196–97.

23. Ibid., pp. 205–7.

24. Anderson, et al. op. cit., pp. 20–21.

25. Ibid., p. 20.

26. Kellen, op. cit., pp. 21–22.

27. Ibid., p. 22.

28. Ibid., p. 23.

29. Ibid., pp. 24–25.

30. Ibid., p. 25.

31. Ibid., p. 25.

32. Ibid.

33. Ibid., pp. 21–25.

34. Gurtov, op. cit., p. 192.

35. Ibid., pp. 48–49.

36. Ibid., pp. 25–26.

37. The Simulmatics Corporation, op. cit., pp. 201–4.

6. EQUIPMENT, ARMS, AND SUPPLIES

1. Darrel R. Lulling, *Communist Militaria of the Vietnam War*, Tulsa, OK: M.E.N. Press, 1980, p. 6.

2. Ibid., p. 15.

3. Ian V. Hogg and John Weeks, *Military Small Arms of the 20th Century*, New York: Hippocrene Books, Inc., 1977, pp. 193–94.

4. *Weapons and Equipment—Southeast Asia*, Washington DC: U.S. Government Printing Office, 1965, pp. 36–37.

5. David Rosser-Owen, *Vietnam Weapons Handbook*, Northants, England: Patrick Stephens Limited, 1986, pp. 16–17.

6. L. P. Holliday and R. M. Gurfield, *Viet Long Logistics*, RAND Corporation Study RM 5423-1-ISA/ARPA, Santa Monica, CA: RAND Corporation, June 1968, p. 41.

7. Frank H. Denton, *Some Effects of Military Operations on Viet Cong Attitudes*, RAND Corporation Study RM-4966-1-ISA/ARPA, Santa Monica, CA: RAND Corporation, November 1966, p. 46.

8. Holliday and Gurfield, op. cit., p. 56.

9. Konrad Kellen, *A Profile of the PAVN Soldier in South Vietnam*, RAND Corporation Study RM-5013-ISA/ARPA, Santa Monica, CA: RAND Corporation, June 1966, p. 56; Tourison interviews.

10. The Simulmatics Corporation, *Improving Effectiveness of the Chieu Hoi Program, Vol. II, The Viet Cong—Organizational, Political and Psychological Strengths and Weaknesses*, New York: The Simulmatics Corporation, September 1967, pp. 148–49.

11. Holliday and Gurfield, op. cit., pp. 20–39.

12. Leon Goure and C. A. H. Thomson, *Some Impressions of Viet Cong Vulnerabilities: An Interim Report*, RM-4699-ISA/ARPA, Santa Monica, CA: RAND Corporation, August 1965, p. 26.

13. Lulling, op. cit., p. 37.

14. The Simulmatics Corporation, op. cit., p. 190.

15. Konrad Kellen, *Conversations with Enemy Soldiers in Late 1968/ Early 1969: A Study of Motivation and Morale*, RAND Corporation Study RM-6131-1-ISA/ARPA, Santa Monica, CA: RAND Corporation, p. 70.

16. Tourison interviews.

17. Department of State Publication 7306, *A Threat to Peace: North Vietnam's Effort to Conquer South Vietnam*, Part II, Washington DC: U.S. Government Printing Office, 1961, p. 61.

18. Michael Lee Lanning, *Vietnam 1969–1970: A Company Commander's Journal*, New York: Ivy Books, 1988, pp. 200–201.

19. Andres Sweetland, *Rallying Potential Among the North Vietnamese Armed Forces*, RAND Corporation Study RM-6375-1-ARPA, Santa Monica, CA: RAND Corporation, December 1970, p. 19.

7. LOGISTICS

1. Vo Nguyen Giap, *People's War, People's Army*, New York: Bantam, 1968, p. 25.

2. Wilfred G. Burchett, *Vietnam North*, New York: International Publishers, 1966, pp. 7, 62, 91, 96, 125, 128.

3. The BDM Corporation, *A Study of Strategic Lessons Learned in Viet-*

nam, Vol. I, *The Enemy*, McLean, VA: The BDM Corporation, 1979, p. 5-1.

4. Bernard G. Fall, *The Two Viet-Nams*, New York: Praeger, 1963, p. 472.

5. King C. Chen, "Hanoi vs. Peking: Policies and Relations—A Survey," *Asian Survey*, September 1972, pp. 806–17.

6. George K. Tanham, *Communist Revolutionary Warfare*, revised edition, New York: Praeger, 1967, pp. 68–69.

7. Chen, op. cit., pp. 806–17.

8. Lt. Col. Lance J. Burton, *North Vietnam's Military Logistics System: Its Contribution to the War, 1961–1969*, Fort Leavenworth, KS: U.S. Army Command and General Staff College, 1977, p. 18.

9. Brig. Gen. Soutchay Vongsavanh, *RLG Military Operations and Activities in the Laotian Panhandle*, Indochina Refugee-Authored Monograph Program, Department of the Army, Office of the Chief of Military History, McLean, VA, 1978, p. 5.

10. Lt. Gen. Sak Sutsakhan, *The Khmer Republic at War and the Final Collapse*, Indochina Refugee–Authored Monograph Program, Department of the Army, Office of the Chief of Military History, McLean, VA, 1978, p. 18.

11. Frank Snepp, *Decent Interval*, New York: Random House, 1977, pp. 19–20.

12. Gen. William C. Westmoreland, *A Soldier Reports*, Garden City, NY: Doubleday & Co., 1976, p. 34.

13. Maj. Gen. Nguyen Duy Hinh, *Lamson 719*, Indochina Refugee–Authored Monograph Program, Department of the Army, Office of the Chief of Military History, McLean, VA, 1977, p. 12.

14. The BDM Corporation, op. cit., pp. 5–17.

15. U.S. Military Assistance Command, Vietnam, Combined Intelligence Center, Study ST 70-05, pp. 3–4.

16. The BDM Corporation, op. cit., pp. 5–22.

17. L. P. Holliday and R. M. Gurfield, *Viet Cong Logistics*, RAND Corporation Study, RM-5423-1-ISA/ARPA, Santa Monica, CA: RAND Corporation, 1968, pp. 4–5.

18. Ibid., p. 6.

19. Ibid., p. 7.

20. David W. P. Elliott and Mai Elliott, *Documents of an Elite Viet Cong Unit*, RAND Corporation Study, RM-5850-ISA/ARPA, Santa Monica, CA: RAND Corporation, 1969, pp. 114–15.

21. Holliday and Gurfield, op. cit., p. 8.

22. Tourison interview, September 9, 1990.

23. Sr. Gen. Van Tien Dung, "Great Spring Victory," Foreign Broadcast Information Service, APA-76-110, June 7, 1976, Vol. IV, No. 110, Supp. 38.

24. Holliday and Gurfield, op. cit., pp. 21–40.

25. Anders Sweetland, *Rallying Potential Among the North Vietnamese*

Armed Forces, RAND Corporation Study, RM-6375-1-ARPA, Santa Monica, CA: RAND Corporation, 1970, p. 2.

26. Lt. Gen. Joseph M. Heiser, Jr., *Vietnam Studies: Logistic Support*, Washington DC: Department of the Army, 1974, pp. 51, 26, 73, 78, 124, 119, 135, 154.

27. Lt. Gen. Carroll H. Dunn, *Vietnam Studies: Base Development in South Vietnam 1965–1970*, Washington DC: Department of the Army, 1972, pp. 40–41, 136.

28. Carl Berger, *The United States Air Force in Southeast Asia*, Washington DC: Office of Air Force History, 1977, pp. 366–67.

29. John S. Bowman, *The World Almanac of the Vietnam War*, New York: Bison Books, p. 358.

30. Holliday and Gurfield, op. cit., pp. 21–40.

31. W. P. Davison and J. J. Zasloff, *A Profile of Viet Cong Cadres*, RAND Corporation Study, RM-4983-1-ARPA, Santa Monica, CA: RAND Corporation, 1966, p. 11.

32. L. Goure, A. J. Russo, and D. Scott, *Some Findings of the Viet Cong Motivation and Morale Study: June–December 1965*, RAND Corporation Study, RM-4911-2-ARPA, Santa Monica, CA: RAND Corporation, 1965, p. 27.

33. Tom Hargrove, "Rice and War in Vietnam: A Rendezvous with the Past," unpublished article, October 26, 1988, author's files.

34. Holliday and Gurfield, op. cit., pp. 28–30.

35. Michael Lee Lanning and Ray W. Stubbe, *Inside Force Recon: Recon Marines in Vietnam*, New York: Ivy Books, 1989, p. 186.

36. Holliday and Gurfield, op. cit., pp. 19–20.

37. Ibid., pp. 40–51.

38. Michael Lee Lanning, *Vietnam 1969–1970: A Company Commander's Journal*, New York: Ivy Books, 1988, pp. 198–201.

39. Holliday and Gurfield, op. cit., pp. 57–60.

40. Melvin Gurtov, *Viet Cong Cadres and the Cadre System: A Study of the Main and Local Forces*, RAND Corporation Study RM-5414-1-ISA/ARPA, Santa Monica, CA: RAND Corporation, 1967, p. 85.

8. LIFE IN CAMP

1. David W. P. Elliott and Mai Elliott, *Documents of an Elite Viet Cong Delta Unit*, Part Five, *Personal Letters*, RAND Corporation Study, RM-5423-1-ISA/ARPA, Santa Monica, CA: RAND Corporation, 1968, p. 7.

2. Interview, Carlton Sherwood, November 16, 1988, Annapolis, MD (see Chapter 11, Voices from the Other Side)

3. Gen. William Westmoreland, *A Soldier Reports*, New York: Doubleday & Co., 1976, p. 56.

4. *RAND Vietnam Interviews*, Series AG, *Active Influence Within the Viet Cong and North Vietnamese Armed Forces*, Santa Monica, CA: RAND Corporation, March 1972, No. 447, p. 24.

5. Ibid., No. 446, p. 43.

6. Ibid., No. 633, p. 28.

7. M. Anderson, M. Arnsten, and H. Averich, *Insurgent Organization and Operations: A Case Study of the Viet Cong in the Delta, 1964–1966* RAND Corporation Study RM-5239-1-ISA/ARPA, Santa Monica, CA: RAND Corporation, 1967, p. 75.

8. Ibid., pp. 76–78.

9. *RAND Vietnam Interviews*, Series AG, No. 623, p. 43.

10. Ibid., No. 593, p. 15.

11. Anderson, Arnsten, Averich, op. cit., pp. 90–92.

12. Ibid., No. 504, p. 30.

13. Ibid., No. 461, pp. 26–27.

14. Ibid., No. 446, p. 43.

15. Elliott and Elliott, *Documents of an Elite Viet Cong Delta Unit*, Part Three: *Military Organization and Activities*, p. 84.

16. Ibid., p. 65.

17. *RAND Vietnam Interviews*, Series AG, No. 534, p. 15.

18. Ibid., No. 503, p. 26.

19. Elliott and Elliott, op. cit., p. 116.

20. 24th Military History Detachment (Airborne), 173rd Airborne Brigade, "Operational Report No. 6, A Monograph of Huynh Nghiep" (DTIC AD 500304), Washington, DC: Department of the Army, February 27, 1969, p. 8.

21. Elliott and Elliott, op. cit., pp. 74–80.

22. Ibid., pp. 61–62.

23. *RAND Vietnam Interviews*, Series AG, No. 517, p. 36.

24. Ibid., No. 503, p. 36.

25. Ibid., No. 579, p. 104.

26. Ibid., No. 513, pp. 28–29.

27. Ibid., pp. 57–58.

28. 24th Military History Detachment (Airborne), op. cit., p. 12.

29. Ibid., p. 9.

30. *RAND Vietnam Interviews*, Series AG, No. 626, p. 28.

31. Ibid., No. 533, pp. 11–12.

32. Ibid., No. 590, pp. 13–14.

33. Michael Charles Conley, *The Communist Insurgent Infrastructure in South Vietnam: A Study of Organization and Strategy* (Department of the Army Pamphlet 550–106), Washington, DC: U.S. Government Printing Office, 1967, p. 250.

34. *RAND Vietnam Interviews*, Series AG, No. 513, p. 53.

35. Ibid., No. 459, p. 23.

36. Ibid., No. 459, p. 23.

37. J. M. Carrier and C.A.H. Thomson, *Viet Cong Motivation and Morale: The Special Case of the Chieu Hoi* (RM-4830-2-ISA/ARPA (AD 032193), Santa Monica, CA: RAND Corporation, May 1966, p. 53.

38. *RAND Vietnam Interviews*, Series AG, No. 535, p. 34.

39. Harvey H. Smith, et al., *Area Handbook for South Vietnam*, Washington, DC: U.S. Government Printing Office, 1967, p. 123.

40. *RAND Vietnam Interviews*, Series AG, No. 593, p. 10.

41. Ibid., No. 458, p. 17.

42. Ibid., No. 3, p. 27.

43. Ibid., No. 459, pp. 10, 12.

44. Ibid., No. 63, p. 31.

45. Ibid., No. 447, p. 20.

46. Ibid., No. 454, p. 36.

47. Ibid., No. 504, p. 24.

48. Ibid., No. 514, p. 39.

49. Ibid., No. 503, p. 25.

50. Ibid., No. 507, p. 40.

51. Ibid., No. 534, p. 20.

52. Ibid., No. 633, p. 19.

53. Ibid., No. 6, p. 25.

54. Ibid., No. 623, pp. 29–30; No. 8, p. 14; Truong Nhu Tang, with David Chanoff and Doan Van Toai, *A Viet Cong Memoir*, New York: Harcourt Brace Jovanovich, 1985, p. 164.

55. *RAND Vietnam Interviews*, Series AG, No. 534, p. 16.

56. Ibid., No. 593, p. 10.

57. Ibid., No. 590, p. 19.

58. Ibid., No. 579, p. 80.

59. Ibid., No. 505, p. 32.

60. Ibid., No. 461, p. 16.

61. Ibid., No. 499, p. 8.

62. Ibid., No. 3, p. 3.

63. Ibid., No. 623, p. 28.

64. The Simulmatics Corporation, *Improving Effectiveness of the Chieu Hoi Program, Vol. II*, New York: The Simulmatics Corporation, September 1967, p. 213.

65. *RAND Vietnam Interviews*, Series AG, No. 459, p. 23.

66. Ibid., p. 24.

67. Ibid., No. 507, p. 64.

68. Elliott and Elliott, *Documents of an Elite Viet Cong Delta Unit*, Part Five: *Personal Letters*, pp. 11–12.

69. Ibid., p. 15.

70. Unless otherwise indicated, this section is based on the Tourison interview conducted September 9, 1990.

71. Elliott and Elliott, op. cit., p. 1.

72. *RAND Vietnam Interviews*, Series AG, No. 626, p. 28.

73. Ibid., No. 539, pp. 3–4.

74. Ibid., No. 447, p. 25.

75. Ibid., No. 504, p. 33.

76. Elliott and Elliott, op. cit., pp. 40, 57.

77. *RAND Vietnam Interviews*, Series AG, No. 520, pp. 29–30.

78. Ibid., No. 535, p. 27.

79. The Simulmatics Corporation, op. cit., p. 87.

80. *RAND Vietnam Interviews*, Series AG, No. 524, p. 15.

81. Ibid., No. 461, p. 46.

82. Ibid., No. 514, p. 35.

83. Ibid., No. 7, p. 4.

84. Leon Goure and C.A.H. Thomson, *Some Impressions of Viet Cong Vulnerabilities: An Interim Report* (RM-4699-1-ISA/ARPA (AD A032189), Santa Monica, CA: RAND Corporation, August 1965, p. 37.

85. *RAND Vietnam Interviews*, Series AG, No. 584, p. 35.

86. Ibid., No. 579, p. 104.

87. Ibid., No. 540, p. 1.

88. Ibid., No. 579, p. 50.

89. Ibid., No. 634, p. 19.

90. Ibid., No. 584, p. 39.

91. Ibid., No. 507, p. 35.

92. The Simulmatics Corporation, op. cit., p. 219.

93. *RAND Vietnam Interviews*, Series AG, No. 505, p. 14.

94. The Simulmatics Corporation, op. cit., p. 253.

95. Conley, op. cit., pp. 152–53.

96. Elliott and Elliott, op. cit., p. 15.

97. The Simulmatics Corporation, op. cit., p. 256.

98. Ibid., p. 223.

99. *RAND Vietnam Interviews*, Series AG, No. 571, p. 16.

100. The Simulmatics Corporation, op. cit., p. 221.

101. Smith et al., op. cit., p. 163.

102. *RAND Vietnam Interviews*, Series AG, No. 529, p. 48.

103. Ibid., No. 535, p. 18.

104. Harvey H. Smith, et al., *Area Handbook for North Vietnam*, p. 412.

105. *RAND Vietnam Interviews*, Series AG, No. 504, p. 36.

106. *Foreign Broadcast Information Service Daily Reports*, No. 33, February 15, 1968, p. KKK7.

107. Ibid., No. 44, March 4, 1968, p. KKK10.

108. Ibid., No. 14, January 19, 1968, p. KKK1.

109. *RAND Vietnam Interviews*, Series AG, No. 590, p. 11.

110. Ibid., No. 539, p. 11.

111. Ibid., No. 3, p. 24.

112. Carrier and Thomson, op. cit., pp. 34–35.

113. *RAND Vietnam Interviews*, Series AG, No. 579, p. 59.

114. Ibid., No. 633, p. 16.

115. Capt. Arthur Mason Ahearn, "Viet Cong Medicine," *Military Medicine*, March 1966, p. 221.

116. *RAND Vietnam Interviews*, Series AG, No. 584, pp. 30–31.

117. Ibid., p. 23.

118. *RAND Vietnam Interviews*, Series SX, No. 33, p. 23.

119. *RAND Vietnam Interviews*, Series AG, No. 634, p. 39.

120. Ibid., No. 633, p. 27.

121. Ahearn, op. cit., p. 220.

122. *RAND Vietnam Interviews*, Series AG, No. 584, pp. 26–27.

123. Ibid., No. 459, p. 15.

124. Ibid., No. 504, p. 40.

125. Truong Nhu Tang, op. cit., pp. 168–70.

9. IN BATTLE

1. P. J. Honey, *Communism in North Vietnam: Its Role in the Sino-Soviet Dispute*, Cambridge, MA: The M.I.T. Press, 1963, p. 168.

2. Gen. William C. Westmoreland, *A Soldier Reports*, New York: Dell, 1980, p. 67.

3. Vo Nguyen Giap, *People's War, People's Army*, New York: Bantam, 1962, p. 42.

4. Dave Richard Palmer, *Summons of the Trumpet: U.S.–Vietnam in Perspective*, Navato, CA: Presidio Press, 1978, p. 62.

5. Ibid., p. 103.

6. Brian Michael Jenkins, *Why the North Vietnamese Will Keep Fighting*, RAND Corporation Study P-4395-1, Santa Monica, CA: RAND Corporation, March, 1972, p. 1.

7. "Viet leaders altered will, death date of 'Uncle Ho,'" *The Arizona Republic*, Sept. 3, 1989, p. A16.

8. Konrad Kellen, *A View of the VC: Elements of Cohesion in the Enemy Camp in 1966–1967*, RAND Corporation Study RM-5462-1-ISA/ARPA, Santa Monica, CA: RAND Corporation, 1969, p. 70.

9. Ibid., pp. 57, 59, 65.

10. Ibid., pp. 57–58.

11. Harry G. Summers, Jr., *On Strategy: The Vietnam War in Context*, Carlisle Barracks, PA: U.S. Army War College, 1981, p. 1.

12. Department of Defense, *Know Your Enemy: The Viet Cong*, Washington, DC: U.S. Government Printing Office, 1966, p. 19.

13. M. Anderson, M. Arnsten, and H. Averich, *Insurgent Organization and Operations*, RAND Corporation Study RM-5239-1-ISA/ARPA, Santa Monica, CA: RAND Corporation, 1967, pp. 59–101.

14. Ibid., p. 90.

15. Ibid., p. 92.

16. Michael Lee Lanning, *The Only War We Had: A Platoon Leader's Journal of Vietnam*, New York: Ivy Books, 1987, p. 131.

17. Lt. Col. David H. Hackworth, "Find 'Em, Fix 'Em, and Then Smash 'Em," *Lessons Learned*, Department of the Army, 173d Airborne Brigade (Separate), Republic of Vietnam, January 28, 1967.

18. Maj. Lane Rogers, "The Enemy," *Marine Corps Gazette*, March 1966, p. 51.

19. Anderson, et al., op. cit., pp. 102–3.

20. Ibid., p. 105.

21. Ibid., p. 107.

22. Col. M. J. Sexton, "Sapper Attack," *Marine Corps Gazette*, September 1969, pp. 30–31.

23. Anderson, et al., op. cit., p. 111.

24. David W. P. Elliott and Mai Elliott, *Documents of an Elite Viet*

Cong Delta Unit, RAND Corporation Study, RM-5850-ISA/ARPA, Santa Monica, CA: RAND Corporation, May 1969, p. v.

25. Anderson, et al., op. cit., p. 115.

26. Douglas Pike, *The Viet Cong Strategy of Terror*, Saigon: U.S. Mission, February 1970, p. 20.

27. Edward S. Herman, *Atrocities in Vietnam: Myths and Realities*, Philadelphia: Pilgrim Press, 1970, p. 35.

28. L. Goure et al., *Some Findings of the Viet Cong Motivation and Morale Study: June–December 1965*, RAND Corporation Study RM 4911-1-ISA/ARPA, Santa Monica, CA: RAND Corporation, February 1966, p. 40.

29. Melvin Gurtov, *Viet Cong Cadres and the Cadre System: A Study of the Main and Local Forces*, RAND Corporation Study RM-5414-1-ISA/ARPA, Santa Monica, CA: RAND Corporation, December 1967, p. 74.

30. Pike, op. cit., p. 53.

31. Ibid., pp. 107–8.

32. Guenter Lewy, *America in Vietnam*, New York: Oxford University Press, 1978, p. 276.

33. W. R. Peers, *Report on the Department of the Army Review of the Preliminary Investigation into the My Lai Incident*, Vol. I, *The Report of the Investigation*, Washington, DC: U.S. Government Printing Office, March 14, 1970, p. A-3.

34. House Armed Services Committee, No. 94-47, Washington DC: U.S. Government Printing Office, 1976.

35. OASD(PA) News Release No. 537-74, "Secretary of the Army Releases the 'Peers Report,' " November 13, 1974.

36. Battelle Columbus Laboratories, *Journal of Defense Research, Series B: Tactical Warfare Analysis of Vietnam Data*, Volume 7B, Number 3, Washington, DC: U.S. Government Printing Office, Fall 1975, p. 804.

37. Ibid., p. 805.

38. Office of the Assistant Secretary of Defense (Comptroller), *Southeast Asia Statistical Summary*, Washington, DC: U.S. Government Printing Office, April 1973, pp. 1–9.

39. The Simulmatics Corporation, *Improving Effectiveness of the Chieu Hoi Program, Vol. II, The Viet Cong—Organizational, Political and Psychological Strengths and Weaknesses*, New York: The Simulmatics Corporation, September 1968, p. 142.

40. W. P. Davison and J. J. Zasloff, *A Profile of Viet Cong Cadres*, RAND Corporation Study RM-4983-1-ISA/ARPA, Santa Monica, CA: RAND Corporation, June 1966, p. 40.

41. The Simulmatics Corporation, op. cit., p. 141.

42. Battelle Columbus Laboratories, op. cit., pp. 774–78.

43. E. O'Ballance, *The Indo–China War 1945–54*, London: Faber and Faber, 1964, pp. 110, 157, 175.

44. Battelle Columbus Laboratories, op. cit., pp. 777–78.

45. Kellen, op. cit., pp. 24, 76.

46. Leon Goure and C. A. H. Thomson, *Some Impressions of Viet Cong Vulnerabilities: An Interim Report*, RAND Corporation Study RM-4699-1-ISA/ARPA, Santa Monica, CA: RAND Corporation, August 1965, pp. 76–77.

47. Konrad Kellen, *A Profile of the PAVN Soldier in South Vietnam*, RAND Corporation Study RM-5013-1-ISA/ARPA, Santa Monica, CA: RAND Corporation, June 1966, p. 41.

48. Konrad Kellen, *Conversations with Enemy Soldiers in Late 1968/Early 1969: A Study of Motivation and Morale*, RAND Corporation Study RM-6131-1-ISA/ARPA, Santa Monica, CA: RAND Corporation, September 1970, p. xvii.

10. VOICES FROM THE OTHER SIDE: THE GENERALS

1. Interview, January 31, 1989, with the company commander of the U.S. unit.

2. Douglas Kinnard, *The War Managers*, Hanover, New Hampshire: University of Vermont, 1977, p. 67.

3. Letter, Gen. (Ret.) W. B. Rosson, September 29, 1988, Roanoke, VA.

4. Letter, Gen. (Ret.) William E. Depuy, July 29, 1988, Delaplane, VA.

5. Letter, Lt. Gen. (Ret.) Julian J. Ewell, July 31, 1988, McLean, VA.

6. Letter, Maj. Gen. (Ret.) Ellis W. Williamson, August 2, 1988, Arlington, VA.

7. Letter, Brig. Gen. (Ret.) James S. Timothy, August 15, 1988, Longboat Key, FL.

8. Letter, Lt. Gen. (Ret.) William J. McCaffrey, August 4, 1988, Alexandria, VA.

9. Letter, Lt. Gen. (Ret.) Elvy B. Roberts, September 2, 1988, San Francisco, CA.

10. Lt. Gen. (Ret.) Willard Pearson, *Vietnam Studies, The War in the Northern Provinces 1966–1968*, Washington, DC: Department of the Army, 1975, pp. 4–5.

11. Letter, Lt. Gen. (Ret.) Willard Pearson, July 27, 1988, Wayne, PA.

12. Letter, Gen. (Ret.) William C. Westmoreland, August 15, 1988, Charleston, SC.

13. Gen. (Ret.) William C. Westmoreland, *A Soldier Reports*, New York: Dell, 1980, p. 330.

14. Letter, Maj. Gen. (Ret.) Paul F. Smith, August 15, 1988, Satellite Beach, FL.

15. Letter, Maj. Gen. (Ret.) George S. Eckhardt, October 25, 1988, Rockport, TX.

16. Letter, Lt. Gen. (Ret.) Fillmore K. Mearns, July 27, 1988, Fripp Island, SC.

17. Letter, Gen. (Ret.) George S. Blanchard, August 9, 1988, McLean, VA.

18. Letter, Gen. (Ret.) Frederick J. Kroesen, Jr., September 5, 1988, Falls Church, VA.

19. Letter, Lt. Gen. (Ret.) William K. Jones, April 8, 1989, Alexandria, VA.

20. Letter, Gen. (Ret.) Michael S. Davison, July 28, 1988, Arlington, VA.

11. VOICES FROM THE OTHER SIDE: THE GRUNTS

1. Interview, James H. Webb, Jr., September 4, 1988, Falls Church, VA.

2. Letter, Maj. Gen. Bernard O. Loeffke, October 1, 1988, Fort Clayton, Canal Zone.

3. Interview, Carlton Sherwood, November 16, 1988, Annapolis, MD.

4. Letter, Al Santoli, July 29, 1988, Brooklyn, NY.

5. Letter, Bill Jayne, August 8, 1988, Washington, DC.

6. Letter, Tom Carhart, August 23, 1988, Alexandria, VA.

7. Letter, David Sherman, July 31, 1988, Philadelphia, PA.

8. Interview, Lt. Col. William J. Morrow, Jr., October 6, 1988, Tacoma, WA.

9. Letter, Lt. Col. (Ret.) Vic Reston, August 29, 1988, Fairfax, VA.

10. Letter, Clarence D. Long III, June 1, 1989, Falls Church City, VA

11. Letters, F. C. Brown, September 19, 1988, and March 10, 1989, Subic Bay, Philippines.

12. Letter, Kenn Miller, May 1, 1989, San Gabriel, CA.

13. Letter, William G. Bainbridge, July 20, 1989, Washington, DC.

14. Letter, Lawrence J. De Meo, November 6, 1989, Rockville, MD.

15. Letter, Sedgwick Tourison, October 21, 1990, Crofton, MD.

12. LOSERS AND LOSERS

1. Thomas G. Tobin, Arthur F. Laehr, and John F. Hilgenberg, *Last Flight from Saigon*, USAF Southeast Asia Monograph Series, Vol. IV, Monograph 6, Washington, DC: U.S. Government Printing Office, 1978, pp. 101–2.

2. William E. Le Gro, *Vietnam from Cease-Fire to Capitulation*, Washington, DC: U.S. Army Center of Military History, 1981, pp. 2–3.

3. Ibid., pp. 39–40.

4. Van Tien Dung, *Great Spring Victory*, Washington, DC: Foreign Broadcast Information Service, Vol. IV, No. 110, Supp. 38, June 7, 1976, p. 3.

5. Ibid., p. 8.

6. Ibid., pp. 56–57.

7. Ibid., pp. 3, 15.

8. Truong Nhu Tang with David Chanoff and Doan Van Toai, *A Viet Cong Memoir*, New York: Vintage Books, 1986, p. 242.

9. Le Gro, op. cit., p. 28.

10. Van Tien Dung, op. cit., p. 18.

11. Le Gro, op. cit., p. 150.

12. Van Tien Dung, op. cit., p. 30.

13. Le Gro, op. cit., p. 151.

14. Ibid., p. 159.

15. Cao Van Vien and Dong Van Khuyen, *Reflections on the Vietnam War*, Washington, DC: U.S. Army Center of Military History, 1980, p. 127.

16. Le Gro, op. cit., p. 171.

17. Ibid., pp. 173–76.

18. Ibid., p. 122.

19. Tiziano Terzani, *Giai Phong! The Fall and Liberation of Saigon*, New York: St. Martin's Press, 1976, p. 94.

20. Stanley Karnow, "'Liberated' But Still Capitalist," *Atlantic Monthly*, November 1981, pp. 10, 15.

21. Stanley Karnow, *Vietnam*, New York: Viking, 1983, p. 669.

22. Terzani, op. cit., p. 97.

23. Ibid., p. 100.

24. Truong Nhu Tang, op. cit., pp. 263–65. This story is told in a somewhat shorter version by Al Santoli in *To Bear Any Burden*, New York: E. P. Dutton, 1985, pp. 18–19.

25. Ibid., p. 268.

26. Nguyen Cong Hoan in Santoli, *To Bear Any Burden*, p. 287.

27. Nguyen Van Canh, *Vietnam Under Communism, 1975–1982*, Stanford, CA: Hoover Institution Press, 1983, pp. 11, 18.

28. [Nguyen Chi Thien], *Prison Songs*, No. 11, "This One Great Mistake," arranged by Pham Duy, translated by Nguyen Ngoc Bich, Philadelphia: Hoi Van-Hoa VN Lai Bac-My (Vietnamese Literary Club of North America), 1982.

29. Bui Diem, "A New Kind of War in Southeast Asia," *Asian Affairs*, May–June 1979, p. 274.

30. Ibid., Doan Van Toai, op. cit., pp. 200–201; John S. Bowman, *The World Almanac of the Vietnam War*, New York: Bison Books, 1985, p. 349; Nguyen Huu Thuy, *Chinese Aggression Against Vietnam*, Hanoi: Foreign Language Publishing House, 1979, p. 37.

31. *Refugee Reports*, December 16, 1988, Table I, p. 7.

32. William J. Duiker, *Vietnam Since the Fall of Saigon*, Athens, OH: Ohio University Center for International Studies, Center for Southeast Asian Studies, 1985, p. 121.

33. Gary Klintworth, "Vietnam's Withdrawal from Cambodia," Canberra, Australia: Australian National University, 1987, p. 24.

34. Bowman, op. cit., p. 349.

35. Duiker, op. cit., p. 121.

36. Tourison interviews.

37. Klintworth, op. cit., p. 13.

38. Nayan Chanda, "The Black Book of Hatred," *Far Eastern Economic Review*, January 19, 1979, pp. 19, 22.

39. Dan Cragg, "An Interview with Son Sann," *The National Vietnam Veteran's Review*, February 1984, p. 27.

40. The Heritage Foundation, "Dealing With a Fast-Changing Indochina," *Backgrounder* No. 87: Washington, DC: The Heritage Foundation, March 23, 1989, p. 8.

41. *Facts on File*, December 31, 1978, pp. 996–997.

42. Bui Diem, op. cit., p. 275.

43. Nayan Chanda, "Cambodia: Fifteen Days That Shook Asia," *Far Eastern Economic Review*, January 19, 1979, p. 11.

44. Duiker, op. cit., p. 122.

45. *Facts on File*, January 12, 1979, p. 9.

46. *Facts on File*, January 19, 1979, p. 27.

47. *Facts on File*, April 20, 1979, p. 278.

48. Duiker, op. cit., p. 117.

49. Ibid.

50. Ibid., p. 121.

51. Cragg, op. cit., 27.

52. Bui Diem, op. cit., p. 276.

53. Ibid., p. 276.

54. Nguyen Huu Thuy, op. cit., p. 36.

55. *Beijing Review*, "Frontier Forces Counterattack Vietnamese Aggressors," February 23, 1979, p. 3.

56. Duiker, op. cit., pp. 241–42.

57. Nguyen Huu Thuy, op. cit., p 46; Bui Diem, op. cit., p. 277.

58. Harlan W. Jencks, "China's 'Punitive' War on Vietnam: A Military Assessment," *Asian Survey*, August 8, 1979, p. 805.

59. Ibid., p. 804.

60. Ibid., p. 803.

61. Duiker, op. cit., p. 134.

62. Jencks, op. cit., p. 805.

63. Li Man Kin, *Sino-Vietnamese War*, transl. Wan Siu Yin and Tina Bailey: Hong Kong: Kingsway International Publications, Ltd., 1982, p. 33.

64. Ibid., p. 807.

65. Nguyen Huu Thuy, op. cit., p. 54.

66. Jencks, op. cit., p. 809.

67. Ibid., p. 811.

68. Duiker, op. cit., p. 137.

69. Nguyen Van Canh, op. cit., p. 243.

70. Jencks, op. cit., p. 812.

71. Li Man Kin, op. cit., p. 33.

72. Ibid., p. 59.

73. Drew Middleton, "How Chinese Performed: Lack of Mobility Evident," *The New York Times*, March 6, 1979, p. A10.

74. Jencks, op. cit., p. 808.

75. Nguyen Huu Thuy, op. cit., p. 57.

76. Duiker, op. cit., p. 138.

77. Klintworth, op. cit., pp. 11–12.

78. [Nguyen Chi Thien], No. 11, "This One Great Mistake."

79. The Heritage Foundation, *The U.S. and Asia: A Statistical Handbook*, Washington, DC: The Heritage Foundation Asian Studies Center, July 29, 1988, p. 74.

80. Klintworth, op. cit., p. 15.

81. *Facts on File*, May 8, 1987, p. 339.

82. The Heritage Foundation, *The U.S. and Asia: A Statistical Handbook*, p. 74.

83. The Heritage Foundation, *Backgrounder* No. 87, p. 5.

84. Don Oberdorfer, "U.S. States Conditions for Ties With Vietnam," *The Washington Post*, December 21, 1988, p. 24.

85. Ibid.

86. *Asian Defence Journal*, "Thailand Says Vietnamese Troops Still in Cambodia," November 1989, p. 94.

87. Ibid., p. 7.

88. Klintworth, op. cit., p. 28.

89. Khien Theeravit, et al., *Research Report on the Vietnamese Army Deserters*, Bangkok: Institute of Asian Studies Chulalongknorn University (Asian Studies Monograph No. 037), July 1987, pp. 46–47.

90. *Facts on File*, Vol. XXVI, p. 247.

91. *Facts on File*, May 8, 1987, p. 339.

92. Harvey H. Smith, et al., *Area Handbook for South Vietnam*, Washington, DC: U.S. Government Printing Office, 1967, pp. 355–56.

93. *Asian Defence Journal*, "Cleaning Up the Economic Mess," July 1989, p. 98.

94. *The Economist Intelligence Unit*, "Indochina: Vietnam, Laos, Cambodia," Country Report No. 2, 1988, pp. 8, 15.

95. The Heritage Foundation, op. cit., p. 6.

96. Vo Van Ai, *Vietnam Today*, Gennevilliers, France: Que Me, Vietnam Committee for Human Rights, 1985, pp. 13–16.

97. Ibid., pp. 7–8.

98. Nguyen Van Canh, op. cit., p. 142.

99. Joseph Cerquone, *Uncertain Harbors: The Plight of the Vietnamese Boat People*, Washington, DC: U.S. Committee for Refugees, October 1987, pp. 1, 4, 9, 11.

100. *Refugee Reports*, Washington, DC: U.S. Committee for Refugees, December 16, 1988, pp. 6, 7; for statistics on Vietnamese refugees, see Cerquone, op. cit., pp. 9, 19.

101. Nguyen Van Canh, op. cit., p. 129.

102. Richard D. Burns and Milton Leitenberg, *The Wars in Vietnam, Cambodia and Laos, 1945–1982*, Santa Barbara, CA: ABC-Clio Information Services, 1984, p. 209.

103. William Branigin, "'Memories Come at Night' for Hanoi's

Disabled Vets,'' *The Washington Post*, October 19, 1990, pp. A25, 29.

104. James Webb to Dan Cragg. Mr. Webb visited Vietnam in the spring of 1991 with Sen. Bob Kerry.

BIBLIOGRAPHY

BOOKS

Berger, Carl. *The United States Air Force in Southeast Asia*. Washington, DC: Office of Air Force History, 1977.

Berman, Paul. *Revolutionary Organization, Institution-Building Within the People's Liberation Armed Forces*. Lexington, MA: Lexington Books, 1974.

Bowman, John S. *The World Almanac of the Vietnam War*, New York. Bison Books, 1985.

Brodrick, Alan. *Little China*. London: Oxford University Press, 1942.

Bui Diem. *In The Jaws of History*. Boston: Houghton Mifflin, 1987.

Burchett, Wilfred G. *Vietnam: Inside Story of the Guerrilla War*. New York: International Publishers, 1965.

————. *Vietnam North*. New York: International Publishers, 1966.

Burns, Richard D. and Milton Leitenberg. *The Wars in Vietnam, Cambodia and Laos, 1945–1982*. Santa Barbara, CA: ABC-Clio Information Services, 1984.

Burton, Lt. Col. Lance J. *North Vietnam's Military Logistics System: Its Contribution to the War, 1961–1969*. Fort Leavenworth, KS: U.S. Army Command and General Staff Office, 1977.

Cao Van Vien and Dong Van Khuyen. *Reflections on the Vietnam War*. Washington, DC: U.S. Army Center of Military History, 1980.

Cerquone, Joseph. *Uncertain Harbors: The Plight of the Vietnamese Boat People*. Washington, DC: U.S. Committee for Refugees, 1987.

Chanoff, David and Doan Van Toai. *Portrait of the Enemy*. New York: Random House, 1986.

Confucius. *See K'ung Fu-tse*.

Conley, Michael Charles. *The Communist Insurgent Infrastructure in South*

Vietnam: A Study of Organization and Strategy. Washington, DC: The American University, 1967.

Duiker, William J. *Vietnam Since the Fall of Saigon.* Athens, OH: Ohio University Center for International Studies, Center for Southeast Asian Studies, 1985.

Dung, Van Tien. *Our Great Spring Victory: An Account of the Liberation of South Vietnam.* New York: Monthly Review Press, 1977.

Dunn, Lt. Gen. Carroll H. *Vietnam Studies: Base Development in South Vietnam 1965–1970.* Washington, DC: Department of the Army, 1972.

Dupuy, R. Ernest and Trevor. *The Encyclopedia of Military History.* New York: Harper & Row, 1970.

Encyclopedia Americana. International Edition. Danbury, CT: Grolier, Inc., 1984.

Encyclopaedia Britannica. Thirteenth Edition. New York: The Encyclopaedia Britannica Co., Ltd., 1926.

Fall, Bernard B. *Hell in a Very Small Place.* New York: J. B. Lippincott Co., 1967.

———. *The Two Viet-Nams.* New York: Praeger, 1963.

———. *Vietnam Witness*, 1953–66. New York: Praeger, 1966.

FitzGerald, Frances. *Fire in the Lake.* Boston: Little, Brown & Co., 1972.

Gerassi, John. *North Vietnam: A Documentary.* New York: The Bobbs-Merrill Company, Inc., 1968.

Giap, Vo Nguyen. *People's War, People's Army.* New York: Bantam, 1962.

———. *Big Victory, Great Task.* New York: Praeger, 1968.

Hammer, Ellen J. *A Death in November.* New York: E. P. Dutton, 1987.

Heiser, Lt. Gen. Joseph M., Jr. *Vietnam Studies: Logistic Support.* Washington, DC: Department of the Army, 1974.

Henderson, William Darryl. *Why the Viet Cong Fought.* Westport, CT: Greenwood Press, 1979.

The Heritage Foundation. *The U.S. and Asia: A Statistical Handbook.* Washington, DC: Asian Studies Center, 1988.

Herman, Edward S. *Atrocities in Vietnam: Myths and Realities.* Philadelphia: Pilgrim Press, 1970.

Hickey, Gerald C. *Village in Vietnam.* New Haven: Yale University Press, 1964.

Hoang Van Chi. *From Colonialism to Communism.* New York: Praeger, 1968.

Hogg, Ian V., and John Weeks. *Military Small Arms of the 20th Century.* New York: Hippocrene Books, Inc., 1977.

Holmes, Richard. *Acts of War.* New York: The Free Press, 1988.

Honey, P. J. *Communism in North Vietnam: Its Role in the Sino-Soviet Dispute.* Cambridge, MA: M.I.T. Press, 1963.

Jones, Bruce E. *War Without Windows.* New York: The Vanguard Press, 1987.

Karnow, Stanley. *Vietnam.* New York: Viking, 1983.

Katallo, Dennis C., and Allen J. Bending. *North Vietnamese Army, Viet*

Cong Uniforms and Field Equipment (1965 1975). Addison, IL: Miltec Enterprises, 1988.

Kinnard, Douglas. *The War Managers.* Hanover, NH: University of Vermont, 1977.

Klintworth, Gary. *Vietnam's Withdrawal from Cambodia.* Canberra, Australia: Australian National University, 1987.

Knoebl, Kuno. *Victor Charlie.* London: Pall Mall Press, 1967.

K'ung Fu-tse. *Analects* (Transl. Arthur Waley). London: George Allen & Unwin, Ltd., 1964.

Lanning, Michael Lee, and Stubbe, Ray W. *Inside Force Recon: Recon Marines in Vietnam.* New York: Ivy, 1989.

Lanning, Michael Lee. *The Only War We Had: A Platoon Leader's Journal of Vietnam.* New York: Ivy Books, 1987.

————. *Vietnam 1969–1970: A Company Commander's Journal.* New York: Ivy Books, 1988.

Le Gro, William E. *Vietnam from Cease-Fire to Capitulation.* Washington, DC: U.S. Army Center of Military History, 1981.

Lenin, V. I. *Collected Works.* English ed. Moscow: Foreign Languages Publishing House, 1962.

Lewy, Gunther. *America in Vietnam.* New York: Oxford University Press, 1978.

Li Man Kin. *Sino-Vietnamese War.* Hong Kong: Kingsway International Publications Ltd., 1982.

Lulling, Darrel R. *Communist Militaria of the Vietnam War.* Tulsa, OK: M.E.N. Press, 1980.

Mao Tse-tung. *Selected Works.* English ed. Peking: Foreign Language Press, 1965.

Marx, Karl. *Capital.* English ed. Moscow: Foreign Languages Publishing House, 1954

McChristian, Maj. Gen. Joseph A. *Vietnam Studies: The Role of Military Intelligence.* Washington, DC: Department of the Army, 1974.

[Nguyen Chi Thien]. *Prison Songs* (Arranged by Pham Duy, translated by Nguyen Ngoc Bich). Philadelphia, PA: Hoi Van-Hoa VN tai Bac-My (Vietnamese Literary Club of North America), 1982.

Nguyen Du. *The Tale of Kieu* (Transl. Huynh Sanh Thong). New Haven: Yale University Press, 1983.

Nguyen Huu Thuy. *Chinese Aggression Against Vietnam.* Hanoi: Foreign Languages Publishing House, 1979.

Nguyen Van Canh. *Vietnam Under Communism, 1975–1982.* Stanford, CA: Hoover Institution Press, 1983.

Nguyen Van Thai and Nguyen Van Mung. *A Short History of Viet-nam.* Saigon: The Times Publishing Co., 1958.

O'Ballance, Edgar. *The Indo-China War 1945–54.* London: Faber and Faber, 1964.

Palmer, Dave Richard. *Summons of the Trumpet: U.S.-Vietnam in Perspective.* Novato, CA: Presidio Press, 1978.

Pearson, Lt. Gen. Willard. Vietnam Studies: *The War in the Northern*

Provinces 1966–1968. Washington, DC: Department of the Army, 1975.

Pike, Douglas. *Viet Cong: The Organization and Techniques of the National Liberation Front of South Vietnam*. Cambridge, MA: M.I.T. Press, 1966.

_____. *The Viet Cong Strategy of Terror*. Saigon: U.S. Mission, 1970.

_____. *PAVN: People's Army of Vietnam*. Novato, CA: Presidio Press, 1986.

Rosser-Owen, David. *Vietnam Weapons Handbook*. Northants, England: Patrick Stephens Limited, 1986.

Salisbury, Harrison E. *Behind the Lines—Hanoi*. New York: Harper and Row, 1967.

Santoli, Al. *To Bear any Burden*. New York: E. P. Dutton, 1985.

Smith, Harvey H., et al. *Area Handbook for South Vietnam*. Washington, DC: U.S. Government Printing Office, 1967.

_____. *Area Handbook for North Vietnam*. Washington, DC: U.S. Government Printing Office, 1967.

Snepp, Frank. *Decent Interval*. New York: Random House, 1977.

Stanton, Shelby L. *Vietnam Order of Battle*. New York: Exeter Books, 1981.

Summers, Harry G., Jr. *On Strategy: The Vietnam War in Context*. Carlisle Barracks, PA: Strategic Studies Institute, 1981.

Tanham, George K. *Communist Revolutionary Warfare*. New York: Praeger, 1967.

Telfer, Gary L., Lane Rogers, and V. Keith Fleming, Jr. *Fighting the North Vietnamese, 1967*. Washington, DC: History and Museums Division, Headquarters, USMC, 1984.

Terzani, Tiziano. *Giai Phong! The Fall and Liberation of Saigon*. New York: St. Martin's Press, 1976.

Theeravit, Khien, et al. *Research Report on the Vietnamese Army Deserters*. Bangkok: Institute of Asian Studies, Chulalongkorn University, 1987.

Tobin, Thomas G., et al. *Last Flight from Saigon*. Washington, DC: U.S. Government Printing Office, 1978.

Truong Nhu Tang, with David Chanoff and Doan Van Toai. *A Viet Cong Memoir*. New York: Harcourt Brace Jovanovich, 1985.

Vietnam: The Anti-U.S. Resistance for National Salvation 1954–1975. Hanoi: People's Army Publishing House, 1980.

Vietnamese Phrase Book. New York: Holt, Rinehart and Winston, Inc., 1966.

Vo Van Ai. *Vietnam Today*. Gennevilliers, France: Que Me, Vietnam Committee for Human Rights, 1985.

Westmoreland, Gen. William C. *A Soldier Reports*. New York: Dell, 1980.

PERIODICALS

Ahearn, Capt. Arthur Mason. "Viet Cong Medicine." *Military Medicine,* March 1966.

Army. "An Anatomy of the Enemy and Why He Is Hurting." October 1967, 124–25.

———. "Illustrations of Camouflage Techniques Used by the Viet Cong," June 1966, 31–33.

Asian Defence Journal. "Vietnam: Cleaning Up the 'Economic Mess'." July 1988, 89.

———. "Thailand Says Vietnamese Troops Still in Cambodia." November 1989, 89.

Beecher, William. "Another Face of the War." *National Guardsman,* February 1971, 2–7.

Beijing Review. "Frontier Forces Counterattack Vietnamese Aggressors." February 23, 1979.

Browning, Joseph. "Women of the Viet Cong." *National Guardsman,* August 1968, 2–6.

Bui Diem. "A New Kind of War in Southeast Asia." *Asian Affairs.* May–June 1979.

Chanda, Nayan. "The Black Book of Hatred." *Far Eastern Economic Review,* January 19, 1979, 19, 22.

———. "Cambodia: Fifteen Days That Shook Asia." *Far Eastern Economic Review.* January 19, 1979, 11.

Chen, King C. "Hanoi vs. Peking: Policies and Relations—A Survey." *Asian Survey.* September 1972, 806–17.

Clapp, Col. Archie J. "Don't Envy the Enemy," U.S. Naval Institute *Proceedings,* November 1966, 49–59.

Cragg, Dan. "An Interview with Son Sann." *The National Vietnam Veteran's Review.* February 1984, 27.

The Economist Intelligence Unit. "Indochina: Vietnam, Laos, Cambodia." Country Report No. 2, 1988.

Facts on File. Dec. 31, 1978; Jan 1–5, 12, 19, 1979; Apr. 20, 1979; May 8, 1987.

The Heritage Foundation. "Dealing With a Fast-Changing Indochina." *Backgrounder* No. 87. March 23, 1987.

Jencks, Harlan W. "China's 'Punitive' War on Vietnam: A Military Assessment." *Asian Survey.* August 8, 1979, pp. 805, 808, 809, 812.

Karnow, Stanley. "'Liberated' But Still Capitalist." *Atlantic Monthly,* November 1981, pp. 10, 15.

Middleton, Drew. "How Chinese Performed: Lack of Mobility Evident." *The New York Times,* March 6, 1979.

Neglia, Capt. Anthony V. "NVA and VC: Different Enemies, Different Tactics," *Infantry,* September–October 1970, 50–55.

O'Ballance, Maj. Edgar. "The Ho Chi Minh Trail," *Army Quarterly and Defense Journal,* April 1967, 105–10.

Oberdorfer, Don. "U.S. States Conditions for Ties with Vietnam." *The Washington Post.* Dec. 21, 1988.

Patton, Lt. Col. George S. "Why They Fight," *Military Review*, December 1965, 16–23.

Peterkin, Frederick. "The Sapper," *Infantry*, November–December 1969, 51–53.

Refugee Reports, Vol. IX, Nos. 2, 3, 12, 1988.

Rogers, Maj. Lane. "The Enemy," Marine Corps *Gazette*, March 1966, 51–55.

Samson, Col. Jack. "Viet Cong Tactics 'Ten Against One,' " *Military Review*, January 1967, 89–93.

Sexton, Col. M. J. "Sapper Attack," Marine Corps *Gazette*, September 1969, 28–31.

Thayer, Thomas C. "How to Analyze a War Without Fronts, Vietnam 1965–1972." *Journal of Defense Research, Series B: Tactical Warfare*. Alexandria, VA: Defense Technical Information Center (DDCOO4262), 1975.

Weller, Joe. "Viet Cong Arms and Men," *Ordnance*, May–June 1966, 602–10.

Simpson, Howard R. "The Guerrilla and His World," U.S. Naval Institute *Proceedings*, August 1969, 42–53.

White, Peter T. "Mosaic of Cultures," *National Geographic*, March 1971, 301–3.

NEWSPAPERS

Arizona Republic, 1989

The New York Times, 1960–1975

Nhan Dan (The Party Worker), 1962–1989

Pacific Stars and Stripes, 1965–1975

The Washington Post, 1990

The Washington Times, 1989

STUDIES, PAMPHLETS, REPORTS, AND DOCUMENTS

Anderson, M., M. Arnsten and H. Averich. *Insurgent Organization and Operations: A Case Study of the Viet Cong in the Delta, 1964–1966*. Santa Monica, CA: RAND Corporation Study RM-5239-1-ISA/ARPA, August 1967.

Armed Forces Information Service. *Why We Fight in Vietnam*, DoD VR-1, Vietnam Review. Washington, DC: U.S. Government Printing Office, September 1967.

Battelle Columbus Laboratories. *Journal of Defense Research, Series B*, Volume 7B, Number 3. Washington, DC: Government Printing Office, Fall 1975.

BDM Corporation. *A Study of Lessons Learned in Vietnam*, Volume I, "The Enemy." McLean, VA: The BDM Corporation, 1979.

Carrier, J. M. and C. A. H. Thomson. *Viet Cong Motivation and Morale:*

The Special Case of the Chieu Hoi. Santa Monica, CA: RAND Corporation Study RM-4830-2-ISA/ARPA, May 1966.

Davison, W. P., and J. J. Zasloff. A Profile of Viet Cong Cadres. Santa Monica, CA: RAND Corporation Study RM 4983-1-ISA/ARPA, June 1966.

Davison, W. Phillips. Users' Guide to the RAND Interviews in Vietnam. Santa Monica, CA: RAND Corporation AD-759 829, November 1972.

Denton, Frank H. Some Effects of Military Operations on Viet Cong Attitudes. Santa Monica, CA: RAND Corporation Study RM-4966-1-ISA/ARPA, November 1966.

———. Volunteers for the Viet Cong. Santa Monica, CA: RAND Corporation Study RM-5647-ISA/ARPA, September 1968.

Department of the Army Pamphlet 550-106. See Conley, Michael.

———. 24th Military History Detachment (Airborne). 173rd Airborne Brigade, "Operational Report No. 6, A Monograph of Huynh Nghiep." Washington, DC: Department of the Army (DTIC AD 500304), February 27, 1969.

Department of Defense. Aggression from the North: The Record of North Vietnam's Campaign to Conquer South Vietnam. DoD Gen-14. Washington, DC: U.S. Government Printing Office, 1965.

———. Communist Dedicated Forces in South Vietnam. DoD VR-3, Vietnam Review. Washington, DC: U.S. Government Printing Office, September 1967.

———. Communist "Wars of National Liberation." DoD VR-10, Vietnam Review. Washington, DC: U.S. Government Printing Office, November 1968.

———. Free World Assistance for South Vietnam. DoD VR-4, Vietnam Review. Washington, DC: U.S. Government Printing Office, September 1967.

———. Ideas in Conflict: Liberty and Communism. DoD Gen-27. Washington, DC: U.S. Government Printing Office, 1962.

———. Know Your Enemy: The Viet Cong. DoD Gen-20. Washington, DC: U.S. Government Printing Office, 1966.

———. Long Live the Victory of the People's War: Red Chinese Blueprint. DoD Gen-17. Washington, DC: U.S. Government Printing Office, 1966.

———. MACV Order of Battle Summary, RG 472, Box 39, "Westmoreland vs. CBS Litigation Collection." Washington National Records Center, Suitland, MD.

———. Manual for Courts-Martial United States 1969 (Revised Edition). Washington, DC: U.S. Government Printing Office, 1969.

———. National Reconciliation in South Vietnam. DoD VR-6, Vietnam Review. Washington, DC: U.S. Government Printing Office, November 1967.

———. North Vietnam. DoD AG-149, Capsule Facts for the Armed Forces. Washington, DC: U.S. Government Printing Office, July 1970.

———. Office of the Assistant Secretary of Defense (Public Affairs). "Secretary of the Army Releases the 'Peers Report.' " News Release No. 537-74, November 13, 1974.

———. *Viet Cong Tactics in South Vietnam.* DoD VR-5, Vietnam Review. Washington, DC: U.S. Government Printing Office, November 1967.

———. *Weapons and Equipment—Southeast Asia.* Washington, DC: U.S. Government Printing Office, 1965.

Department of State. *A Threat to the Peace: North Vietnam's Effort to Conquer South Vietnam.* Washington, DC: U.S. Government Printing Office, 1961.

Document Exploitation Report, 199th Light Infantry Brigade, RVN. "Diary of Nguyen Van Nhuong," August 1969.

Donnell, John C. *Viet Cong Recruitment: Why and How Men Join.* Santa Monica, CA: RAND Corporation Study RM-5486-1-ISA/ARPA, December 1967.

Dung, Sr. Gen. Van Tien. *Great Spring Victory.* Washington, DC: Foreign Broadcast Information Service, 1976.

Elliott, David W. P., and Mai Elliott. *Documents of an Elite Viet Cong Delta Unit: The Demolition Platoon of the 514th Battalion—Part Three: Military Organization and Activities.* Santa Monica, CA: RAND Corporation Study RM-5880-ISA/ARPA, May 1969.

———. *Documents of an Elite Viet Cong Delta Unit: The Demolition Platoon of the 514th Battalion—Part Five: Personal Letters.* Santa Monica, CA: RAND Corporation Study RM-5852-ISA/ARPA, May 1969.

Foreign Broadcast Information Service Daily Reports, January–March 1968.

Goure, L., A. J. Russo, and D. Scott. *Some Findings of the Viet Cong Motivation and Morale Study: June–December 1965.* Santa Monica, CA: RAND Corporation Study RM-4911-2-ISA/ARPA, February 1966.

Goure, Leon. *Some Impressions of the Effects of Military Operations on Viet Cong Behavior.* Santa Monica, CA: RAND Corporation Study RM-4717-1-ISA, August 1965.

Goure, Leon, and C. A. H. Thomson. *Some Impressions of Viet Cong Vulnerabilities: An Interim Report.* Santa Monica, CA: RAND Corporation Study RM-4699-1-ISA/ARPA, August 1966.

Gurtov, Melvin. *Viet Cong Cadres and the Cadre System: A Study of the Main and Local Forces.* Santa Monica, CA: RAND Corporation Study RM-5414-1-ISA/ARPA, December 1967.

Hackworth, Maj. David H. "Find 'Em, Fix 'Em, and Then Smash 'Em," Republic of Vietnam: 173rd Airborne Brigade *Lessons Learned*, January 28, 1967.

Holliday, L. P. and R. M. Gurfield. *Viet Cong Logistics.* Santa Monica, CA: RAND Corporation Study RM-5423-1-ISA/ARPA, June 1968.

Joint United States Public Affairs Office, Saigon. "Diary of an Infiltrator,"

Vietnam Documents and Research Notes, Document No. 1, October 1967.

———. "Out of Rice, Ammunition and Bandages: Notes of a VC Veteran," *Vietnam Documents and Research Notes*, Document No. 13, January 1968.

———. "The Problems of a Dispensary," *Vietnam Documents and Research Notes*, Document No. 16, January 1968.

———. "Women in the Winter–Spring Campaign," *Vietnam Documents and Research Notes*, Document No. 24, April 1968.

———. "Fighting at Tet: A Viet Cong 'After-Action Report,' " *Vietnam Documents and Research Notes*, Document No. 27, April 1968.

Jenkins, Brian Michael. *Why the North Vietnamese Will Keep Fighting.* Santa Monica, CA: RAND Corporation Paper P-4395-1, March 1972.

Kellen, Konrad. *A Profile of the PAVN Soldier in South Vietnam.* Santa Monica, CA: RAND Corporation Study RM 5013-1-ISA/ARPA, June 1966.

———. *A View of the VC: Elements of Cohesion in the Enemy Camp in 1966–1967.* Santa Monica, CA: RAND Corporation Study RM-5462-1-ISA/ARPA, November 1969.

———. *Conversations with Enemy Soldiers in Late 1968/Early 1969: A Study of Motivation and Morale.* Santa Monica, CA: RAND Corporation Study RM-6131-1-ISA/ARPA, September 1970.

———. *1971 and Beyond: The View from Hanoi.* Santa Monica, CA: RAND Corporation Paper P-4634-1, June 1971.

Ketchum, MacLeon and Grove, Inc. *Youth Attitude Trend Survey.* U.S. Army Recruiting Command, May 1967.

Nguyen, Maj. Gen. Duy Hinh. *Lam Son 719.* McLean, VA: Office of the Chief of Military History, Department of the Army, 1977.

Peers, W. R. *Report on the Department of the Army Review of the Preliminary Investigation into the My Lai Incident, Volume I: The Report of the Investigation.* Washington, DC: U.S. Government Printing Office, 1970.

RAND Corporation. *RAND Vietnam Interview Series, Active Influence Within the Viet Cong and North Vietnamese Army,* Series AG. Santa Monica, CA: RAND Corporation, 1972.

———. *Infiltration Routes and Methods,* Series SX. Santa Monica, CA: RAND Corporation, 1972.

Simulmatics Corporation. *Improving Effectiveness of the Chieu Hoi Program,* New York: The Simulmatics Corporation, September 1967.

Sak, Lt. Gen. Sutsakham. *The Khmer Republic at War and the Final Collapse.* McLean, VA: Office of the Chief of Military History, Department of the Army, 1978.

Soutchay, Brig. Gen. Vongsavanh. *RLG Military Operations and Activities in the Laotian Panhandle.* McLean, VA: Office of the Chief of Military History, Department of the Army, 1978.

Sweetland, Anders. *Rallying Potential Among the North Vietnamese Armed*

Forces. Santa Monica, CA: RAND Corporation Study RM-6375-1 ARPA, December 1970.

United States Congress. House Committee on Armed Services. *Investigation of the My Lai Incident.* H.A.S.C. No. 94-47, 91st Cong. 2d Sess. 1976.

United States Office of the Assistant Secretary of Defense (Comptroller). *Southeast Asia Statistical Summary.* Washington, DC: U.S. Government Printing Office, April 1973.

United States Military Assistance Command, Vietnam. STUDY ST 70-05. Saigon: Combined Intelligence Center, 1970.

Westmoreland, William C. *Report on the War in Vietnam.* Washington, DC: U.S. Government Printing Office, 1968.

UNPUBLISHED PAPERS

Hargrove, Tom. ''Rice and War in Vietnam: A Rendezvous with the Past.'' October 26, 1988. Lanning's files.

COLLECTIONS AND ARCHIVES

Indochina Archive, University of California, Berkeley, CA.

Westmoreland Vs. CBS Litigation Collection, National Archives, Suitland, MD. (see *MACV Order of Battle Summary*)

Wilson Center for Scholars, Newspaper files, Smithsonian Institution, Washington, DC.

INTERVIEWS AND CORRESPONDENCE

SMA (Ret.) William G. Bainbridge	Washington, DC	July 20, 1989
Gen. (Ret.) George S. Blanchard	McLean, VA	August 9, 1988
Lt. Cdr. F. C. Brown	Subic Bay, P.I.	March 10, 1989
Tom Carhart	Alexandria, VA	August 23, 1988
Gen. (Ret.) Michael S. Davison	Arlington, VA	July 28, 1988
Capt. (Ret.) Lawrence J. DeMeo	Rockville, MD	November 6, 1989
Gen. (Ret.) William E. Depuy	Delaplane, VA	July 29, 1988
Maj. Gen. (Ret.) George S. Eckhardt	Rockport, TX	October 25, 1988
Lt. Gen. (Ret.) Julian J. Ewell	McLean, VA	July 31, 1988
Bill Jayne	Washington, DC	August 8, 1988

Maj. Gen. (Ret.) William Jones	Alexandria, VA	April 8, 1989
Gen. (Ret.) Frederick J. Krosen	Falls Church, VA	September 5, 1988
Lt. Col. (Ret.) James W. Lanning	Winters, TX	January 31, 1989
Maj. Gen. Bernard O. Loeffke	Fort Clayton, CZ	October 1, 1988
C. D. Long	Falls Church, VA	June 1, 1989
Lt. Gen. (Ret.) William J. McCaffrey	Alexandria, VA	August 4, 1988
Lt. Gen. (Ret.) Fillmore K. Mearns	Fripp Island, SC	July 27, 1988
Kenn Miller	San Gabriel, CA	May 1, 1989
Lt. Col. William J. Morrow, Jr.	Tacoma, WA	October 6, 1988
Lt. Gen. Willard Pearson	Wayne, PA	July 27, 1988
Lt. Col. (Ret.) Vic Reston	Fairfax, VA	August 29, 1988
Lt. Gen. (Ret.) Elvy B. Roberts	San Francisco, CA	September 2, 1988
Gen. (Ret.) W. B. Rosson	Roanoke, VA	September 29, 1988
Al Santoli	Brooklyn, NY	July 29, 1988
David Sherman	Philadelphia, PA	July 31, 1988
Carlton Sherwood	Annapolis, MD	November 16, 1988
Maj. Gen. Paul F. Smith	Satellite Beach, FL	August 15, 1988
Brig. Gen. (Ret.) James S. Timothy	Longboat Key, FL	August 15, 1988
CW3 (Ret.) Sedgwick Tourison, Jr.	Crofton, MD	June–October 1990
James H. Webb, Jr.	Falls Church, VA	September 4, 1988
Gen. (Ret.) William C. Westmoreland	Charleston, SC	August 15, 1988
Maj. Gen. (Ret.) Ellis W. Williamson	Arlington, VA	August 2, 1988

Look for these titles on Vietnam
written by a soldier who was there.
LT. COL.
MICHAEL LEE LANNING

Published by Ivy Books.